Decoupled Drupal in Practice

Architect and Implement Decoupled Drupal Architectures Across the Stack

Preston So

Foreword by Dries Buytaert

Apress®

Decoupled Drupal in Practice: Architect and Implement Decoupled Drupal Architectures Across the Stack

Preston So
Ridgewood, NY, USA

ISBN-13 (pbk): 978-1-4842-4071-7   ISBN-13 (electronic): 978-1-4842-4072-4
https://doi.org/10.1007/978-1-4842-4072-4

Library of Congress Control Number: 2018964944

Managing Director, Apress Media LLC: Welmoed Spahr
Acquisitions Editor: Louise Corrigan
Development Editor: James Markham
Coordinating Editor: Nancy Chen

Cover designed by eStudioCalamar

Cover image designed by Freepik (www.freepik.com)

Distributed to the book trade worldwide by Springer Science+Business Media New York, 233 Spring Street, 6th Floor, New York, NY 10013. Phone 1-800-SPRINGER, fax (201) 348-4505, e-mail orders-ny@springer-sbm.com, or visit www.springeronline.com. Apress Media, LLC is a California LLC and the sole member (owner) is Springer Science + Business Media Finance Inc (SSBM Finance Inc). SSBM Finance Inc is a **Delaware** corporation.

For information on translations, please e-mail rights@apress.com, or visit http://www.apress.com/rights-permissions.

Apress titles may be purchased in bulk for academic, corporate, or promotional use. eBook versions and licenses are also available for most titles. For more information, reference our Print and eBook Bulk Sales web page at http://www.apress.com/bulk-sales.

Any source code or other supplementary material referenced by the author in this book is available to readers on GitHub via the book's product page, located at www.apress.com/9781484240717. For more detailed information, please visit http://www.apress.com/source-code.

Printed on acid-free paper

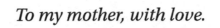

To my mother, with love.

Table of Contents

About the Author

© Terrell Woods

Preston So has been a web developer since 2001, a Drupal developer since 2007, a Drupal contributor since 2009, and a globally recognized expert on decoupled Drupal since 2015. Currently, he works as Director of Research and Innovation at Acquia, where he is the primary subject-matter expert and evangelist for decoupled Drupal and API-first approaches. Previously, he led the Entertainment Weekly development team at Time Inc. (now Meredith). Over the last decade, he has given talks at more than 50 conferences on five continents in multiple languages on a variety of topics, including front-end development, responsive design, user experience, Drupal development, open source innovation, emerging technologies (conversational interfaces, augmented reality), the decentralized web, and decoupled Drupal. He has presented at SXSW Interactive twice (2017, 2018) and at industry conferences around the world, including Frontend United, Great Wide Open, and others. He has also delivered keynotes at conferences on four continents in multiple languages on the subject of decoupled Drupal.

About the Technical Reviewer

**Brandon Scott** is a software architect with a passion for improving experiences for both end users and engineers alike. Over his career Brandon has built his experience across many industries including finance, entertainment, and education. His primary focuses have been creating distributed systems, developing coaching strategies for engineers, and leading experience design workstreams. Recently he has partnered with Razer, Inc., focusing on the design of their SDK products and open source libraries. Brandon has also previously worked with Microsoft on exploring their Microsoft Store capabilities with the education sector.

Foreword

When I started the Drupal project 18 years ago in a cramped Belgian dorm room, working nights and weekends on what was originally supposed to be a message board for my friends, I could never have imagined the impact that my software project would have. Today, Drupal powers a full 2 percent of web sites online, and it has a devoted open source community of more than a million people from all walks of life around the world.

Nor could I have imagined back then the variety of places where we encounter Drupal today, beyond the web sites that used to be Drupal's primary focus. In just the last few years, we have seen Drupal used to power digital signage on university campuses, in-flight entertainment systems, interactive kiosks on cruise ships, and even real-time updates about the next arriving train in a major transit system.

A little over two years ago, on my blog, *https://dri.es*, I wrote about how Drupal is for ambitious digital experiences. When we talk about ambitious digital experiences, though, we aren't just concerned with web sites; we mean virtual and augmented reality, conversational interfaces, and Internet of Things applications that are only now getting started.

Now that Drupal has a strong API-first focus with web services available out of the box, decoupled Drupal is a critical component of making it easy to build the ambitious digital experiences we want to see in the world. It is no accident that Drupal is today considered a leader in decoupled architectures among content management systems. Thanks to Drupal's web services, any application can create and edit content on Drupal. We have well-known standards like JSON API, GraphQL, and CouchDB, and a growing ecosystem of tools around decoupled Drupal that make it simple for developers to build applications in any technology.

That is why this book, which I'm excited to see published, is so important. Preston So is a respected voice in the Drupal community, with expertise in Drupal dating back to 2007. I first worked directly with him in 2012 on the Spark initiative, a community effort to improve the user experience of Drupal's editorial interface, back when he was a college student. Since three years ago, when he first began to explore decoupled Drupal, Preston has become well-known worldwide through his writing and speaking on the topic, and he spearheaded the effort to adopt React to build new administrative interfaces in Drupal core. He has been instrumental in driving adoption of decoupled architectures in the Drupal community. I've been working alongside Preston on these efforts, and I can tell you there is no one better to write this book.

The book you hold in your hands is a must-have guide to decoupling Drupal, from the history and background of how this trend came to be all the way to the details of how to work with the nuances of Drupal's web service APIs. When you finish reading, I think you will agree that decoupled Drupal is an essential element of the bright future in front of Drupal.

If you're new to Drupal, I give you my warm welcome and invite you to report issues on Drupal.org, join us at one of our many Drupal events, and consider contributing just a little of your time, no matter whether you work with code, documentation, design, usability testing, or anything else. I'm thrilled that this book is now available for the Drupal community and the wider web development universe, who can now discover Drupal in a new light.

Dries Buytaert

Boston

September 15, 2018

Dries Buytaert is the original creator and project lead for the Drupal open source web publishing and collaboration platform. He is cofounder and chief technology officer of Acquia, a venture-backed software company that offers products and services for Drupal. A native of Belgium, Buytaert holds a PhD in computer science and engineering from Ghent University and a Licentiate Computer Science (MsC) from the University of Antwerp. In 2008, Buytaert was elected Young Global Leader at the World Economic Forum as well as MIT TR 35 Young Innovator.

Acknowledgments

Authoring a book, particularly on a rapidly evolving and maturing subject area like decoupled Drupal, is a demanding endeavor fraught with challenges and rewards as well as highs and lows. I have been incredibly fortunate to have the support of a great many individuals and organizations in crafting this work. There are far too many names to fit in this space, and although it is an unwritten law that all acknowledgments sections suffer from incompleteness, I will do my best here.

First, I would like to express my gratitude to Acquia and my teammates in the Office of the CTO (OCTO), who have been wonderful throughout this undertaking. In particular, my thanks to Dries Buytaert, Drupal project lead and Acquia CTO, for his unwavering support over the course of this project. Thank you also to my dear friend Wim Leers, who was among the very first confidants to whom I revealed my plans long ago and whose healthy skepticism as an engineer paired with moral support as a friend has both moderated and buoyed my efforts. I also wish to thank Terrence Kevin O'Leary (tkoleary), who was an amazing mentor during my first stint at Acquia and continues to boost all of my professional pursuits today.

I express my fond thanks to all of my other former and current OCTO colleagues, who are nothing short of extraordinary in every sense of the word: Alex Bronstein (effulgentsia), Angie Byron (webchick), ASH Heath, Chris Hamper (hampercm), Emilie Nouveau (dyannenova), Gabe Sullice (gabesullice), Gábor Hojtsy, Jess (xjm), Jesse Beach (jessebeach), Lauri Eskola (lauriii), Leah Magee, Mark Winberry (markwin), Matt Grill (drpal), Michael Meyers (michaelemeyers), Moshe Weitzman (weitzman), Sam Mortenson (samuel.mortenson), Ted Bowman (tedbow), and Tim Plunkett (tim.plunkett).

Second, I wish to express my appreciation to all the contributors involved in two strategic initiatives that are mapping the future of Drupal even as the ink dries on this page: the API-first Initiative and the Admin UI and JavaScript Modernization Initiative. Thank you to the coordinators of the API-first Initiative not already mentioned, without whom this book would be impossible: Daniel Wehner (dawehner), Mateu Aguiló Bosch (e0ipso), and Sebastian Siemssen (fubhy). My thanks also to the coordinators of the Admin UI and JavaScript Modernization Initiative not yet mentioned: Cristina Chumillas (ckrina) and Sally Young (justafish).

ACKNOWLEDGMENTS

Third, I want to thank the entire Drupal community in Colorado, whose tireless efforts to cultivate the local community spurred my own involvement in Drupal and professional growth over the last 11 years. I especially wish to express my gratitude to the late Rick Nashleanas, who hired me at Monarch Digital in Colorado Springs and promptly shifted our entire web business to Drupal, and Matt Tucker (ultimateboy), who first introduced me to the inner workings of Drupal over a decade ago. My gratitude also goes to my high school English teacher Jeff Flygare, who encouraged me to pursue interests in web development and writing. Who would have thought these two hobbies of mine would come together in this way?

Thank you to the editorial staff at Apress for facilitating an excellent author experience from start to finish, especially Nancy Chen, Louise Corrigan, and James Markham. Fond thanks also to technical reviewer Brandon Scott, who provided actionable and insightful feedback throughout the process.

I also wish to express my deep appreciation for the members of the Acquia Marketing team who have supported my book project since day one, including Andrea Rosmarin, DC Denison, and David Churbuck. My fond respect and gratitude also go to Christopher Rogers, David Butler, Drew Robertson, Eric Williamson, Gigi Anderson, Lynne Capozzi, Molly Sloan, Reena Leone, and Saša Zelenović.

I am grateful for all of my friends and family spread throughout New York City, Boston, and the globe that have supported me in innumerable ways over the course of this past year. Your friendship and love mean the world to me.

Last but not least, I also wish to express my unending appreciation for the worldwide Drupal community, without whom the software underpinning this book would not exist. This incredibly open, welcoming, and quirky open source community has galvanized an inestimable passion in my heart for the ideals of free and open source software and the principles that have guided Drupal throughout its history and continue to do so today.

I wish to close with a few words of encouragement to all those, like me, who have been marginalized, underrepresented, and often oppressed in our industry. It is my sincere hope that this work inspires you to pursue your own addition to our discourse and introduce your invaluable perspective and unique expertise. We urgently need more voices like yours, front and center, on stage at conferences, and at our local bookstores and libraries; and we must continue to broaden the space for contributions like yours to flourish and inspire.

Introduction

At no point in the history of content management has there been such a dizzying proliferation of devices in our lives and of the digital experiences we encounter and consume. Long the most critical element of an organization's digital presence, the web site is increasingly treated as just a single facet in a kaleidoscope of content channels and form factors. Many of today's users, in the course of acquiring content or data, never even touch a traditional web browser.

On a daily basis, users interact with a staggering array of different clients, also known as consumers: native mobile applications on smartphones, native desktop applications on personal computers, over-the-top boxes on televisions, chat applications, conversational interfaces, and Internet of Things (IoT) devices. Today, these consumers tend to interact with a single server that acts additionally as a content repository or data store.

This phenomenon has upended architectural paradigms and prior approaches across the industry. Traditionally, web sites, especially larger ones, are administered through a content management system (CMS), software that enables the creation and manipulation of content and its formatting and layout. Many traditional CMSs, having long specialized in web site administration, are underprepared for the ongoing explosion of content channels.

Drupal, a free and open source CMS created by Dries Buytaert, is a notable exception to this trend. In recent years, Drupal has been recasting itself as a CMS that can be employed not just as an end-to-end system for traditional web sites, but also for communication with clients ingesting data and other servers—as well as a cohesive hybrid of both. This portends exciting new possibilities for one of the most commonly used content management frameworks in existence today.

Other CMSs on the market suffer from certain disadvantages in the new digital landscape. WordPress, which offers a RESTful API known as WP-API, nonetheless lacks a flexible content model like Drupal's and employs a homegrown specification that enforces a learning curve for developers building data consumers. Meanwhile, proprietary alternatives such as Contentful and Prismic, although quickly gaining market share, are suboptimal for those who prefer to work with open source from end to end.

In these pages, we will inspect concepts and ideas in decoupled Drupal from the minutest details, such as how to issue requests that yield desired responses on the consumer, to the bigger picture, including the implications of decoupled Drupal for the future of Drupal and CMS architectures in general. By the end of this book, you will gain an idiomatic understanding of Drupal's APIs and their consumption and successfully build simple content applications in a variety of technologies.

Part 1, "Decoupled Drupal Fundamentals," outlines a trajectory for how monolithic CMS architectures have increasingly evolved into decoupled or "headless" CMS architectures for the demands of today's multichannel world. Drawing a parallel between the history of the CMS and the evolution of the web page, the first three chapters outline how decoupled CMS architectures surfaced from the need to break architectural and technical barriers. From there, we will define decoupled Drupal as comprehensively as possible, evaluate its most common architectural approaches, and enumerate the risks and rewards of decoupling Drupal. Part 1 can be safely skipped for those already familiar with RESTful approaches and decoupled CMS architectures.

Part 2, "Decoupling Drupal," scrutinizes Drupal in its capacity as a content service, web service provider, and content repository. In those chapters, we will examine web services solutions available in Drupal 8, both within Drupal core as a result of the Web Services and Context Core Initiative (WSCCI) and among contributed modules. Configuring Drupal as a RESTful data service will be described in detail, along with available authentication mechanisms.

Part 3, "Consuming and Manipulating Drupal 8," introduces how to bridge the gap between Drupal and its API consumers, which typically occurs through XMLHttpRequests (XHR). These chapters deal with how to form requests that will create, read, update, and delete data on Drupal's server side using core REST and contributed solutions such as JSON API, RELAXed Web Services, and GraphQL.

Part 4, "The Decoupled Drupal Ecosystem," deals with the emerging ecosystem surrounding Drupal with regard to API-first distributions, which aid developers that are new to Drupal, as well as software development kits (SDKs) and reference applications, which furnish boilerplates for developers to build on and bridge the gap between Drupal and consumer technologies. In the process, we identify projects such as Contenta, Reservoir, Headless Lightning, and the Waterwheel ecosystem.

Part 5, "Integration with Consumers," explores the development of Drupal-backed (i.e., consuming or manipulating data from Drupal) applications themselves rather than solely the requests and responses that underpin them. Using a variety of widespread technologies, these chapters explain how to integrate decoupled Drupal with JavaScript-based consumers.

Part 6, "Advanced Topics in Decoupled Drupal," deals with issues of decoupled Drupal in production, such as the REST plug-in system, self-documenting APIs, code generation, and caching. In addition, these chapters assess questions about the future of decoupled Drupal, content management, and decoupled CMSs from a critical standpoint.

This book illuminates decoupled Drupal as an expanding paradigm ready for prime time but also answers the increasing need to provide greater clarity, standardization, and best practices around emerging approaches. Decoupled Drupal invites exciting new advancements in user experience and digital ecosystems, but risks and drawbacks limit its appropriateness for all use cases. Straddling two wildly different epochs in content management, decoupled Drupal is a critical turning point not only in how we conceptualize and deliver content, but also how we envisage our relationship to those experiences.

PART I

Decoupled Drupal Fundamentals

In Part 1, we will establish an important conceptual foundation for decoupled Drupal, a paradigm witnessing vast popularity but not without its risks. First, we will inspect how the changing web has impacted the evolution of the content management system by locking open the door to digital experiences in other technologies. Concurrent changes in the server side and client side, most importantly universal JavaScript, have encouraged even web practitioners to explore decoupled CMS architectures for more than just native applications.

We define decoupled Drupal as the use of Drupal as a content service for consumption by other applications, identifying two major architectural paradigms in the process. The first, fully decoupled Drupal, a complete separation between Drupal's default front end and consumer applications, is increasingly employed not only to satisfy the requirements of native and IoT applications but also JavaScript applications. Another, progressively decoupled Drupal, provides a middle ground by interpolating JavaScript frameworks into the Twig-driven front end.

Finally, after diving into the use cases and motivations for decoupling Drupal, we will analyze some of the key advantages and disadvantages of these approaches, which include considerations not only for developers but also the content editors, site builders, site administrators, and end users who will inevitably forge and manipulate the resultant experiences. Due to the relative immaturity of decoupled Drupal, I encourage you to evaluate these risks and rewards carefully during project discovery, as these architectural decisions may have outsized ramifications later in the process.

CHAPTER 1

The Changing Web

Perhaps the most compelling fact about the Cambrian explosion, a seminal event in Earth's history, was that extant life forms diversified from mostly unicellular organisms into multicellular organisms that came to represent most of the present-day animal kingdom—all at one moment in the fossil record 541 million years ago. In the last several years, digital experiences and content management are in the midst of another Cambrian explosion—not in life forms, but in form factors.

In the present day, users are presented with a fast-growing buffet of options to interact with organizations. A typical university student experience in the United States, for instance, can potentially involve a range of touchpoints including a web site, a mobile application, digital signage, and interactive kiosks. This phenomenon engenders a fundamental question of how to prepare and architect for a widening range of experiences that comes close to approaching the optimal state of *content everywhere*. Before leaping headlong into how we can conceive and construct these experiences, it is useful to zoom out and take stock of where we have been and how digital experiences have evolved and will progress in the future. We can only build what we can clearly define.

Web Sites Are Now Just the Starting Point

Until the late 1990s, the vast majority of web site content was made up of text, images, and, infrequently, other media assets. This original state of web content consisted of large chunks of narrative or long-form text, with images and other media punctuating this text. From the perspective of user experience on the Web, most users interacted with these experiences with the sole help of the mouse and keyboard that were the primary means of interfacing with a desktop computer.

© Preston So 2018
P. So, *Decoupled Drupal in Practice*, https://doi.org/10.1007/978-1-4842-4072-4_1

As late as the end of the First Browser War, standards for writing web sites were not codified evenly across vendors responsible for web browsers, even after the Cascading Style Sheets (CSS) standards promulgated by Håkon Wium Lie in 1994 emerged as a widely understood specification by the late 1990s. The slow adoption of well-established World Wide Web Consortium (W3C) standards for some time stunted the growth of best practices in the realm of web development such as the jettisoning of table-based layouts and the introduction of CSS-based layouts. In the meantime, strong competition between browser makers Netscape and Microsoft overshadowed the emergence of JavaScript, a programming language initially prototyped in a mere ten days in 1995 by Brendan Eich that later saw itself implemented in profoundly different ways in distinct browsers.

The free and open source Drupal content management system (CMS) played a role in the evolution toward server-side dynamic web pages between its version 1.0 and 3.0 releases. The advent of server-side dynamism, which allowed a server-side implementation—such as a CMS—to create markup and concatenate templates with user-generated content retrieved from a database, overturned the previous approach of uploading flat Hypertext Markup Language (HTML) files and media assets via File Transfer Protocol (FTP). In turn, server-side dynamism was an important antecedent for the migration of such application logic to the client side in the 2000s. More detail on this can be found in Chapter 3.

For many web developers, it can be hard to grasp that web sites are considered only the starting point in the current state of our industry. Nonetheless, there are innumerable other formats where the codification of best practices and standards similar to what transpired in the early-2000s Web remains in its initial stages.

From Web Sites to Web Applications

Web 2.0 and Dynamic HTML (DHTML) heralded the entry of interactive elements on web sites, marking the beginning of the era of web applications. In the early 2000s, in contrast to its previous infamy as an inconsistently implemented language from browser to browser, JavaScript was utilized to enhance interactions via Asynchronous JavaScript and XML (Ajax), which facilitated dynamic markup changes on the client side after a web page was flushed to the browser.

With the help of the Ajax paradigm, front-end developers benefited from the `XMLHttpRequest` (XHR) application programming interface (API), a core feature of JavaScript in the browser, to retrieve data from servers asynchronously and provide for background operations that did not require full page refreshes. This transition can be considered the moment when web sites truly became web applications rather than flat assets delivered to a browser, solidifying the move away from flat-file HTML or markup cobbled together on the server side. The "new" web page was one with dynamic portions that would obviate the necessity of full round trips back to the server.

At this point in the history of web development, the distinction between web sites and web applications becomes increasingly ambiguous, and it remains difficult to codify such a differentiation today. See Chapter 3 for more about the evolution of client-side JavaScript, the resulting JavaScript renaissance, and universal (isomorphic) JavaScript.

Responsive Web Design

The late 2000s saw the advent of responsive web design (RWD), which emerged as a method of offering web sites the capability to seamlessly transition across desktop, tablet, and mobile without requiring that distinct versions of the page itself be provided. By conceiving of content as a fluid ("content is like water") that adapts to the vessels in which it sits, responsive web design, a term coined by Ethan Marcotte in 2010 but already present on some web sites even in the early 2000s, removed the desktop–mobile divide from web design and is today ubiquitous around the Web and an important exemplar of user interface plasticity.[1]

In RWD, web content can adhere to the confines of a typical web site or take on many of the traits of native mobile applications when viewed on a mobile device. From the perspective of the user, the experience on a mobile device is similar but distinguishable, as on mobile, most assets such as text and images span the entire viewport.

Native Desktop and Mobile Applications

Native desktop and mobile applications—and frameworks to build them—have existed for many years, but they were typically proprietary ecosystems coupled with platform-specialized technologies. Developers needed to engage with two starkly different ecosystems and communities to write iOS applications in Objective-C as opposed to Android applications in Java.

---

[1]Marcotte, Ethan. "Responsive Web Design." *A List Apart*. 25 May 2010. Accessed 1 April 2018. http://alistapart.com/article/responsive-web-design

By the late 2000s, frameworks endeavoring to facilitate cross-device native mobile application implementations began to appear. These tended to be based on nonnative code, as seen in the example of Xamarin, which translated applications written in C# to native-ready code. The releases of Titanium and Cordova (formerly known as PhoneGap), which are web application frameworks optimized for building native mobile applications, reflected a new tendency toward web-to-native frameworks enabling developers to write code familiar to them before compiling it to native code. By 2013, Titanium powered applications on approximately 10 percent of all smartphones around the world.[2]

In light of the JavaScript renaissance, JavaScript frameworks and libraries like React and Angular have immersed themselves in the web-to-native paradigm by providing vanilla JavaScript-to-native frameworks like React Native, Electron, and Ionic. Some of these frameworks also offer features that enable developers to build native desktop applications through web technologies. As such, JavaScript-to-native frameworks emphasize cross-platform similarity in applications by touting the desire for web applications to be indistinguishable from their native equivalents.

Zero User Interfaces

Beyond the realm of web development, user interfaces are evolving in similarly disruptive ways, staking their claim to the range of channels that organizations are asked to consider outside of web sites, web applications, and native applications. Some user interfaces used today on a day-to-day basis no longer rely on manual—or visual—user interface components. Such **zero user interfaces** lack screens and physically manipulated elements entirely.[3]

Voice assistants such as the Amazon Echo and Google Home both fit the zero user interface paradigm, but other interfaces depending on aural or gestural manipulation are also part of this paradigm, such as ambient and haptic interfaces that react to surrounding stimuli rather than explicit user input on a screen or manual input.

---

[2]Bort, Julie. "Microsoft Might Buy a Startup that Powers 10 Percent of the World's Smartphones." *Business Insider*. 1 February 2013. Accessed 1 April 2018. http://www.businessinsider.com/ microsoft-eyes-appcelerator-acquisition-2013-2#ixzz2YmNSFhT7

[3]Brownlee, John. "What Is Zero UI? (And Why Is It Crucial to the Future of Design?)." *Fast Company*. 2 July 2015. Accessed 1 April 2018. https://www.fastcodesign.com/3048139/ what-is-zero-ui-and-why-is-it-crucial-to-the-future-of-design

Although well beyond the scope of this book, zero user interfaces and their interaction design will demand a rethinking of usability testing as interfaces become increasingly adaptive and intelligent in their own right.

Conversational Content

Conversational content, which entails interaction with content through dialogues in text or voice, has been a favorite target of marketing teams and organizations in the last few years. The aforementioned voice assistants occupy one side of the conversational interface spectrum, but traditional chatbots, Short Message Service (SMS) textbots, and messenger bots like those encountered on Facebook and Slack are also changing the face of content access. Some voice assistants such as Amazon Echo and Google Home can be programmed with custom functionality, whereas device assistants such as Cortana and Siri reflect more closed ecosystems that limit custom code.

Conversational content is inaccessible without an information architecture that provides forks in the road leading to one's desired content. It tends toward single utterances limited in length to maintain attention and cannot depend on media assets outside of audio. Users can only interact with conversational interfaces in verbal forms that are spoken or written.

For many organizations, serving web-based content as conversational content without any change through a rudimentary chatbot might satisfy the need for centralized content but is wholly inadequate for customers that require more conversation-friendly content resembling authentic human interlocution. Crafting conversational content remains a relatively unexplored wilderness where platform agnosticism is beginning to take shape, with the help of new businesses such as Dialogflow (formerly known as api.ai).

Content in Augmented and Virtual Reality

Even as content is becoming increasingly conversational, content is also more and more contextual. Nascent technologies such as machine vision (detecting and identifying items in view of a device) and augmented reality (AR; superimpositions of media over a projection of the real world) portend a future in which content will be a fixture in our physical world as much as it is in our digital world.

Particularly important for marketing teams and organizations is an emphasis on location-specific content that can also reside in the context of a user's physical surroundings, whether that entails a projection of the user's actual surroundings (as in AR) or a fictional presentation (as in virtual reality [VR]). Forrester Research claimed in 2016 that "companies will continue to experiment with AR and VR, setting the foundation for larger implementations in 2018 and 2019."[4] On the heels of the Consumer Electronics Show (CES) 2018, a survey commissioned by Accenture also buttressed this view,[5] indicating that users are becoming more comfortable with interfaces in AR and VR that offer information about their surroundings or help them improve their performance in certain tasks. The usefulness of AR and VR now stretches well beyond their gaming-oriented trappings.[6]

Such superimposed content provided to AR and VR interfaces is not only contextual but overlain or projected on top of the user's view. As such, unlike web content or conversational content, any limited amount of text or media needs to complement the preexisting visual elements of the user experience. Unlike conversational interfaces or manual interfaces where interactions take place via explicit input, AR and VR interfaces typically rely on user perspective or gestures to move across application states.

Situational Content

With the growing maturity of geolocation technology, pinpointing a user's location allows for improved targeting of content according to where a user is at the current moment. There are many ways to triangulate the location of a user, but the most commonly used methods today are via location services on smartphones or Bluetooth Low Energy (BLE) proximity beacons such as those produced by Estimote. Today, this is something wifi is capable of as well.

---

[4]"2017 Predictions: Dynamics that Will Shape the Future in the Age of the Customer." *Forrester*. October 2016. Accessed 1 April 2018. https://go.forrester.com/wp-content/uploads/ Forrester-2017-Predictions.pdf

[5]"Time to Navigate the Super My Way: Give Digital Consumers Exactly What They're Looking For." *Accenture*. 2018. Accessed 1 April 2018. https://www.accenture.com/us-en/ event-digital-consumer-survey-2018

[6]Martin, Chuck. "Consumers Warm to Virtual, Augmented Reality: CES Study." *MediaPost*. 10 January 2018. Accessed 1 April 2018. https://www.mediapost.com/publications/ article/312758/consumers-warm-to-virtual-augmented-reality-ces.html

Recently, proximity marketing that delivers personalized content with the aid of beacons and other Internet of Things (IoT) hardware is gaining prominence. The content we consume in our daily lives is increasingly geospatial, locational, and situational. Enabling such content delivery is a range of technologies that function in tandem to facilitate more situational digital experiences. A 2015 report from ABI Research contends that shipments of Bluetooth-enabled beacons will exceed 400 million by 2020.[7] Concurrently, businesses such as Walmart, Target, and Macy's have adopted beacons to enhance their sales floor experiences, and 14 Marriott hotels are now using beacons as a means to deliver promotional messages showcasing available guest amenities.[8]

Nevertheless, this form of situational content often remains prohibitively difficult due to the complexity of orchestrating devices across the spectrum of hardware, each with its own software development kit (SDK). The dream of augmenting a user's perspective and surroundings with content—rather than the inverse—is remarkably distant from the manner in which content-first web sites are designed and architected, however.

Other Channels

We cannot account for all possible channels where content can be delivered, but three channels are particularly prominent in the wider industry, namely wearable technology, digital signage, and set-top boxes such as Apple TV and Roku.

In all of these, limitations intrinsic to these digital experiences restrict how content can be served. For instance, digital signage prizes legibility above all, resulting in a lower quantity of content so that it can be visible from large distances. At the other extreme, because real estate is at a high premium on smartwatches, content must consist of text at small sizes. Set-top boxes, meanwhile, contend with design limitations that encapsulate content in prefabricated templates adhering to a rigid set of rules.

---

[7]"BLE Beacon Shipments Break 400 Million in 2020." *ABI Research.* 30 July 2015. Accessed 1 April 2018. https://www.abiresearch.com/press/ ble-beacon-shipments-break-400-million-in-2020/

[8]Schumacher, Frederic. "Interaction, Personalization, and Tech: The 3 Biggest Trends in the Hospitality Industry 2017." *Metro Accelerator.* 21 April 2017. Accessed 1 April 2018. https:// metroaccelerator.com/blog/3-biggest-trends-in-the-hospitality-industry-2017/

Conclusion

The channel explosion continues unabated, and the interwoven narratives of content delivery and its technical paradigms challenge the very nature of what "content" truly entails in a world of digital experiences that are increasingly off the screen. In this chapter, we have inspected the range of dimensions along which content must succeed to better separate the content we need to present from the mechanisms by which we deliver it.

Whereas Drupal historically has focused on delivering content for consumption on web sites, decoupled Drupal asks developers, designers, and architects alike to reconsider this emphasis and move toward a more channel-agnostic stance where content is no longer coupled to strict mechanisms of presentation. In the next chapter, we dive deeper into the evolution of the CMS itself and how decoupled content management has become a compelling paradigm.

CHAPTER 2

The Server Side: From Monolithic to Decoupled CMS

Two long-term trends have led to the promulgation of decoupled Drupal as a viable approach rather than an unrealistic idea. These processes are essential to understand how CMSs are evolving to embrace a channel-agnostic approach by default.

First, in response to the channel explosion and the trend toward multichannel publishing workflows, CMSs, like many other software projects, have gradually adopted RESTful APIs as a means to serve data to many different consumers rather than a single presentation layer tightly coupled to the back end. These decoupled architectures, in which many consumers rely on a single data service, reflect the disentangling of the CMS (server side) from its front end (client side) to deliver data to diverse consumers.

Second, the tendency for the client side to become less static and more dynamic has upended both user experience and web development paradigms in recent years, as discussed in Chapter 1. Most efforts to create interactive experiences involved enriching web pages with more application-like behavior, seen in the seamless user experience features found on native applications such as transitions across states and the real-time appearance of new content without an explicit user request. Most web CMSs were built in the early Web 2.0 era (see Chapter 3), when editorial interfaces needed to contend with just display rather than behavior.

The CMS has traditionally consisted of a monolithic rather than decoupled architecture, in which the software governs all elements of content management, from database access to string concatenation in templates to page rendering and everything in between. This characterization is true of many long-standing CMSs like WordPress and Joomla. However, the spread of new devices and applications has encouraged many

11

© Preston So 2018
P. So, *Decoupled Drupal in Practice*, https://doi.org/10.1007/978-1-4842-4072-4_2

in the CMS landscape to repurpose extant means of communicating with other systems, typically used for server-to-server communication, to serve content to an array of front-end consumers.

Drupal, the free and open source CMS created by Dries Buytaert in 2001, is a framework written in PHP and distributed under the GNU General Public License. Historically, Drupal has been used for a variety of web sites such as personal blogs, complex corporate and government sites, and knowledge management sites. The Drupal community is global, with thousands of contributors around the world.

Monolithic Content Management

In the past, these web-based implementations tended to be unitary in that native mobile applications or other experiences were unavailable to users; in short, the only form of access was the web browser through traditional means. However, because these web sites now often have other applications in parallel, providing a single source of content as a centerpiece for an application ecosystem has become a paramount concern.

Drupal, however, has historically employed a *monolithic* architecture, meaning that it is a contiguous end-to-end system with no ability to decouple subsystems from one another, particularly the Drupal theme layer, which encapsulates the Drupal front end. This tight coupling led to symptoms such as *Drupalisms* on the front end, a phenomenon in which opaque Drupal terminology is exposed as HTML and CSS classes, puzzling front-end developers less familiar with Drupal who are tasked with building a Drupal theme.

As an example of how tight this coupling was with regard to multiple clients, in versions of Drupal prior to version 7, it was not possible to serve raw Drupal content, rather than HTML pages fully rendered by Drupal, to other systems or front ends. In other words, it was not possible to use Drupal solely for its database abstraction layer or for its Views collections.

Decoupled Content Management

In contrast, *decoupled* CMS architectures involve components of a system that interact with each other through machine-to-machine interfaces such as web services rather than explicitly depending on each other as Drupal's subsystems do. Whereas some service-oriented systems consist entirely of small components that communicate without interdependencies, most CMSs that can be decoupled tend to exercise this separation of concerns between the *front end* (or client side) and *back end* (or server side) to enable greater flexibility on either side.

A useful way to illustrate the difference between monolithic and decoupled CMSs is through astronomical metaphors. We can imagine monolithic CMSs as resembling planet Earth, a single contiguous unit with many interdependent subsystems. Meanwhile, decoupled CMSs can be thought of as individual Earths having many satellites that transmit and receive messages between the CMS and decoupled consumers, as seen in Figure 2-1.

Figure 2-1. *In this illustration, Mars represents "decoupled" bases that exchange data through requests to and responses from a "monolithic" Earth, in this case, monolithic Drupal*

Consider, for instance, a scenario where a Martian base with a limited capacity to store information must retrieve certain data from mission control on Earth to keep functioning properly. Rather than housing all of the mechanisms required to store and prepare these data on Mars itself, the Martian base can request only the small mission-critical pieces of information from Earth that it immediately requires. In that way, the Martian base can operate in a much more lightweight fashion, as mission control on Earth is the unit that is solely responsible for all of the other concerns with the required data, such as its archival and preparation for transmission.

In the case of Drupal, this analogy additionally succeeds because Drupal 8 is not built in a services-oriented fashion. That is, when Drupal 8 is decoupled, this does not mean that its subsystems are separated from one another. Instead, the Drupal theme layer is left *unused* as other decoupled systems take its place as consumers of data. As we'll see later, this is why such a diverse and flexible range of architectural approaches (see Chapter 4) is possible with Drupal.

For this reason also, the monikers *decoupled* and *headless* Drupal, both frequently used interchangeably to describe Drupal, are not as accurate as they seem. In short, Drupal in its traditional form is a monolithic CMS backing decoupled applications, but it is not decoupled itself insofar as its internal dependencies disappear. Instead, traditional Drupal is decoupled in the sense that its communication interfaces enable it to operate as a web service and without a front end enabled.

Note   Some practitioners prefer to call decoupled Drupal headless. In its broadest meaning, *headless software* is software that does not make use of a graphical user interface (GUI). However, such an interface already exists for Drupal, namely the command-line interfaces Drush and Drupal Console, which enable administration of Drupal solely through a terminal. Nonetheless, *headless* does effectively illustrate the lack of use of Drupal's coupled front end. Both terms suffer from imprecision and connotations conferred by other terminology.

Figure 2-2 is a simple rendering that depicts a basic architecture for decoupled Drupal. We'll be revisiting this diagram in Chapter 3.

Site or repository built in
Drupal

Consumer
application

Figure 2-2. *In this diagram, a Drupal site acting as a traditional site or content repository contains a web service (often a RESTful API) that accepts HTTP requests and issues HTTP responses in JSON or XML to an HTTP client located on a decoupled application, which might be server side or client side*

Web Services

Today, *RESTful APIs,* a particular subset of web APIs, are the most common communication interface between Drupal and other systems or applications. There are several important terms here to decode, namely *API, REST,* and *RESTful API.*

An API consists of a set of defined methods and object classes that collectively describe the expected behavior of a framework such as Drupal when certain actions are undertaken. In simple terms, an API abstracts the underlying implementation of the framework by exposing just the classes or methods that a developer might require in building an application that builds on that framework.

Note   The API reference for all Drupal versions is located at `api.drupal.org`. More in-depth API documentation is located at `drupal.org/docs/8/api` for Drupal 8 (including documentation about the RESTful API) and at `drupal.org/docs/7/api` for Drupal 7.

Drupal has many APIs that govern the process of extending and reusing the existing implementation, such as the Database API, Entity API, and Form API, but it did not have a web service and corresponding API until Drupal 8. *Web service APIs* are APIs that allow for machine-to-machine communication among web servers like Drupal's or between web servers and clients.

In the early 2000s, many web service APIs were built atop the available open standards at the time: Extensible Markup Language (XML), the data format; Simple Object Access Protocol (SOAP), the transfer protocol for communication; and Web Services Description Language (WSDL), a means of describing web APIs in XML. Later, JavaScript Object Notation (JSON) became a popular format for encoding data over web service APIs, because of its natural fit for client-side JavaScript code and the challenges of parsing XML effectively.

Note   The W3C defined *web services* in 2002 as "designed to support interoperable machine-to-machine interaction over a network."[1] However, this is a narrower definition than the one provided earlier and encompasses several requirements, most notably the use of SOAP over HTTP rather than REST.

REST and RESTful APIs

Many web service APIs today adhere to the ideas of *Representational State Transfer* (REST) and are known as *REST-compliant*. REST is a term promulgated by Roy Fielding in his dissertation on the subject and consists of a set of architectural principles for designing web services. REST-compliant, or RESTful, web services permit other systems to query and modify *web resources*, which are stateful representations of data located at particular uniform resource identifiers (URIs), through a limited and unchanging range of stateless operations. These web resources are representations of the underlying data, usually serialized as JSON or XML.

A RESTful API must adhere to certain architectural constraints, commonly known as *Fielding constraints* after their promulgator, to be considered REST-compliant or RESTful:

- *Client/server separation:* The client/server model is one of the most prominent examples of separation of concerns in web architecture. A RESTful API presumes that the data are eventually destined for a consumer that includes a user interface displaying those data. The RESTful API itself is located on the server side, where data storage occurs.

- *Stateless:* A REST client, which is a consumer of the RESTful API, should not pass information about the client application's state to the server for storage and use on the server. Each request issued by the consumer should contain all information necessary to execute on the request on the server side, such that all state is retained on the consumer.

- *Cacheable:* Responses from RESTful APIs should include information about the cacheability of that response. This is to disallow clients from employing stale or unsuitable data when responding.

---

[1]"Web Services Glossary." World Wide Web Consortium. 11 February 2004. Accessed 17 May 2018. `https://www.w3.org/TR/ws-gloss/`

- *Layered system:* A RESTful API must be able to function where there is middleware or intermediaries such as a cache system or load balancer. This is because clients are typically unaware of the nature of the destination of requests they issue.

- *Code on demand:* Although optional, a server might also transmit through a RESTful API additional executable code in the form of client-side JavaScript. This is to allow for clients to be extended by logic located on the server.

- *Uniform interface:* The most important of all the Fielding constraints, clients must be able to rely on a uniform and unchanging interface to query and manipulate data on the server side. Resources are typically identified in requests by their URIs, and they are manipulated solely through their representations (e.g., in JSON or XML). A client must have enough information about the resource through its representation to perform operations that modify or delete it and to process it on the client, such as an Internet media type. Finally, a RESTful API must adhere to standards of *hypermedia as the engine of application state* (HATEOAS), in which a REST client should be able to use links provided by the initial response of the server to understand how to interact with the API solely through the API's response rather than any hard-coded information.

RESTful APIs are those APIs that are REST-compliant; that is, they follow the architectural principles laid out by REST. RESTful APIs operate using HTTP methods (GET, POST, PATCH, and DELETE, among others) and define a specific Internet media type (e.g., application/vnd.collection+json) in which representations will be formatted. They also have a base URI that serves as an initial entry point for REST clients.

RESTful and API-First Drupal

Now that we've introduced the key principles of REST and some of the fundamentals of web APIs, we can examine Drupal and how it characterizes itself as RESTful or non-RESTful. The wide use of REST has led to some confusion in terms of identifying which web services solutions are RESTful or not in the Drupal community.

In Drupal 6 and 7, web service API capabilities were limited solely to contributed modules, most notably *Services,* which provided an API specifically for performing operations against a Drupal site efficiently. However, due to its wide range of capabilities that go well beyond normal RESTful API functionality, Services does not explicitly follow the Fielding constraints, which means that it is not strictly RESTful. Nonetheless, other modules are available in Drupal 7, such as **restWS** and **Restful**, which do adhere to the REST constraints.

During the development of Drupal 8, the Web Services and Context Core Initiative (WSCCI) endeavored to allow server-to-server communication over a network using Drupal. This community initiative, coordinated by Larry Garfield, led to the creation of several modules, most notably the **REST** module, which provides the foundation for RESTful APIs in Drupal. The default REST API available out-of-the-box in Drupal 8 Core is REST-compliant (see Chapter 7).

In Drupal 8's contributed module ecosystem, there are several important additional modules available, including non-RESTful Services for Drupal 8. The first of the REST-compliant modules, **RELAXed Web Services**, is a module that follows the CouchDB API specification, with an eye toward content staging, content workflow, and PouchDB- and Hoodie-oriented use cases (see Chapters 8 and 13). At the time of print, **JSON API**, a module that implements the eponymous RESTful API specification in Drupal, is slated for inclusion in Drupal core as a stable module in a forthcoming release (see Chapters 8 and 12).

In recent years, other options have surfaced that do not adhere to REST and promise certain functionality beyond what REST-compliant solutions provide, most notably **GraphQL** (see Chapters 8 and 14), a query language specialized for consumer-driven queries (and therefore responses tailored for the consumer). Because of the confusion around what constitutes a REST-compliant module, from this point forward we refer to RESTful Drupal solely as a Drupal implementation using those modules with RESTful functionality.

In this case, *API-first Drupal* refers to a Drupal implementation using those modules with any web services functionality, irrespective of whether the module is REST-compliant or not. It also includes the notion that Drupal is *API-first,* where the web services are counted as Drupal's most essential features and consumers using the APIs are Drupal's most important users. Indeed, this is the reason for the Drupal community's ongoing *API-first initiative,* a direct successor to WSCCI working to advance Drupal as a web service provider.

Content as a Service

The story of decoupled management doesn't end here. An additional development, extrinsic to the broad range of web services solutions in Drupal, has galvanized the community to acknowledge and address the importance of developers of other applications who might wish to rely on Drupal solely as a back-end web service provider.

The earliest nominal examples of decoupled content management originate from a preexisting category of platforms known as *mobile back end as a service* (mBaaS or simply BaaS), which aim to provide a centralized data repository for native mobile applications. Typical functionality not only included data storage and access, but also mobile-specific capabilities such as push notifications and integration with other systems, often depending on SDKs for use on the client side. Examples of mBaaS vendors include Kinvey and Built.io.

Whereas mBaaS platforms are specialized for native mobile applications, *content as a service* (CaaS) encompasses all use cases involving content and content applications. In a CaaS model, content is delivered on demand to client applications that consume web APIs licensed under a hosting subscription. The platform serves as the content repository for any consumer applications and typically offers additional content management features such as content workflow and user management. Examples of CaaS vendors include Contentful and Prismic.

Many opt to decouple Drupal because they wish to harness both Drupal's extensive content management capabilities and the greater flexibility that decoupled front ends can provide. Others do so because they might need applications beyond Drupal to view and manipulate a single collection of content. Whatever the case, although Drupal might not be as specialized as mBaaS or CaaS providers, Drupal does benefit from its commitment to being free and open source software from end to end, including the Waterwheel SDKs that are suited specifically for decoupled use cases (see Chapter 16).

This means that if you host Drupal and any Drupal-backed (i.e., consuming or manipulating Drupal data) applications yourself, you can take advantage of Drupal as a back-end web service provider without paying a penny.

Conclusion

Web service APIs undergird all decoupled CMS architectures because they are the conduit through which data travel on its way from the server to the consumer. Some web service APIs are also RESTful, which means that they adhere to certain constraints that characterize a range of widely used APIs. Nevertheless, in recent years, non-RESTful web service solutions have also become popular both inside and outside the Drupal community.

The CMS, historically a monolithic entity, has become decoupled because of the exigencies of multichannel content workflows that publish content to many different presentation layers. In this chapter, we examined how this evolution occurred and how Drupal's efforts have led to its favorable positioning as a decoupled CMS in the wider industry. In the next chapter, we turn to the client side to explain how the evolution in technologies such as JavaScript has engendered a wholesale shift in how data are handled and ultimately presented.

## CHAPTER 3

The Client Side: From Static to Dynamic Pages

The introduction of new digital experiences and content channels, and the underlying software evolution that made it possible, is one important factor that led to the interest in decoupling content management paradigms, as discussed in Chapter 1. Nonetheless, changes in the architecture of web pages—both in terms of what users demand from them and how they are composed—directly encouraged some to decouple Drupal from its front end to use JavaScript-driven front ends instead.

From Web 1.0 to Web 2.x

In the 1990s, during the Web 1.0 era, web pages tended to be flat files, located on servers and administered through code editors. These *static pages* were each representations of state, but state changes could only occur through a server round trip, initiated through a full-page refresh in the browser, as illustrated in Figure 3-1. In Web 1.0 pages, this is how HTML forms such as newsletter subscription forms would deliver feedback to the user. In Drupal's case, this would entail two bootstraps of Drupal.

© Preston So 2018
P. So, *Decoupled Drupal in Practice*, https://doi.org/10.1007/978-1-4842-4072-4_3

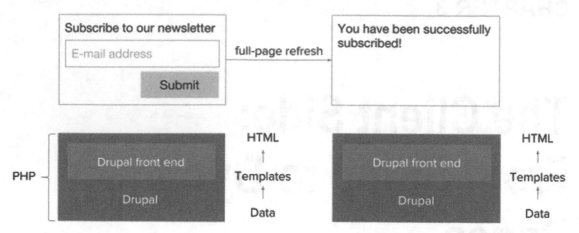

Figure 3-1. *In the Web 1.0 era, applications typically articulated application state as static pages*

The early 2000s brought a new approach to working with web pages: CMSs such as Drupal. In Web 2.0, web sites that enabled user-generated content, a straightforward user experience, and interoperability across devices were valued. With its early focus on user-generated content and editorial experience, Drupal's administrative pages can be considered part of this trend.

Concurrently with the dissemination of Web 2.0 as an ideal, the concept of *dynamic pages* appeared. Dynamic pages can mean one of two things: On the server side, dynamic pages are composed by a framework such as Drupal according to a variety of conditions, such as the logged-in user and the particular search parameters entered. Server-side dynamic pages also used relational databases like MySQL instead of flat file assets. On the client side, dynamic pages are those that are manipulated or otherwise rendered by client-side JavaScript, which could parse HTML attributes such as onMouseOver.

In the later 2000s, web pages gradually became increasingly dynamic not only on the server side—thanks to frameworks like Drupal, which used PHP to preprocess data for pages—but also on the client side. Asynchronous JavaScript and XML (Ajax) is a collection of client-side techniques to asynchronously retrieve and manipulate data on a server and to inject those data dynamically without the need for a page reload.

Through Ajax, vast improvements to user experience were made possible, and this is clearly seen in Drupal's own Ajax framework for dynamic client-side updates. In the case of a lowly newsletter subscription form, this meant that on submission, an Ajax spinner could appear signifying the journey to the server, and a subsequent overwriting of the form could indicate success or failure, as seen in Figure 3-2. Each change in the application state would not require a full-page refresh.

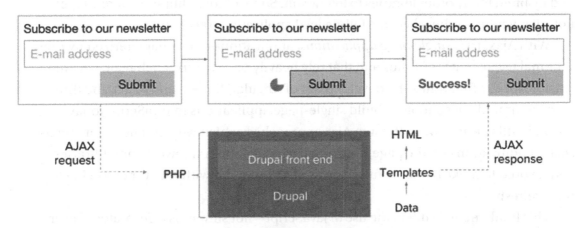

Figure 3-2. *In Ajax, a small portion of the page is replaced with an Ajax spinner indicating a change in progress and reinjected with new information requested from the server*

The principles that governed Ajax were quickly applied to increasingly larger scopes. It was not only forms that experienced this kind of dynamic replacement and such state changes without page refreshes; entire layout components of the page, and gradually even the entirety of the page, became fodder for client-side dynamic behavior. With the need for alternatives to JavaScript due to inadequate browser support now dwindling, client-side techniques are quickly gaining momentum as JavaScript adoption widens and user experience requirements become more demanding.

The JavaScript Renaissance

One of the effects of the Ajax movement was an explosion of growth in the wider JavaScript community, thanks to the "professionalization" of this once-lowly language. In the 2000s, JavaScript was often denigrated as a programming language used by nonprogrammers, due to the limited scope possible for JavaScript applications along with proprietary influence.

In the late 2000s and early 2010s, use of JavaScript began to be codified and reformulated in unprecedented ways. First, John Resig's creation of jQuery, a document object model (DOM) manipulation library, led to the normalization of Ajax techniques and inspired many other libraries to follow suit. Some of these libraries were widget libraries, whereas others became full-fledged application frameworks.

With Ajax, true *single-page applications,* applications often characterized by their minimal use of page refreshes and that rely heavily on JavaScript behavior, became feasible for the first time. The development of Angular, Ember, and React, the three most commonly used tools to build single-page applications in JavaScript today, began in this period. In contrast to Ajax approaches, which were intended for small-scale modifications on the page, single-page application frameworks and libraries endeavored to make dynamic full-page renders possible, without ever enforcing a page refresh.

This fundamental shift in the use of JavaScript—not simply as a decorator of user interfaces, but as a page renderer—also resulted in the expansion of JavaScript to realms outside the web browser, especially to the server side. In 2009, Node.js, an open source JavaScript runtime environment, was released. Beyond the revolution in front-end build tools that Node.js engendered through the Node Package Manager (NPM), Node.js also made server-side JavaScript possible.

Some practitioners in the JavaScript community have treated the "professionalization" of JavaScript as emblematic of a larger *JavaScript renaissance* that includes the transition of small-scale Ajax to large-scale JavaScript frameworks and of JavaScript limited to the browser to JavaScript available during the build process, and most impactfully, on the server.

Universal (Isomorphic) JavaScript

Because JavaScript was formerly only executable on the client side, if JavaScript were responsible for the entire page rendering process, this code would need to be downloaded, parsed, and executed by the browser before most functionality would be available. Two metrics for determining perceived page performance are *time to first paint,* ending when the user begins to see content on the page, and *time to first interaction,* ending when the user is able to interact with the application's user interface.

In 2010, Twitter, in the midst of a redesign, architected a new client-side interface that required substantial execution of JavaScript to render and enrich the user interface. Client-side JavaScript would retrieve the data from a web service API optimized for a variety of devices and populate the page, largely with client-side logic. In the end, the interface's time to first interaction suffered considerably, particularly on underprepared mobile devices. In 2012, Twitter employed a new approach in which the initial pages were rendered server-side and the client side bootstrapped an application with more limited scope that furnished the expected behavior after rendering was complete.

In 2013, Airbnb reinvented JavaScript application architectures by using Node.js for *universal* (also known as *shared*) JavaScript, in which at least some JavaScript is executed identically on both client and server—although this code is replicated on both, it is, in effect, shared. On the server side, an application framework composes an initial render of the page using data provided through RESTful API calls or a NoSQL database such as MongoDB. Once the initial render appears in the browser, the same application framework begins "rehydrating" the server-side render by performing asynchronous RESTful API calls and injecting updated data into the DOM.

Consider Figure 3-3, which depicts a typical isomorphic JavaScript implementation.

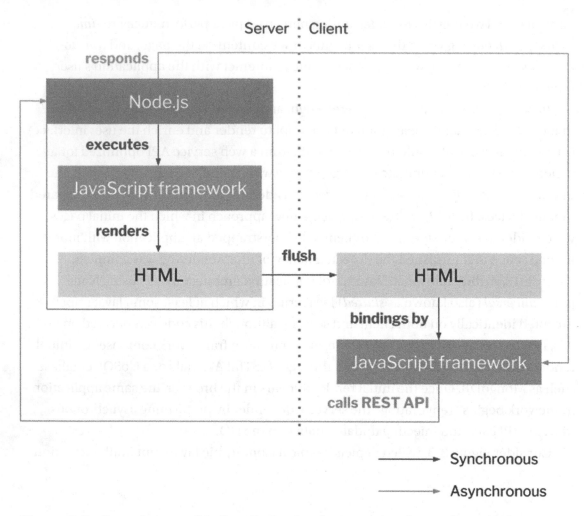

Figure 3-3. *In an isomorphic JavaScript implementation focused on rendering shared across client and server, Node.js executes a framework, which composes an initial application state in client-ready markup. This initial application state is handed to the client side, which initializes the framework to facilitate additional client-side rendering that is needed, especially to "rehydrate" or update the initial state issued by the server side.*

Airbnb's most important invention was a completely reusable rendering system. Because the JavaScript framework is the same on the server and client sides, it's much more convenient to debug or maintain the rendering code. As such, the main difference between server-side and client-side rendering in the universal context is not the templating language used, but instead what data derive from the server and how.

Apart from the modernization of JavaScript occurring presently through the solidifying ECMAScript 6 (ES6) specification, universal JavaScript is one of the most important motivations for the increased adoption of JavaScript-driven front ends. This means that monolithic Drupal, with its focus on PHP-rendered pages, might be cast as a second choice. Decoupling Drupal enables access to Node.js and JavaScript isomorphism.

Figure 3-4 depicts a typical isomorphic JavaScript implementation that consumes a CMS (in this case, Drupal).

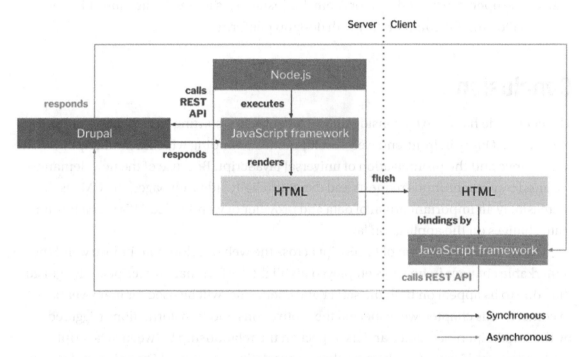

Figure 3-4. *In an isomorphic JavaScript implementation served data by a CMS, Node.js executes a framework, which retrieves data from a CMS such as Drupal and thereafter composes an initial application state in client-ready markup. Any asynchronous requests issued by the client side are directed to the CMS.*

JavaScript-to-Native Applications

One final aside to highlight is the growing need for unity across applications that comprise an application ecosystem, including not only traditional web applications but also native applications on mobile and desktop. This is both to maintain parity across disparate user experiences and developer experiences, but also to allow development teams to go to market more rapidly. To this end, many JavaScript frameworks now offer *JavaScript-to-native* compilation, in the sense that code in JavaScript-driven single-page applications can be rewritten as machine code.

Native mobile applications for Android and iOS typically require the use of Java (for Android), or languages like Objective-C and Swift (for iOS). Angular and React use Ionic and React Native, respectively, to compile single-page JavaScript applications into native code. Meanwhile, for desktop applications, where still other technologies are often used, solutions like Electron allow for single-page applications in JavaScript to be compiled to native. The open source code editor Atom, for instance, is a web application at its core but uses Electron for compatibility with desktop platforms.

Conclusion

The client side has evolved considerably in recent years, starting with the proliferation of Ajax and jQuery in front-end web development and ending with the JavaScript renaissance and the promulgation of universal JavaScript. Because of the new demands required by asynchronous requests and dynamic client-side web pages, the CMS is increasingly an important origin of data and provider of web service APIs that allow for state changes on the application layer.

The wide dissemination of JavaScript across the web development industry and the remarkable changes in how it is employed highlight the fact that JavaScript is a language that, due to its appeal on both the server and client side, will be used for many years to come. In this chapter, we inspected the motivations and transformations triggered by the JavaScript renaissance and its impact on the relationship between JavaScript applications and Drupal. In the next chapter, we define decoupled Drupal more formally as a set of architectural paradigms and describe each of the most common decoupled Drupal approaches in turn.

CHAPTER 4

Decoupled Drupal

Simply put, *decoupled Drupal* is the process of employing Drupal as a web service provider that exposes data for consumption by other applications (Figure 4-1). Drupal can be used to back other server-side applications, native desktop and mobile applications, single-page JavaScript applications, over-the-top applications, and IoT applications. Indeed, any application that can perform requests against a web service can be a consumer of the APIs exposed by a decoupled Drupal implementation.

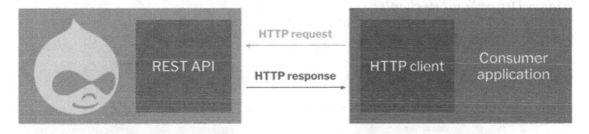

Site or repository built in Drupal   Consumer application

Figure 4-1. *In its simplest form, decoupled Drupal involves communication via HTTP requests and responses between a web service in a Drupal site or content repository (such as a RESTful API) and an HTTP client in a Drupal-backed consumer application (such as a single-page JavaScript application).*

We can see the distinction between monolithic and decoupled Drupal in Figure 4-2. In monolithic Drupal, the Drupal front end is part and parcel of the overarching Drupal bootstrap; as such the entirety of the implementation is written in Drupal's native PHP. In the decoupled case, a consumer application is written in an arbitrary language, such as JavaScript, Java, or even PHP, and interacts with Drupal through a RESTful API present on the server side, as seen in Figure 4-3.

© Preston So 2018
P. So, *Decoupled Drupal in Practice*, https://doi.org/10.1007/978-1-4842-4072-4_4

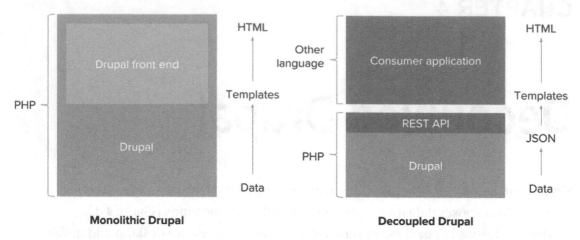

Figure 4-2. *In monolithic Drupal (left), the entire bootstrap, from data retrieval to template rendering, is written in PHP, and the Drupal front end (the theme layer) is inseparable from other Drupal subsystems. In decoupled Drupal (right), an arbitrary language can be used for the consumer application, and the RESTful API bridges Drupal and its clients.*

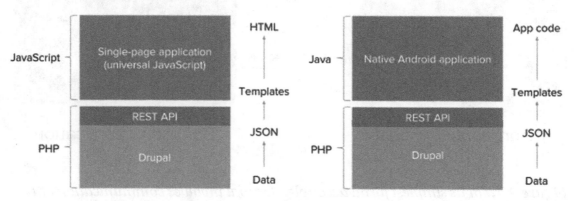

Figure 4-3. *A decoupled Drupal implementation can serve any manner of Drupal-backed consumers, including a single-page application written in JavaScript (left) or a native mobile application written in Java for Android (right).*

One crucial note is that a single Drupal repository or decoupled Drupal back end can serve as the centerpiece of an application ecosystem where many applications rely on data originating from Drupal, as illustrated in Figure 4-4. For purposes of content syndication, where a unitary source of content is important to keep data in sync across all applications, an architecture where a single Drupal implementation feeds many applications can be optimal.

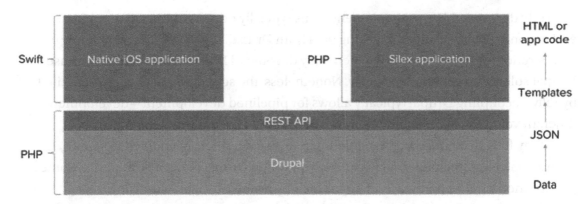

Figure 4-4. *A single Drupal site or repository can serve as a hub of data that serves information to a variety of applications collectively consuming the same API*

Fully Decoupled Drupal

In *fully decoupled Drupal,* a decoupled Drupal installation serves as a data repository for consumption by Drupal-backed applications. In other words, there is a complete separation between the client side and server side, resulting in differing experiences for Drupal users and developers (see Figure 4-5). For developers, whereas the back end remains intact, the front end requires expertise not traditionally found in Drupal. For end users, the front end might be either the administrative interfaces that Drupal provides on the back end or the user-facing front end that replaces the Drupal theme.

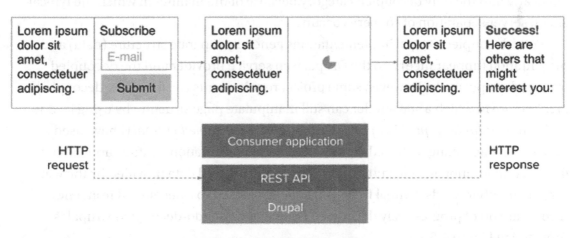

Figure 4-5. *In this example of fully decoupled Drupal, a consumer application (in this case a single-page JavaScript application) performs all rendering on both the server side and client side. Drupal is consulted solely via HTTP requests.*

Fully decoupled Drupal implementations typically do not expose a Drupal front end beyond the applications receiving data from Drupal, either due to redundancy or a preference for other front ends. Often, fully decoupled Drupal implementations use Drupal solely as a content repository. Nonetheless, the separation of concerns entailed by fully decoupling Drupal typically allows for pipelined development—development at different velocities by differently specialized teams—to occur (see Chapter 5).

Many fully decoupled implementations consist of a single decoupled front end, such as one implemented in a JavaScript framework, connected to a Drupal site. Some practitioners choose to replace a Drupal site's front end outright to transform the branded experience into a more application-like experience. This kind of architecture, however, means that without the need for the original Drupal front end, the decoupled front end merely replaces rather than augments Drupal's capabilities.

Pseudo-Decoupled Drupal

When it comes to site building and assembly, this can present a particularly intractable challenge. Site builders prefer to have control over the layout and structure of their pages by using Drupal modules such as Panels, but decoupled front ends do away with this capability. For the use case where decoupling is desired but layout control is also required, there is a category of fully decoupled Drupal implementations that do not fall neatly into the fully decoupled category because of the manner in which the typical client/server separation of concerns occurs.

Fully decoupled Drupal implementations generally separate structure (data) and presentation (appearance) into the Drupal web service provider and the decoupled front end, respectively. However, some project requirements call for a fully decoupled architecture in which a site builder can still manipulate page structure by using layout tools. In *pseudo-decoupled Drupal* or *Drupal-aware decoupled Drupal* (I have used both terms interchangeably in the past), additional presentational information about layout configuration is transmitted alongside the structured data provided by the web service. In other words, Drupal front-end logic is exposed to a decoupled front end. A comparison of progressively decoupled Drupal and pseudo-decoupled Drupal is provided in Figure 4-6.

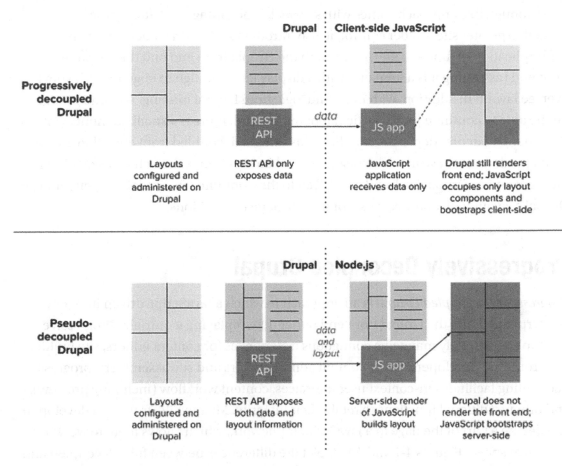

Figure 4-6. *An illustration of the differences between progressively decoupled Drupal and pseudo-decoupled Drupal*

As an example, RESTful Panels, a module that translates Panels configuration into JSON, provides JSON-encoded layout component names, which contain the data that will populate that layout component in the consumer application. As a result, the consumer application interprets both the structure (data) and some presentation (layout), even though the vast majority of presentational information is already present in the consumer application. Moreover, rendering is now split between the exterior render accomplished by the consumer application's own paradigms and the interior render that depends on information from Drupal before proceeding.

Although this approach comes with several key advantages, including but not limited to greater site builder control, it also introduces a few drawbacks. First, there is a duplication of functionality in that both the Drupal front end and the decoupled front end (assuming it is a front end with a display large enough to engender a layout) oversee layout. In addition, with front-end logic from Drupal missing, the render might not be able to continue past a particular point. Second, there is a small but nontrivial potential for circular dependencies. If, for instance, a decoupled front end allowed users to manipulate layout structure on itself rather than on Drupal, then changes on either the front end or Drupal back end could lead to the front-end layout tool's dependency on Drupal's layout tool, and vice versa, or introduce race conditions.

Progressively Decoupled Drupal

Progressively decoupled Drupal is an approach in which a JavaScript-driven front end is interpolated into the Drupal front end rather than replacing it outright. Progressive decoupling uniquely maintains contiguous experiences for content editors, site builders, and front-end developers. As for content administrators and site assemblers, progressive decoupling facilitates in-context user interfaces, content workflow (including preview), and other traditional functions to retain their integrity. Meanwhile, front-end developers can devote a part of the page to a JavaScript framework, which allows them to work at their own speed. Figures 4-7 and 4-8 depict the differences between fully decoupled and progressively decoupled Drupal.

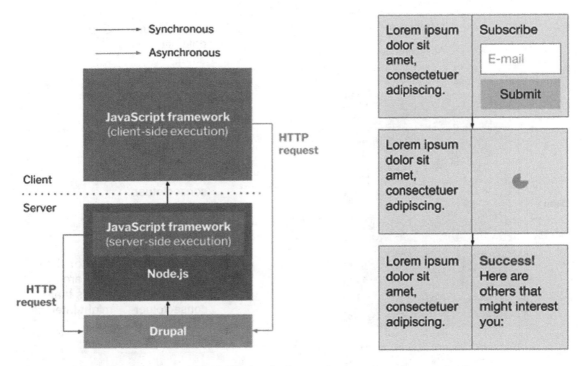

Figure 4-7. *In fully decoupled Drupal, the entire rendered page is the responsibility of a JavaScript framework. However, this means that you cannot leverage Drupal layout tools that would allow you to swap the columns or add a third column to this layout.*

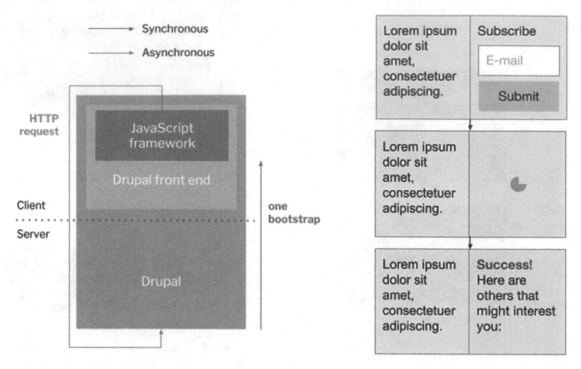

Figure 4-8. *In progressively decoupled Drupal, Drupal's page structure is intact, and by limiting the JavaScript framework's scope to just those dynamic components, you can retain layout because some of the page is fully under Drupal's control*

There are two primary motivations for this architectural approach that derive from both server-side and client-side issues, although progressive decoupling is more optimal for cases where greater power is required on the front end than Drupal provides by default. On the server side, some hosted platforms do not have a Node.js offering that would allow for JavaScript isomorphism to occur, despite a strong desire to use a JavaScript framework. Many Drupal hosting providers, for instance, only offer hosting for the LAMP stack that powers Drupal.

Meanwhile, on the client side, progressive decoupling is optimal for cases where greater power is required on the front end than Drupal provides by default. First, many of Drupal's features rely on the ability to effect changes in the front end, such as preprocessing data before it enters templates or displaying system notifications. Many who implement Drupal often don't want to see these features go. Second, although Drupal's front-end capabilities are strong, particularly with the arrival of Drupal 8, some practitioners prefer to use a more JavaScript-driven approach, even if server-side JavaScript execution is unavailable. In this case, a handover is possible between the server and client; Drupal renders the initial state of the page, then a JavaScript framework takes over once it has initialized.

Of course, because progressive decoupling is an approach that relates to the foregoing trend of *progressive enhancement*, it is only relevant for Drupal front ends. That is, progressively decoupled Drupal does not resolve the question of content syndication; rather, it is intended to enrich Drupal as is to introduce some of the novel functionality that galvanizes many architects to fully decouple Drupal instead.

Crucially, however, because progressive decoupling involves the interpolation of JavaScript into Drupal's front end, whose administrative interfaces already make considerable use of JavaScript, a spectrum of possibilities is possible, as seen in Figure 4-9. Although a JavaScript framework can occupy a very small portion of the page, it can also serve to dynamize ever-larger portions of the page. For instance, a minimal progressively decoupled implementation could scope JavaScript components tightly to individual blocks on the page.

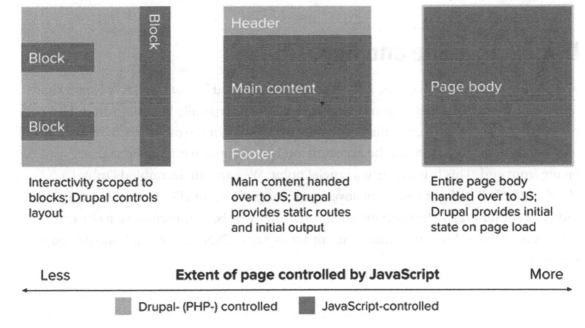

Figure 4-9. *This spectrum of progressively decoupled approaches demonstrates that dynamic components of a page can occupy solely a block in Drupal, leaving the majority of the page content in Drupal's hands; or it can encompass the entire page body, in a fashion almost indistinguishable from fully decoupled JavaScript applications.*

Meanwhile, other progressively decoupled implementations have explored placing the entire content area within a JavaScript framework while leaving the header and footer intact. The header and footer on pages tend to contain navigational elements that are not mutable across different pages and do not need substantial rerendering. In this way, Drupal can provide solely the static portions of the page, dedicating the dynamic portions to JavaScript, and simultaneously dictating static fallbacks for routes and furnishing an initial server-side output.

Finally, on the extreme end of the spectrum, some progressively decoupled implementations opt instead to replace the entire page body with a JavaScript framework, thus leaving Drupal with solely those portions outside the `<body>` element. Drupal provides an initial state, but a JavaScript framework subsequently exerts full control over the page. Most implementations of this nature use Drupal because of its rich and extensible `drupalSettings` JavaScript object (`Drupal.settings` in Drupal 7), which is usually served on first page load and can contain critical information about translations or configuration.

Drupal as a Site and Repository

Throughout these first chapters, I've referred to decoupled Drupal alternately as a site and a repository. This distinction is made because sites typically benefit from public, user-facing front ends like the default Drupal front end. On the other hand, repositories are usually data stores that can be accessed but lack their own endogenous user-facing front end. This brings me to a crucial point: We can call decoupled Drupal a *site* if and only if its front end is still leveraged alongside other clients; otherwise, it is merely a content *repository* serving clients. In other words, in this context, a site can act as a repository, but a repository cannot act as a site. This distinction is illustrated in Figure 4-10.

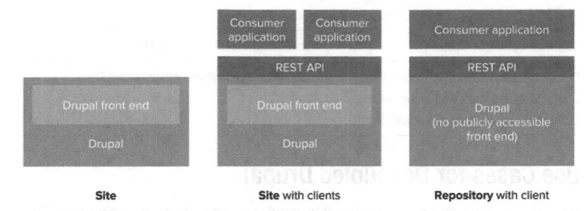

Figure 4-10. *In these three examples, Drupal is a site with a publicly accessible front end but no decoupled clients (i.e., monolithic Drupal, left), a Drupal site with an accessible front end with decoupled clients (i.e., fully decoupled Drupal with the Drupal portion intact, center), and a Drupal repository without an accessible front end but with a consumer client (i.e., fully decoupled Drupal where the client is the only front end available, right).*

Because of Drupal's rich capabilities and the functional losses incurred when decoupling Drupal, the risks and rewards of decoupling Drupal (see Chapters 5 and 6) must be carefully considered. Relegating Drupal to solely a repository role means that none of Drupal's features are accessible to the public, especially if an incident incapacitates all consumer applications. Meanwhile, retaining Drupal as a full-fledged site in addition to decoupled front ends, especially if there is only a single web-based client fitting this bill, can lead to confusion among users.

Although the distinction is small, conceptualizing Drupal in this bifurcated manner can help to isolate the use cases where decoupling Drupal is truly necessary. If you are using Drupal as a repository that serves only one client, Drupal might or might not be the most appropriate for your needs. For instance, there might be a way to address the client's needs within a monolithic implementation, such as through progressive decoupling.

As we can see in Table 4-1, most decoupled Drupal use cases are appropriate, as long as the Drupal site is accessible in the case of one or more clients, or it is the central repository in the case of many clients. However, a Drupal repository with only one client should raise the question of why a monolithic architecture is not pursued.

Table 4-1. *Use Cases for Decoupled Drupal*

Common Valid Use Cases	Use Cases Needing Discussion
Drupal as a site with one or many clients	Drupal as a repository with only one client
Drupal as a repository with many clients	
Drupal as a stand-alone site (monolithic)	

Use Cases for Decoupled Drupal

Because decoupled Drupal as a set of architectural approaches is still maturing, there is comparatively little guidance on how to decide whether an implementation should use decoupled or monolithic Drupal. Architects must weigh many advantages and disadvantages, such as the ones outlined in Chapters 5 and 6, before settling on a way forward. Decoupling Drupal is not a decision to be taken lightly, because it has vast ramifications on the nature of a project and the teams working on it.

A summary of the approaches discussed so far in this chapter follows, and is also illustrated in Figure 4-11.

- *Monolithic Drupal* consists of one single, contiguous site that does not expose data to other applications.

- *Progressively decoupled Drupal* entails the interpolation of a JavaScript framework into Drupal's front end to access its front-end developer experience and dynamic page capabilities without jettisoning Drupal's front end entirely.

- *Fully decoupled Drupal* comprises a Drupal site or repository that exposes data to other applications for consumption or manipulation. These applications can be any server-side or client-side application.

- *Pseudo-decoupled Drupal* involves fully decoupled Drupal, with the exception that presentational information such as layout configuration is exposed to other applications for consumption or manipulation. These applications tend to be those that make heavy use of layout, such as JavaScript applications.

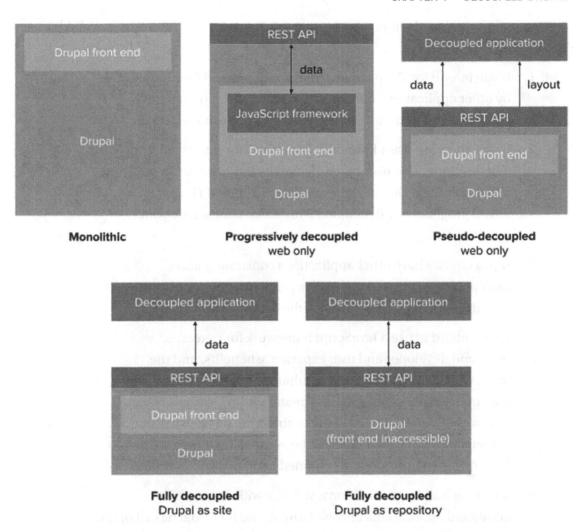

Figure 4-11. *A comprehensive comparison of all common approaches to decoupled Drupal, including (clockwise from top left) monolithic (traditional), progressively decoupled with a JavaScript framework, pseudo-decoupled with presentational exports, fully decoupled Drupal as a repository (with an inaccessible Drupal front end), and fully decoupled Drupal as a site*

Generally speaking, the following broad guidelines can be followed when making decisions around projects.

1. If you intend for Drupal data to be consumed and manipulated by other applications outside of Drupal, and you do not need Drupal's front-end functionality, use fully decoupled Drupal.

2. If you intend to use a JavaScript framework for perceived front-end developer and user benefits, and the framework will consume and manipulate Drupal data, use fully decoupled Drupal if and only if progressively decoupled Drupal does not satisfy your requirements.

3. If you already have other applications consuming and manipulating Drupal data besides your JavaScript application, fully decoupled Drupal is usually the better option.

4. If you intend to use a JavaScript framework for perceived front-end developer and user experience benefits, and the framework will consume and manipulate not only Drupal data but also presentational information from Drupal such as layout configuration needed to construct the page, use pseudo-decoupled Drupal. Nonetheless, be aware of the potential pitfalls from using this approach, as outlined earlier.

5. If you are building a traditional web site with no need for additional applications beyond Drupal, and if Drupal has all of the functionality you need, use monolithic Drupal.

To sum up these guidelines through a single dichotomy, if you need non-web-based applications outside of Drupal such as native applications to consume and manipulate Drupal data, fully decoupled Drupal is the best choice. On the other hand, if you need web-based applications in JavaScript to consume and manipulate Drupal data, you can choose between progressively and fully decoupled Drupal. If you prefer to retain all of Drupal's existing functionality, including aspects of the Drupal front end, and you do not require substantial evolution in your front-end developer experience and end-user experience, monolithic Drupal might be the right choice.

In Figure 4-12, these guidelines are applied within the context of a helpful flowchart for decision making when it comes to decoupled Drupal, taken from Dries Buytaert's blog post "How to decouple Drupal in 2018," which outlines several trajectories that decoupled Drupal architectures can pursue.

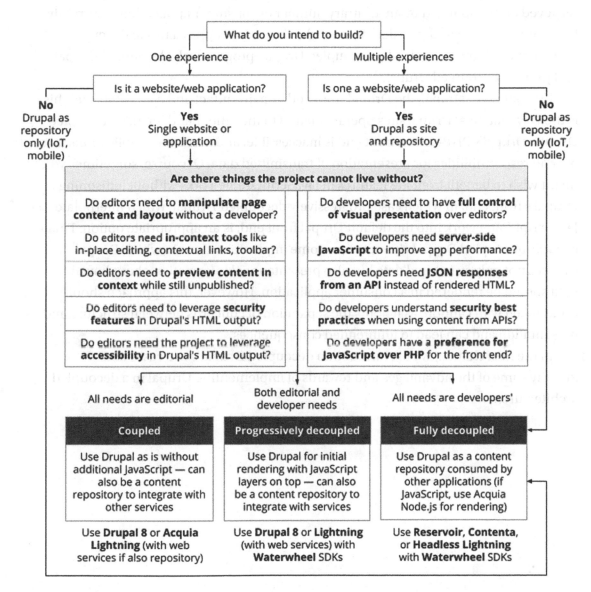

Figure 4-12. *A flowchart for decision makers considering decoupled Drupal architectures, reprinted with permission from Dries Buytaert (`https://dri.es/ how-to-decouple-drupal-in-2018`).*

Conclusion

In this chapter, we defined decoupled Drupal more formally and examined the most common approaches and use cases to decouple Drupal. As mentioned earlier, decoupled Drupal is the use of Drupal as a web service provider that allows data to be retrieved or manipulated by an arbitrary number of consumer applications. Currently, four architectural paradigms demonstrate the diversity of approaches in decoupled Drupal: monolithic Drupal, fully decoupled Drupal, progressively decoupled Drupal, and pseudo-decoupled Drupal.

In monolithic Drupal, the Drupal front end remains intact and accessible, and this is the way that most Drupal sites operate today. On the other hand, in fully decoupled Drupal, Drupal's PHP-driven front end is inaccessible, and consumer applications take over all responsibilities for presentation of transmitted data. Of course, sometimes you might wish to benefit from the features of JavaScript frameworks without jettisoning Drupal's front end, in which case progressively decoupled Drupal, which interpolates a JavaScript framework into the default Drupal front end, is an appropriate option. Finally, pseudo-decoupled Drupal characterizes some implementations in which Drupal exposes not only structured data but also presentational information about how the data should be rendered in a consumer application. However, this approach should be undertaken with caution, as it flouts the separation of concerns between structure and presentation and can lead to unintended consequences.

In the next chapter, we dig further into decoupled Drupal's use cases and identify some of the advantages and rewards of implementing Drupal in a decoupled architecture.

## CHAPTER 5

Advantages of Decoupled Drupal

There are many advantages of decoupling Drupal in your own implementation, but there are a few that are particularly valuable to marketing teams, to developers, and to businesses: namely content syndication ("write once, publish everywhere"), an architectural separation of concerns (structured data as distinct from presentation), and pipelined development. Employing Drupal as a web service provider is particularly beneficial if you have a team that specializes in JavaScript or in other front-end technologies besides Drupal.

Progressively decoupled Drupal has its own benefits, which are outlined throughout this chapter. These include pipelined development, but also the ability to maintain a monolithic architecture without multiple points of failure, as well as mixed experiences in which differentiated levels of interactivity can be provided for the benefit of the user.

Content Syndication

"Write once, publish everywhere" is rapidly becoming a popular tenet in marketing and publishing in the omnichannel landscape. Increasingly, content providers and publishers are seeking to take advantage of diverse mediums to deliver their content to a growing array of experiences. In these scenarios, Drupal is the hub for a constellation of experiences, all ingesting content from a single source of truth, whether that hub is a full Drupal site (with optional progressive decoupling) or a fully decoupled Drupal repository.

It is important to emphasize here that Drupal does not need to be fully decoupled for content syndication to succeed when it comes to building experience ecosystems. Many Drupal sites that are monolithic and end-to-end also expose data for consumption by

© Preston So 2018
P. So, *Decoupled Drupal in Practice*, https://doi.org/10.1007/978-1-4842-4072-4_5

other applications. Indeed, this is how Drupal project lead Dries Buytaert recommends that architects use Drupal in a decoupled way: as a public-facing Drupal site that also acts as a central data source for consumer applications. This maintains Drupal's end-to-end contiguity and also retains Drupal's front-end benefits on the Drupal web site itself.

Separation of Concerns

Web development has long contended with the issues surrounding the separation of concerns between structured data and its presentation layer. Whereas structured content and its delivery constitute the structural skeleton of Drupal, templates and their logic make up the presentation of Drupal content. Even in monolithic Drupal, one can easily draw a distinction between the layers that make up key back-end features of Drupal (e.g., the database itself, the database abstraction layer) and its front-end functions (e.g., the Twig theme layer).

Although in monolithic and progressively decoupled Drupal, this separation of concerns is implicit and largely invisible to the user, in fully decoupled Drupal it becomes an explicit split between structured content, handled by Drupal, and its presentation, handled by consumer applications. As such, by exposing data to the front end in JSON or in XML, presentation and aesthetics become the domain of the consumer applications that create their own experiences using Drupal content, separately from the default Drupal front end.

The RESTful Panels module challenges this paradigm in the fully decoupled context, but the injection of presentational logic from Drupal alongside structured content challenges the separation of concerns that fully decoupled Drupal touts in the first place.

User-Centered User Experiences

The benefit of improved user experiences is perhaps the most polemical of the advantages that decoupled Drupal confers, because a good user experience results from effective design and development, not necessarily from architectural decisions. Nonetheless, decoupled Drupal does confer the advantage of an improved user experience because experiences better catered to users' needs can be crafted by undertaking a decoupled Drupal architecture.

The question of user experience in this case is closely intertwined with the issues surrounding the front-end developer experience (see the next section). For instance, an interactive application requiring frequent rerenderings of content might not be as effective in Drupal as in a JavaScript framework better oriented to the task. Nevertheless, for consumer applications built for mobile audiences, the user experience must be well-suited to the task, and Drupal's responsive design might not be sufficient to provide a user-centered experience.

In progressively decoupled Drupal, a JavaScript framework is employed to enhance the existing user experience provided by Drupal, whether that means replacing as much of it as possible or adding interactivity to a section of a single page. In this way, a more user-centered experience can be applied selectively to an existing Drupal front end in an incremental fashion.

Front-End Developer Experience

For many front-end developers, especially those well-versed in JavaScript, the Twig-driven front end of Drupal could be complex and distinct from the paradigms they have worked with in the past. Some teams are made up of primarily JavaScript developers for whom modern front-end development requires ample use of NPM and other JavaScript development tools. In addition, Twig and Drupal's Ajax frameworks are ill-suited for highly interactive applications that might be requested by business stakeholders.

Decoupling Drupal, whether fully or progressively, offers developer teams the ability to apply specialized knowledge in a differentiated fashion to desired functionality. For instance, the use of a JavaScript framework with which a developer team is intimately familiar can accelerate development on a progressively decoupled project. By the same token, a fully decoupled Drupal implementation with a JavaScript consumer opens access to a JavaScript framework's features.

This is particularly true given the immense advancement that JavaScript as a language has seen in recent years and its favorable positioning for use in interactive client-side settings. New features in ES6, the current version of JavaScript seeing widening browser support, such as arrow functions, destructured assignment, the spread operator, and classes, among others, offer a much more pleasant experience for developers than ever before.

Pipelined Development

In pipelined development, teams with different skill sets can work in parallel on different components of the implementation without impeding each other's work or compromising the integrity of the project. Decoupled Drupal also opens the door to a pipelined development process in which a front-end team can build applications against a dummy web service API used solely for testing but not actually completed, and a back-end team can construct the back end that exposes that API and the underlying processes yielding it.

Fully decoupled and progressively decoupled Drupal architectures both allow teams to produce work at their own respective velocities. For instance, whereas an Ember developer would be proficient with Handlebars, he or she might not understand the systems that provision web service APIs in Drupal, at which point a Drupal developer can contribute. In this fashion, a front-end developer is no longer hamstrung by the complexities of Drupal's theme layer and can control markup and rendering, and Drupal developers can focus on their expertise on the back end and craft a robust RESTful API.

Conclusion

In this chapter, we examined some of the rewards incurred when decoupling Drupal, whether in the fully decoupled or progressively decoupled way. These include content syndication, where an omnichannel landscape helps realize the dream of "write once, publish everywhere," and a separation of concerns, where structured content is distinct from its presentation.

In addition, both developers and users benefit from experiences that are fine-tuned to their requirements, whether it is greater interactivity, a particular device, or a set of technologies. Finally, perhaps the most relevant for both fully decoupled and progressively decoupled approaches is the promise of pipelined development, where developers of different specializations can work in parallel on distinct components.

CHAPTER 6

Disadvantages of Decoupled Drupal

With all of the buzz and favorable attention surrounding decoupled Drupal at present, it can be easy to sidestep the pitfalls of decoupling Drupal without evaluating them intensively. Choosing to use Drupal only for its web service capabilities and as a content repository can endanger your entire architecture if you need Drupal's front-end functionality or other critical functions that rely on the presence of Drupal's default front end. Other risks apply as well.

Additional Point of Failure

Typically, monolithic Drupal implementations are hosted on LAMP (Linux, Apache, MySQL, PHP) stacks, which are ubiquitous on today's Web. On the other hand, JavaScript consumer applications that are clients in a fully decoupled architecture obligate the use of Node.js stacks like MERN (MongoDB, Express, React, Node.js) or MEAN (Angular in lieu of React). Other solutions entirely might be necessary for native mobile or IoT applications that have different demands.

As a result, introducing an additional hosting stack into your organization's infrastructure might not only be difficult for those of more modest means; it also introduces an additional point of failure in your architecture. For instance, if the Drupal site acting as a web services provider fails without proper caching, the data your application conveys to the user might be outdated or inaccessible. By the same token, consumer applications that are the sole conduit for Drupal content and experience downtime will lead to a situation where users have no means of accessing your content, unless your Drupal site is also publicly accessible.

© Preston So 2018
P. So, *Decoupled Drupal in Practice*, https://doi.org/10.1007/978-1-4842-4072-4_6

Security and Input Sanitization

Whereas the vast majority of modern JavaScript and application frameworks contain means to combat cross-site scripting attacks, including measures like input sanitization, both fully decoupled and progressively decoupled Drupal require that you carefully scrutinize the security implications of your architecture. For example, even though Drupal offers form validation and text sanitization out of the box for all form fields, this is only available in a monolithic architecture.

If you or your organization opts to use a bespoke framework—or "vanilla" JavaScript without the aid of a framework—the security of user-generated input becomes a potentially massive risk, a hazard that warrants strong emphasis here. Instead of allowing Drupal to do the heavy lifting, your homegrown approach will require ample research to evaluate whether you have taken satisfactory steps to ensure the security of users, the consumer applications, and ultimately the entire architecture.

Contextualized Editing and Administration

Some of Drupal 8's most compelling functions include in-place editing (known as the Quick Edit module) and configuration menus accompanying certain page components (known as Contextual Links), a few of the modules that comprise contextualized tools for Drupal administration. During content preview in a monolithic architecture, these interfaces permit site builders and content editors to adjust content while viewing its live result or to access administration pages from the comfort of the visual preview.

These contextualized tools, in a fully decoupled Drupal architecture, are no longer available, unless they are reconstructed on the consumer application, which leads to a duplication of functionality. As such, employing a distinct front end from Drupal's for the web experience transfers responsibility for deploying such interfaces to the front-end developer, who can either provide replacements or replicas of these tools or note their unavailability in the editor's experience. The progressively decoupled approach somewhat mitigates this, although it suffers from a "black box" problem in which material contained within decoupled areas of the page cannot be edited or administered according to normal Drupal administrators' expectations.

Layout and Display Management

Among Drupal 8's features are core and contributed modules that confer features for layout and display management, which offer a spectrum of options to provide variable content displays (Display Suite) or construct layouts consisting of content panes (Panels). Because they require significant control over Drupal's markup, these modules need to be tightly coupled to Drupal's presentation layer.

Removing modules like Panels and Display Suite from the editorial equation means that layout management becomes a developer concern, not that of an editor. This results in considerable challenges for marketing teams that do not have access to developers who can assist in implementing layout changes. To allow editors to continue manipulating layouts rather than just content, your organization will either need to employ Drupal's presentation layer, rebuild layout management as a feature in the consumer application, or expose layout configuration in the form of ingestible data via modules like RESTful Panels.

Previewable Content Workflows

Among the most important underpinnings of a robust CMS is the capability to create and operate along editorial content workflows, whereby one can conveniently preview content states such as drafts and "in review" without prematurely posting potentially embargoed content.

Jettisoning Drupal's functionality for content previews and content workflow by employing a different front end from Drupal's translates into considerable challenges if an editorial team desires a previewable content workflow, to which they might be accustomed after years of working within a traditional CMS. Several alternatives exist, such as provisioning an additional private staging environment to allow for different content to be deployed, or extending web services to expose differentiated content accessible via secondary authentication or unique query parameters.

System Notifications

Another key feature of Drupal is its robust notification system, which displays information about any issues arising during a Drupal system process, especially severe system errors that demand immediate attention. Although a REST resource is available

51

within Drupal to fetch watchdog logs, these provide only a limited amount of the possible issues that administrators should scrutinize. Moreover, Drupal system messages frequently highlighted at the top of rendered pages are inaccessible in a fully decoupled Drupal environment.

To maintain unimpeded awareness of potential problems that occur in Drupal, especially ones that could affect the transmission of data to consumer applications, it is important to watch system messages within the Drupal back-end interface carefully, as without substantial custom code, these messages will be unavailable. In a progressively decoupled setting, providing these messages is less of a concern, as Drupal does handle some of the rendering and only requires an area where such system messages can be visible.

Monolithic Performance Benefits

One of the most compelling features of Drupal 8 is cache tags (see Chapter 25), also known as cacheability metadata, which allow developers to define dependencies on data managed by Drupal and permit cache invalidation of items that rely heavily on granular content contained within them. For instance, the BigPipe contributed module abbreviates the time to first paint by providing progressive loads of pages based on the differentiated cacheability of respective page components.

Such capabilities give Drupal the means to achieve significant performance improvements during the page load. Sometimes, BigPipe can alleviate developers' concerns about monolithic Drupal performance by benefiting from a similar page load performance as that expected in JavaScript applications. This type of progressive loading dependent on cacheability metadata is not available to developers of fully decoupled implementations, but progressively decoupled builds can in certain cases leverage this feature. Of course, for those who lack preexisting Drupal sites or are less accustomed to Drupal's feature set, this disadvantage might be less relevant.

Accessibility and User Experience

Finally, but perhaps most important, Drupal's efforts on accessibility and user experience have included utmost consideration for markup and how it is presented to people living with disabilities and users of assistive technologies. For example, Drupal's use of ARIA roles and other techniques ensure that all Drupal content is available for users of screen readers. Moreover, Drupal's focus on usability across its history means that anyone using Drupal's Form API is certain to benefit from a set of standardized and battle-tested best practices.

In the fully decoupled and progressively decoupled setting, when it comes to JavaScript applications, markup and user experience require considerably more thought, because Drupal no longer provides ready-made front-end code or a roster of core interface components and interactions to rely on. This results in the front-end developer needing to craft a suitable user experience and robust accessibility without the aid of Drupal. Fortunately, JavaScript frameworks have made significant strides in accessible markup in recent years.

Conclusion

Although decoupling Drupal can translate into wide-ranging dividends for your team and for your goals in building digital experience ecosystems, it comes with certain trade-offs, particularly if you employ Drupal as a stand-alone content service without a corresponding front end. In the fully decoupled case, abandoning the Twig-driven front end enables a better separation of concerns and pipelined development, but it forces developers to be far more attentive to issues of accessibility and user experience.

Fully decoupling Drupal introduces considerable problems that should give pause to any stakeholder and demand frank assessment. For instance, an additional hosting stack introduces a second point of failure (although this is the case with each infrastructurally distinct consumer you add). Issues of security such as sanitization of user-generated content also deserve close examination. More relevant for editors and administrators, key functions of Drupal that rely on its presentation layer such as contextual tools, layout and display management, previewable content workflows, and system notifications disappear except within the administrative interface, unless resurrected as replicas in the consumer application.

Progressive decoupling mitigates some of these concerns by providing some solutions; for instance, contextual tools, layout and display management, previewable content, and system notifications remain intact, although the "black box" problem is a source of concern for editors.

In other words, if you opt to decouple Drupal, whether fully or progressively, be ready to work with a highly competent development team with specialties in both Drupal and front-end technologies and to experiment with custom or contributed solutions as you progress with your decoupled Drupal architecture.

In Part 2, we decouple Drupal by digging into the details behind Drupal's web services. We turn first to the core REST modules in Drupal core, which include capabilities for HAL-compliant JSON responses adhering to Drupal's data model and RESTful principles. Then, we turn our attention to major contributed modules like JSON API, GraphQL, and RELAXed Web Services, which each provide different capabilities to interact with Drupal content, as well as authentication mechanisms.

PART II

Decoupling Drupal

In Part 1, we examined decoupled Drupal from a conceptual and historical perspective by following its trajectory on the server side and client side and analyzing common decoupled Drupal approaches and motivations for using a particular paradigm over another. In these chapters, we dive into how Drupal core provides web services for consumers, how Drupal's contributed ecosystem has fostered a substantial ecosystem surrounding core features, and how to authenticate requests against Drupal's web services.

In the process, we will enumerate a large variety of technologies, including modules in Drupal core (Serialization, RESTful Web Services, HAL), Drupal contributed modules (JSON API, RELAXed Web Services, GraphQL, REST UI), and authentication methods (OAuth 2.0, JSON Web Tokens).

From the standpoint of out-of-the-box web services, Drupal 8 Core offers a robust variety of features for handling the encoding and serialization of API responses that consumers require. In Drupal 8 Core, four key modules, when enabled, collectively facilitate the provisioning of RESTful APIs out of the box: HAL, Serialization, REST, and Basic Authentication. Some of these modules provide foundations that underpin important contributed modules also useful for Drupal such as JSON API, RELAXed Web Services, and GraphQL. For instance, while the JSON API contributed module depends on Serialization, it does not depend on REST.

In addition, the RESTful Web Services module integrates tightly with Drupal's Entity Access system to provide granularly permissioned access to resources. Finally, with more recent developments such as the inclusion of CORS support and the future incorporation of JSON API into Drupal core, the advantages of employing Drupal off the shelf to provide web services become more compelling.

After examining these modules and setting up Drupal 8 as a web service provider, we'll configure Drupal 8 to be an effective web service provider and back end before turning to the contributed ecosystem of web services modules. Many developers may find that Drupal's contributed ecosystem offers more flexible and extensible solutions for providing web services, as well as user interfaces and additional features that enhance existing web services.

For instance, JSON API, CouchDB, and GraphQL are all widely understood standards that have witnessed significant adoption due to their emphasis on a positive developer experience. In Drupal's case, the REST UI module furnishes a more user-friendly experience for REST resource configuration.

This and other useful contributed modules offer convenient user interfaces for esoteric configuration tasks.

Finally, one of the most critically important elements of any decoupled Drupal architecture is authentication to ensure that data remains private and protected. While Drupal offers several built-in mechanisms in core that we can employ in a decoupled Drupal architecture, namely Basic Authentication and cookie-based authentication, these are much less secure than contributed alternatives. In the contributed landscape, the Simple OAuth (Drupal's OAuth 2.0 implementation) and JSON Web Tokens modules implement more modern standards.

Because Drupal 8 Core is the most common point of entry for those experimenting with Drupal as a decoupled back end, we'll start there.

## CHAPTER 7

Decoupling Drupal 8 Core

Thanks to the work of the WSCCI, Drupal 8 today provides a capable REST server out of the box that includes the ability to retrieve and modify content entities—such as nodes, users, taxonomy terms, and comments—through broadly understood create, read, update, and delete (CRUD) operations within HTTP requests.

The Web Services and Context Core Initiative

For Drupal to truly embrace the future web, we need to fundamentally rethink how Drupal responds to an incoming HTTP request. We need to treat HTML pages as what they are: A particularly common form of REST response, but only one among many. To that end, Drupal needs to evolve, and quickly, from a first-class web CMS into a first-class REST server that includes a first-class web CMS.

—Larry Garfield, WSCCI lead[1]

As we saw in Chapters 2 and 3, Drupal emerged during a more traditional time when static pages drove application state and CMSs were monolithic by nature. In recent years, however, increasing dynamism in web applications and unprecedented new channels for content delivery are spotlighting Drupal's increasing challenges when it comes to honoring requests intended for a diverse array of sources.

---

[1]Garfield, Larry. "Announcing the Web Services and Context Core Initiative." *GarfieldTech.* 11 April 2011. Accessed 12 March 2018. `https://www.garfieldtech.com/blog/web-services-initiative`

© Preston So 2018
P. So, *Decoupled Drupal in Practice*, https://doi.org/10.1007/978-1-4842-4072-4_7

These requests can run the gamut between partial page requests (e.g., edge side includes), RESTful API calls, and even requests originating from command-line interfaces such as Drush and Drupal Console.[2] Nevertheless, requests like these were not particularly well-suited for Drupal during a time when Drupal placed a much greater emphasis on building and rendering HTML pages rather than data needing to be presented in various formats. As late as Drupal 7, the core installation of Drupal solely provided an XML-RPC (remote procedure calls in XML) layer in lieu of a bonafide web services layer.[3]

The *Web Services and Context Core Initiative* (WSCCI) was launched in 2011 during the Drupal 7 release cycle and became an official Drupal 8 initiative. Owing to the need to circumvent the HTML rendering processes in Drupal, the objective of the WSCCI team was to modernize Drupal's handling of requests and serving of pages to anticipate the myriad use cases that would emerge further along in the Drupal 8 development cycle.

To accommodate all of the kinds of responses that Drupal needs to serve for consumers, as part of the effort to include more of the Symfony PHP framework in Drupal core, WSCCI advocated the incorporation of the Symfony HTTPFoundation component (an HTTP request processing library written in PHP) into Drupal core. In addition, in 2012, due to the vast scope of the initiative, it scaled down to occupy itself solely with web services concerns.[4, 5]

With the entry of the Serialization module, WSCCI enabled Drupal to *serialize,* meaning to transform structured data into a storable format (e.g., files or transmissions across networks), and to *deserialize,* meaning to reconstruct Drupal data structures from data formatted for storage. For the first time, modules could serialize content entities into XML, JSON, and the HAL+JSON format based on the HAL normalization, which adheres to the Hypertext Application Language (HAL) specification.

---

[2]Catchpole, Nathaniel. "Componentized Drupal: Drupal 8 and Symfony2." *Drupal Watchdog.* 1 March 2013. Accessed 12 March 2018. https://www.drupalwatchdog.com/volume-3/issue-1/componentized-drupal

[3]Sánchez, Valentin. "Drupal 8 Web Services and Context Core Initiative." *Conocimiento Plus.* 6 January 2015. Accessed 12 March 2018. https://conocimientoplus.wordpress.com/2015/01/06/drupal-8-web-services-and-context-core-wscci-initiative/

[4]Kudwien, Daniel F. "Drupal 8: The path forward." *Unleashed Mind.* 20 February 2012. Accessed 12 March 2018. http://www.unleashedmind.com/en/blog/sun/drupal-8-the-path-forward

[5]Buytaert, Dries. "The future is a RESTful Drupal." *Dries Buytaert.* 16 February 2012. Accessed 12 March 2018. https://dri.es/the-future-is-a-restful-drupal

---

Note   The Drupal community chose to replace JSON-LD with HAL in 2013.
For more information, visit `https://www.drupal.org/project/drupal/`
`issues/1924220`.

The Serialization Module

The Serialization module permits modules that cite it as a dependency (like the
RESTful Web Services or REST module) to employ serializers contained therein to
transform Drupal data into formats consumable by other applications. Built with the
Symfony Serializer component as a foundation, the Serialization module provides an
API for developers to introduce additional serialization formats via the installation
of contributed modules. Prominent modules using the Serialization API include the
aforementioned HAL module in Drupal 8 Core (supports the HAL+JSON format) and the
CSV Serialization contributed module (supports data in CSV format).

When different standards and specifications inevitably enter the picture, the
Serialization module also handles *normalization,* the process by which data in
a particular format are structured or exposed differently to adhere to particular
requirements without changing their format (*denormalization* is the process in reverse).
For instance, the HAL+JSON format provided by the HAL module uses data structures
and exposes pieces of information that are different from the default JSON encoding in
Drupal, including links to other resource URIs that adhere to the HAL specification.

To satisfy the need for both normalization and serialization, the Serialization
module offers other modules a default serializer and default normalizer. In addition,
other modules can also employ their own homegrown *encoders,* which transform arrays
generated by normalizers into serialization formats, or normalizers. Custom encoders
for JSON and XML are unnecessary, as default JSON and XML encoders are already
present in the Symfony Serializer format.

As Figure 7-1 indicates, a serialization process in Drupal consists of a normalization
process and an encoding process in succession.

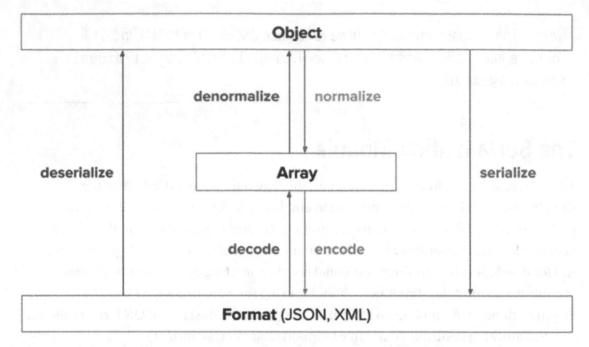

Figure 7-1. *This figure, adapted from a diagram in the Symfony Serializer documentation, demonstrates how serializers create consumable data in JSON and XML based on two constituent processes: normalization and encoding*

How Serialization Works

Although most developers will choose to employ the serializer as is, each serialization (or deserialization) process actually consists of both normalization (or denormalization) and encoding (or decoding). This provides for a separation of concerns between a *normalization* of an object into a nested array and an *encoding* of that same array into the required format. Figure 7-2 digs deeper into this dual process with an example serialization process.

Node: Article

Title: Title
Body: Lorem ipsum dolor sit amet

normalize()
calls HAL normalizers

```
[
  '_links' => [
    'self' => [
      'href' => 'http://drupal.dev/node/1?_format=hal_json'
    ],
    'type' => [
      'href' => 'http://drupal.dev/rest/type/node/article'
    ],
    ...
  ],
  ...
  'title' => [
    ['value' => 'Title', 'lang' => 'en']
  ],
  ...
];
```

encode()
calls JSON encoder

```
{
  "_links": {
    "self": {
      "href": "http://drupal.dev/node/1?_format=hal_json"
    },
    "type": {
      "href" => "http://drupal.dev/rest/type/node/article"
    },
    ...
  },
  ...
  "title": [
    {"value": "Title", "lang": "en"}
  ],
  ...
}
```

Figure 7-2. *This diagram illustrates how normalization needs to occur before encoding to satisfy certain specifications like HAL, which dictate certain elements that should be part of the encoded format. In this example serialization, a node entity is normalized into a HAL-compatible structure before being encoded into the HAL+JSON format.*

We can introspect the methods used to detail this process even further. When the `Serializer::serialize()` method is invoked, the Serializer iterates through all available Normalizer services to determine which Normalizer it should use, invoking `Normalizer::supportsNormalization($object, $format)` on each Normalizer (from highest to lowest priority) until it discovers a Normalizer returning TRUE. If a Normalizer is not found, Drupal returns an error.

The Serializer service undertakes exactly the same process to choose the right Encoder, iterating through the Encoders and invoking `EncoderInterface::supportsEncoding($format)` every time until it encounters the particular Encoder that satisfies the stipulations of the format provided as an argument.

Adding a New Encoding

Drupal ships with the core-supported formats JSON, XML, and HAL+JSON, but sometimes you might wish to add a new encoding altogether, assuming the available formats are unsuitable for your project. To that end, you can add an Encoder as long as the data structure provided by core's default Normalizers is appropriate for your encoding as well.

First, create an encoder that implements `EncoderInterface` and define the obligatory `encode()` and `decode()` methods. Then, you can register the encoder using a `*.services.yml` file in your module. This example is taken from the HAL module's `hal.services.yml` file:

```
services:
  # ...
  serializer.encoder.hal:
    class: Drupal\hal\Encoder\JsonEncoder
    tags:
      - { name: encoder, priority: 10, format: hal_json }
  # ...
```

Note   You can find the full example of this YAML file at `https://api.drupal.org/api/drupal/core%21modules%21hal%21hal.services.yml/8.6.x`.

The Serialization API

There are several key APIs that can aid you in constructing new serializers and normalizers and in handling entities with references to other entities using entity resolvers.

Serializing and Deserializing

You can use the `serialize()` and `deserialize()` methods in Drupal 8's `serializer` service (`\Symfony\Component\Serializer\SerializerInterface`) to either serialize an entity into JSON or XML output or to deserialize incoming JSON or XML into a Drupal entity:

```
$output = $this->serializer->serialize($entity, 'json');
$entity = $this->serializer->deserialize($output, \Drupal\node\Entity\
Node::class, 'json');
```

In the first line shown, an entity is serialized into JSON output. In the second, a JSON data structure is deserialized into an entity that can then be manipulated normally by Drupal code.

Encoding and Decoding Serialization Formats

Each serializer implementation makes use of an encoder (`\Symfony\Component\
Serializer\Encoder\EncoderInterface`) and decoder (`\Symfony\Component\
Serializer\Decoder\DecoderInterface`) that can be used to add support for encodings to and decodings from new serialization formats (e.g., CSV or something else).

As an educational example, the `encode()` implementation in the CSV Serialization module identifies the type of input data and encodes that data into CSV that can then be consumed outside of Drupal's own understanding of entities.

Note   See the CSV Serialization module's implementation of `encode()` at
`https://cgit.drupalcode.org/csv_serialization/tree/src/
Encoder/CsvEncoder.php#n108`.

Normalizing and Denormalizing

To reconcile the differences between a particular encoding and a specific normalization, such as the distinctions between the raw JSON data structures and the HAL+JSON normalization, the Symfony Serializer component introduces normalizer (`\Symfony\Component\Serializer\Normalizer\NormalizerInterface`) and denormalizer (`\Symfony\Component\Serializer\Normalizer\DenormalizerInterface`) interfaces.

In Drupal, the default normalization is as close to an identical replication of the object data as possible and merely applies the JSON and XML encoders to the default normalization (`json` and `xml` formats). Other normalization formats written by developers might wish to apply specific constraints to incoming object data, such as the omission of local IDs in favor of universally unique identifiers (UUIDs) or the addition of new metadata that satisfies specifications like JSON-LD or HAL.

The `normalize()` implementation in the HAL module, which is discussed further shortly, demonstrates how adherence to specifications must be captured by normalizers and not encoders, whose responsibilities do not include the inclusion of metadata such as that required by the HAL specification. In this example, the normalization is prepended with a `_links` key that begins every HAL response.

Note   See the HAL module's implementation of `normalize()` at `https://github.com/drupal/drupal/blob/8.5.x/core/modules/hal/src/Normalizer/ContentEntityNormalizer.php#L57`.

Using Entity Resolvers

Although content entities are the most common data structures to be serialized, you might also find that a particular entity references other entities. When that is the case, as is common in complex Drupal content models, you can resolve those referenced entities by invoking `resolve()` with their UUIDs (`\Drupal\serialization\EntityResolver\UuidResolver`) or local Drupal identifiers (`\Drupal\serialization\EntityResolver\TargetIdResolver`).

The RESTful Web Services Module

On the shoulders of the RESTful Web Services module in Drupal 7, Drupal core's REST module also depends on the Serialization module. In its standard usage, the REST module exposes a customizable and extensible REST API that exposes data housed in Drupal. In this section, I discuss the REST module and its API; see Chapter 10 for retrieving and manipulating data through CRUD operations, and see Chapter 22 for more advanced features of the REST module such as resource plug-ins.

By default, the REST module permits developers to work with Drupal data using HTTP methods (like GET, POST, and DELETE) on content entities (including nodes, users, and comments). Moreover, issuing GET requests against configuration entities (e.g., vocabularies, user roles, and site configuration) and Watchdog database log entries is now supported as of Drupal 8.2.0.[6]

Note   The RESTful Web Services module for Drupal 7 is available on the Drupal. org project page located at `https://www.drupal.org/project/restws`.

The RESTful Web Services API

The REST module makes a few APIs available to developers who wish to extend the feature set of Drupal's default core REST API. Not to be confused with the REST API exposed for consumer applications, the RESTful Web Services module's API refers to the internal interfaces available for Drupal developers to extend core functionality.

This section delves into one of the two key APIs that Drupal developers have access to and by far the most important: REST resource configuration. The other available API, which handles resource plug-ins that add additional resources to defaults available out of the box, is covered in Chapter 25.

---

[6]"RESTful Web Services module overview." Drupal.org. 9 November 2016. Accessed 23 March 2018. `https://www.drupal.org/docs/8/core/modules/rest/overview`

Configuring REST Resources

To begin, each REST resource, irrespective of whether it represents a content entity or configuration entity, has its own configuration entity (`\Drupal\rest\RestResourceConfigInterface`) that corresponds to a `@RestResource` plug-in. Without the REST resource configuration entity, the REST resource plug-in is unavailable for use.

Because all REST resources have corresponding configuration entities, we can configure them in the same way as other configuration entities. As an example, you can designate particular HTTP methods, serialization formats, and authentication methods that a given REST resource is intended to support. Through this process, the chosen serialization formats and authentication methods are exposed to the selected HTTP methods in configuration.

REST resources can be configured by either using the REST UI module, which offers a GUI, or by modifying and importing configuration YAML by hand. Many developers, myself included, use existing configurations of REST resources, such as `core/modules/rest/config/optional/rest.resource.entity.node.yml` as a handy reference that can be copied and pasted.[7]

Using the RESTful Web Services Module

Typically, when you are building out an architecture with multiple consumers that require data from Drupal, you would expose these data by permitting access to resources by certain user roles with specific permissions and by designating a REST resource's serialization format and authentication method as you see fit.

Exposing Resources with Entity Access

One key advantage of Drupal 8 is that it contains a granular and robust user roles and permissions system that works effectively with permissions for accessing exposed REST resources. In Drupal 8, for REST resources exposing content entities, the Entity Access API determines whether a user role has the correct permissions to retrieve or manipulate content entities.

---

[7]"RESTful Web Services API overview." Drupal.org. 5 March 2018. Accessed 23 March 2018. `https://www.drupal.org/docs/8/api/restful-web-services-api/restful-web-services-api-overview`

For instance, to issue GET requests on a node (i.e., read or view it), a user—which in this case might simply be a consumer application, represented on Drupal as an anonymous user—needs to be granted the *Access content* permission by a Drupal administrator. Similarly, the *Create article* content permission must be enabled for a user to be able to issue a POST request against a node of type Article.

The reuse of the Entity Access system by REST resources is a critical feature for consumers handling sensitive private data and as such should be employed with appropriate authentication methods like that provided by the Simple OAuth module, which couples user roles and their designated permissions with individually identifiable consumer applications. I discuss authentication methods in greater detail in Chapter 9.

Note   The Simple OAuth module for Drupal 8 is available on the Drupal.org project page located at `https://www.drupal.org/project/simple_oauth`.

Customizing a REST Resource's Format and Authentication Method

Out of the box, the REST module contains support for the two most commonly used formats on the Web: json and xml. By enabling core's HAL module (see next section), developers can also use the hal_json format. With the assistance of other contributed modules, still other formats can be added, such as csv. The REST module also allows developers to provide distinct authentication methods depending on the resource in question, so developers can differentiate between requiring Basic Authentication for certain resources and OAuth2 authentication for more sensitive resources. See Chapter 8 for a more comprehensive discussion of authentication in decoupled Drupal.

Here is an example of how to configure available formats and authentication mechanisms on a per-resource basis using YAML:

```
granularity: resource
configuration:
  methods:
    - ...
```

```
formats:
  - hal_json
  - xml
  - json
authentication:
  - cookie
```

Note   The preceding example uses cookie-based authentication, which is relevant in the progressive decoupling case, because the consumer application and Drupal front end are both active in a single browser session. In cookie-based authentication, a cookie set during an authenticated user session can be employed by a JavaScript application to perform authentication against Drupal's REST API.

All of this configuration can also be done using the REST UI module.

Hypertext Application Language

When consumer applications ingest data normalized as HAL-compliant JSON (HAL+JSON), the appearance of data structures adhere to the HAL specification, which underpins the HAL module. When enabled, Drupal 8's HAL module normalizes entities according to the HAL specification.

Much like JSON-LD, the HAL specification addresses one particular requirement that many web service APIs grapple with: the ability to hyperlink across multiple resources to include links or references to other relevant resources in a single API response that provides greater usefulness to consumer applications. Indeed, HAL itself is a generic media type the purpose of which is to comprise "series of links" within web service APIs. Armed with these links, API consumers can then traverse them to progress through a variety of application states.

The availability of surrounding tooling remains among the most obvious benefits of adopting a specification like HAL to serve API responses. For example, a HAL browser offers developers the means to "test drive" their applications and inspect how their JSON is formatted through a convenient user interface.

> **Note**   The HAL specification is located at `https://tools.ietf.org/html/draft-kelly-json-hal-08`.

Setting Up Drupal 8 as a Web Service Provider

With some of the key foundations established, we can now turn our attention to setting up Drupal 8 as a web services provider. In this section, we acquire, install, and generate content for Drupal before moving into core REST configuration, both manually and using the REST UI module. First, though, we'll need a local copy of the most recent version of Drupal.

Installing Composer

If you have never installed Drupal or worked with Drupal 8 before, the new dependency management system in Drupal might be unfamiliar. If you have already worked with Composer-based workflows in the past, this section can be safely skipped.

Composer is a dependency manager in PHP, analogous to package managers like NPM and Yarn in JavaScript and Bundler in Ruby. Based on a `composer.json` file located in your PHP code base, Composer fetches and installs the dependencies listed therein.

Unless you have specific requirements that obligate unique versions of Composer on a per-project basis, it is a best practice to install Composer globally. If you are using Linux, Unix, or OSX, navigate to `https://getcomposer.org/installer` to download a convenient installer. Once it is installed, use the following command to move Composer to a directory in your PATH. This will allow you to use `composer` commands globally.

```
$ mv composer.phar /usr/local/bin/composer
```

If you are using Windows, navigate to `https://getcomposer.org/Composer-Setup.exe` to download an executable that will install Composer such that it will be available on any directory.[8]

---

[8]"Introduction." Composer. 18 February 2012. Accessed 8 September 2018. `https://getcomposer.org/doc/00-intro.md`

> **Note**   For more information about installing Composer including manual installation and local installation, consult the Composer documentation at `https://getcomposer.org/doc/00-intro.md`.

Downloading Drupal and Drupal Dependencies with Composer

In the directory where you wish to house Drupal, run the following. This command also executes `composer install`, which will download Drupal 8 and all dependencies.

```
$ composer create-project drupal-composer/drupal-project:8.x-dev core-rest
--stability dev --no-interaction
$ cd core-rest
```

> **Note**   For more information about the `drupal-composer/drupal-project` Composer template for Drupal 8 projects, consult the README at `https://github.com/drupal-composer/drupal-project/blob/8.x/README.md`.

For developers familiar with past development workflows for Drupal, one of the unique aspects of Composer is the ability to add new dependencies from the command line using the command shown here, where `{module_name}` is the name of the module you wish to add. Composer will automatically add the dependency to your `composer.json` file.

```
$ composer require drupal/{module_name}
```

If you open your `composer.json` file, you will see something like the following added.

```
{
  "require": {
    "drupal/{module_name}": "1.x-dev"
  }
}
```

If you see errors while running `composer require`, you might need to add Drupal.org as a Composer repository such that Composer recognizes that Drupal packages need to be fetched from `https://packages.drupal.org/8`. We can use `composer config` to set this, as you can see in the following command. Note that if you are using the installation method detailed earlier or if you are on Drupal 8.3.0 or later, this step should be unnecessary.

```
$ composer config repositories.drupal composer https://packages.drupal.
org/8
```

When you open `composer.json` again, you will see the following appear.

```
{
  "repositories": {
    "drupal": {
      "type": "composer",
      "url": "https://packages.drupal.org/8"
    }
  }
}
```

Note   If you are running Composer and encounter a memory limit error, there are several resolutions available. The most common is to configure the `memory_limit` within your `php.ini` file to be larger than the default. Another option is to temporarily configure PHP's memory limit to be infinite, as seen in the following version of the `composer create-project` command. For more information, consult the Composer documentation regarding PHP memory limits at `https://getcomposer.org/doc/articles/troubleshooting.md#memory-limit-errors`.

```
$ php -d memory_limit=-1 composer.phar create-project
drupal-composer/drupal-project:8.x-dev core-rest --stability
dev --no-interaction
```

Provisioning a Drupal Site

After downloading Drupal and its dependencies, you can provision a new site in your designated local development environment using the existing code base you just acquired. In these examples I am using Acquia Dev Desktop, but you can use any local development environment you prefer, such as Lando, Docker for Drupal, or MAMP. In Acquia Dev Desktop, selecting the + button in the lower left opens a menu of options, including the one we want: *Import local Drupal site*. Once you have inputted all the information, as shown in Figure 7-3, we can move ahead to installing Drupal.

Note   Acquia Dev Desktop can be downloaded at `https://dev.acquia.com/ downloads`.

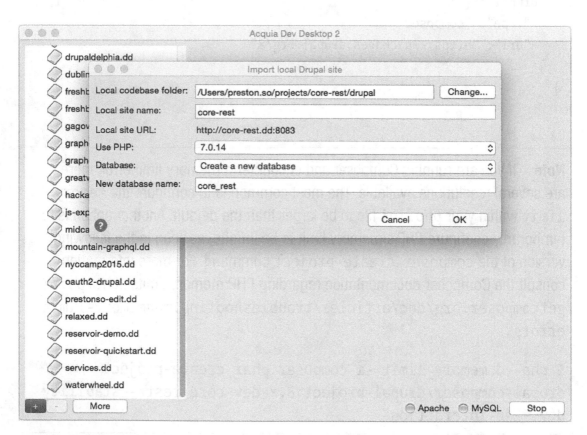

Figure 7-3. *In this screenshot, we have opted to import a local Drupal site that already exists in the* core-rest *directory. This Drupal site will use PHP version 7.0.14, and a new database will be created.*

Now, you can install Drupal in the normal way, whether through Drush, Drupal Console, or manually using the web interface at `/core/install.php`. If you encounter a White Screen of Death—an empty error screen that might include unformatted errors at the top of the page—at `/core/install.php` with errors regarding `autoload.php`, you might need to rerun `composer install`.

Note   More information about Drush and Drupal Console can be found at their sites, `http://www.drush.org` and `https://drupalconsole.com`, respectively.

Generating Content and Enabling Core REST Modules

Next, we'll want to create some content that we can test through the API, a process that can be done manually or using the Devel Generate submodule of Devel. The following commands create 20 nodes and 20 users (both examples of content entities).

```
$ composer require drupal/devel
$ drush en -y devel devel_generate
$ drush genc 20 && drush genu 20
```

Note   Devel's project page on Drupal.org is at `https://www.drupal.org/project/devel`.

Once you have installed the site and added a modicum of content, you now have a fully functional Drupal site. However, we have yet to enable the modules that are responsible for exposing the core REST API. Because these modules are already part of core but not enabled, we simply need to navigate to the *Extend* page (`/admin/modules`) or enable them via Drush. The following Drush command, for instance, enables Drupal Core's Serialization, HAL, Basic Authentication, and REST modules.

```
$ drush en -y serialization hal rest basic_auth
```

At this point, we can navigate to `core-rest.dd:8083/node/1?_format=json` to test our shiny new REST API. Unfortunately, when we do navigate to that path (seen in Chrome in Figure 7-4), we see an error stating "Not acceptable format: json". This

means there is still more work we have to do, namely configuring the REST resources
that we want exposed in the API.

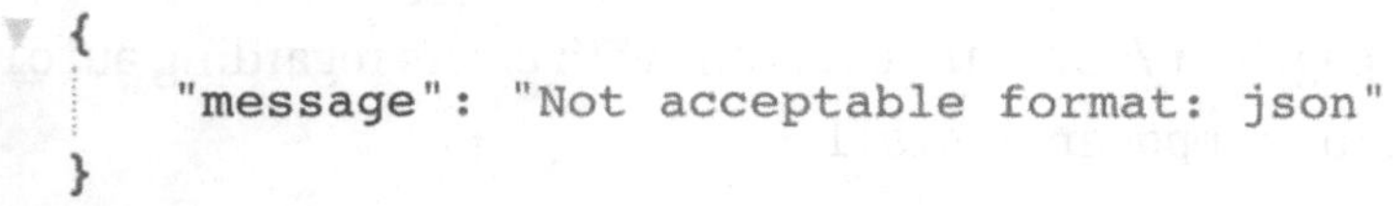

```
{
    "message": "Not acceptable format: json"
}
```

Figure 7-4. *There's a step missing here, as our REST resources are not yet
configured*

Configuring Core REST

To expose our REST resources in a Drupal-exposed REST API, we need to configure
those REST resources using Drupal's configuration management system. As an example,
if our requirement is to expose nodes of content type Article to the API, we need to
ensure that we have assigned HTTP methods, formats, and authentication methods to
the content type's corresponding REST resource.

As mentioned previously, an example configuration YAML file that can serve as
a reference for others is located at /core/modules/rest/config/optional/rest.
resource.entity.node.yml. By using Drupal's configuration import system, we can
copy the following YAML into Drupal to provide a newly configured REST resource.

```
langcode: en
status: true
dependencies:
  module:
    - basic_auth
    - hal
    - node
id: entity.node
plugin_id: 'entity:node'
granularity: resource
configuration:
  methods:
    - GET
    - POST
```

```
  - PATCH
  - DELETE
formats:
  - hal_json
authentication:
  - basic_auth
```

To make Drupal aware of this configuration, we can navigate to Manage ➤ Configuration ➤ Development ➤ Configuration synchronization (`/admin/config/development/configuration`), where we can choose to import a single item, as shown in Figure 7-5.

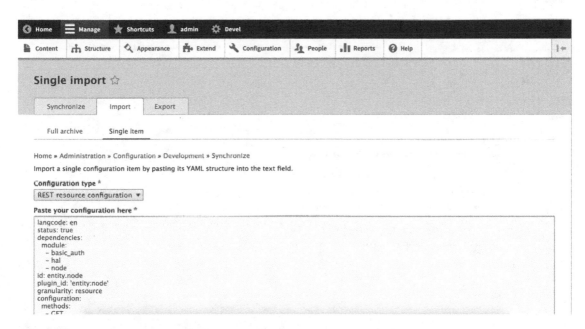

Figure 7-5. *The Single import page is used to import individual configuration items. We need to import a configuration item each time we designate another REST resource for each content type.*

Once we have imported the configuration for our Articles, we can test requests against the REST API that is now properly configured. Although we can do this using the cURL command-line interface or in the browser, I recommend the Postman REST client, which is a tool that issues and saves arbitrary requests against HTTP APIs. Postman is quite powerful with many useful features, so we will be using it throughout this chapter to test requests.

Note   Postman can be downloaded at `https://www.getpostman.com`.

In Postman, we can create and issue requests like the one shown in Figure 7-6, which depicts a GET request against `core-rest.dd:8083/node/1?_format=hal_json`. All we need to do is insert the correct URL, choose the HTTP method, and click *Send*. The resulting response is a HAL-compliant JSON payload that contains all of the information contained in a node (content item) having a node ID of 1.

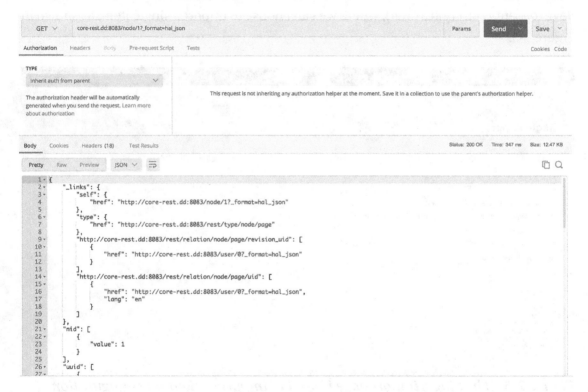

Figure 7-6. *Postman is a powerful HTTP client that can replace cURL in your developer toolbox. In this example, we are issuing a* GET *request against the node (a content item in Drupal) that has a node ID (identifier) of 1.*

Congratulations! You have just successfully issued your very first GET request against the core REST API in Drupal 8. In other words, you have just taken the first steps to implement decoupled Drupal.

Configuring CORS

Even though we now have a fully functional REST API after having configured REST resources, we should not deploy this API to production as it currently stands. If we were to attempt to access this domain from an application on a different domain, our requests would all fail due to the *same-origin policy,* a principle that forbids requests from other domains from retrieving content on a home domain for security reasons. The same-origin policy prevents data housed on one domain from falling victim to exploits or distributed denial-of-service (DDoS) attacks conducted by another.

To mitigate this risk, *cross-origin resource sharing* (CORS) allows user agents (for our purposes, API consumers or consumer applications) to access designated resources via particular HTTP headers from a domain that is distinct from the originator of the request. As an example, a request to my-decoupled-backend.com from my-consumer-app.net would be blocked by default unless the appropriate headers are present in the request.

Note   For more information about both principles, the Mozilla Developer Network has well-maintained documentation about the same-origin policy (`https://developer.mozilla.org/en-US/docs/Web/Security/Same-origin_policy`) and CORS (`https://developer.mozilla.org/en-US/docs/Web/HTTP/CORS`).

By default, Drupal blocks every request that originates from different domains for security purposes. However, using Drupal's site settings, which drive behavior across an entire installation of Drupal, we can permit select domains (or all domains on the web) access to particular methods or routes in Drupal. This allows us to expose our API for consumers on different origins, and we can make particular methods or routes available in an arbitrary manner.

Consider the following selection from sites/default/default.services.yml, which contains Drupal's default site settings; this section deals specifically with CORS settings.

```
# Configure Cross-Site HTTP requests (CORS).
# Read https://developer.mozilla.org/en-US/docs/Web/HTTP/Access_control_CORS
# for more information about the topic in general.
# Note: By default the configuration is disabled.
```

```
cors.config:
  enabled: false
  # Specify allowed headers, like 'x-allowed-header'.
  allowedHeaders: []
  # Specify allowed request methods, specify ['*'] to allow all possible
  ones.
  allowedMethods: []
  # Configure requests allowed from specific origins.
  allowedOrigins: ['*']
  # Sets the Access-Control-Expose-Headers header.
  exposedHeaders: false
  # Sets the Access-Control-Max-Age header.
  maxAge: false
  # Sets the Access-Control-Allow-Credentials header.
  supportsCredentials: false
```

CORS is disabled by default. To override the default and enable it, we need to copy
default.services.yml into a new file named services.yml in the same directory.
By doing so, we instruct Drupal to overrule the default settings with our bespoke file
where we have provided our own CORS configuration. In the process, we can designate
specific HTTP headers, HTTP methods, or origins that we wish to grant access to our
new API. For instance, the following YAML characterizes a public API against which any
consumer from any origin can issue requests that have direct ramifications on Drupal
content.

```
cors.config:
  enabled: true
  allowedHeaders: ['*']
  allowedMethods: ['GET', 'POST', 'PATCH', 'DELETE']
  allowedOrigins: ['*']
  exposedHeaders: false
  maxAge: false
  supportsCredentials: false
```

That CORS configuration is overly lax and should not be used in production. In the following example, the API is much more private and only allows incoming requests accompanied with certain headers. Moreover, it restricts all possible HTTP methods to GET only and allows only requests from a single consumer application's origin to proceed.

```
cors.config:
  enabled: true
  allowedHeaders: ['x-csrf-token', 'authorization', 'content-type',
  'accept', 'origin', 'x-requested-with']
  allowedMethods: ['GET']
  allowedOrigins: ['https://my-decoupled-app.net']
  exposedHeaders: false
  maxAge: false
  supportsCredentials: false
```

Although Drupal significantly eases the process with the help of YAML, your infrastructure might obligate you to perform additional steps, especially if you are using Apache or Nginx. If you run into CORS issues even after saving `services.yml` and rebuilding the cache registry (`drush cr`), you might be encountering an upstream issue in your web server's configuration and its issuance of CORS header responses.

Note   A CORS contributed module (`https://www.drupal.org/project/cors`) existed previously for the benefit of Drupal 8 implementations prior to Drupal 8.2.0. However, as of Drupal 8.2.0, the introduction of opt-in CORS support has led to the deprecation of the CORS module in favor of Core's native CORS support. For more information, see the change record at `https://www.drupal.org/node/2715637`.

Conclusion

In this chapter, we investigated the availability of web services in core and the foundations that underpin how we provision APIs in core REST. As you can see, the history is quite complicated and indicates an early emphasis on the availability of web services during the Drupal 8 development cycle, although the original motivation behind efforts to foster core support was cross-site content synchronization rather than decoupled Drupal use cases.

Owing to the baseline drawn by the WSCCI, web services are now an integral piece of Drupal 8 Core, albeit not enabled by default. Thanks to the Serialization module, furthermore, we can now access a broad range of features that handle a variety of encodings and normalizations, with the possibility of extending those through the Serialization API.

With RESTful Web Services and HAL in Drupal 8 Core, we can easily expose REST APIs for consumer applications without adding a single module to core as it exists. In this chapter, we also covered setting up and installing Drupal 8 to provide web services, configuring REST resources, and configuring CORS support. In the following chapter, we turn to contributed modules for providing web services and how they dovetail with core REST capabilities.

## CHAPTER 8

Decoupling Drupal 8 with Contributed Modules

In Chapter 7, we examined the existing web services ecosystem within Drupal core thanks to the introduction of the Serialization, HAL, and RESTful Web Services modules during the Drupal 8 development cycle. However, many of the rationales that justified the adoption of HAL are no longer as relevant as they were, and many new API specifications that are better suited to decoupled Drupal architectures have emerged since.

In this chapter, we zoom out from the capabilities available by default in Drupal 8 to inspect the wider Drupal web services ecosystem, focusing on four modules in particular. Three of them, JSON API, RELAXed Web Services, and GraphQL, are already used in production by early adopters. A fourth, REST UI, is a tool that provides a GUI for configuring core REST and can be easier for many users than writing YAML by hand to configure REST resources.

The Drupal Web Services Ecosystem

One of the most striking characteristics of Drupal in the decoupled sense is that it benefits from a wide and diverse array of web services that support interoperable machine-to-machine interaction between Drupal and consumer applications. In the Drupal ecosystem, web services are typically provided in the form of contributed modules. The most commonly seen in production builds are core REST, JSON API, RELAXed Web Services, and GraphQL (see Figure 8-1).

81

© Preston So 2018
P. So, *Decoupled Drupal in Practice*, https://doi.org/10.1007/978-1-4842-4072-4_8

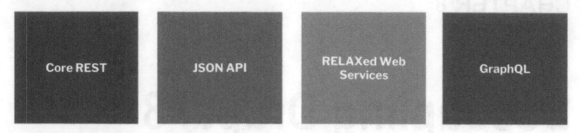

Figure 8-1. *The four most commonly used web services in Drupal 8*

Although most of these web services are RESTful APIs, which adhere to REST principles and operate using HTTP methods, some web services modules, most notably the GraphQL module, do not provide an HTTP API following REST principles and therefore cannot be considered RESTful. For this reason, it is generally preferred to use the term *web services* to describe all of the APIs available to Drupal rather than the narrower term *RESTful APIs*.

Consider Figure 8-2, which consists of a Euler diagram delineating the most common web services modules available in Drupal 8, including core REST and contributed solutions JSON API, RELAXed Web Services, and GraphQL. Whereas JSON API and RELAXed Web Services both implement API specifications that are specifically RESTful, GraphQL is a query language in addition to a web service and is therefore categorized differently.

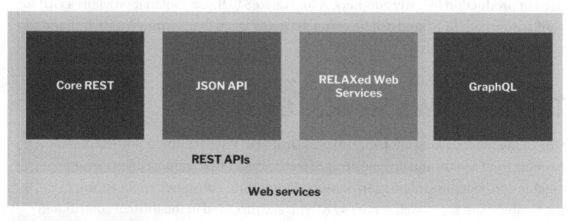

Figure 8-2. *This Euler diagram shows which of Drupal 8's web services are RESTful; GraphQL is non-RESTful but is still a web service*

Drupal's web services ecosystem consists of modules that vary in their dependencies. Some modules, such as RELAXed Web Services, depend on the RESTful Web Services module in addition to the Serialization module available in Drupal 8 Core (among other modules related to content staging). Others, such as JSON API, depend on Serialization for features such as the JSON encoder but not the REST module. A final outlier is GraphQL, which relies on none of the aforementioned modules.

Figure 8-3 demonstrates the variation in dependencies across the Drupal web services ecosystem. Note that this illustration only considers modules available for Drupal 8.

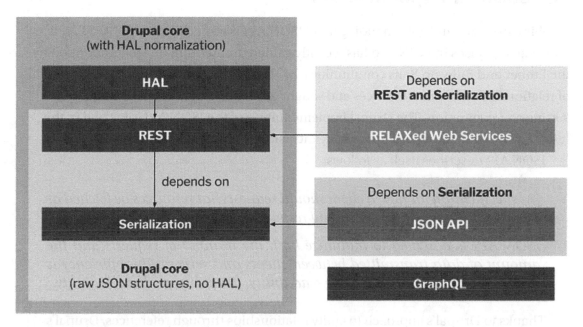

Figure 8-3. *Core web services capabilities form the foundation of contributed web services modules. Whereas RELAXed Web Services depends on the RESTful Web Services module, JSON API implements its own approach and only relies on the Serialization module.*

JSON API

In this section, we describe and examine the most stable and widely used of all four web services modules, JSON API. The JSON API specification is among the most recognizable in the web services landscape, with communities such as Ember and Ruby on Rails adopting it for their own REST APIs. JSON API is favorable for many developers because of its focus on facilitating highly relational queries with rich operations provided in query string parameters.

As of this writing, the Drupal 8 implementation of JSON API is slated for inclusion in an upcoming minor version release of Drupal core as a stable module. The JSON API module is maintained by Mateu Aguiló Bosch (e0ipso), Wim Leers, and Gabriel Sullice (gabesullice).

The JSON API Specification

Dubbing itself an "anti-bikeshedding tool," JSON API is a specification for REST APIs emitting responses in JSON and has recently gained momentum due to its adoption by the Ember and Ruby on Rails communities. JSON API also benefits from robust handling of relationships between resources and sought-after query operations like built-in sorting and pagination. The Drupal implementation of the JSON API is located in the JSON API module, which is approaching inclusion in Drupal 8 Core.

JSON API describes itself as follows:

> *[A] specification for how a client should request that resources be fetched or modified, and how a server should respond to those requests.*
>
> *JSON API is designed to minimize both the number of requests and the amount of data transmitted between clients and servers. This efficiency is achieved without compromising readability, flexibility, or discoverability.*

Thanks to Drupal's approach to entity relationships through references, Drupal's data structures (e.g., entity types, bundles, and fields) are well-suited for consumption and manipulation in conjunction with the JSON API specification and module.[1]

Note   The JSON API specification is located at `http://jsonapi.org`, and the JSON API module's project page is available on Drupal.org at `https://www.drupal.org/project/jsonapi`.

---

[1]"JSON API." Drupal.org. 18 December 2017. Accessed 10 May 2018. `https://www.drupal.org/docs/8/modules/json-api/json-api`

JSON API Document Structure

Unlike the HAL specification or many common APIs in JSON in the wild, the JSON API specification is highly opinionated about how data should be provided within a JSON API response. This section does not treat the JSON API specification exhaustively and should not be considered as authoritative a resource as the formal specification itself.

Every request and response body, no matter what the method, consists of a single JSON object. Any data specific to a resource lie under this object under the key `data`, which can represent either an object or array value. However, JSON API has strict rules for the typing of the data value: When creating or updating an entity resource, the value will be an object containing a single value; only when retrieving collections of more than one resource (see Chapter 12) does the value become an array. Compare the following two examples:

```
{
  "data": {
    // Single resource
  }
}
{
  "data": [
    {
      // One of multiple resources
    }
  ]
}
```

Apart from `data`, other top-level *members*, or predefined keys within the JSON object, include `errors`, `meta`, `links`, and `included`. The most frequently used member, as you might expect, is `included`, which contains all resources fetched via includes in query arguments.[2] See Chapter 12 for more information about JSON API includes.

---

[2]"Core Concepts." Drupal.org. 17 April 2018. Accessed 11 May 2018. `https://www.drupal.org/docs/8/modules/json-api/core-concepts`

JSON API Resource Objects

The JSON API specification also defines *resource objects* that represent the content of the relevant entities that the JSON API module treats as resources. These are contained within the data and included members. Within the context of Drupal, resource objects correspond to JSON representations of individual entities, such as content entities like users and nodes.

The specification requires that two members must be represented in every resource object: type and id. All identifiers in JSON API are UUIDs.

Note   Because the creation of entities via POST generally relies on Drupal to generate a unique identifier, the id is not required for POST requests that create resources through JSON API. Nonetheless, a consumer application is at liberty to provide a UUID for the resource when issuing a POST request.

The type member, which is always in kebab case (i.e., custom-entity-type) is always necessary as it indicates to JSON API how the resource should be treated and operated on. We cover how the JSON API module provides type information later in this chapter. For now, the most important fact you need to know is that the value for the type member consists of the entity type name and bundle name separated by two hyphens.

Theoretically, on an entity without any required fields, you could create an entity simply by issuing a POST request from the consumer application with the following object.

```
{
  "data": {
    "type": "node--airport",
  }
}
```

This would create an entity with no values filled in, though, as we're missing two additional important members: attributes and relationships.

JSON API Attributes and Relationships

To house values, the JSON API specification defines two members: `attributes`, which stores values specific to the resource in question, and `relationships`, which stores values that are provided by another resource in the system. Within the Drupal context, relationships are usually represented by values that are available via entity reference.

As an example, consider a bundle Airport on type Node that has a `uid` property representing the creator of the node. This could correspond to a user whose information would be presented to the Airport entity via entity reference. The following document showcases a more complete object with `attributes` and `relationships` represented:

```
{
  "data": {
    "type": "node--airport",
    "id": "5c11bcce-dd2f-43b3-9925-c85036b7fcc0",
    "attributes": {
      "title": "Daniel K. Inouye International Airport"
    },
    "relationships": {
      "uid": {
        "data": {
          "type": "user--user",
          "id": "ffe4bcbe-4aef-4676-9d22-c63cfac51d56"
        }
      }
    }
  }
}
```

In this example, the `relationships` member contains a reference to the property that contains the related entity. Within the `uid` property, another data object is defined, along with the required `type` and `id` members that indicate it is a unique resource also accessible through JSON API at its own URL.

As you might have noticed, whereas the surrounding resource contains attributes of the entity in question, the related resource does not have any `attributes` or `relationships` itself, because JSON API will only provide a related resource's contents if it is specifically requested by the consumer through the `include` query parameter. See Chapter 12 for more on includes.

The JSON API Module

The vision of the JSON API module is to require the user to perform the minimum amount of configuration possible. As such, on installing and enabling the JSON API module, you make a REST API immediately available for every content type within your Drupal installation. To do this, the JSON API module traverses entity types and bundles to generate URLs where it can retrieve and manipulate entities via safe and unsafe HTTP methods.

This mission of "no configuration" and off-the-shelf readiness for production does come with several drawbacks, namely that the JSON API is necessarily opinionated about the paths at which resources are made available, methods against which you can issue requests, and permissions by which entities can be retrieved and otherwise modified. This is because permissions for the JSON API module always fall back to default permissions in the core user system rather than relying on a unique configuration page (as core REST does).

To enable JSON API, use the following commands:

```
$ composer require drupal/jsonapi
$ drush en -y jsonapi
```

The JSON API Module API

The API within the JSON API module makes heavy use of Drupal's entity type and bundle system. Every available bundle within the Drupal application is assigned a unique URL that follows strict patterns. Unlike the core REST modules, JSON API's paths cannot be configured and are enabled by default. This is because the JSON API specification sets out rules that cover much more territory than specifications such as HAL, given that it dictates how HTTP methods should be used, which HTTP response codes are issued, and how resources should be formatted in responses and linked to others.

JSON API Types

The reliance on bundles means that the JSON API module requires that every resource have a globally unique type property, the value of which is populated by the entity type machine name and bundle type machine name separated by two hyphens. Consider Table 8-1, which contains examples of how types and bundles are translated into the JSON API-compliant type property.

Table 8-1. *Drupal Entity Types and Bundles as JSON API types*

Type	Bundle	JSON API **type**
Article (article)	Node (node)	node--article
Basic page (page)	Node (node)	node--page
User (user)	None (defaults to Type user)	user--user

As you can see from Table 8-1, when an entity type lacks a bundle, the entity type is repeated for consistency's sake.

JSON API URLs

For disambiguation from other web services modules and also from Views REST exports (see Chapter 11), the JSON API module requires that all resource URLs be prefixed with /jsonapi.

In addition, the module requires that every resource type represented in Drupal must be "uniquely addressable" within the API, meaning that every Drupal type has to live at its own path. This is to prevent collisions between two bundles (Drupal content types) having distinct sets of fields at the same URI. This condition in the JSON API module also means that each resource URL only handles requests for a single type of resource. As such, the Drupal implementation of JSON API follows the pattern seen in Table 8-2.

Table 8-2. *JSON API Resources in Drupal and Available HTTP Methods*

Method	URL	Example
GET, POST	/jsonapi/{entity_type_id}/{bundle_id}	/jsonapi/node/article
GET, PATCH, DELETE	/jsonapi/{entity_type_id}/{bundle_id}/ {entity_id}	/jsonapi/node/ article/{{uuid}}

GET appears twice in Table 8-2 because of JSON API's provision of optionality when it comes to retrieving an individual entity or a collection of entities. For more information, see Chapter 12.

Note   There is no valid resource URL at /jsonapi/node, because if it were allowed, the resource URL would serve multiple resource types (due to the potential presence of multiple bundle types within the entity type) from a single URL, which violates the JSON API specification.

After the entity type and bundle are provided, there is an optional component for the entity identifier. In the JSON API case, this is the UUID, not the node ID as seen in core REST modules. When working with a single resource, whether it is to retrieve it or manipulate it, you must include the UUID in the URL. When creating resources, however, the UUID must be excluded so that Drupal is responsible for generating the UUID on creating the entity.

JSON API Request Headers and Response Codes

Where appropriate, the JSON API specification asks clients that are issuing requests to include Content-Type and Accept headers that indicate that the request adheres to the JSON API specification, such as the sample headers here:

```
Accept: application/vnd.api+json
Content-Type: application/vnd.api+json
```

The JSON API specification also includes information about what responses can be issued as acceptable. The Drupal module makes use of the codes illustrated in Table 8-3.

Table 8-3. *Response Codes Issued by the JSON API Module*

Response Code	Condition
200 OK	Successful GET and PATCH requests
201 Created	Successful POST requests (just-created resource is also included in response body)
204 No Content	Successful DELETE requests

For examples of requests against Drupal's JSON API implementation, see Chapter 12. Now, we turn to RELAXed Web Services, another major web services provider in Drupal 8.

RELAXed Web Services

The RELAXed Web Services module, maintained by Tim Millwood (timmillwood) and Andrei Jechiu (jeqq), is unique among the most popular web services solutions available in Drupal 8 because of its use of the CouchDB specification and its emphasis on content staging use cases rather than content delivery to multiple channels. In this sense, it is closest in orientation to the original efforts of the WSCCI, whose initial mission was to foster better content staging across Drupal sites.

Content staging is a loosely defined range of features that include editorial workflows, content previews, and most important, the ability to draft and test content in a nonproduction environment in cases where the content needs to remain embargoed or otherwise private. When content has been sufficiently vetted and is greenlit to go live, content synchronization must occur between the staged content and live content. In Drupal, this is typically done through content *workspaces*, which are collections of content that should be synced across environments as a group. Content staging is a common feature in most CMSs.

The RELAXed Web Services module is part of the Drupal Deploy ecosystem, which we discuss in detail in this section. In addition, we cover the CouchDB specification and PouchDB client, which facilitates offline-enabled consumers. More details on RELAXed Web Services and Drupal's CouchDB implementation can be found in Chapter 13.

The Drupal Deploy Ecosystem

The Drupal Deploy ecosystem consists of several key modules that ease the process of content staging from one Drupal site to another. The centerpiece of the Drupal Deploy ecosystem is the Deploy module, which manages any dependencies that entities might have to one another and includes a robust API that handles a variety of content staging use cases, including the following.[3]

---

[3]"Drupal Deploy." Drupal Deploy. Accessed 24 August 2018. http://www.drupaldeploy.org

- *Cross-site content staging:* Deploy and RELAXed Web Services are well-suited for content staging across multiple Drupal sites.

- *Single-site content staging:* The Workspace module integrates with the Deploy module and offers a previewing system for a variety of workflow states.

- *Fully decoupled content delivery:* RELAXed Web Services also supports content delivery to consumers operating in non-web channels.

The Deploy module depends on the Multiversion and RELAXed Web Services module. The Multiversion module makes all content entities in Drupal revisionable, namely nodes, taxonomy terms, users, comments, and block content. It also adds a new unique identifier for revisions to the Entity API in Drupal that facilitates effective handling of revision trees and restoration of deleted revisions.

Meanwhile, RELAXed Web Services implements the CouchDB specification and provides a REST API that we can employ both for traditional cross-site content staging and decoupled consumers. For many architects, using RELAXed Web Services will only make sense in conjunction with the other modules that are part of the Drupal Deploy ecosystem, such as Replication, Conflict, Trash, and Workbench Moderation.

Note   The full scope of the Drupal Deploy ecosystem is far too large for full coverage in this volume. For more information, refer to the Drupal Deploy web site at `www.drupaldeploy.org`.

The CouchDB Replication Protocol

CouchDB is not a traditional specification for REST APIs; rather, it is a NoSQL database tool. CouchDB stores data within JSON documents that are accessible via web browser and via HTTP requests issued from consumers written in languages like JavaScript.[4] Each of these documents (resources) has a unique name within a CouchDB

---

[4]"Multiversion." Drupal.org. 31 May 2014. Accessed 24 August 2018. `https://www.drupal.org/project/multiversion`

database, which is exposed through a RESTful API that permits resource retrieval and manipulation.[5]

Like JSON API in Drupal, CouchDB supports certain HTTP methods such as GET, POST, PUT, and DELETE. However, CouchDB also supports other HTTP methods excluded from core REST such as PUT and COPY. A list of the most common request methods and expected responses follows.

- GET: In CouchDB, GET requests retrieve items, which can be documents (resources), static items, or introspective information such as configuration, returned as JSON.

- POST: In CouchDB, POST is used for updating values in documents, uploading new documents, and triggering certain remote procedures.

- PUT: Excluded from Drupal's core REST, PUT in CouchDB allows us to create new objects such as databases, documents, and others.

- DELETE: In CouchDB, DELETE requests delete the resource in question.

- COPY: Special to CouchDB, COPY requests can be used to reproduce documents and objects in the database.

If a disallowed method is used, CouchDB returns a 405 Method Not Allowed response code and lists the allowed methods in the response body.[6]

Note   For more information about the CouchDB API, consult the API reference located at http://docs.couchdb.org/en/latest/api/index.html.

---

[5]"1. Introduction." Apache CouchDB. 2018. Accessed 24 August 2018. http://docs.couchdb.org/en/latest/intro/index.html

[6]"10. API Reference." Apache CouchDB. 2018. Accessed 24 August 2018. http://docs.couchdb.org/en/latest/api/index.html

The RELAXed Web Services Module

To install the RELAXed Web Services module, be sure to include the third-party dependency manually or use Composer Manager to ensure the `relaxedws/replicator` library is present.

```
$ composer require relaxedws/replicator:dev-master
$ composer require drupal/relaxed
$ drush en -y relaxed
```

Once RELAXed Web Services is installed, navigate to Configuration ➤ Relaxed settings (`/admin/config/relaxed/settings`), where you will find a RELAXed Web Services settings page. During installation, RELAXed Web Services generates a new *Replicator* user that is responsible for content replication across sites. This is afforded by the *Perform pull replication* and *Perform push replication* permissions specific to RELAXed Web Services.

If you do not need content staging functionality, you can skip ahead to the next section. If you do plan to stage content across Drupal sites, create a new user with the Replicator role or update an existing user with the role. Remember that the Replicator user needs to be present on all Drupal sites that are conducting content replication. On the RELAXed Web Services settings page, provide the Replicator user's credentials and set the root path for all resources exposed through RELAXed Web Services, as seen in Figure 8-4.

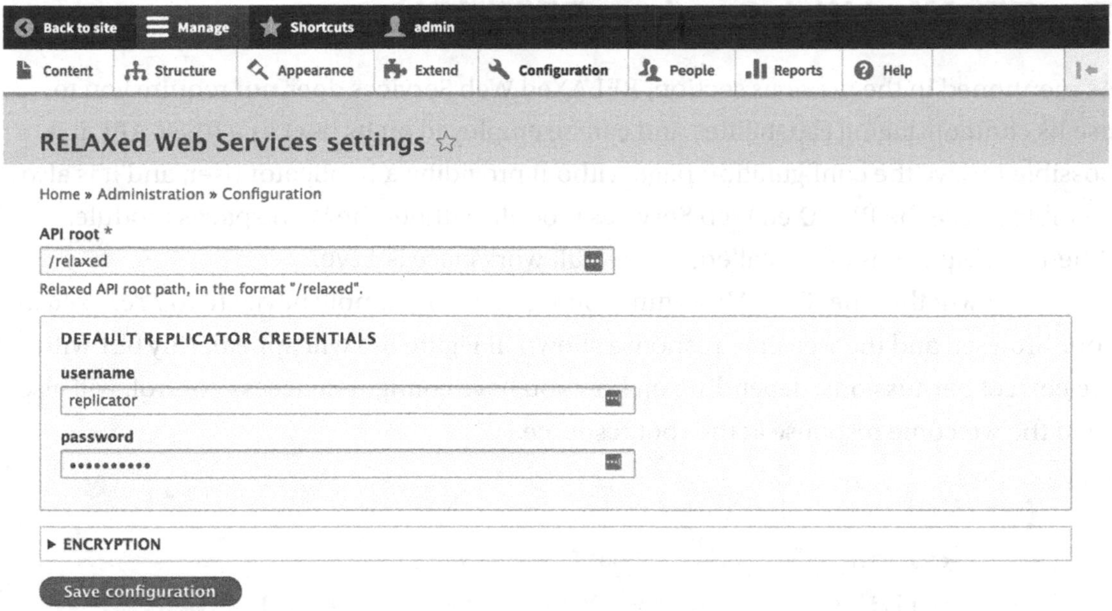

Figure 8-4. *If you are staging content across multiple sites, assign the Replicator role to a user and provide that user's credentials on the RELAXed Web Services settings page*

If you are performing content replication across multiple Drupal sites, you will also need to configure a remote by navigating to Configuration ➤ Relaxed remotes (/admin/config/services/relaxed), where you can add new remote Drupal sites, a process that requires the Workspace module. You will need to provide the credentials of the Replicator user responsible for content replication.

Finally, navigate to Structure ➤ Workspaces (/admin/structure/workspace) to add and edit the workspace that should connect to the remote Drupal site.

Note   For more information about using the Drupal Deploy suite, see the RELAXed Web Services module configuration page on Drupal.org, located at `https://www.drupal.org/docs/8/modules/relaxed-web-services/module-configuration`.

The RELAXed Web Services REST API

As mentioned in the previous section, RELAXed Web Services does not require you to use its content staging capabilities and can be employed on its own as a REST API. It is possible to save the configuration page without providing a Replicator user, and it is also possible to use the RELAXed Web Services module without the Workspaces module. When Workspaces is not installed, the default workspace is live.

To test whether the REST API is functioning correctly, simply navigate to /relaxed in your browser, and the welcome response shown in Figure 8-5 will appear. Any GET with the correct permissions, depending on how you have configured access control, will also yield the welcome response at the root resource.

```
{
    "couchdb": "Welcome",
    "uuid": "02286a1b231b68d89624d281cdfc0404",
    "vendor": {
        "name": "Drupal",
        "version": "8.5.6"
    },
    "version": "8.5.6"
}
```

Figure 8-5. *A GET request against the root CouchDB resource in RELAXed Web Services will yield a welcome response*

To obtain a list of all available workspaces on the Drupal back end, we can issue a GET request against the /relaxed/_all_dbs resource, which will return a response containing the workspaces present on Drupal. If you have not installed the Workspaces module, this will return the default workspace live.

To obtain a collection of all the Drupal entities (CouchDB documents) available in a workspace, we can issue a GET request against /relaxed/{workspace}/_all_docs, where {workspace} is the desired workspace. For instance, on a Drupal site

without Workspaces installed, the resource would be located at the path /relaxed/
live/_all_docs.[7]

For example requests that demonstrate RELAXed Web Services functionality,
see Chapter 13.

Note   A full accounting of the available REST resources and supported methods
in RELAXed Web Services is available on Drupal.org at https://www.drupal.
org/docs/8/modules/relaxed-web-services/available-rest-
resources-and-supported-http-methods.

PouchDB and Hoodie

One of the most important reasons that decoupled Drupal practitioners choose
RELAXed Web Services over the other options is not solely because of its content staging
capabilities; it is also because other databases can integrate richly with data contained
in RELAXed Web Services. Most compellingly, client-side technologies such as PouchDB
and Hoodie can be used to provide offline-enabled features.

PouchDB is the JavaScript analogue of Apache CouchDB and is designed specifically
to work locally in the browser. PouchDB enables applications to house local data in an
offline database, which is then synchronized with an available CouchDB database once
the user regains connectivity.

Note   A comprehensive introduction to PouchDB is beyond the scope of this
volume. For more information about PouchDB, consult the web site at https://
pouchdb.com.

Hoodie, which depends on PouchDB, more overtly embraces offline-first and no-
back-end principles. Written in JavaScript, Hoodie is based on CouchDB and Node.
js and can also integrate with a Drupal-powered CouchDB database for content
synchronization.

---

[7]"Available REST Resources and Supported HTTP Methods." Drupal.org. 8 June 2018. Accessed
25 August 2018. https://www.drupal.org/docs/8/modules/relaxed-web-services/
available-rest-resources-and-supported-http-methods

> **Note**   A comprehensive introduction to Hoodie is beyond the scope of this volume.
> For more information about Hoodie, consult the web site at `http://hood.ie`.

GraphQL

Within the Drupal web services ecosystem, perhaps the most futuristic solution available to decoupled Drupal practitioners is GraphQL, a declarative query language and application-level protocol created by Facebook to power its extensive mobile application ecosystem. Thanks to the work of maintainers Sebastian Siemssen (fubhy) and Philipp Melab (pmelab), Drupal has its own implementation of GraphQL.

GraphQL is quite similar to previous query languages like SPARQL insofar as it describes function calls and does not directly query a database; instead, the GraphQL server acts as an additional abstraction layer and is responsible for handling incoming requests from consumers. GraphQL servers should be agnostic to data storage and are typically proxies or relay systems that forward API calls.

The most important principle in GraphQL is that client requests and server payloads adhere to a shared shape. In other words, the client provides a structure of the data that it requires, and the server returns the data according to the client-declared structure.

Motivating GraphQL

GraphQL's recent success in the JavaScript community and beyond has much to do with the limitations of traditional RESTful architectures found in today's CMS landscape. Typical RESTful architectures rely on many endpoints, suffer from response bloat, require many round trips to the server, lack backward compatibility, and often provide insufficient introspection.

In REST APIs, individual resources tend to be overly specific and yield responses that are ill-suited for highly relational resource trees. This often leads to bespoke or homegrown API resources that satisfy developers of consumer applications but increase maintenance costs. For these developers, this issue can be particularly damaging because they have the responsibility to traverse undesirable or convoluted responses without control over the response object's structure. To alleviate this, GraphQL provides a single URL that provides a unified response even if a GraphQL server needs to perform constituent operations to acquire those data.

Today, we often employ REST APIs for vast collections of consumer applications, without due attention to the fact that consumers are highly distinct and should not receive the same response, especially low-level consumers such as Raspberry Pi. In addition, due to changing business requirements, consumers might need to contend with ever-larger payloads without the ability to control the quantity of incoming data. GraphQL's tailored responses allow for consumers themselves to dictate precisely the amount of data they need—no more, no less.

Many REST APIs also enforce multiple requests to the server to provide a complex or highly relational application view on the consumer. In Drupal's case, this also means additional bootstraps. Unlike JSON API, which uses query parameter strings to dictate how relationships or includes should figure in the response payload, GraphQL allows consumers to cater the response to their request structure in a flexible way.

When it comes to maintenance, REST APIs suffer considerably from a lack of industry cohesion around a solution for API versioning. This leads to convoluted solutions such as the provisioning of multiple APIs with version-specific paths (e.g., /api/v1, /api/v2). When changes occur in the API and how it responds to requests, consumers must be updated manually to new API versions. GraphQL obviates the need for API versioning by allowing consumers to submit identical queries to multiple versions without a difference in the response, thanks to the consumer-tailored structure of the response.

Finally, many REST APIs contend with challenging developer experiences by not providing a full introspection layer within the API. GraphQL has a native and extensible schema and type system that developers can introspect in the same way as they query a GraphQL API. This aids client-side tooling and validation downstream.[8]

Table 8-4 summarizes the preceding information by enumerating each disadvantage of traditional RESTful architectures and GraphQL's mitigation.

---

[8]So, Preston, and Sebastian Siemssen. "An Introduction to GraphQL and What It Means for Drupal." Acquia. 10 March 2016. Accessed 25 August 2018. https://www.acquia.com/resources/webinars/introduction-graphql-and-what-it-means-drupal

Table 8-4. *Limitations in Typical RESTful Architectures and GraphQL Mitigations*

REST Limitation	GraphQL Mitigation
Many endpoints	Fewer endpoints
Response bloat	Tailored responses
Many round trips	Fewer round trips
No backward compatibility	Inherent backward compatibility
No native introspection layer	Full introspection layer

Nonetheless, GraphQL does have its disadvantages, which decoupled Drupal practitioners should consider as well. For instance, many of the features available in GraphQL are also available in HTTP, such as parallel network requests (varies across browsers), content negotiation (which allows clients to request multiple versions of a resource at a single path), and a native content type system (which is analogous to GraphQL's own type system). In addition, many architects might find that the learning curve of GraphQL is overly steep and might favor simply provisioning additional REST API endpoints.

The GraphQL Specification

In this section, we embark on a rapid introduction to some of the most important key concepts in GraphQL. We apply this knowledge when we implement requests against Drupal's GraphQL server in Chapter 14.

Note   A comprehensive account of GraphQL's syntax is beyond the scope of this volume. For more information about GraphQL syntax, refer to `https://graphql.org/learn`.

GraphQL Operations

GraphQL models two types of operations: queries and mutations. *Queries,* which are read-only retrievals of data, can be named case-sensitively or anonymous. *Mutations* are write queries. Consider the following examples and note the comment syntax.

```
query {
  # Read-only fetch
}
```

This anonymous query has a shorthand.

```
{
  # Read-only fetch
}
```

Queries can be named.

```
query getUscr {
  # Read-only fetch
}
```

Note   These are hypothetical examples solely for illustrative purposes and not functional queries that would yield responses from Drupal.

GraphQL Selection Sets and Fields

Consider the following hypothetical query. In GraphQL, the *field* is the most important irreducible unit within a requested object, and *selection sets* define which fields from objects should be present in a response payload. In selection sets, fields are separated by carriage returns (\n). Top-level fields (e.g., entity in this example) are typically globally accessible.

```
{
  entity {
    user(id: "123") {
      name
    }
  }
}
```

If it were functional, this query would return a response object from the GraphQL server whose structure mirrors that of the original query, such as the following.

```
{
  "data": {
    "entity": {
      "user": {
        "name": "Preston So"
      }
    }
  }
}
```

Fields are also capable of describing relationships with other data. For instance, we can consider fields to be much like functions insofar as they return values and can carry an arbitrary number of arguments. Consider the following example.

```
{
  entity {
    user(id: "3") {
      firstName
      lastName
      email
      avatar(height: "72", width: "72")
    }
  }
}
```

Fields can also be aliased, which is useful for disambiguating identically named fields.

```
{
  entity {
    user(id: "3") {
      firstName
      lastName
      email
```

```
      thumbnail: avatar(height: "72", width: "72")
      profileImage: avatar(height: "250", width: "250")
    }
  }
}
```

GraphQL Fragments

GraphQL also allows for the definition of *fragments,* which are reusable selection sets that can help keep queries from becoming unmaintainable. As a note, fields present in fragments are included in the query at the same level of invocation as adjacent fields. For instance, in the following example, title and body occupy the same hierarchical plane.

```
{
  entity {
    article: node(id: "992") {
      title
      ...content
    }
  }
}

fragment content on Page {
  body
}
```

This hypothetical query might yield a response like this:

```
{
  "data": {
    "entity": {
      "article": {
        "title": "GraphQL and Drupal ..."
        "body": "... go together like peas in a pod!"
      }
    }
  }
}
```

Fragments are required to declare types so that when objects of different types are fetched, their fields are conditionally applied. For example, consider a query that includes two fragments, each dedicated to a particular type of view on the article. When the object selected by a query is a Teaser, the body is excluded and a smaller image is chosen.

```
{
  entity {
    article: node(id: "992") {
      title
      ...content
    }
  }
}

fragment content on Page {
  heroImage: image(width: "960")
  body
}

fragment content on Teaser {
  thumbnail: image(width: "100")
}
```

Fragments are also nestable.

```
{
  entity {
    article: node(id: "992") {
      title
      ...content
    }
  }
}

fragment content on Page {
  ...heroImage
  body
}
```

```
fragment heroImage on Page {
  image(width: "960")
}
```

Fragments can be inlined to improve code legibility, and in this usage they can be nameless.

```
{
  entity {
    article: node(id: "992") {
      title
      ... on Page {
        body
        image(width: "960")
      }
      ... on Teaser {
        image(width: "100")
      }
    }
  }
}
```

GraphQL Variables and Directives

In GraphQL, *directives* alter query behavior and can be used to conditionally include or exclude fields based on *variables* that are defined in the query definition and the values of which are passed into the query. For instance, consider the following hypothetical query.

```
query getArticle($hasBody: Boolean) {
  article: node(id: "992") {
    title
    ... @include(if: $hasBody) {
      body
      image(width: "960")
    }
  }
}
```

The GraphQL specification recommends supporting directives such as @skip and @include.

```
query getArticle($hasBody: Boolean, $anonymous: Boolean = true) {
  article: node(id: "992") {
    title
    author @skip(if: $anonymous)
    ... @include(if: $hasBody) {
      body
      image(width: "960")
    }
  }
}
```

To pass in variables, the GraphQL server also needs to accept a JSON payload that contains the variables defined with values.

```
{
  "hasBody": true,
  "anonymous": true
}
```

GraphQL Mutations

In GraphQL, *mutations* are write operations that instruct the GraphQL server to perform the operation named with the fields contained in the selection set. Consider the following mutation query, in which the exclamation mark indicates that an argument is required. In this hypothetical scenario, we have predefined an Article object type in GraphQL having several fields.

```
mutation CreateArticle($article: Article!) {
  createArticle(article: $article) {
    id
    title
    body
  }
}
```

We can then execute this mutation query with the following arguments, under the assumption that this data structure mirrors the `Article` type definition.

```
{
  "article": {
    "title": "GraphQL and Drupal ...",
    "body": "... go together like peas in a pod!"
  }
}
```

This query would then yield the following response, which would confirm the article's creation.[9]

```
{
  "data": {
    "createArticle": {
      "id": "992",
      "title": "GraphQL and Drupal ...",
      "body": "... go together like peas in a pod!"
    }
  }
}
```

The GraphQL Module

The GraphQL module is Drupal's authoritative implementation of GraphQL and permits the creation and exposure of a schema reflecting a Drupal 8 site's content. Because the module depends on the `webonyx/graphql-php` library, a PHP implementation of GraphQL, it satisfies the full feature set of the GraphQL specification.

The GraphQL module can be used as a baseline for constructing schemas via custom code, but there is a default generated schema that is extensible through plug-ins within

---

[9]"Queries and Mutations." GraphQL. 2018. Accessed 25 August 2018. `http://graphql.github.io/learn/queries`

the GraphQL Core submodule. In addition, GraphiQL, a debugger for GraphQL queries, is built into the GraphQL module and is available at the path /graphql/explorer on module installation.[10]

The GraphQL module has a unique installation method that can be confusing to developers new to Drupal. Because it relies on an external repository hosted on GitHub, the first step is to open our composer.json file in the root of our Drupal installation and add the following as a member of the repositories array.

```
{
  "type": "vcs",
  "url": "https://github.com/drupal-graphql/graphql"
}
```

Once you save your composer.json file, you will be able to use a normal Composer workflow or Composer Manager to handle dependencies. Note that we are also enabling the GraphQL Core module, which provides, among other things, the GraphiQL debugger.

```
$ composer require drupal/graphql
$ drush en -y graphql graphql_core
```

For examples that demonstrate how consumers can retrieve Drupal content through GraphQL, see Chapter 14.

Note   The GraphQL module is available on GitHub at https://github.com/drupal-graphql/graphql. The project page is available on Drupal.org at https://www.drupal.org/project/graphql.

REST UI

Although it is essential to understand the underpinnings of REST resource configuration in Drupal 8 and how it integrates with the Drupal configuration system (see Chapter 7), the REST UI module, maintained by Juampy NR (juampynr) and Clemens Tolboom (clemens.tolboom), accelerates your configuration process thanks to a convenient user

---

[10]"GraphQL." Drupal.org. 20 March 2015. Accessed 25 August 2018. https://www.drupal.org/project/graphql

interface that alleviates the need to perform single imports on Drupal's configuration synchronization page. For users who are less experienced with Drupal, such an interface can be particularly useful.

Use the default approach (i.e., downloading, extracting into the /modules directory, and installing on the Extend page) or dependency management in Composer. A cache registry rebuild might be necessary.

```
$ composer require drupal/restui
$ drush en -y restui
$ drush cr
```

On navigating to Manage ➤ Configuration (/admin/config), you will encounter a new user interface with a list of enabled REST resources, as seen in Figure 8-6. If you followed our steps in Chapter 7 to import configuration for entities that are nodes, you will already see nodes represented as an enabled resource within the interface.

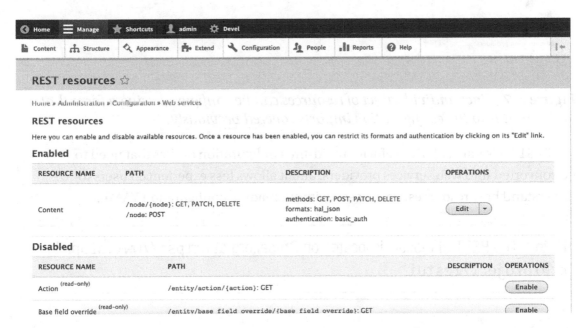

Figure 8-6. *The REST resources configuration page in the REST UI modules takes into account resources that you have already configured. Here, we have configured all node resources to be made available for retrieval and manipulation.*

Adjacent to each resource type represented, you can edit its configuration via an interface that replicates the structure of configuration imports in the appearance of a form, as seen in Figure 8-7.

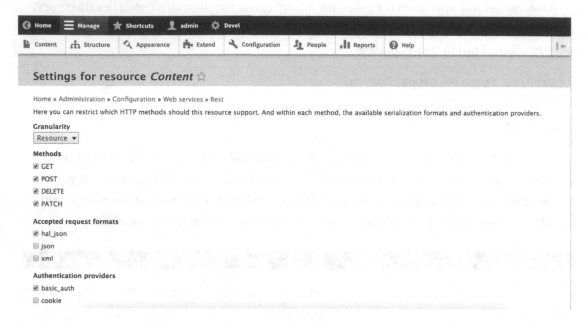

Figure 8-7. *Each individual set of resources can be configured using a form that looks similar to the configuration imports covered previously*

REST UI is particularly useful for rapid-fire configuration of sites that need to be converted into web services providers, and it allows less experienced users to understand how resources are exposed without reading configuration YAML.

Note   The REST UI module is located on Drupal.org at `https://www.drupal.org/project/restui`.

Conclusion

In this chapter, we've covered the most stable and popular contributed solutions for web services available in Drupal 8—namely JSON API, RELAXed Web Services, and GraphQL—along with the REST UI module, which can help to accelerate your progress. In addition, we have become familiar with concepts across all three specifications that will be useful when we turn to developing applications against these modules in later chapters.

In the next chapter, we orient ourselves toward an area of critical importance in decoupled Drupal architectures: authentication. First, we'll look at the authentication methods that Drupal core provides out of the box: Basic Authentication and cookie-based authentication. Luckily, more secure contributed solutions exist, such as Simple OAuth and JSON Web Tokens. As we learn, protecting the security and privacy of users in your decoupled Drupal architecture is just as mission-critical as delivering content to the devices they use.

## CHAPTER 9

Authenticating Requests in Drupal 8

Among the most important areas of concern for decoupled Drupal architecture is security. By nature, decoupled Drupal introduces substantial security concerns that have implications for the data stored in Drupal as well as the safety of users who access Drupal content through a consumer. Indeed, one of the drawbacks of decoupled Drupal cited in Chapter 6 was the increased onus on developer teams to build in robust authentication.

There are three approaches in Drupal 8 for authentication that are relevant to decoupled Drupal. Basic Authentication and OAuth2 Bearer Token authentication are the most commonly used for decoupled Drupal architectures, whereas cookie-based authentication is important for progressively decoupled Drupal implementations in which consumers make use of the user session cookie on a Drupal-rendered page. Other approaches exist as well, most notably JSON Web Tokens (JWT), which is implemented in a Drupal contributed module.

Basic Authentication

The Basic Authentication module is by far the easiest to use, but it is also rather insecure. Available in Drupal 8 Core, Basic Authentication (commonly abbreviated *Basic Auth*) processes an incoming request, isolating the provided username and password and authenticating them against Drupal to ensure that the user in question has the correct permissions to retrieve or manipulate requested content.[1]

---

[1]"HTTP Basic Authentication Overview." Drupal.org. 22 December 2016. Accessed 7 August 2018. `https://www.drupal.org/docs/8/core/modules/basic_auth/overview`

© Preston So 2018
P. So, *Decoupled Drupal in Practice*, https://doi.org/10.1007/978-1-4842-4072-4_9

113

Nonetheless, you should exercise extreme caution when using Basic Authentication with decoupled Drupal, because the username and password are protected in a limited fashion. In Basic Authentication, credentials are transmitted over the wire in base64 encoding (i.e., not encrypted or hashed), which is straightforward to convert into exploitable plain text. In addition, every request typically includes credentials, meaning that this sensitive information is transmitted repeatedly, creating a larger attack window.[2] Due to these concerns, Basic Authentication should be used only together with HTTPS on the Drupal back end.

Warning   Due to the inherent vulnerabilities of Basic Authentication, it is a best practice to use either Simple OAuth or JSON Web Tokens (covered later in this chapter) in production where sensitive data needs to be retrieved. However, for authenticated requests against nonsensitive data, Basic Authentication can offer a more convenient developer experience and is thus used frequently during development or technical demonstrations.

HTTP Basic Authentication

The Basic Authentication module implements the HTTP Basic protocol, which dictates how to conduct *basic access authentication.* The HTTP Basic protocol allows user agents to issue requests that include a standard provision of a user's username and password. HTTP Basic is often desirable because it enforces access controls without requiring cookies (see next section) or session identifiers and because it employs HTTP headers, eliminating the need for handshakes.[3]

The HTTP Basic protocol stipulates how to construct an *Authorization* field to transmit authentication credentials to Drupal. According to RFC 7617 (2015), we can construct the Authorization field as follows:[4]

---

[2]"Is BASIC-Auth Secure if Done over HTTPS?" Stack Overflow. 5 December 2010. Accessed 7 August 2018. `https://security.stackexchange.com/questions/988/is-basic-auth-secure-if-done-over-https`

[3]"Basic Access Authentication." Wikipedia. 10 July 2018. Accessed 7 August 2018. `https://en.wikipedia.org/wiki/Basic_access_authentication`

[4]Reschke, J. "The 'Basic' HTTP Authentication Scheme." Internet Engineering Task Force. September 2015. Accessed 7 August 2018. `https://tools.ietf.org/html/rfc7617`

1. Both the username and the password are concatenated together and separated by a colon, which means that the username cannot contain a colon.

2. The concatenated string is then encoded into an octet sequence. The character set for this encoding step can be unspecified by default or dictated by a charset parameter originating from the server.

3. This encoded string is then encoded using a variant of base64 encoding.

4. The base64-encoded string is then prepended with the authorization method in question (e.g., "Basic") followed by a space.

The Authorization Header

In Drupal, if a request exercises some permissioned action unavailable for anonymous users, it must include an Authorization header containing credentials for a user that has a role with the sufficient permissions to conduct the action, whether it is an update or deletion of an entity. Within any sensitive request that travels to Drupal, the Authorization header must be set by the consumer, which additionally needs to handle the aforementioned preparation steps itself.

As an example, consider the username and password combination admin and admin. Consider the following JavaScript function, which returns a correctly formatted Authorization field thanks to string concatenation and JavaScript's native btoa() function:

```
function encodeBasicAuth(user, pass) {
  var creds = user + ':' + pass;
  var base64 = btoa(creds);
  return 'Basic ' + base64;
}
```

Then, within an XMLHttpRequest (XHR), you can invoke the function. As we will see in later chapters, many JavaScript frameworks accelerate this process by providing their own XHR API, as does Waterwheel.js (see Chapter 16). Note that the Drupal back end referred to in the following example is the same one we set up in Chapter 7.

```
var req = new XMLHttpRequest();
req.open('GET', 'https://core-rest.dd:8083/node/1');
req.setRequestHeader('Authorization', encodeBasicAuth('admin', 'admin'));
req.send('_format=hal_json');
```

This request can also be written as follows, which reflects a Drupal back end where Basic Authentication is required for retrieval of content entities. As you can see, our base64-encoded `Authorization` field is `YWRtaW46YWRtaW4=`.

```
GET /node/1?_format=hal_json HTTP/1.1
Content-Type: application/json
X-CSRF-Token: SDEEgyW_n2vI3GygOI2Y-W7VRrfIiN8gk3PdO1O3vHo
Authorization: YWRtaW46YWRtaW4=
Host: core-rest.dd:8083
```

Cookie-Based Authentication

In Drupal, *cookie-based authentication* is an additional method to authenticate user credentials during the issuance of a request. The primary distinction between Basic Authentication and cookie-based authentication is the latter's use in Drupal's normal operations. Whereas Basic Authentication focuses on third-party applications, in cookie-based authentication, Drupal uses cookies on the browser to preserve a user's session.

As a result, cookie-based authentication is particularly useful in instances of progressive decoupling, because any Drupal page that requires authentication will refer to the session cookie housed in the browser. Because progressive decoupling involves the interpolation of a JavaScript framework into Drupal's front end, the framework has access to the authenticated cookie as well, absolutely free of charge. This is because both the framework and the surrounding Drupal front end have access to the `document. cookie` object, where the cookie is located.

For fully decoupled implementations, cookie-based authentication is roughly analogous to Basic Authentication, except for the crucial fact that the value of an active session cookie can easily be stolen and subsequently employed to exploit a Drupal back end. As such, although I am including it for the sake of completeness to illustrate the functionality, you should leverage this approach with extreme caution.

Retrieving Cookies in Fully Decoupled Consumers

It is possible to replace Basic Authentication in fully decoupled Drupal architectures with cookie-based authentication, particularly if your authentication needs are relatively simple and your data are less sensitive. Whereas in Basic Authentication, a username and password are transparently available on the client, in a fully decoupled implementation of cookie-based authentication, the session cookie is stored on the client and transmitted on every request.

Warning   Due to the inherent vulnerabilities of cookie-based authentication, it is a best practice to use either Simple OAuth or JSON Web Tokens (covered later in this chapter) in production where sensitive data need to be retrieved. However, for authenticated requests against nonsensitive data, cookie-based authentication can offer a more convenient developer experience and is thus used frequently during development or technical demonstrations.

To retrieve the session cookie for cookie-based authentication, we need a user session. To acquire a user session, you can issue a POST request against the login form (/user/login?_format=json) of the Drupal back end serving your content, submitting alongside it the following request body[5]:

```
{
  "name": "admin",
  "pass": "admin"
}
```

As you can see in Figures 9-1 and 9-2, the response to this request will have a 200 OK response code and contain a session cookie, as well as a response object containing information about the user whose session has begun and tokens that can be used to issue requests using unsafe HTTP methods (see Chapter 10 for more about the X-CSRF-Token) or to log the user out.

---

[5]Kandyba, Igor. "Playing with Web Services API in Drupal 8. Theory and Practice." Just Drupal. 23 May 2017. Accessed 7 August 2018. https://justdrupal.com/web-services-drupal-8/

```
{
  "current_user": {
    "uid": "1",
    "roles": [
      "authenticated",
      "administrator"
    ],
    "name": "admin"
  },
  "csrf_token": "SDEEgyW_n2vI3GygOI2Y-W7VRrfIiN8gk3PdO1O3vHo",
  "logout_token": "jW66ozYwAe_D_rj2sY61WfuzPW9ft91ei6vngUhoYms"
}
```

Note   In these examples, we are using Postman, an HTTP client. For more information about Postman and its usage, see Chapter 10.

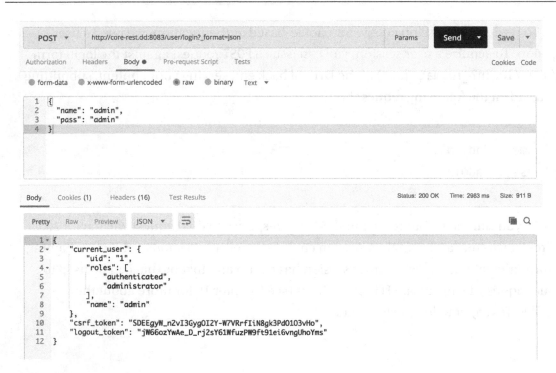

Figure 9-1.   *We can issue a POST request against Drupal's login form to retrieve the cookie that we need to conduct cookie-based authentication. The response also includes useful information about the user's roles and tokens for other purposes.*

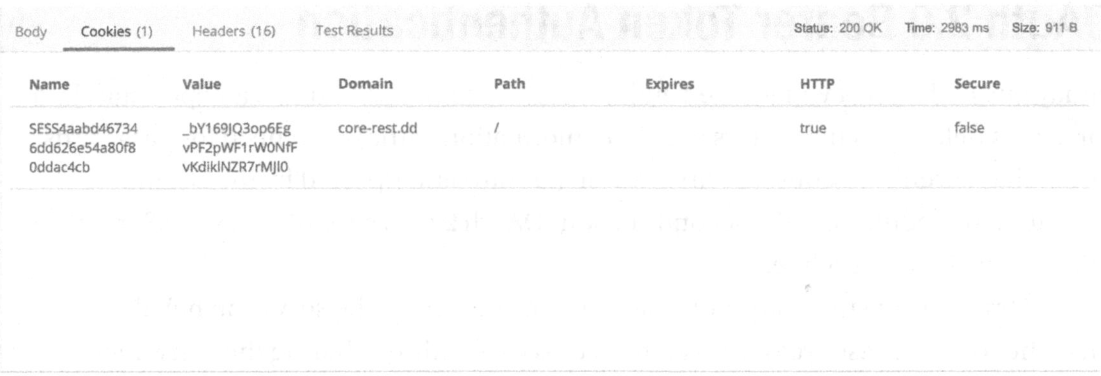

Body	Cookies (1)	Headers (16)	Test Results			Status: 200 OK	Time: 2983 ms	Size: 911 B
Name	Value	Domain	Path	Expires		HTTP	Secure	
SESS4aabd46734 6dd626e54a80f8 0ddac4cb	_bY169JQ3op6Eg vPF2pWF1rWONfF vKdikINZR7rMJl0	core-rest.dd	/			true	false	

Figure 9-2. *The session cookie can be used to authenticate requests from consumer applications through a logged-in user's session*

Authenticating Using Cookies

In fully decoupled Drupal implementations, the steps undertaken in the previous section are required to access the session cookie. However, in progressively decoupled implementations, the session cookie is available in document.cookie, as the JavaScript framework and Drupal-rendered front end occupy the same DOM.

You can include the cookie name (e.g., SESS4aabd467346dd626e54a80f80ddac4cb) and value (e.g., _bY169JQ3op6EgvPF2pWF1rWONfFvKdiklNZR7rMJl0), separated by =, in the request headers of any subsequent request that requires authentication to proceed. For instance, consider the following headers for a POST request that creates a node. For further examples of POST requests against core REST, see Chapter 10.

```
POST /entity/node?_format=json HTTP/1.1
Content-Type: application/json
X-CSRF-Token: SDEEgyW_n2vI3GygOI2Y-W7VRrfIiN8gk3PdO1O3vHo
Cookie: SESS4aabd467346dd626e54a80f80ddac4cb=_
bY169JQ3op6EgvPF2pWF1rWONfFvKdiklNZR7rMJl0
Host: core-rest.dd:8083
```

To log the user out, simply issue a POST request to /user/logout?_format= json&token=jW66ozYwAe_D_rj2sY61WfuzPW9ft91ei6vngUhoYms (using the previously retrieved logout_token as the second query string parameter), on which you will receive a 204 No Content response code that indicates termination of the user session.[6]

---

[6]"Additional RPC Endpoints: user/login user/login/status user/logout user/password." Drupal. org. 28 July 2016. Accessed 9 August 2018. https://www.drupal.org/node/2720655

OAuth 2.0 Bearer Token Authentication

Today one of the most widely used authentication methods, OAuth is an open standard for access delegation that grants access to information without the need for passwords. OAuth has several versions; the first version (OAuth) is supported by the OAuth contributed module, and the second version (OAuth 2.0) is supported by the Simple OAuth contributed module.

In OAuth, a consumer is granted access to resources on the server on behalf of an owner of those resources, who authorizes access without sharing the consumer credentials. OAuth issues access tokens over HTTP to consumers via an authorization server. From there on, the consumer employs the access token to retrieve or manipulate protected resources in requests that it issues.[7]

Because the first version of OAuth is less secure and is not backward compatible with OAuth 2.0, we focus solely on the second version in this section. Some developers might opt to use OAuth 1 to avoid an HTTPS server requirement, but this is no longer advisable.[8]

Note   The Simple OAuth module (OAuth 2.0) is available on Drupal.org at `https://www.drupal.org/project/simple_oauth`. The OAuth module (OAuth 1) is available on Drupal.org at `https://www.drupal.org/project/oauth`.

Warning   OAuth 1 is now considered less secure than OAuth 2.0 and should not be used in production where using OAuth 2.0 is possible instead.

---

[7]"OAuth." Wikipedia. 30 July 2018. Accessed 7 August 2018. `https://en.wikipedia.org/wiki/OAuth`

[8]"OAuth 2.0." Drupal.org. 18 February 2018. Accessed 7 August 2018. `https://www.drupal.org/project/simple_oauth`

OAuth 2.0 Grants

In OAuth 2.0, a *grant* is a means of acquiring an access token that can be used by consumers to access protected resources. There are various ways to communicate with a back end from the consumer's standpoint via API, but depending on the relationship between the consumer and the server, one particular grant type might be better than others. The *authorization code grant* type, for instance, is used to build many custom third-party applications that consume GitHub data.[9]

The PHP League establishes four OAuth 2.0 grant types that map neatly onto the five grant types cited in the OAuth 2.0 Authorization Framework RFC (RFC 6749). In the process, the PHP League also introduces several justifications for a particular grant type. In what follows, *first-party* refers to a consumer sufficiently trusted to handle an end user's credentials, whereas a *third-party* consumer is untrusted.[10]

- *Authorization code grant:* If the permission of a user (the access token owner) is required to access resources, and if the consumer is a web application or a third-party native application, you can use the authorization code grant type.

- *Implicit grant:* If the permission of a user is required to access resources, and if the consumer is a third-party browser-based application, you can use the implicit grant type.

- *Client credentials grant:* If the permission of a user is not required to access resources, you can use the client credentials grant type.

- *Password grant:* If the permission of a user is required to access resources, and if the consumer is a first-party application, you can use the password grant type.

The Simple OAuth module emphasizes the password grant, as it is a convenient catchall for trusted first-party applications that potentially require access to any operation possible in Drupal, including creating and deleting users. Nonetheless, the password grant might allocate excessive power to the consumer application. In that case, consider one of the other grant types.

---

[9]"OAuth 2.0 Server: Terminology." The League of Extraordinary Packages. Accessed 7 August 2018. http://oauth2.thephpleague.com/terminology

[10]"Which OAuth 2.0 Grant Should I Implement?" The League of Extraordinary Packages. Accessed 10 August 2018. https://oauth2.thephpleague.com/authorization-server/which-grant

---

Warning   There is considerable debate about whether the password grant type is truly secure enough for consumers like single-page applications, which need to store client secrets within readable code, and even native applications. The additional requirement of user credentials (see upcoming sections) might be sufficiently secure for your needs, but not all implementations consider this a best practice. See this GitHub issue for more context and insight: `https://github.com/thephpleague/oauth2-server/issues/889`.

Installing Simple OAuth and Generating Keys

To install Simple OAuth, you can execute the following Composer commands.

```
$ composer config repositories.drupal composer https://packages.drupal.org/8 && composer require drupal/simple_oauth:^3
```

This will install both the Simple OAuth module and the OAuth2 Server package by the PHP League, which is a strict dependency. You can also install Simple OAuth using Drush or the Drupal user interface, but installing the OAuth2 Server is a required step, whether you manage it with Composer or you download it directly.

Once you have installed Simple OAuth, you will need to generate a pair of keys to encrypt the tokens that Simple OAuth generates. For security reasons, store these keys outside of your Drupal document root, while ensuring you save the respective paths to the keys.

```
$ openssl genrsa -out private.key 2048
$ openssl rsa -in private.key -pubout > public.key
```

> **Note**   If you run into errors while attempting to use the keys you generated, your permissions might not be set correctly on those files. Use the chmod command to set the octal code on your keys directory to 0600.

OAuth 2.0 Scopes and Drupal Roles

In OAuth 2.0, *scopes* are permissions and can help define the operations to which an OAuth 2.0 token ought should access. In Drupal, they are synonymous with *user roles*. It is generally good practice to associate every consumer with a single user role, such as an explicit role for our "Swift app" alongside the existing Administrator and Authenticated user roles.

In Figure 9-3, we have created a new Swift app role, and we have given it the same permissions as an administrator in Figure 9-4.

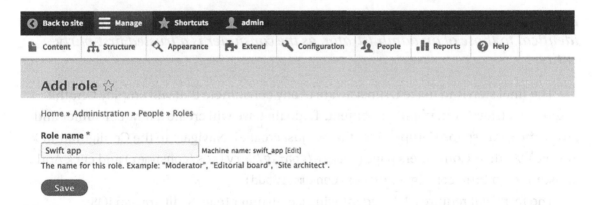

Figure 9-3.   *Create a new role with its own permissions to reflect the scope that a consumer can access. It is a best practice to make consumers synonymous with their roles.*

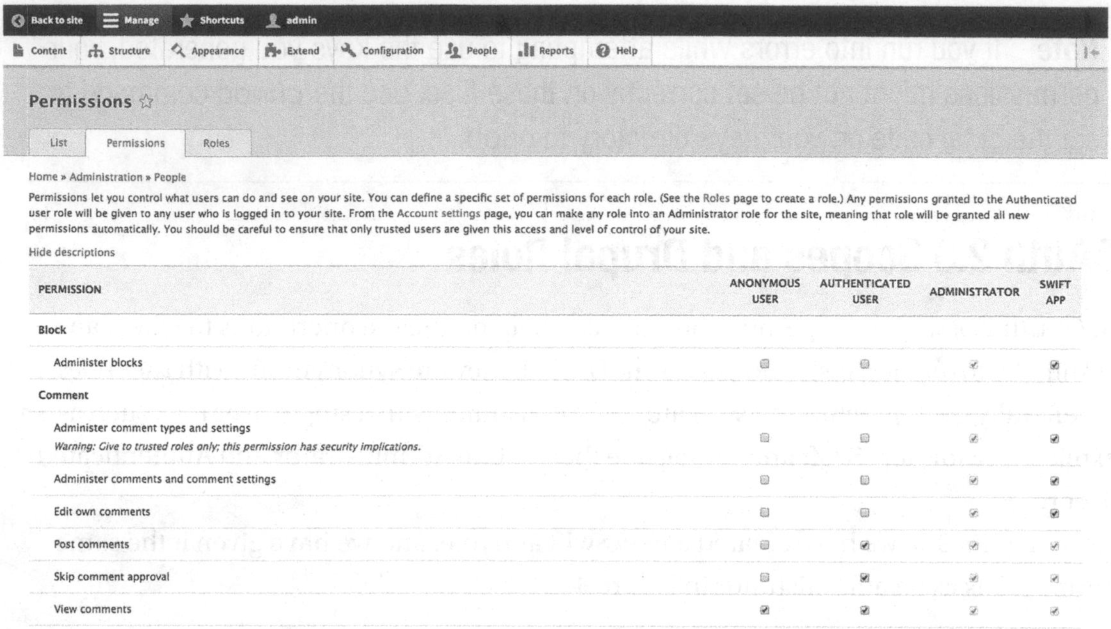

Figure 9-4. *In this example, we have set all of the consumer's permissions to be identical to those of an administrator, as the consumer is a trusted first-party entity*

The final step is to make Drupal aware of any consumers that will employ OAuth2 tokens to retrieve or manipulate content. To do that, we will create a new consumer and give it the same scope (Drupal role) that we just created. Navigate to the Configuration ➤ Simple OAuth ➤ Consumers page (/admin/config/services/consumer) and click Add consumer (/admin/config/services/consumer/add).

The form will require a label identifying a consumer (e.g., Swift app, an iOS application written in Swift) and a new secret (a new password that the consumer will use, hashed in Drupal; e.g., l0r3m1psum). There are other optional fields as well, covered in the subsequent sections. On saving the form, Drupal will generate a consumer identifier, a UUID by which the consumer will be identifiable (e.g., 24ac1dc6-9cd3-11e8-98d0-529269fb1459). This is what you will see on the Consumers page of the Simple OAuth module (Figure 9-5).

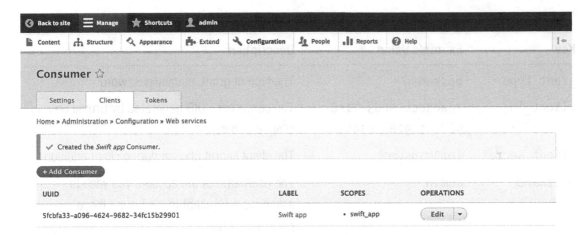

Figure 9-5. *Once we have created the consumer, it will appear in our list of consumers along with its UUID and assigned scope(s)*

Navigate to the Simple OAuth configuration page (`/admin/config/people/simple_oauth`) and insert the paths to the public and private key that you saved earlier. Optionally, you can also set a higher expiration time for tokens (e.g., 870000 instead of 300 seconds) for testing purposes, but you should not do this in production.[11]

Creating and Verifying Access Tokens

We can now issue our first request, which is for an access token that Drupal grants us to perform operations against the Drupal back end. The resource against which we will need to issue our request is the access token resource provided by Simple OAuth, located at `/oauth/token`. Our request body will need to contain all of the elements required for Drupal to identify the client.

Because the OAuth 2.0 specification requires that the OAuth token resource accept only POST requests formatted in `form-data` or `x-www-form-urlencoded`, we cannot use a traditional JSON-formatted request body to retrieve an access token. (In fact, JSON-formatted responses will be rejected.) Fortunately, Postman provides a convenient interface to insert request bodies in `form-data` or `x-www-form-urlencoded`.

Each POST request needs to contain the encoded information required by OAuth 2.0 shown in Table 9-1.

---

[11]Aguiló Bosch, Mateu. "2. Installation and Set Up." YouTube. 30 November 2016. Accessed 10 August 2018. `https://www.youtube.com/watch?v=SI60hF4n8U8`

Table 9-1. *Required Parameters in Request Body to Retrieve an OAuth 2.0 Token*

Key	Example Value	Description
grant_type	password	The type of grant, usually password
client_id	24ac1dc6-9cd3-11e8-98d0-529269fb1459	The consumer UUID generated by Drupal on client creation
client_secret	l0r3m1psum	The client secret chosen during client addition
Username	admin	The username of the account you wish to associate your client to (and grant those permissions to)
Password	admin	The password of the user account

Issuing this POST request will yield a response containing a JSON object with two important keys: access_token and request_token. A sample response from an OAuth token resource follows, with tokens truncated in the interest of brevity.

```
{
  "token_type": "Bearer",
  "expires_in": 870000,
  "access_token": "eyJOeXAiOiJKV1Qi[...]",
  "refresh_token": "uAXzh+B/7kCxsXkl[...]",
}
```

To verify that our access token indeed works with Drupal's OAuth 2.0 server, we can issue a GET request against the /oauth/debug resource, with ?_format=json appended. Issuing a GET request without an Authorization header would yield a response containing a typical anonymous user's Drupal roles and permissions as encoded in JSON.

We can use the debug endpoint /oauth/debug to verify that our access token is correct. Add an Authorization header containing "Bearer " (note the space following the prefix) followed by the access token copied from the response from /oauth/token and issue a GET request.

```
GET /oauth/debug?_format=json HTTP/1.1
Authorization: Bearer eyJOeXAiOiJKV1Qi[...]
```

The response will contain a JSON object with the submitted access token, and if the authentication was successful, the identifier of the user whose credentials were supplied during access token retrieval. In addition, Drupal's OAuth 2.0 server provides in the response a listing of the user's roles and permissions.[12]

Issuing OAuth 2.0-Authenticated Requests

Once your keys are saved in the Simple OAuth configuration page, you can instruct Drupal to allow certain methods and resources to be exposed through OAuth2 authentication using either the configuration import approach (see Chapter 7) or the REST UI contributed module (see Chapter 8) to enable the `oauth2` authentication method.

We can enable both the core REST modules and REST UI as follows.

```
$ composer require drupal/restui
$ drush en -y rest restui
```

Then, navigate to Configuration » REST (`/admin/config/services/rest`) in Drupal to access REST UI, where the list of resources available to core REST is available. For now, we can focus our attention solely on the settings under the category Content. On the Settings for resource Content page (`/admin/config/services/rest/resource/entity%3Anode/edit`), assuming you have configured the Simple OAuth module correctly, an `oauth2` option will be available in the Authenticated providers list. Enabling the `oauth2` option permits OAuth 2.0-authenticated requests from consumers to access the correct resource.

To retrieve the token, issue a `POST` request against `/oauth/token` with the request body containing the following parameters as `form-data`.

```
grant_type: password
client_id: 24ac1dc6-9cd3-11e8-98d0-529269fb1459
client_secret: l0r3m1psum
username: admin
password: admin
```

---

[12]Aguiló Bosch, Mateu. "3. Password Grant." YouTube. 30 November 2016. Accessed 10 August 2018. `https://www.youtube.com/watch?v=BEKKFExaBMM`

Finally, add an `Authorization` header to your consumer's request with the `Bearer` prefix, as you can see next. Once Drupal receives the consumer's request that contains an OAuth 2.0 token in the `Authorization` header, Drupal will serve the request after validating the token.

```
Authorization: Bearer eyJ0eXAiOiJKV1Qi[...]
```

> **Note**   For more resources about Drupal's OAuth 2.0 implementation, Mateu Aguiló Bosch has a well-made video series on YouTube detailing some of the Simple OAuth module's functionality, particularly its handling of other grant types, at `https://youtu.be/rTcCOmaPLSA`.

Handling Expired Tokens

During development, having a high length of time until an OAuth 2.0 token is expired is perfectly appropriate. However, once your consumer and server are live in production, it is inadvisable to have overly lengthy times to expiration for your OAuth 2.0 token. After all, if your token expires within 120 seconds, all operations requiring that token must transpire during that span of time; otherwise, your token will have expired.

If your token has expired, you can follow these steps to generate a new token to continue issuing requests against Drupal. When Simple OAuth generates an access token, which needs to be used in all OAuth 2.0-authenticated requests (see previous section), it also generates an authentication token known as the *refresh token*. Refresh tokens last longer and are associated with another access token that can replace the expired access token. To acquire a new access token, we need to use the refresh token grant rather than the password grant.

To make use of the refresh token grant, you will need to enable the Simple OAuth Extras module, which comes downloaded with the Simple OAuth module.

```
$ drush en -y simple_oauth_extras
```

To retrieve a new access token using the refresh token provided in the initial response (containing the expired access token), issue a POST request against /oauth/ token with the request body containing the following parameters as form-data.

```
grant_type: refresh_token
refresh_token: uAXzh+B/7kCxsXkl[...]
client_id: 24ac1dc6-9cd3-11e8-98d0-529269fb1459
client_secret: l0r3m1psum
```

You can also require that the new access token be limited to a particular scope (Drupal role). Note that scope is optional but can be used to associate the newly generated token with a different scope than before, which we can express using the machine name of the Drupal role under which all access should occur.

```
scope: swift_app
```

In response, Drupal's OAuth 2.0 implementation will return a JSON object containing the keys token_type (having the value Bearer), expires_in (with the new TTL of the access token), access_token (a new access token signed with the private key recognized by Drupal), and refresh_token (a new refresh token with which to refresh access tokens).[13]

If your refresh token has also expired, there is no option but to generate a new token from scratch, which is problematic because it requires the transmission of user credentials across the wire. You can automate the process of refreshing an access token by always ensuring that your consumer issues a request for a new access token just before the refresh token expires based on the duration provided in the original access token response.

Note   You can debug existing tokens directly on your Drupal site by navigating to Configuration ➤ Simple OAuth ➤ Tokens (`/admin/config/people/simple_oauth/oauth2_token`), where you will find a list of existing tokens that Drupal has generated.[14]

The PHP League's implementation of OAuth 2.0 uses JSON Web Tokens (JWT) to articulate all authentication tokens. For more about JWT, continue to the next section.

---

[13]"Refresh Token Grant." The League of Extraordinary Packages. Accessed 22 August 2018. `http://oauth2.thephpleague.com/authorization-server/refresh-token-grant`

[14]Aguiló Bosch, Mateu. "6. Debugging Existing Tokens." YouTube. 30 November 2016. Accessed 22 August 2018. `https://www.youtube.com/watch?v=Xpv6x2hAktQ`

JSON Web Tokens

Defined by RFC 7519, JSON Web Tokens (JWT) is a rapidly maturing open standard for authentication via JSON objects, implemented in the JSON Web Token Authentication module, or JWT module for short. The Drupal implementation, authored by Jonathan Green (jonathan.green) and Gabe Sullice (gabesullice), provides an authentication provider in Drupal that allows for information to be verified through a digital signature.

In JWT, tokens are *signed* either through a secret using the HMAC algorithm or a typical public and private key pair through RSA or ECDSA. The JWT standard is particularly useful for authorizing user sessions through transmission of tokens on each request and for facilitating information exchange between parties through verification of signed tokens.[15]

Note   The JSON Web Tokens (JWT) specification is located at `https://jwt.io`.

The JSON Web Tokens Standard

Individual JSON Web Tokens (JWTs, pronounced *jots*) are made up of three components that are dot-separated—the header, payload, and signature—and adhere to this format:

```
header.payload.signature
```

The first part of a JWT is the *header*. JWT headers are generally split into two parts: the type of the token (JWT) and the chosen hashing algorithm employed to encrypt the payload (e.g., HMAC SHA256 or RSA), expressed in a JSON object as in the following example.

```
{
  "alg": "HS256",
  "typ": "JWT"
}
```

This object is then base64url-encoded to constitute the first portion of the JWT.

```
eyJhbGciOiJIUzI1NiIsInR5cCI6IkpXVCJ9
```

---

[15]"Introduction to JSON Web Tokens." JWT. Accessed 20 August 2018. `https://jwt.io/introduction/`

The second part is the *payload,* which expresses *claims* (or statements of information) about a consumer's identity, the information we wish to transmit, and other information about the token in question.[16] There are three different types of claims:

- *Registered claims:* Registered claims are key/value pairs in the payload that are recommended but not mandatory and adhere to certain predefined, interoperable claims, including `iss` (the issuer of the token), `exp` (time of expiration), `sub` (the subject of the token), `aud` (the audience of the token), `nbf` (the time before which the JWT must not be accepted), `iat` (issuance time of the JWT), and `jti` (unique token identifier).

- *Public claims:* Public claims are those that JWTs can define at will. The authoritative list of public claims is the IANA JSON Web Token Registry, which lists all claims already defined. This is to avoid collisions in the event that two JWTs define identical public claims. An alternative approach is to define a public claim through a URI that is resistant to collision (e.g., a URI containing a UUID).

- *Private claims:* Private claims are custom claims that parties agree to define to share information privately. These are neither registered nor public, as they are not part of the IANA registry nor the shortlist of registered claims.

An example JSON object representing a payload follows.

```
{
  "iss": "jwt-drupal-backend.net",
  "exp": 1534864265,
  "name": "Preston So",
  "admin": true
}
```

---

[16]Chan, Edward. "Using JSON Web Tokens (JWT) to Authenticate Requests to REST Resources in Drupal 8." Mediacurrent. 23 March 2017. Accessed 21 August 2018. `https://www.mediacurrent.com/blog/using-json-web-tokens-jwt-authenticate-requests-rest-resources-drupal-8/`

Like the JWT header, the JWT payload is also base64url-encoded. For signed tokens, the header and payload are both globally readable, a situation that is only resolved if the information housed in the header and payload are encrypted before base64url encoding.

ewogICJpc3MiOiAiandoLWRydXBhbC1iYWNrZW5kLm5ldCIsCiAgImV4cCI6IDE1MzQ4NjQy
NjUsCiAgIm5hbWUiOiAiUHJlc3RvbiBTbyIsCiAgImFkbWluIjogdHJ1ZQp9

The third and last part is the *signature,* which is comprised of a hash of the encoded header, the encoded payload, and secret (the signature available to the server that verifies existing tokens and signs new ones). You must use the algorithm specified in the JWT header to generate the signature. The signature guarantees that any data in the payload were not modified.

For instance, if you are using HMAC SHA256 as your chosen algorithm, you can create methods that handle base64url encoding and HMAC SHA256 hashing and employ them as in the following example, where secret is a secret key, provided by the consumer and validated by the server, used to create a digitally signed token.

```
const signature = HMACSHA256(
  base64url(header) + '.' + base64url(payload),
  secret
);
```

An example signature can be seen here:

jIyIIA6wMwGCLE2fyIU1f_Y9e3Nn4rPC3Ta1MzoAKLA

Once you have the hashed signature, you can now concatenate all three strings together, separated by periods, to form the completed JWT.

eyJhbGciOiJIUzI1NiIsInR5cCI6IkpXVCJ9.ewogICJpc3MiOiAiandoLWRydXBhbC1iYWNr
ZW5kLm5ldCIsCiAgImV4cCI6IDE1MzQ4NjQyNjUsCiAgIm5hbWUiOiAiUHJlc3RvbiBTbyIsCi
AgImFkbWluIjogdHJ1ZQp9.jIyIIA6wMwGCLE2fyIU1f_Y9e3Nn4rPC3Ta1MzoAKLA

Note   The IANA JSON Web Token Registry is located at https://www.iana.org/assignments/jwt/jwt.xhtml. The jwt.io Debugger is located at http://jwt.io.

How JSON Web Tokens Work

Several advantages characterize the JWT standard over alternatives such as HTTP Basic Authentication and OAuth 2.0. First, JWTs are compact in size with limited overhead, especially when compared to alternative approaches such as Security Assertion Markup Language (SAML)—this means that JWTs can be sent within a URL, POST parameter, or HTTP header. Second, JWTs are self-contained, and all required information about the consumer is present in the JWT payload. Finally, JWTs are fully functional in CORS, as token-based authentication systems permit calls to any server when the token is in the HTTP header.

JWTs are considered more secure than session-based authentication mechanisms like cookies and OAuth 2.0 because they do not require session data to be maintained on the server, obviating the need to share such session data between servers that provide the same application. In addition, JWTs express their own expiry date within the payload so that garbage collection is not required on session expiry.

Perhaps more relevant to decoupled Drupal practitioners, however, is the fact that JWT is *stateless*, as RESTful communication between consumer and server requires that a valid JWT accompany every request issued. Because JWTs can be transmitted with each request and already express all information about users and consumers, there is no need to perform any fetches from a database for these details.

Figure 9-6 illustrates a typical authentication workflow, in which the authentication provider (in this case Drupal) receives a request for a JWT, creates a digitally signed JWT using the secret key provided, and issues the JWT to the consumer to be stored client-side. From that point on, the consumer issues requests to the server, where the JWT is verified and validated. The server then transmits the response to the consumer.

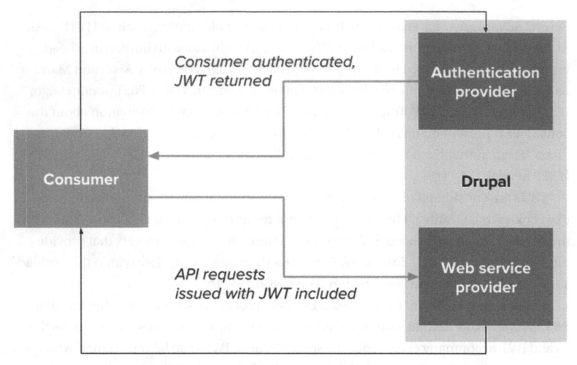

Consumer requests new token

Consumer authenticated, JWT returned

API requests issued with JWT included

Server verifies JWT and issues response

Figure 9-6. *A JWT authentication workflow in Drupal, which serves as both the authentication and web service provider. When the consumer requests a new token with valid credentials, Drupal's JWT authentication provider creates and issues a new JWT to the consumer. The consumer then employs this JWT in every request to the API that it issues.*

Installing JSON Web Tokens

The Drupal implementation of JSON Web Tokens requires the Key module and can be installed through the normal module installation process, with one important caveat. Because JWT comes with its own composer.json file and has a dependency on the firebase/php-jwt PHP library, you can either use the Composer Manager module to install the third-party library or your own Composer-based approach, such as the following.

```
$ composer config repositories.drupal composer https://packages.drupal.org/8
$ composer require drupal/jwt
$ drush en -y jwt
```

We also need to enable the JWT module's two inner modules handling Drupal's issuance and consumption of JWTs.

```
$ drush en -y jwt_auth_consumer jwt_auth_issuer
```

As seen in previous sections, Drupal's primary responsibility besides issuing responses to consumer requests is to provide secrets that are capable of signing or validating JWTs, functionality handled by the Key module. Once installation of the JWT module is complete, we need to create a new key by navigating to Configuration ➤ System ➤ Keys (`/admin/config/system/keys`), where we can add new or existing keys.

JWT offers us a choice when it comes to the hash algorithm used, and the Drupal implementation of JWT includes two of those options: JWT HMAC Key and JWT RSA Key. We cover each of those in turn in the next section.

Note   The JSON Web Token Authentication module, Drupal's JWT implementation, is available on Drupal.org at `https://www.drupal.org/project/jwt`. The Key module is available on Drupal.org at `https://www.drupal.org/project/key`. The `firebase/php-jwt` library is available on GitHub at `https://github.com/firebase/php-jwt`.

Warning   The JWT module in Drupal remains an alpha release and should not be used live in production without extreme care and caution.

Creating JWT HMAC and JWT RSA Keys

The JWT module documentation recommends file-based keys, regardless of whether you are using HMAC or RSA. Recall that in Drupal, keys are synonymous with JWT secrets.

To issue and validate your JWTs in Drupal using HMAC, you can generate a file-based key consisting of 256 bits, base64-encoded.

```
$ head -c 64 /dev/urandom | base64 -w 0 > /path/to/private/keys/jwt.key.txt
```

A sample HMAC key follows:

```
md64thgkOicWTrZ5B4Yb45nvYwPcaWnrn/82lJWODW4piGQcU2TC/BL/
lOZLsiwnSnOdinr1rZOmwwOnZ9Aurg==
```

Note   If you receive an error base64: invalid option, you might need to use the -b (--break) option instead of -w (--wrap), depending on the version of the base64 command-line interface you are using. BSD allows -w, whereas GNU allows -b. In both versions, the -b and -w flags handle line wrapping during encoding.

To issue and validate your JWTs in Drupal using RSA, you can generate a file-based key consisting of 2,048 bits.

```
$ openssl genrsa -out private.key 2048 > /path/to/private/keys/jwt.key.txt
```

Once you have created the key you plan to provide to your consumers, and once you have designated if it should be stored as configuration or referred to in a file, navigate to Configuration ➤ System ➤ Keys (/admin/config/system/keys), where you can designate if the key should be stored as configuration (in which case you need to directly provide the value in the form) or referred to as a file (already located on the server). This is illustrated in Figure 9-7.

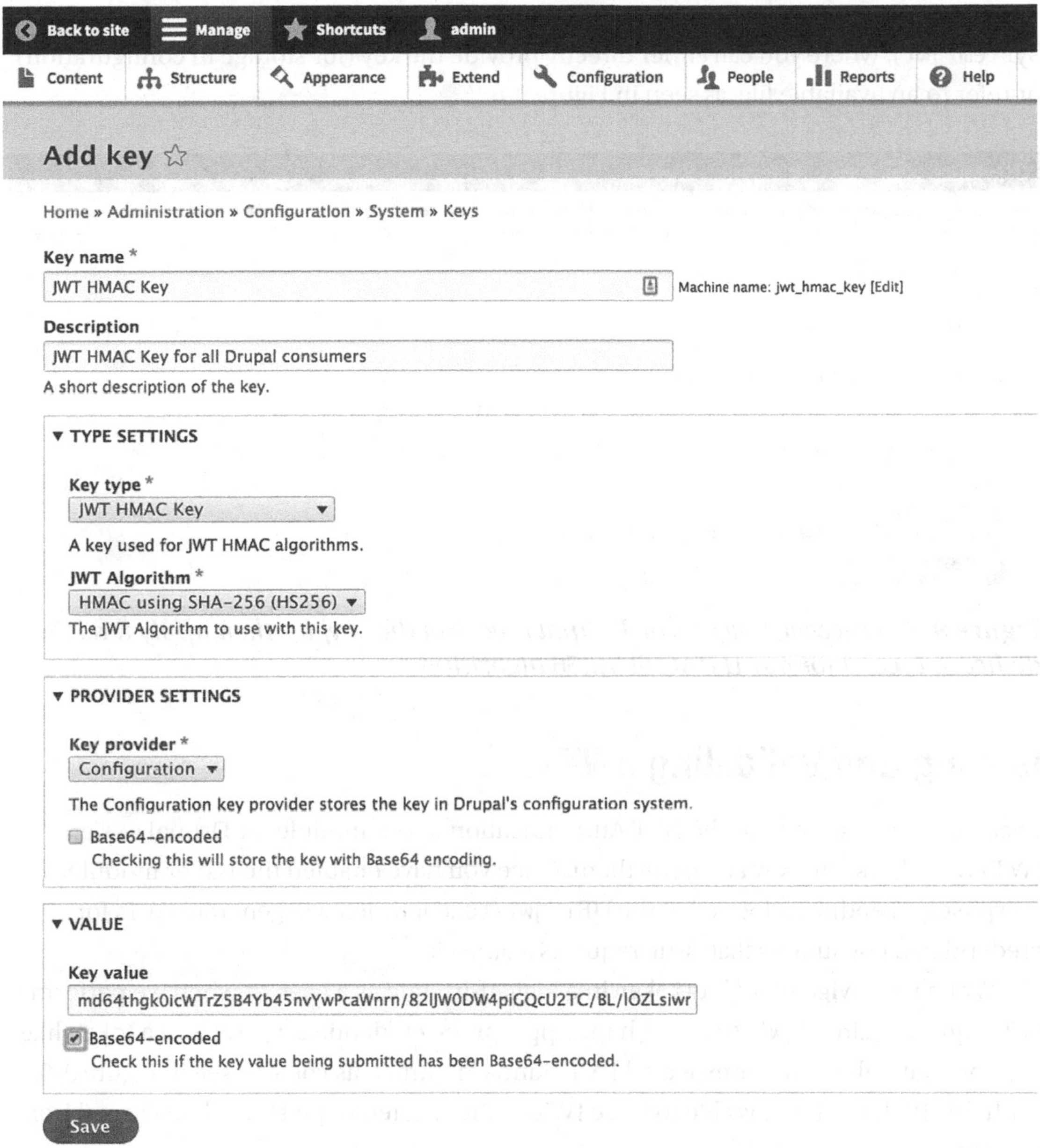

◀ Back to site	☰ Manage	★ Shortcuts	👤 admin				
📄 Content	🎛 Structure	🎨 Appearance	🧩 Extend	🔧 Configuration	👥 People	📊 Reports	❓ Help

Add key ☆

Home » Administration » Configuration » System » Keys

Key name *

| JWT HMAC Key | 🗒 |

Machine name: jwt_hmac_key [Edit]

Description

| JWT HMAC Key for all Drupal consumers |

A short description of the key.

▼ TYPE SETTINGS

Key type *

| JWT HMAC Key | ▼ |

A key used for JWT HMAC algorithms.

JWT Algorithm *

| HMAC using SHA-256 (HS256) ▼ |

The JWT Algorithm to use with this key.

▼ PROVIDER SETTINGS

Key provider *

| Configuration ▼ |

The Configuration key provider stores the key in Drupal's configuration system.

☐ Base64-encoded
  Checking this will store the key with Base64 encoding.

▼ VALUE

Key value

| md64thgk0icWTrZ5B4Yb45nvYwPcaWnrn/82lJW0DW4piGQcU2TC/BL/lOZLsiwr |

☑ Base64-encoded
  Check this if the key value being submitted has been Base64-encoded.

(Save)

Figure 9-7. *In this example, we are using configuration to provide the key, which means we need to store it in Drupal's configuration rather than as a file. The result of our earlier HMAC key creation command is reflected in the Key value field.*

Then, navigate to Configuration ➤ System ➤ JWT Authentication (`/admin/config/system/jwt`), where you can either directly provide the key (for storage in configuration) or refer to an available file, as seen in Figure 9-8.[17]

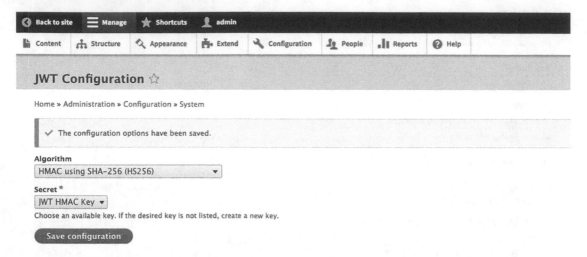

Figure 9-8. *Once we have made Drupal aware of the key, we then apply it as the dedicated secret for our HMAC SHA256 algorithm*

Issuing and Validating JWTs

Recall that we must enable the JWT Authentication Issuer module for Drupal to sign JWTs with this secret key and issue them. Once you have enabled the Issuer module, it exposes an endpoint located at the URI `/jwt/token`, which will generate JWTs for credentialed consumers that issue requests against it.

When we navigate to `/jwt/token` in a logged-in state as a user, or when we perform a `GET` request against `/jwt/token` with the appropriate credentials, we receive a token like the one that follows, in the expected JWT standard format, as you can see in Figure 9-9. With this JWT, we are now able to issue JWT-authenticated requests against Drupal from consumers.

```
eyJ0eXAiOiJKV1QiLCJhbGciOiJIUzI1NiJ9.eyJpYXQiOjE1MzQ4ODc2MzMsImV4cCI6MTUz
NDg5MTIzMywiZHJ1cGFsIjp7InVpZCI6IjEifX0.jIyIIA6wMwGCLE2fyIU1f_
Y9e3Nn4rPC3Ta1MzoAKLA
```

---

[17]"JSON Web Token Authentication (JWT)." Drupal.org. 19 February 2016. Accessed 21 August 2018. `https://www.drupal.org/project/jwt`

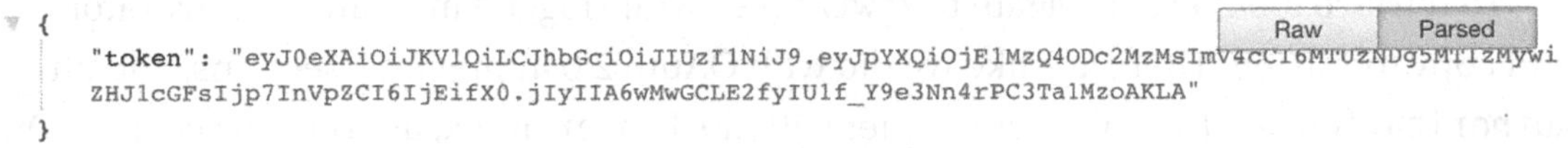

```
▼ {                                                               [ Raw ] [ Parsed ]
    "token": "eyJ0eXAiOiJKV1QiLCJhbGciOiJIUzI1NiJ9.eyJpYXQiOjE1MzQ4ODc2MzMsImV4cCI6MTUzNDg5MTIzMywi
    ZHJ1cGFsIjp7InVpZCI6IjEifX0.jIyIIA6wMwGCLE2fyIU1f_Y9e3Nn4rPC3TalMzoAKLA"
  }
```

Figure 9-9.   *To get to your token, navigate to /jwt/token in the browser after providing your key (JWT secret) and enabling the JWT Authentication Issuer module*

Issuing JWT-Authenticated Requests

The next step is for us to issue a JWT-authenticated request to retrieve content on the consumer. Although our Drupal site is now configured to issue and accept JWTs, we have not yet configured our REST resources to be available for use with Drupal's JWT authentication. To remedy this, we need to follow the same steps that we followed in Chapter 7 to configure how Drupal will serve authenticated requests. Fortunately, REST UI, covered in Chapter 8, can make this process much easier, as we also saw earlier in this chapter with OAuth 2.0.

Recall how we install and enable both the core REST modules and REST UI.

```
$ composer require drupal/restui
$ drush en -y rest restui
```

Navigate to Configuration ➤ REST (/admin/config/services/rest) in Drupal to access REST UI, where we can choose any of the resources available to core REST. For our limited purposes, we can choose to edit the settings for Content. On the Settings for resource Content page (/admin/config/services/rest/resource/entity%3Anode/edit), assuming you have configured the JWT module correctly, you will see an additional jwt_auth option in the Authenticated providers list. Enabling the jwt_auth option will allow for all content resources to be authenticated via JWT.

To test JWT-authenticated requests, we can modify permissions for accessing content such that anonymous users cannot perform retrievals (GET) of content without a role with greater access. Navigate to People ➤ Permissions (/admin/people/permissions) and disable the View published content permission for anonymous users.

To retrieve the token, navigate to /jwt/token while logged in as an administrator and copy the string. Then, just like we did with OAuth 2.0 in previous sections, add an Authorization header to your consumer with the Bearer prefix, as you can see here. On receipt of the JWT-authenticated request, Drupal will validate the token and serve the appropriate response.

```
Authorization: Bearer eyJ0eXAiOiJKV1QiLCJhbGciOiJIUzI1NiJ9.eyJpYXQiOjE1MzQ4
ODc2MzMsImV4cCI6MTUzNDg5MTIzMywiZHJ1cGFsIjp7InVpZCI6IjEifX0.jIyIIA6wMwGCLE
2fyIU1f_Y9e3Nn4rPC3Ta1MzoAKLA
```

Note   For more information about the inner workings of Drupal's JWT implementation and how it generates and validates JWTs from the PHP standpoint, see Edward Chan's excellent tutorial on issuing JWT-authenticated requests against Drupal at https://www.mediacurrent.com/blog/using-json-web-tokens-jwt-authenticate-requests-rest-resources-drupal-8.

Conclusion

Authentication is critical for ensuring users' privacy and security, particularly in a more services-oriented—and therefore intrinsically less secure—architecture like decoupled Drupal. In this chapter, we scrutinized the most common approaches for authenticating requests to Drupal 8, including Basic Authentication, OAuth2 Bearer Token authentication, and JWT. In addition, we covered cookie-based authentication in Drupal 8, which is useful for progressively decoupled implementations that require use of a Drupal-rendered page.

In Part 3, we leap headlong into how Drupal's web services modules, whether in core or contributed, handle and respond to requests from consumers. We will cover two highly distinct approaches to using core REST for retrieving and manipulating content: a more traditional developer-focused approach and an approach utilizing the Views module that is friendlier for site builders and content creators. Then, we will discuss each of the aforementioned contributed modules, namely JSON API, RELAXed Web Services, and GraphQL, in turn to evaluate their similarities and differences so we can make educated decisions about which web service solutions to select.

PART III

Consuming and Manipulating Drupal 8

In Part 2, we discussed the most important building blocks of any decoupled Drupal architecture, from the web services that expose Drupal content to the reference applications that can serve as the foundation of API consumers. In the process, we also inspected API-first distributions in Drupal, authentication methods, and in particular the core and contributed modules that facilitate decoupling Drupal 8.

In these chapters, we move from the what to the how and bridge the gap between client applications and the APIs they consume by providing a comprehensive view of how to issue requests to serve a variety of requirements. We will examine how we can directly apply the web services Drupal and its contributed ecosystem make available through both retrieval and manipulation of Drupal entities. Through this approach, we will apply our understanding of the web services ecosystem in Drupal (core REST, JSON API, RELAXed Web Services, and GraphQL) to demonstrate how they are similar and distinct from one another. We also will explore a built-in feature of core REST, Views REST exports, which allows for the rapid-fire construction of read-only APIs.

Like the previous chapters, we turn first to core REST, which introduces Drupal's own X-CSRF-Token header and allows for serialization formats to be customized during the request so that JSON, XML, or other responses can be served. In the process, we will also explore the unique content modeling features in Drupal and how they can be leveraged to design rich content APIs thanks to the Drupal core module Views.

Though core REST can sometimes provide a less ideal experience for those building consumer applications, it underpins many of the other web services solutions available in Drupal and allows for architects to provision a robust CRUD-enabled API out of the box with no additional code required. This is also true of Views REST exports, meaning that a Drupal site on its own can provide a fully functional RESTful API without the need to install additional modules.

Then, we will redirect our attention to the contributed modules providing web services for Drupal 8, namely JSON API, GraphQL, and RELAXed Web Services. Each of these modules provides a different set of features for developers of consumer applications, and as such their mechanisms of data access vary. In particular, because GraphQL cannot be considered a typical RESTful web service and obligates learning its specification, we treat each of these web services modules differently.

Besides its substantial adoption by other open-source communities and the robust means by which we can retrieve and manipulate content, JSON API also offers a significantly better experience when it comes to retrieving relationships and performing complex filtering on read queries to Drupal. This means that we can fetch not only a content entity but also information about the user who authored it, which would require two successive requests in core REST. While JSON API's query string-focused approach can quickly become convoluted, it has the highest level of adoption in the Drupal community and widest-ranging ecosystem of surrounding tools out of all available web services solutions, as we will see in Chapter 23.

Sometimes, it is also useful for us to pair a RESTful API with other tools and features that serve other purposes in our Drupal architectures. This is the case with RELAXed Web Services, Drupal's implementation of the CouchDB specification and part of the Drupal Deploy ecosystem for content staging and synchronization. Paired with client-side technologies that provide offline-enabled features, RELAXed Web Services can be a powerful solution for content ecosystems that require complex editorial workflows. Nonetheless, RELAXed Web Services can also be employed on its own as well.

Finally, we will inspect one of the more intriguing characters in the web services landscape when it comes to decoupled Drupal: GraphQL. While Drupal's implementation of GraphQL lacks write query functionality off the shelf, its unique approach to read queries that curate responses can serve as an improvement over some of the complicated queries that other web services obligate us to issue. Today, the GraphQL module robustly addresses a range of needs in typical read queries, such as sorting, filtering, and condition groups.

Because contributed modules evolve rapidly, we will start with the most stable of the web services solutions available in Drupal 8, namely core REST.

CHAPTER 10

Core REST

As we witnessed in previous chapters, because Drupal includes a HAL-compliant REST API out of the box with minimal configuration, it is easy to provision a web service API that developers can use to consume content entities and manipulate them from consumer applications. In Chapter 7, we exposed content entities as REST resources, employed Entity Access to manage permissions, and configured the serialization formats and authentication methods to be used in the core REST API. Now it's time to retrieve and manipulate those data as a consumer.

Fortunately, if you are already familiar with other REST APIs, writing and issuing HTTP requests against Drupal core to ascertain the data you require in your application is simple. In this chapter, we examine the key components of every request that hits the core REST API, how to retrieve and manipulate content entities through core REST, and how to add and remove them from Drupal.

Issuing REST Requests Against Drupal Core

As REST is an architectural pattern that functions across HTTP, it extensively uses HTTP verbs, which fall into two categories: *safe* and *unsafe* methods. In addition, Drupal provides an additional mechanism to protect the back end from potential vulnerabilities—the X-CSRF-Token *request header*—to prevent attackers from using unsafe methods nefariously. For instance, without CSRF protection, an attacker could issue a POST request that introduces executable code if CORS (see Chapter 7) is not applied correctly. Finally, because Drupal serves responses flexibly across a variety of serialization formats, it expects a query argument in the request that describes the desired serialization format for consumption.

143

© Preston So 2018

P. So, *Decoupled Drupal in Practice*, https://doi.org/10.1007/978-1-4842-4072-4_10

Safe and Unsafe Methods

In HTTP, *verbs* (also known as *request methods*) include GET, HEAD, POST, PUT, DELETE, TRACE, OPTIONS, CONNECT, and PATCH. Some of these request methods are defined as *safe* because they describe read-only operations and cannot manipulate the data in question. From this list of HTTP verbs, HEAD, GET, OPTIONS, and TRACE are safe methods. On the other hand, all of the other methods listed are *unsafe*, because they perform write operations against the data exposed by the API and thus data stored in Drupal.

In this chapter, we only cover GET, POST, DELETE, and PATCH among the aforementioned methods, because they correspond to the fundamental CRUD operations that permit us to retrieve and manipulate content. In the case of Drupal and many other such systems, GET means *read*, POST means *create*, DELETE means *delete*, and PATCH means *update*.[1]

Whereas PUT and POST in REST parlance both translate to updates of data, PUT is problematic for Drupal as its request body generally incorporates the entire data structure that will overwrite the existing data. Due to this trait, requests that include relationships to other entities in addition to a single content entity introduce considerable complexity to the API. In addition, the HAL normalization in core, per the specification, includes link relations that must precisely reflect the data returned in response to a GET request.

Other motivations specific to Drupal exist for the exclusion of PUT support that have to do with field-level permissioning in content entities. To issue a well-formed PUT request, a consumer application would need write access on every field present in a content entity rather than only the select few it truly needs. As a result, Drupal maintainers would potentially need to expand permissions much more widely than would be considered safe under normal circumstances. Luckily, because PATCH supports partial write operations, updates to content entities by the consumer can occur when only certain fields are writeable—by excluding fields for which consumers have insufficient permissions from the request altogether.[2]

---

[1]"Getting Started: REST Configuration & REST Request Fundamentals." *Drupal.org.* 17 May 2017. Accessed 2 April 2018. https://www.drupal.org/docs/8/core/modules/ rest/1-getting-started-rest-configuration-rest-request-fundamentals

[2]Garfield, Larry. "Putting off PUT." *Drupal.org.* 26 February 2013. Accessed 2 April 2018. https://groups.drupal.org/node/284948

The **X-CSRF-Token** Header

As we saw in Chapter 7, Drupal has built-in tools for CORS that protect the underlying data. Another potential vulnerability results from *cross-site request forgery* (CSRF), a scenario in which a consumer application that has permissions to modify data behind the API could issue malicious requests against the same API even without the consumer application's awareness. This is possible because the consumer application might not have the protections available to validate user-generated input and filter potentially damaging data contained therein.

To guard itself from CSRF attacks, Drupal 8 requires that all requests define an X-CSRF-Token request header whenever they employ an unsafe HTTP method like POST, PATCH, or DELETE. To retrieve the token, you should issue a preliminary GET request against the path /session/token or /rest/session/token. In forthcoming examples, we witness directly how the use of unsafe methods differs from safe methods thanks to the X-CSRF-Token request header's presence.

Specifying Serialization Formats

Because Drupal can serve and accept multiple serialization formats, including HAL+JSON, JSON, and XML, every request to the core REST API has to specify a query argument that designates the serialization format desired or used in the request. This remains the case even if the Drupal back end's core REST API only supports a single serialization format (e.g., JSON).

When you issue a request against Drupal's core REST API, you must append the query argument ?_format to each URI. As an example, on the test site we installed in Chapter 7, we would point a GET request to retrieve HAL-compliant JSON for a node with an ID of 1 toward the URI core-rest.dd:8083/node/1?_format=hal_json.

When a request body presents data in a particular serialization format, such as node objects in the case of unsafe methods like POST and PATCH, developers should specify the Content-Type request header indicating the corresponding serialization method, as demonstrated over the next several sections.

Note Although Drupal 8 made `Accept` header-based content negotiation available previously, due to poor support by browsers and proxies, it was removed from Drupal. As a result, Drupal 8 today requires the serialization format to be indicated via query arguments rather than allowing it to be specified solely in the `Accept` request header.[3] See the following change record for more information: `https://www.drupal.org/node/2501221`.

Retrieving Content with Core REST

If you currently lack a test site similar to the one we installed in Chapter 7, you can return to that chapter and set up a site like `core-rest.dd:8083`. As a note, all subsequent paths in examples throughout this chapter are domain-relative. Near the end of Chapter 7, we used Postman to issue a GET request to retrieve a content entity.

Let's repeat that same request to show the process once more in detail. As mentioned previously, issuing successful GET requests against core REST requires the following REST resource configuration:

```
granularity: resource
configuration:
  methods:
    - GET
  formats:
    - hal_json
  authentication:
    - basic_auth
```

In Postman, it is possible to issue a GET request against `/node/1` having the query parameter `?_format=hal_json` (resulting in the final path `/node/1?_format=hal_json`). If you issue this request without any headers, you will receive the response in Figure 10-1 with a `200 OK` status code. Success!

---

[3]Wehner, Daniel. "Accept Header Based Routing Got Replaced by a Query Parameter." *Drupal.org*. 6 July 2015. Accessed 2 April 2018. `https://www.drupal.org/node/2501221`

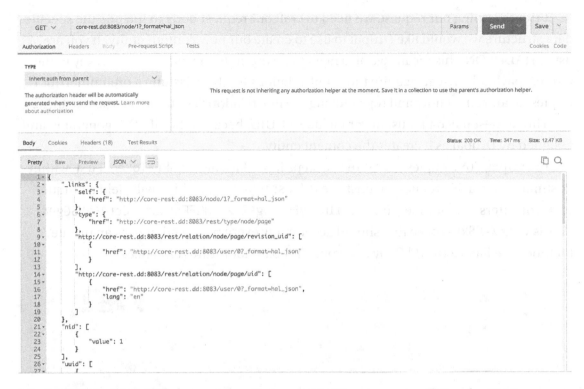

Figure 10-1. *This GET request results in a 200 OK response code and a HAL-compliant JSON payload containing a single content entity, in this case a node with an nid of 1.*

Creating Content with Core REST

To issue POST requests against core REST, we need the following REST resource configuration:

```
granularity: resource
configuration:
  methods:
    - POST
  formats:
    - hal_json
  authentication:
    - basic_auth
```

Prior to issuing our request, we need to craft our request body to include the specific data structure we would like Drupal to use to create our new content entity. If you are using HAL+JSON, this means we also need to incorporate the correct _links key in the request payload. We can acquire those link relations easily by issuing a preliminary GET request against the entity and reproducing the link relations contained in the response.

The request payload must never include a UUID, because the UUID is generated and assigned by Drupal as it creates the content entity.

In Drupal, POST requests require two steps if you lack an X-CSRF-Token. First, within Postman, issue a GET request against /rest/session/token, which will yield a unique string of letters and numbers (e.g., Eh1INrGyEUNBog5ZL2o-dHFPnLoseIKCcL35aVSGg94). This is your X-CSRF-Token that should accompany every request that uses an unsafe method (see Figure 10-2).[4] Copy it to your clipboard for future reference.

Figure 10-2. *In this GET request, we've merely requested the* X-CSRF-Token *that we will need to include in any request using an unsafe method*

---

[4]"POST for Creating Content Entities." *Drupal.org*. 14 March 2018. Accessed 24 April 2018. https://www.drupal.org/docs/8/core/modules/rest/3-post-for-creating-content-entities

To create a new article, create a POST request that contains a JSON data structure for a new article with a test title such as *My snazzy new article*. Drupal needs an interpretable data structure within the request payload that it can use to create a new article node, like the following (see Figure 10-3).

```json
{
  "_links": {
    "type": {
      "href": "http://core-rest.dd:8083/rest/type/node/article"
    }
  },
  "title": [
    {
      "value": "My snazzy new article"
    }
  ],
  "type": [
    {
      "target_id": "article"
    }
  ]
}
```

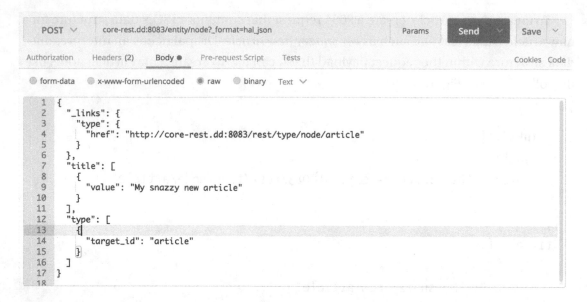

Figure 10-3. *In this POST request, we include the data that we want Drupal to use to populate the article during creation. Note in particular that we are also specifying link relations and the content type in this request.*

Because we are focused on forming requests properly and want to avoid distractions, we do not use built-in authentication methods for now. This is extremely dangerous and inadvisable live in production, but in a local development environment we can do this safely.

For the purposes of this chapter, we can enable an anonymous user to create content by navigating to People ➤ Permissions in the administration toolbar. To proceed, grant the following permissions to the Anonymous user role on the appropriate content types (for now, we are only working with Articles and Basic pages). These permissions encompass Create new content (i.e., POST), Delete any content (i.e., DELETE), and Edit any content (i.e., PATCH).

Afterward, back in Postman, we will want to incorporate the X-CSRF-Token that we retrieved via GET earlier (X-CSRF-Token: Eh1INrGyEUNBog5ZL2o-dHFPnLoseIKCcL35aVSGg94) as well as the correct Content-Type header (Content-Type: application/hal+json) into the request headers, as shown in Figure 10-4.

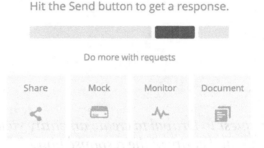

Figure 10-4. *Postman allows you to specify arbitrary request headers. In this case, we've included the X-CSRF-Token and Content-Type headers so that Drupal accepts our request and also associates it with the correct serialization format.*

Next, in Postman, we can issue a POST request against /entity/node?_format=hal_ json (recall that the _format query parameter is required for every request to Drupal irrespective of the method). Drupal responds with a 201 Created response code and response payload containing the data structure of the just-created entity. Success again! Figure 10-5 shows the result of the request in Postman.

Figure 10-5. *A POST request to Drupal to create an entity yields a 201 Created response code and the created entity in the response body*

Drupal's home page, on installation, displays content ordered by descending recency by default. If we take a moment and navigate to our home page for testing purposes (see Figure 10-6), we see our new article is present with Anonymous as the author. Because we only provided a title and didn't fill in any of the other fields, the article has a title only.

Figure 10-6. *Our Drupal home page, which is a list of content ordered by most to least recent, shows our newly created article, but there is no body as we did not provide one in the request*

Note   As of Drupal 8.3.0, you can issue requests against the path /node instead with the format query parameter appended. For all intents and purposes, that path is identical to the resource at /entity/node in versions of Drupal 8.3.0 and later.

Updating Content with Core REST

With our snazzy new article created and available for consumption in Drupal, we can now turn to the question of updating that content, such as in cases when our marketing colleagues need to adjust the title to different text. To issue successful PATCH requests against core REST, you will need the following REST resource configuration YAML:

```
granularity: resource
configuration:
  methods:
    - PATCH
  formats:
    - hal_json
  authentication:
    - basic_auth
```

Before we issue our request, just as we witnessed in POST requests, we must include the _links key to ensure our request body adheres to the HAL specification. Moreover, because the entity has already been created, the request payload should not include a UUID, which is an immutable value within Drupal generated on entity creation.

Whereas content creation via POST obligates us to provide the entity we wish to create in its entirety, PATCH only asks us to describe the *changes* we want to see reflected in the entity on Drupal, and this is the key difference between the two methods. This means we have fewer data we need to transmit, and our requests can shrink in size as a result. However, several new challenges emerge, such as the fact that a 403 Forbidden response code will not be sent when the PATCH request is only successful for certain fields due to favorable permissioning as others remain unchanged due to lack of permissions. Due to this, some PATCH requests can succeed only partially and fail silently from the consumer's perspective.

On the other hand, certain components within a PATCH request, such as the content type, are required and cannot be absent, even if that information never changes. This is because the Drupal server cannot understand under which content type (also known as a bundle in Drupal) an entity should be created when it deserializes a request body. As a result, any required information like the content type's machine name (e.g., article or page) must be present in the request.

Note   As of Drupal 8.1.0, every successful PATCH request returns a 200 OK response status code alongside a response body containing the serialized entity. Prior to Drupal 8.1.0, such requests would yield a 204 No Content code alongside an empty response body.[5]

Now that we understand the particularities of PATCH requests, we can update content on Drupal from consumer applications. To begin, we need a request header containing our X-CSRF-Token. For this example, we have generated a new token that is represented in Figure 10-7 (i7GUIxfEYRR3nzcNyremz9Q73sdyTpStSoCsU7JONQw). Armed with our new token, we need to populate the request body with the fields we are modifying and HAL-compliant link relations:

---

[5]"PATCH for Updating Content Entities." *Drupal.org*. 9 November 2016. Accessed 24 April 2018. https://www.drupal.org/docs/8/core/modules/rest/4-patch-for-updating-content-entities

```
{
  "_links": {
    "type": {
      "href": "http://core-rest.dd:8083/rest/type/node/article"
    }
  },
  "title": [
    {
      "value": "My snazzy and snappy new article"
    }
  ],
  "type": [
    {
      "target_id": "article"
    }
  ]
}
```

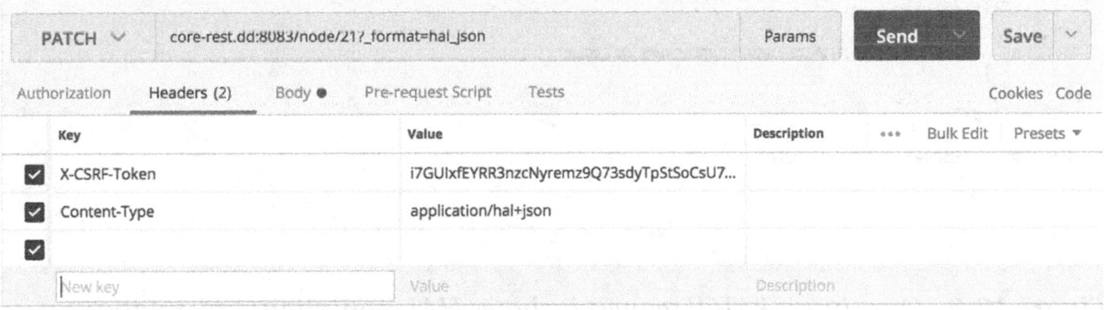

Key	Value	Description	
✓ X-CSRF-Token	i7GUIxfEYRR3nzcNyremz9Q73sdyTpStSoCsU7...		
✓ Content-Type	application/hal+json		
✓			
New key	Value	Description	

Figure 10-7. *Our PATCH request with X-CSRF-Token and Content-Type headers*

In this example, because we are modifying only the title field (we are adding only the words "and snappy" to the title), there are no other fields of which Drupal needs to be aware. Like POST requests, in this example we also see represented the target_id field indicating the content type Drupal should use when deserializing this data structure appropriately.

Because we are not creating a new entity, we point the request to the resource we created in the previous section rather than a generic catchall resource. To match the request to the resource we wish to modify, we need to provide the identifier of the node (the nid) and target our request toward that URI. In our case, as we already used Devel Generate to randomly create 20 nodes, that URI is /node/21?_format=hal_json, as the article we created in the last section was assigned an nid of 21.

First, we populate the appropriate request headers, including the X-CSRF-Token and Content-Type headers.

In the request body, we provide the changes we desire to see on the server, highlighted in Figure 10-8.

Figure 10-8. *Our simple PATCH request includes HAL-compliant link relations, the fields we wish to update (in this case only the title), and the content type of the Drupal entity*

Figure 10-9 depicts the response, consisting of a 200 OK response and a response body that includes the updated entity, which indicates a successful PATCH.

Figure 10-9. *In response, Drupal returns a 200 OK response code and a response body that contains the updated entity*

On refreshing the Drupal home page, we see before our own eyes in Figure 10-10 that the article we created in the previous section has now been updated with our new title. Pretty snappy!

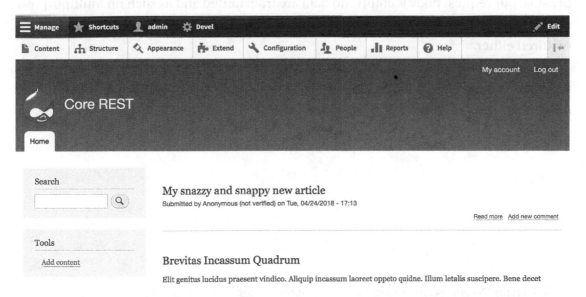

Figure 10-10. *The Drupal home page shows that our article is updated to reflect the new title*

Deleting Content with Core REST

Unfortunately, our customer has returned to us stating that they aren't fans of the new article and we need to delete the article so it will not appear in the consumer application. This situation calls for a DELETE request, which will remove the article from Drupal. To issue successful DELETE requests against core REST, we need the following REST resource configuration YAML:

```
granularity: resource
configuration:
  methods:
    - DELETE
  formats:
    - hal_json
  authentication:
    - basic_auth
```

With the exception of GET requests, among all methods, DELETE requests might be the easiest to compose from the consumer application's standpoint. Most of the required elements of other methods are unnecessary here, as we solely need to provide a clear indication of which entity to delete rather than any information within it. Moreover, because our request body is empty, no data are transmitted and as such no Multipurpose Internet Mail Extensions (MIME) type designated by a Content-Type request header is required either.[6]

Simply point your request at the resource in question and append the format query parameter—forming /node/21?_format=hal_json—along with the X-CSRF-Token header, as seen in Figure 10-11.

---

[6]"DELETE for Deleting Content Entities." *Drupal.org*. 11 July 2017. Accessed 24 April 2018.
https://www.drupal.org/docs/8/core/modules/rest/5-delete-for-deleting-content-entities

Figure 10-11. *There is no need to designate a MIME type for our request body in a DELETE request, as it remains empty*

Drupal responds with an empty response body and the 204 No Content response code, as shown in Figure 10-12, confirming that the entity is now deleted.

Figure 10-12. *Drupal responds with 204 No Content and an empty response body. Our entity has disappeared!.*

Sure enough, our Drupal home page again, when refreshed, shows only the generated content, and the entity has now disappeared, as illustrated in Figure 10-13. Success!

Figure 10-13. *The DELETE request has led to our entity's removal from the Drupal home page*

Conclusion

In this chapter, I introduced you to the key approaches in retrieving and manipulating content entities in Drupal through the core REST API. This encompasses simple use cases like getting and deleting content in Drupal or more complex situations involving creating and modifying content.

As you can see, working with the core REST API is straightforward as long as the correct permissions and REST resources are configured. Although these examples were trivial to demonstrate a consistent process to API testing that we reuse later, the immediacy and directness of the core REST API are part of what make it so appealing.

## CHAPTER 11

Using Views with Core REST

Sometimes, the core REST API isn't adequate for your needs, whether due to the fact that it is ill-equipped to issue collections of resources or because you cannot get out of Drupal the information that you require in your consumer. Many of the same motivations that lead decision makers to choose Drupal as a CMS—namely the Views module and its flexible query building—transfer to decoupled Drupal implementations as well. Fortunately, Views contains a REST export display type that can be employed to provide custom-designed, read-only APIs.

Using Views for Content Listings

For those less familiar with Drupal as a monolithic CMS, Views is a query builder and tool that facilitates the creation of arbitrary listings of entities in Drupal 8 Core. Many of Drupal's administrative user interfaces, in fact, are themselves Views and customizable, such as the home page that we saw in earlier chapters while manipulating our new article. You can use Views to create lists of content in various displays (including page and block) and in various formats (including table and unformatted list).

Many developers and site builders find Views useful to create listings of content such as a table of logged-in users, a teaser list of recent articles, or an alphabetically sorted list of taxonomy terms. In the decoupled Drupal context, this information is highly useful and valuable for consumer applications as well. Instead of using the page or block display, though, which limits the use of these content listings to the native Drupal front end, you can use the *REST export* display type to easily create read-only APIs based on Views output.

© Preston So 2018
P. So, *Decoupled Drupal in Practice*, https://doi.org/10.1007/978-1-4842-4072-4_11

Creating Views for REST Export Displays

Because Views is packaged with Drupal 8 Core, you shouldn't have to enable the relevant modules, but just in case, you should verify that Views and Views UI, the module that provides a user interface for Views, are both installed and enabled. Using REST exports in Views also requires the RESTful Web Services and Serialization modules to be enabled.

We can then navigate to Structure ➤ Views ➤ Add new view to create a new View (`/admin/structure/views/add`). You can also repurpose one of the existing Views that comprise certain listings on the Drupal administrative interface by creating an additional REST export display, but for this example we take a View from start to finish by building a View of articles alphabetized by their titles. On the *Add view* page, shown in Figure 11-1, you'll need to set a name and View settings, which include configuration of content types and sort criteria.

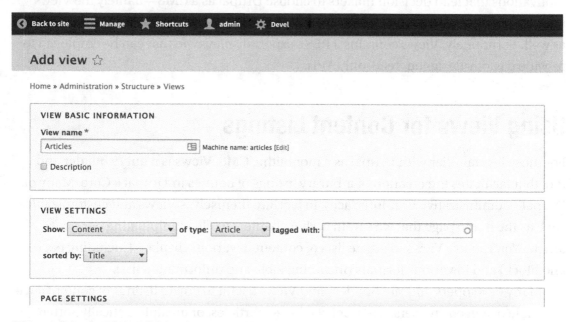

Figure 11-1. *The Add view page allows you to create Views, which are content listings that can be exposed not only as pages and page blocks, but also as REST exports*

Then, we need to create a REST export and provide some initial settings, most importantly a path where this Views display can be accessed. Many API designers prefer to version their APIs by prefixing their resource paths with `/api/v1`, which indicates the first version of an API. This allows for architects to release new versions of APIs, such that new consumers can depend on the improved version while leaving consumers still relying on the prior version unaffected. Because we anticipate this scenario, we'll use api/v1/articles, as shown in Figure 11-2.

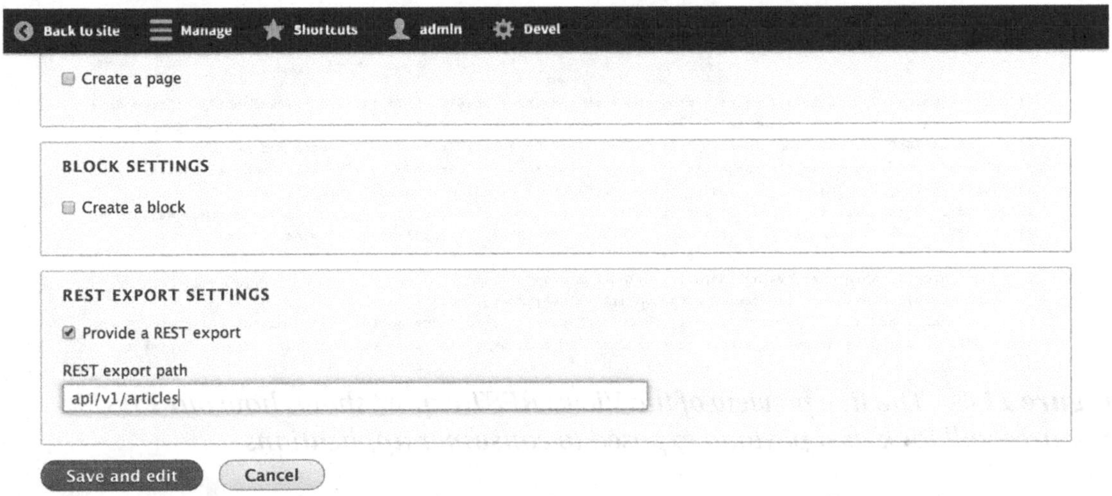

Figure 11-2. *You can set an arbitrary path at which your Views-created REST API will be available when exposing a new View as a REST export. This can aid with a rudimentary versioning system for consumer applications.*

Clicking *Save and edit* brings us to the Views configuration interface, which allows us to set various conditions on our REST export display and offers us a live preview of our API resource as well (see Figure 11-3).

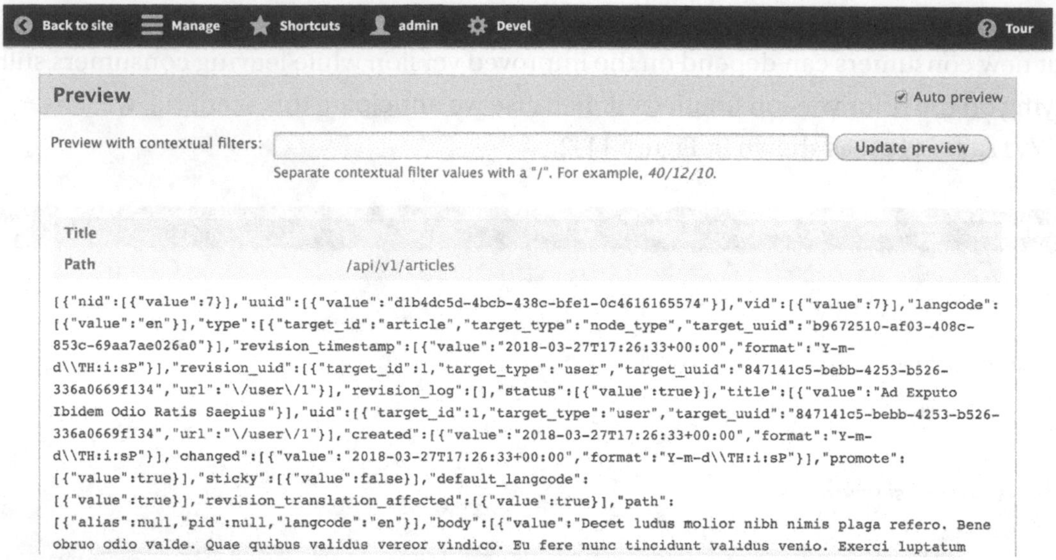

Figure 11-3. *The live preview of the Views REST export shows how our REST resource will look as a payload exposed to consumer applications*

You can use the Add filter criteria modal (see Figure 11-4), for instance, to facilitate the sorting of articles by their number of comments, by updated date, by author name, by published status, or by any of a variety of criteria.

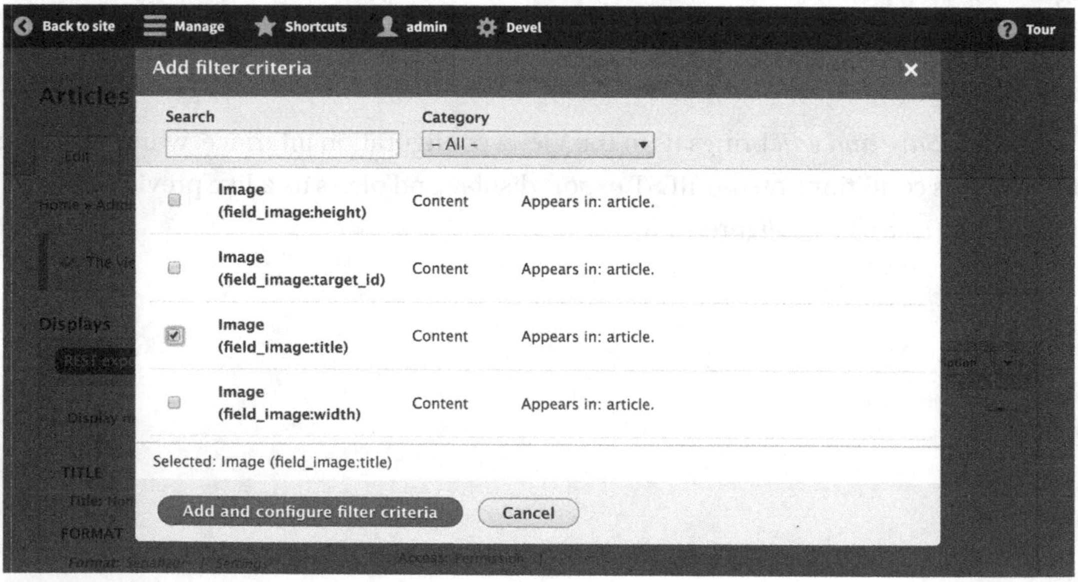

Figure 11-4. *In Views, we can add filter criteria that determine how content items should be sorted based on fields contained therein*

164

Let's examine a real use case for adding a new filter criterion to our Views configuration. Although our web site contains articles that might or might not have articles, our consumer application is designed for a client that requires an image to be present on every content item issued. This means that our API must take into account only articles that have images. Fortunately, our Devel Generate command (see Chapter 7) created some articles with and without images.

Because every image that was generated also has a title, we'll add a filter criterion that ensures that the image's title is not empty, as seen in Figure 11-5.

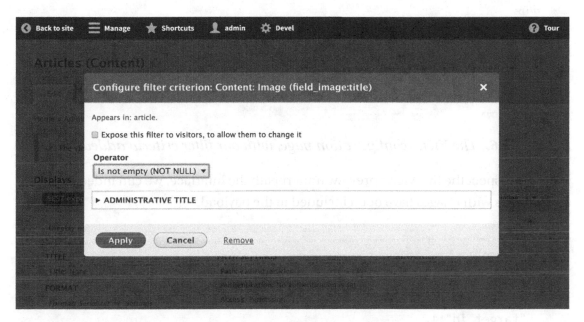

Figure 11-5. *In this filter criterion, we are designating only content items that have images to be included in the REST export display*

Our Views configuration now looks like Figure 11-6, with our filter criteria stating that we only want published articles that contain images with some sort of title filled in.

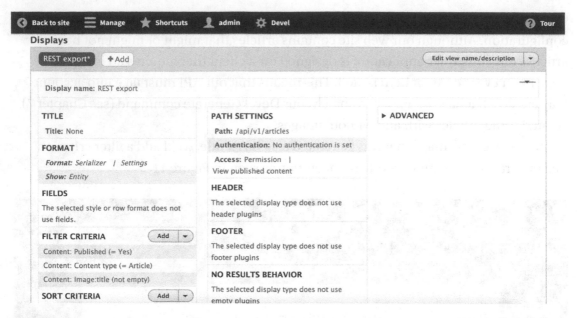

Figure 11-6. *The Views configuration page, with our filter criteria added*

If we inspect the live Views preview underneath the interface, we can indeed see that only articles with images have been included in the payload.

```
...
"field_image":
  [
    {
      "target_id":1
      "alt":"Abbas distineo neo. Importunus luctus nutus turpis ullamcorper
          ymo.",
      "title":"Abbas magna utrum. Distineo gemino interdico lobortis natu
          nibh nimis similis typicus.",
      "width":481,
      "height":563,
      "target_type":"file",
      "target_uuid":"376df8ce-f1f3-474c-94ae-7f4816be67c6",
```

```
      "url": "http:\/\/core-rest.dd:8083\/sites\/core-rest.dd\/
            files\/2018-03\/generateImage_dZ02Dw.png"
   }
]
...
```

Now, we can consume this content normally as an API resource, but not through the typical means in the core REST API; our API, on saving the View, will be available at the path that we defined during the initial Views creation process.

Instead of alphabetizing by article title, the client has requested that we alphabetize by the image title instead. We can apply a new sort criterion based on the image title in ascending order and remove the existing title sort criterion. This leads to the configuration in Figure 11-7.

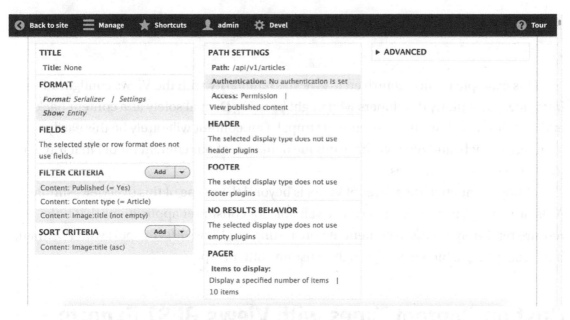

Figure 11-7. *In this example Views configuration, we have limited the View to display only published articles with images, based on the ascending order of the image title within the article*

When we inspect the live preview underneath our configuration, we can see that after the preceding entity, which contains an image whose title begins with "Abbas," a new entity has taken the place of the second content entity. In our generated content, the second presented entity has the title "Laoreet Refero," but the referenced image has a title of "Accumsan augue …."

```
...
"field_image": [
  {
    "target_id": 7,
    "alt": "Abico nimis nunc pecus persto suscipere utinam.",
    "title": "Accumsan augue caecus dolus luctus mauris plaga suscipere
              valde venio.",
    "width": 317,
    "height": 128,
    "target_type": "file",
    "target_uuid": "63bafb27-944a-4484-a991-f8601b1517c8",
    "url": "http:\/\/core-rest.dd:8083\/sites\/core-rest.dd\/
           files\/2018-03\/generateImage_xCOP2i.gif"
  }
]
...
```

This example is fairly contrived to give you familiarity with the Views configuration interface, particularly developers who might be using Drupal solely as a content back end and don't yet have the exposure to Drupal. Our content will rarely be this easily handled, though, and often we have unique demands of our content model that force us to use custom content types.

Although much of the power of Views is beyond the scope of this overview, simple APIs providing Views resources can be valuable for consumer applications that only require read-only access to content. Before testing our Views REST export with Postman, however, we dig a bit deeper through a custom content type.

Custom Content Types with Views REST Exports

Much of Drupal's powerful tooling for content models revolves around the ability to create new custom content types and to designate particular fields for them. This is available out of the box in Drupal and means that, unlike WordPress, which requires custom plug-ins to enable this feature, an arbitrary content model and corresponding schema can be constructed with content types such as Product, FAQ, Train Model, Portfolio Item, and others, depending on the unique requirements of your content. These types can then be customized with fields according to a variety of field types.

In this example, our Basic page and Article types no longer suffice for our content model's needs. Now that our client has decided that they will build a travel site cataloguing airports around the world, we need to create an API that provides a list of airports, which can be sorted via IATA code or via the location of the airport.

We need to create a new Airport content type that contains the following fields:

- Airport (content entity)

  - Name (field)

  - IATA code (field)

  - Location (field)

Navigate to Manage ➤ Structure ➤ Content types (`/admin/structure/types/add`) to add a new content type. In Figure 11-8, we've provided the content type with a name ("Airport"), given it a description that will be used as help text on the Add content page, and changed the default title field label to "Name" to better reflect the specifics of our content type.

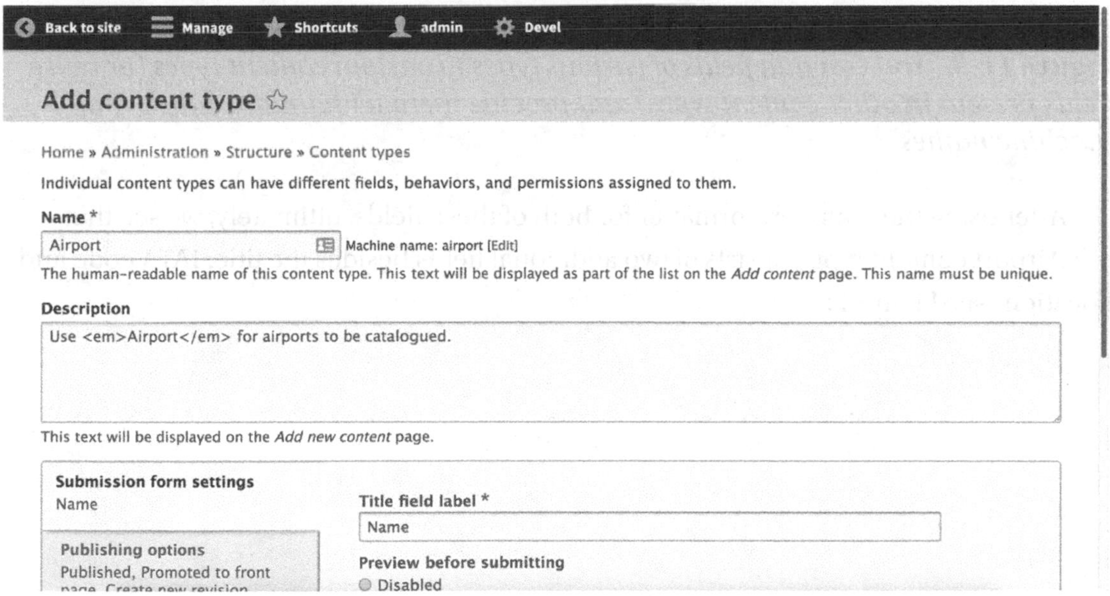

Figure 11-8. *One of the most powerful features of Drupal is the ability to create custom content types that have arbitrary fields. In this screenshot, we are creating a new Airport content type.*

The next page, displayed in Figure 11-9, gives us the ability to add fields to and remove fields from the content type. We don't need the Body field, so we can remove that to focus on just the IATA code field and the Location field.

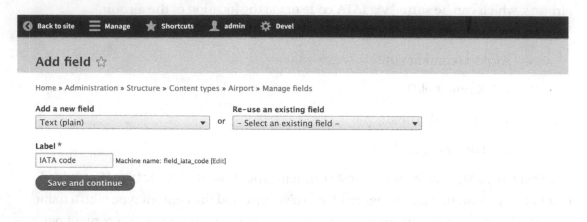

Figure 11-9. *You can add fields of various types to custom content types (or reuse fields present in other content types) and provide them with unique labels and machine names*

After using the plain text formatter for both of these fields, ultimately, we see that our Airport content type consists of two additional fields besides the title: IATA code and Location (see Figure 11-10).

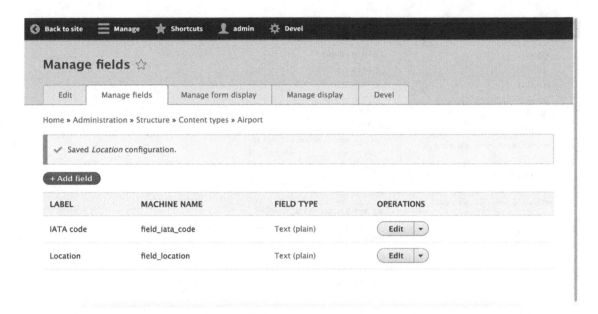

Figure 11-10. *Our completed Airport content type, with IATA code and Location fields*

Now, we can create some content. Add ten content entities of type Airport with the information filled in. Once that is complete, we can create our View and the corresponding REST export. Navigate to Manage ➤ Structure ➤ Views (`/admin/structure/views`) and click Add view (`/admin/structure/views/add`). Give the View a name (e.g., "Airports"), and ensure that the Views settings are set to show content of type Airport sorted by Title. Next, we ensure that a REST export is present that will give us the ability to target the API in our consumer application at the path `api/v1/airports`.

As you might have noticed, our Views configuration does not allow us to delineate which fields we want to include or how to include them. This is because we are using the default Entity formatter to display entities rather than relying on Field formatters. However, we can customize our Views REST export to display individual fields instead of the entire entity in Drupal's entity structure (see Figure 11-11).

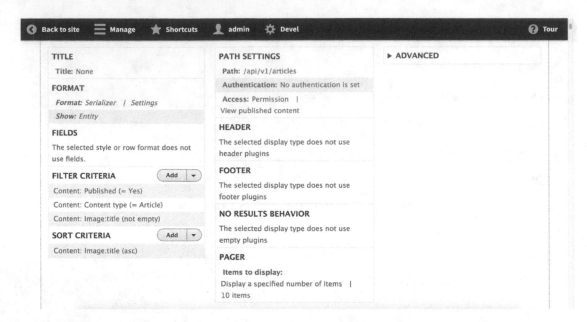

Figure 11-11. *By default, Views formats REST exports to display all fields using the default entity data structure, as seen in the value Entity in the Show field*

Instead, we can change the formatter to show individual fields, which gives us much more flexibility. If we choose, we can ask Views to only provide a REST export that contains an individual field, such as the IATA code and the location, but without any of the others, such as the title. This is particularly useful if you have content that contains fields that you wish to expose in the editorial back end or in your Drupal site but not on your consumer front end.

For our purposes, we'll only export the IATA code and the Location fields, leaving the Title field hidden and only visible when browsing content on the Drupal site. Our new Views configuration shows the IATA code and Location fields but not the Title field—even though the airports are still sorted by their names, as we see in the sort criteria in Figure 11-12.

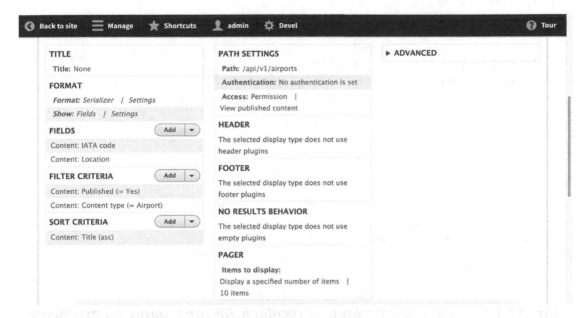

Figure 11-12. *Instead, by setting the REST export to display individual "Fields" instead, we can designate which fields we want to display, instead of all node information generally*

Now we have a lightweight API resource that is only providing individual field data, and the live preview in Figure 11-13 shows that our limiting the exported data solely to IATA code and location has significantly reduced the payload size.

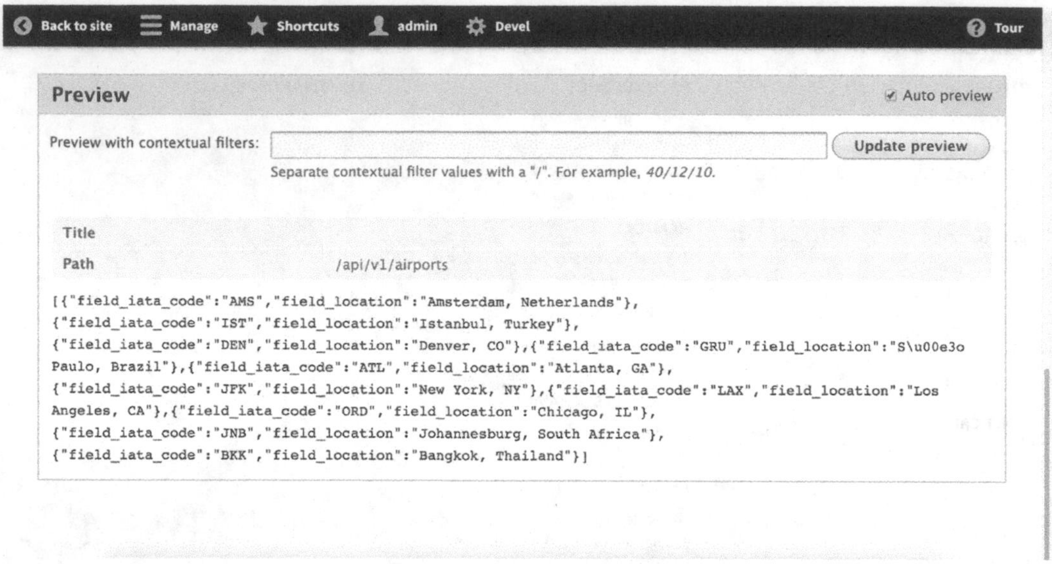

Figure 11-13. *Limiting the display to particular fields can improve the experience of developers building consumer applications with payloads that are less complex and easier to traverse*

Here is how the payload in Figure 11-13 looks when prettified:

```
[
  {
    "field_iata_code": "AMS",
    "field_location": "Amsterdam, Netherlands"
  },
  {
    "field_iata_code": "IST",
    "field_location": "Istanbul, Turkey"
  },
  {
    "field_iata_code": "DEN",
    "field_location": "Denver, CO"
  },
  {
    "field_iata_code": "GRU",
    "field_location": "S\u00e3o Paulo, Brazil"
  },
```

```
  {
    "field_iata_code": "ATL",
    "field_location": "Atlanta, GA"
  },
  {
    "field_iata_code": "JFK",
    "field_location": "New York, NY"
  },
  {
    "field_iata_code": "LAX",
    "field_location": "Los Angeles, CA"
  },
  {
    "field_iata_code": "ORD",
    "field_location": "Chicago, IL"
  },
  {
    "field_iata_code": "JNB",
    "field_location": "Johannesburg, South Africa"
  },
  {
    "field_iata_code": "BKK",
    "field_location": "Bangkok, Thailand"
  }
]
```

There is one issue that gives us pause, though. Drupal indicates every custom field that is not part of its standard core data model with the field_ prefix. All else unchanged, this means that every developer who consumes this API must be aware and write their applications according to the nomenclature provided by Drupal. Fortunately, Drupal also allows us to provide aliases for these custom field names, allowing us to give our fields names that are much easier to remember. Clicking Settings next to the Fields formatter allows us to alias our fields, as you can see in Figure 11-14.

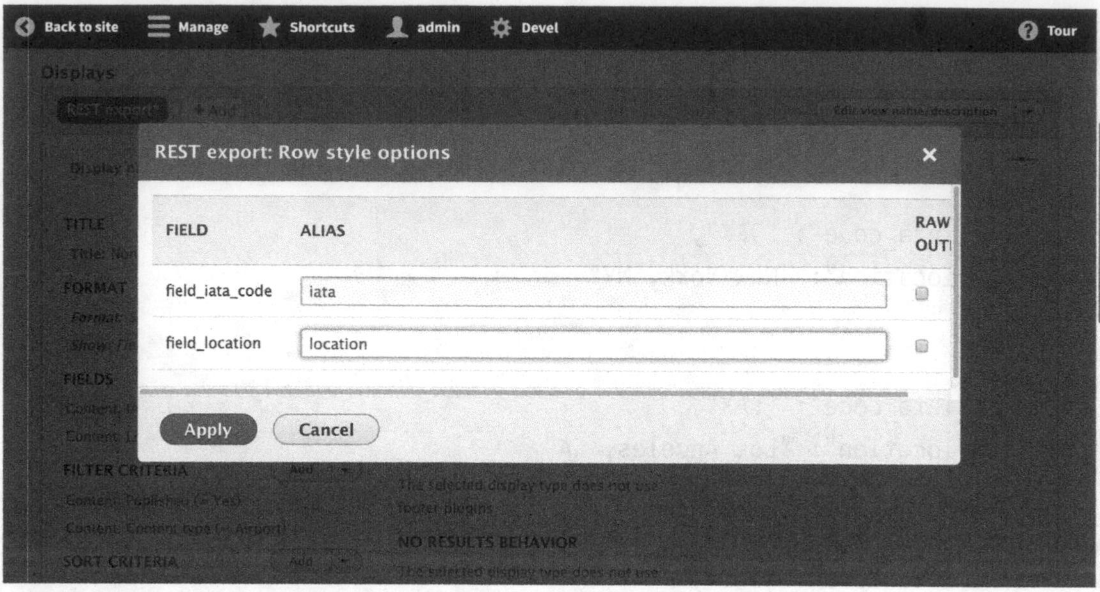

Figure 11-14. *Thanks to Views, we can set aliases on field names that can make the consumer application developer experience better still*

Now our exported data looks even better for consumers that need particular field labeling and also small payload sizes.

```
[
  {
    "iata": "AMS",
    "location": "Amsterdam, Netherlands"
  },
  {
    "iata": "IST",
    "location": "Istanbul, Turkey"
  },
  {
    "iata": "DEN",
    "location": "Denver, CO"
  },
```

```
{
  "iata": "GRU",
  "location": "S\u00e3o Paulo, Brazil"
},
{
  "iata": "ATL",
  "location": "Atlanta, GA"
},
{
  "iata": "JFK",
  "location": "New York, NY"
},
{
  "iata": "LAX",
  "location": "Los Angeles, CA"
},
{
  "iata": "ORD",
  "location": "Chicago, IL"
},
{
  "iata": "JNB",
  "location": "Johannesburg, South Africa"
},
{
  "iata": "BKK",
  "location": "Bangkok, Thailand"
}
]
```

Note   This section was partially inspired by Kevin Blanco's excellent tutorial "Build a Quick RESTful View in Drupal 8," which can be found at https://medium.com/kevinblanco-io/build-a-quick-restful-view-in-drupal-8-56203ea63b88.

As a final step, we can also make our REST export available in serialization formats other than JSON if we have defined them. For instance, we can include the ability to request the data via XML or via CSV, assuming that we have a serializer for CSV in place. In Figure 11-15, we have enabled all three available formats (hal_json, json, and xml), although leaving all boxes unchecked will also make all three available.

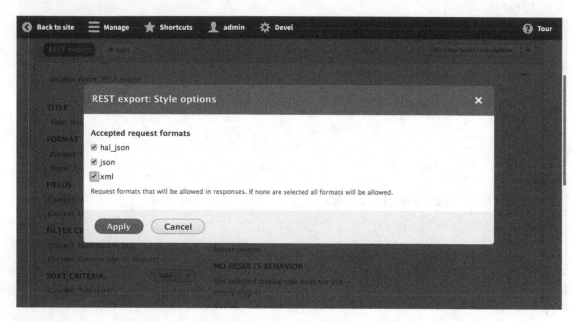

Figure 11-15. *With style options, we can allow consumers to retrieve data in HAL+JSON, JSON, XML, or any other serialization format we have defined*

Retrieving Views REST Exports with Core REST

Over the course of the last several sections, we have used core REST modules like Serialization and Views REST exports to provide us with two API resources, located at /api/v1/articles and /api/v1/airports. Now, we can retrieve both of our Views REST exports by using Postman as we saw previously to issue GET requests against Drupal.

One important note about Views REST exports is that their permissions are defined distinctly from typical REST resources such as the individual entities we have been working with previously. Views REST exports do not make use of REST resource plug-ins, which means that the permissions defined by REST do not apply to Views.[1]

---

[1]"GET on Views-Generated Lists." *Drupal.org.* 12 February 2018. Accessed 26 April 2018. https://www.drupal.org/docs/8/core/modules/rest/get-on-views-generated-lists

When we issue a GET request against /api/v1/articles?_format=hal_json, even without any headers (an X-CSRF-Token is unnecessary here as GET is a safe method), Drupal responds with HAL-compliant article entities, just as we expected. Using the value json gives us a pure representation of the entities in question, as does xml, which can be seen in Figure 11-16.

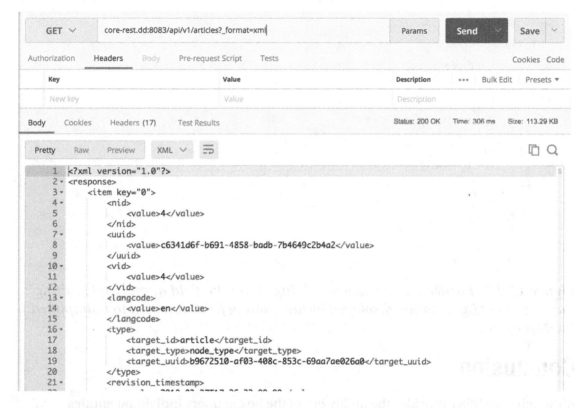

Figure 11-16. *With our Views REST export configured to serve XML responses when requested, we can successfully retrieve our View in XML format*

When we issue a GET request against /api/v1/airports?_format=json, we receive in response the data that we just previewed during our configuration of Views REST exports, displayed in Figure 11-17. Not too shabby!

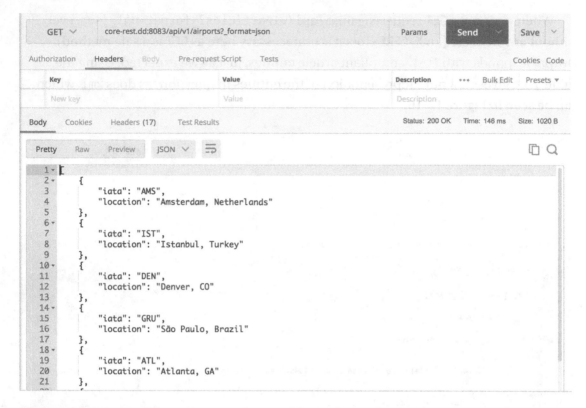

Figure 11-17. *Earlier actions such as adding aliases for field names and limiting the amount of information displayed by designating fields have led to a simplified JSON payload*

Conclusion

Although core REST provides the ability out of the box to query individual entities and to manipulate them, sometimes that is insufficient for the use cases that we are presented with as architects and developers. It often makes sense to manipulate entities individually given the impact of unsafe HTTP methods, but when it comes to read-only operations, individual entities are simply inadequate.

Thanks to Views REST exports, provisioning APIs that expose collections of content can be a painless and quick process. For many lightweight applications that only need to retrieve content, Views can be a powerful alternative to core REST modules. However, Views was originally built to provide content listings for the Drupal front end, which means there are limitations to what it can accomplish.

In addition, there are often situations where you need a more robust API specification that others have worked with before or where you cannot provision two separate API endpoints for the purposes of complex operations you wish to perform against the exposed data. Drupal has a solution to this problem: JSON API, which we discuss at length in coming chapters.

CHAPTER 12

JSON API in Drupal

As we witnessed in Chapter 8, JSON API is a powerful alternative to core REST because it is a widely understood specification, it benefits from robust means of specifying relationships and query operations, and it is one of the most stable of the contributed web services solutions available to Drupal. Although JSON API is slated for inclusion in core as a stable module in Drupal 8.7.0, it might be less of interest to architects focused first and foremost on stability.

The Drupal implementation of JSON API differs significantly from core REST in several key ways. First, the `_format` query parameter that decorates each of our requests against core REST is unnecessary in JSON API, as the serialization format is assumed to be JSON exclusively. Second, the formation of resource URIs differs from core REST and noticeably so from typical routes used to access content on a Drupal site.

In this chapter, we review these differences as well as procedures to issue successful requests against JSON API in Drupal to create, read, update, and delete content.

Note For file upload functionality, refer to the JSON API File module, a contributed solution that is beyond the scope of this volume. The JSON API File module is available on Drupal.org at `https://www.drupal.org/project/jsonapi_file`. Documentation is available on Drupal.org at `https://www.drupal.org/docs/8/modules/json-api/working-with-files-post`.

© Preston So 2018
P. So, *Decoupled Drupal in Practice*, https://doi.org/10.1007/978-1-4842-4072-4_12

Retrieving Resources with JSON API

The JSON API specification recommends that every request include an `Accept` header containing the correct MIME type for JSON API, but the JSON API module accepts requests without any request headers present.[1]

```
Accept: application/vnd.api+json
```

Retrieving Single Resources

Retrieving a single resource requires its identifier, with the caveat that unlike core REST, the identifier is not an `nid` as we saw in core REST, but rather a UUID. To retrieve a single article, all we need to do is issue a `GET` request against the following URI, supplying the UUID in lieu of `{{node_uuid}}`.

```
/jsonapi/node/article/{{node_uuid}}
```

Also, the bundle referred to in the path (i.e., `article`) must reflect the same bundle (content type) as the entity in question, as otherwise an error will be thrown. When you issue the request, the ensuing response will include a response code of `200 OK`, and the response body will contain the JSON API object of the node you requested, including attributes (i.e., fields), any available relationships, and link relations.[2]

Note   To retrieve a particular node's UUID, you can use debugging tools available such as the Devel module, which we installed in Chapter 7 to provide automatic content generation. Navigate to the node you need to identify in Drupal, toggle from the View to the Devel tab, and the UUID is available under the Variable section, as seen in Figure 12-1. Alternatively, you can enable the core REST modules from Chapters 7 and 10 and issue a GET request against the entity, and the resulting response will include the UUID.

---

[1] "Fetching Resources (GET)." *Drupal.org.* 3 April 2018. Accessed 10 May 2018. `https://www.drupal.org/docs/8/modules/json-api/fetching-resources-get`

[2] "Pagination." *Drupal.org.* 29 May 2018. Accessed 26 August 2018. `https://www.drupal.org/docs/8/modules/json-api/pagination`

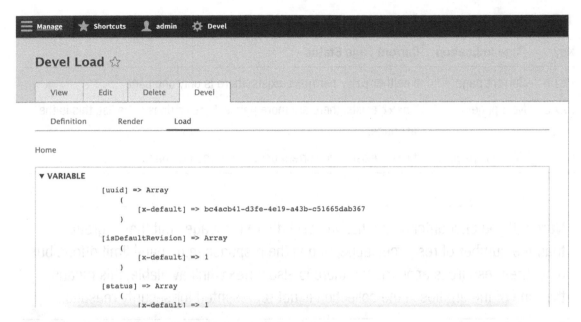

Figure 12-1. *With the help of the Devel module, you can introspect any entity and ascertain its UUID for use in retrieving single entities*

Retrieving Resource Collections

Among the most important motivations for employing JSON API in lieu of core REST is the capability of retrieving multiple resources in a single request via JSON API collections. In Drupal 8 Core, although we can retrieve individual entities using core REST, Views REST exports (see Chapter 11) are the only means by which we can retrieve entity collections out of the box. In JSON API, we simply need to remove the UUID in our GET request. After issuing this request, JSON API responds with a collection of article nodes.

`/jsonapi/node/article`

In the resulting response, we find a 200 OK response code and a data object containing a maximum of 50 articles, accompanied by a link to the following page of available articles in the collection.

Paginating Resource Collections

One best practice when paginating resource collections is to use JSON API's built-in pagination links rather than generating bespoke pagination URLs. Every collection retrieved from JSON API includes the following information under the links key, captured in Table 12-1.

Table 12-1. *JSON API Pagination Links and Definitions*

Key	Page Indication	Current Page Status
self	Current page	If neither prev nor next exists, there is only one page.
next	Next page	If next exists, there are more pages. If next does not exist, this is the last page.
prev	Previous page	If prev exists, the current page is not the first page.

Note   If you encounter a situation in which there is a page limit that is greater than the number of resources appearing in the response (e.g., page limit offour, but only three resources appear), and there is also a next link available, this means that one of the entities in the collection is not represented for security reasons.

In addition to the pagination links, the JSON API specification also facilitates certain query parameters that operate on collections we retrieve through the API. As an example, a request to the following path specifies a limit of 25 articles, and the response will contain a link to the next page of articles in the collection.

```
/jsonapi/node/article?page[limit]=25
```

We can use page[offset] to retrieve the second page of 25 articles so that only articles 26 through 50 are present in the response from the server.

```
/jsonapi/node/article?page[limit]=25&page[offset]=25
```

Note   Due to the need to avoid DDoS and similar attacks that would damage performance on the Drupal back end, the JSON API module enforces an upper page limit of 50 to avoid performing access checks on too many resources. This is also the motivation for the inability to retrieve a total page count. For more information about JSON API pagination in Drupal, see https://www.drupal. org/docs/8/modules/json-api/pagination.

Sorting Resource Collections

We can also perform sort operations on the fly within our requests by making use of the sort query parameter, which recognizes attributes as the value by which to sort results. In the following examples, we sort the collection in the response by the `title` field and `nid` identifier.

```
/jsonapi/node/article?sort[sort-title][path]=title
/jsonapi/node/article?sort[sort-nid][path]=nid
```

There is also a shorthand for these sorts.

```
/jsonapi/node/article?sort=title
/jsonapi/node/article?sort=nid
```

We can reverse the order by providing another parameter.

```
/jsonapi/node/article
?sort[sort-title][path]=title
&sort[sort-title][direction]=DESC
```

```
/jsonapi/node/article
?sort[sort-nid][path]=nid
&sort[sort-nid][direction]=DESC
```

There is also a shorthand that can be leveraged by prefixing the value with a hyphen, which indicates that an ascending order should be reversed and be descending instead.

```
/jsonapi/node/article?sort=-title
/jsonapi/node/article?sort=-nid
```

Where there are attributes available within a field that we are using to sort our collection, we can refer to those by adding a period (.) to access the attributes that are one level down. In the following example, we are sorting the collection by the article author's name, and `sort-author` is the arbitrary name we have given our sort to disambiguate from other sorts.

```
/jsonapi/node/article?sort[sort-author][path]=uid.name
```

The shorthand for this path is as follows.

```
/jsonapi/node/article?sort=uid.name
```

187

It is also possible to sort by multiple fields, which are considered in the order in which they are expressed.

```
/jsonapi/node/article
?sort[sort-title][path]=title
&sort[sort-title][direction]=DESC
&sort[sort-author][path]=uid.name
```

In the shorthand form, you can reverse the order in the same way as we have seen previously.[3]

```
/jsonapi/node/article?sort=-title,uid.name
```

Filtering Resource Collections

When we issue a GET request against a resource collection such as /jsonapi/node/ article, we retrieve every resource that we have the permissions to retrieve. Often, however, consumer applications need filtered responses that adhere to a certain set of characteristics, such as all articles written by a particular author or all articles past a certain date.

In Drupal's JSON API implementation, we can use *filters* to designate which resources should be part of a response. The simplest method of using a filter is by selecting particular resources based on the values of fields, taking the following format in the path, where {field_name} and {other_field_name} are fields available for use in filtering, and {value} represents values based on which to filter.

```
/jsonapi/node/article
?filter[{field_name}]={value}
&filter[{other_field_name}]={value}
```

Unlike Views REST exports (see Chapter 11), which rely on a user interface for exposing customized resources, the filtering system Drupal's JSON API implementation makes available consists of two fundamental ideas: conditions and groups. In JSON API, *conditions* represent expressions that are asserted to be true. A condition indicates that something about a resource is true or false, such as: "Was this article created this week?" When the condition returns FALSE for a resource, JSON API excludes it from the collection.

---

[3]"Collections and Sorting." *Drupal.org.* 22 March 2018. Accessed 26 August 2018. https://www. drupal.org/docs/8/modules/json-api/collections-and-sorting

Meanwhile, *groups* are logical sets composed of the assertions in conditions that facilitate larger condition groups. These condition groups can be nested to craft fine-grained queries with a great deal of granularity. For instance, consider the following example, which illustrates the tree relationships established when we nest condition groups. We can easily express a hierarchy of conditions this way.

```
v( w() && x( y() || z() ) )
```

In this example, conditions y() and z() are members of group x() in an OR relationship. Conditions w() and x() are members of group v() in an AND relationship. Figure 12-2 illustrates this condition group as a tree.

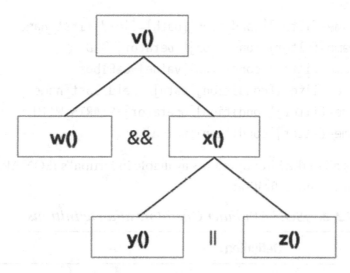

Figure 12-2. *Example condition groups are represented in a hierarchical tree*

Conditions have three components: a path, an operator, and a value. *Paths* identify specific fields on a particular resource. *Operators* are methods of comparison to verify that a condition is satisfied. *Values* are what we need to compare the resource against. Due to the limitations of URL query strings, we represent every condition as a key/value pair.[4]

Consider the following filter, which we have given a random identifier. This filter finds all resources that satisfy the condition that the user's first name is "Gábor" and nothing else. Note in this example that special characters like = (%3D) and á (%E1) are required due to their use in URL query strings.

---

[4]"Filtering." *Drupal.org.* 4 May 2018. Accessed 26 August 2018. `https://www.drupal.org/docs/8/modules/json-api/filtering`

```
/jsonapi/user/user
?filter[my-custom-filter][condition][path]=field_first_name
&filter[my-custom-filter][condition][operator]=%3D
&filter[my-custom-filter][condition][value]=G%E1bor
```

Every condition or group must have an identifier, which we can arbitrarily define, so that JSON API successfully disambiguates it from other conditions and groups. For example, consider that we might wish to also filter by last name such that we only retrieve resources whose last name starts with the letter H. To do this, we need to differentiate our conditions.

```
/jsonapi/user/user
?filter[first-name-filter][condition][path]=field_first_name
&filter[first-name-filter][condition][operator]=%3D
&filter[first-name-filter][condition][value]=G%E1bor
&filter[last-name-filter][condition][path]=field_last_name
&filter[last-name-filter][condition][operator]=STARTS_WITH
&filter[last-name-filter][condition][value]=H
```

Table 12-2 lists all of the filter operators available in Drupal's JSON API implementation and their definitions.

Table 12-2. *JSON API Filter Operators and Definitions*

Operator	Definition
=	Equals
<>	Not equal to
>	Greater than
>=	Greater than or equal to
<	Less than
<=	Less than or equal to
STARTS_WITH	Starts with the provided value
CONTAINS	Contains the provided value
ENDS_WITH	Ends with the provided value

(continued)

Table 12-2. (*continued*)

Operator	Definition
IN	Checks that the provided value is present in an array
NOT_IN	Checks that the provided value is absent from an array
BETWEEN	Checks that the provided value is within a range
NOT_BETWEEN	Checks that the provided value is outside of a range
IS_NULL	Is null (no value required)
IS_NOT_NULL	Is not null (no value required)

Filtering Resource Collections with Condition Groups

We have now applied two conditions to our query, but we have not yet grouped them together to reflect Figure 12-2. To construct a *condition group*, we need to create a *conjunction* between conditions using either AND or OR. Now we can check to see if the user's first name in the resource collection is "Gábor" or "Gabe."

To create a condition group, we define a condition group name and assign our desired filters to that group using the memberOf key and the condition group name. Groups can also have their own memberOf keys, which means we can nest condition groups within one another. Consider the following example, which constructs a condition group selecting users having the first names Gábor or Gabe and employs an additional filter selecting last names beginning with H.

```
/jsonapi/user/user
?filter[g-condition-group][group][conjunction]=OR
&filter[gabor-filter][condition][path]=field_first_name
&filter[gabor-filter][condition][operator]=%3D
&filter[gabor-filter][condition][value]=G%E1bor
&filter[gabor-filter][condition][memberOf]=g-condition-group
&filter[gabe-filter][condition][path]=field_last_name
&filter[gabe-filter][condition][operator]=%3D
&filter[gabe-filter][condition][value]=Gabe
&filter[gabe-filter][condition][memberOf]=g-condition-group
```

```
&filter[last-name-filter][condition][path]=field_last_name
&filter[last-name-filter][condition][operator]=STARTS_WITH
&filter[last-name-filter][condition][value]=H
```

Figure 12-3 depicts these conditions in a hierarchical tree.

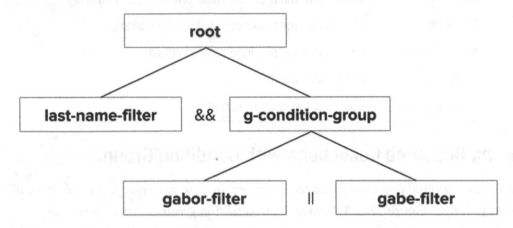

Figure 12-3. *JSON API condition groups can be arbitrarily nested*

Conditions also include another powerful feature captured in paths, much like we saw at the end of the section concerning sorting operations. Paths provide a means for us to filter based on the values present in related entities and use dot (.) notation to traverse those relationships. Consider the following example, which filters articles based on the beginning of the author's name.

```
/jsonapi/node/article
?filter[author_name][condition][path]=uid.name
&filter[author_name][condition][operator]=STARTS_WITH
&filter[author_name][condition][value]=Angie
```

Note   If there are multiple related entities, as in the case of a field with multiple values, you can also use positive integers to indicate which related entity you wish to target. For instance, the path `related_entity.1.field` would filter based on the second related resource.

If the verbosity of some of these filters is worrying, it will come as a comfort that JSON API provides certain shorthands that make writing filters more efficient. For instance, the following filter can be reduced to the filter immediately following, because the equals (=) is assumed when another operator is not provided.

```
/jsonapi/user/user
?filter[first-name-filter][condition][path]=field_first_name
&filter[first-name-filter][condition][operator]=%3D
&filter[first-name-filter][condition][value]=G%E1bor
```

```
/jsonapi/user/user
?filter[first-name-filter][condition][path]=field_first_name
&filter[first-name-filter][condition][value]=G%E1bor
```

If you do not need to filter by the same field multiple times, we can use the path as the identifier for the filter. In the following filters, we have reduced URL verbosity by replacing a custom filter name with the field name itself.

```
/jsonapi/user/user
?filter[first-name-filter][condition][path]=field_first_name
&filter[first-name-filter][condition][value]=G%E1bor
```

```
/jsonapi/user/user
?filter[field_first_name][value]=G%E1bor
```

Finally, we can exclude value altogether in this scenario.

```
/jsonapi/user/user
?filter[field_first_name]=G%E1bor
```

Note Filters on Drupal's JSON API implementation should not be confused with Drupal's access control, governed by user roles and permissions. A best practice is to always verify access on the back end rather than on queries from the consumer and to filter inaccessible resources out of the response ahead of time. Most important, JSON API will not return resources if the user issuing the request lacks access to that resource.

Examples of Common Filtering Scenarios

In this section, we identify some common scenarios and provide filters for each.
Consider the following example, which fetches only those articles that are published.
The shorthand version follows the longhand version in each of the following examples.

```
/jsonapi/node/article
?filter[status-filter][condition][path]=status
&filter[status-filter][condition][value]=1
```

```
/jsonapi/node/article
?filter[status][value]=1
```

We can also filter based on whether a referenced entity is present or not by targeting
the referenced entity UUID. In this case, we are targeting a particular user's articles.

```
/jsonapi/node/article
?filter[author-filter][condition][path]=uid.uuid
&filter[author-filter][condition][value]=360427cb-96be-459f-a0d9-
8fe9bc5164a4
```

```
/jsonapi/node/article
?filter[uid.uuid][value]=360427cb-96be-459f-a0d9-8fe9bc5164a4
```

We might also wish to filter an article collection based on whether the user is one
of several in a list of users. To do this, we use the IN filter operator and a special array
notation to determine whether an article has been written by admin or average_joe.

```
/jsonapi/node/article
?filter[name-filter][condition][path]=uid.name
&filter[name-filter][condition][operator]=IN
&filter[name-filter][condition][value][]=admin
&filter[name-filter][condition][value][]=average_joe
```

Note   For other examples that increase in complexity beyond those presented
here, see the documentation on Drupal.org available at `https://www.drupal.`
`org/docs/8/modules/json-api/filtering`.

Retrieving Limited Subsets of Fields

If you need to serve content to a variety of diverse clients, including consumers that traffic in small payload sizes for performance reasons, the complete response from the JSON API module can often be overwhelmingly large. To alleviate this, the JSON API specification includes the ability to retrieve a limited subset of fields from resources through query parameters that enumerate the fields that we wish to include in the response.

As an example, we can provide a `fields` query parameter that instructs the API to only serve us the title, created and changed timestamps, and body of the article.

```
/jsonapi/node/article?fields[node--article]=title,created,changed,body
```

Retrieving Entity References

Quite often, a final desired feature of retrieving data through APIs is the ability to request not only the individual resource but also fields that contain entity references. For instance, a consumer application might wish, just like many Drupal sites do on a regular basis, to include not only the content originating from the author, but also the full author entity representing the user who created the content.

If we issue a GET request against `/jsonapi/node/article/{{node_uuid}}`, we will receive in the response a `uid` field that includes the identifier of the user who created the article, but no other information that originates from the user entity, such as their e-mail address. To resolve this, we can include the `include` parameter, which defines which relationships to include in the ultimate response.

```
/jsonapi/node/article?include=uid
```

Creating Resources with JSON API

Thanks to the JSON API specification, it is possible for us to create individual resources through an API, but we cannot create multiple resources like we can retrieve collections. This is also true of updates and deletions of resources through JSON API.[5] For information on how to mitigate this limitation, see Chapter 23 for a description of the Subrequests module.

---

[5]"Creating New Resources (POST)." *Drupal.org*. 22 March 2018. Accessed 10 May 2018. `https://www.drupal.org/docs/8/modules/json-api/creating-new-resources-post`

JSON API requires the following request headers on every POST request to yield a standard response:

```
Accept: application/vnd.api+json
Content-Type: application/vnd.api+json
```

To create the article, we can use the same URI we used to retrieve collections of articles when we issue a POST request against JSON API in Drupal.

```
/jsonapi/node/article
```

Just as we saw with entity creation in core REST, we need to include any required fields in the request payload:

```
{
  "data": {
    "type": "node--article",
    "attributes": {
      "title": "My snazzy new article",
      "body": {
        "value": "Hello world! Lorem ipsum dolor sit amet consectetur
                  adipiscing elit",
        "format": "plain_text"
      }
    }
  }
}
```

Often, when creating an entity, we might wish to also include a relationship that identifies a user as the author of an article. In the following request payload, we include in this POST request a relationship that assigns the entity to an existing user with the identifier {{user_uuid}}.

```json
{
  "data": {
    "type": "node--article",
    "attributes": {
      "title": "My snazzy new article",
      "body": {
        "value": "Hello world! Lorem ipsum dolor sit amet consectetur
                  adipiscing elit",
        "format": "plain_text"
      }
    },
    "relationships": {
      "uid": {
        "data": {
          "type": "user--user",
          "id": "{{user_uuid}}"
        }
      }
    }
  }
}
```

Both of these POST requests will yield a 201 Created response code in the response, and JSON API additionally presents us with the created entity (with its Drupal-generated UUID) in the response body, just as if we had retrieved it as a single resource. Figure 12-4 depicts a sample response in Postman.

Figure 12-4. *On creating the article, Drupal's JSON API implementation responds with a response body that contains the created entity*

Note   If you are faced with a 403 Forbidden response code and an error message that requires Administer nodes permissions, you can assign that capability to anonymous users for testing, but this is not advisable in production.

Updating Resources with JSON API

PATCH requests also require Accept and Content-Type request headers.[6]

```
Accept: application/vnd.api+json
Content-Type: application/vnd.api+json
```

---

[6]"Updating Existing Resources (PATCH)." *Drupal.org.* 29 May 2017. Accessed 10 May 2018.
https://www.drupal.org/docs/8/modules/json-api/updating-existing-resources-patch

To issue a PATCH request against Drupal to update an entity, we first need to ascertain the UUID of the resource in question.

```
/jsonapi/node/article/{{node_uuid}}
```

Within the request payload, just like core REST, we include only the fields that we wish to modify, along with the UUID of the entity in question.

```
{
  "data": {
    "type": "node--article",
    "id": "{{node_uuid}}",
    "attributes": {
      "title": "My even snazzier new article"
    }
  }
}
```

PATCH requests also allow us to include a relationship to a user who authored the article, whom we identify by their UUID in the request body. The following object shows a relationship that links the entity to an existing user identified by {{user_uuid}}.

```
{
  "data": {
    "type": "node--article",
    "id": "{{node_uuid}}",
    "attributes": {
      "title": "My even snazzier new article"
    },
    "relationships": {
      "uid": {
        "data": {
          "type": "user--user",
          "id": "{{user_uuid}}"
        }
      }
    }
  }
}
```

Each of these requests yields a 200 OK response code with the JSON API response containing the full updated entity. Figure 12-5 depicts the result of the request.

Figure 12-5. *Just as with POST requests, a PATCH request yields a response from JSON API that includes the updated entity in the response body*

Deleting Resources with JSON API

Now that we have updated the article, we can also delete the article including only the Content-Type request header in the DELETE request.

```
Content-Type: application/vnd.api+json
```

Just as with core REST, unlike the other unsafe HTTP methods, we do not need to provide any request payload when issuing a DELETE request. All we need to do is target the resource with its UUID and issue the DELETE request against that URI.[7]

```
/jsonapi/node/article/{{node_uuid}}
```

---

[7]"Removing Existing Resources (DELETE)." *Drupal.org.* 13 May 2017. Accessed 10 May 2018.
`https://www.drupal.org/docs/8/modules/json-api/removing-existing-resources-delete`

This request yields a 204 No Content response code with a response payload devoid of any content, indicating that our article has been removed from Drupal. Figure 12-6 depicts a sample response in Postman.

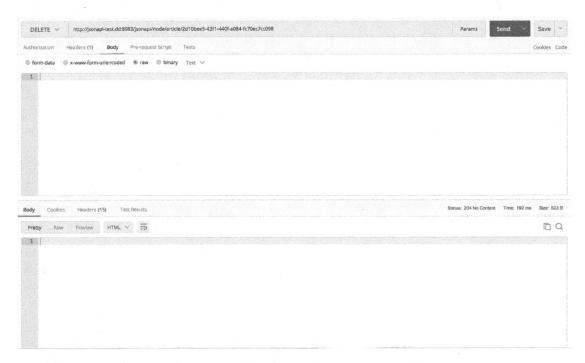

Figure 12-6. *In response to our DELETE request, Drupal's JSON API implementation responds with an empty response body and a 204 No Content response code, proving the deletion of our entity from Drupal*

Conclusion

In this chapter, we covered performing basic CRUD operations with JSON API in Drupal. Although JSON API is a complex and robust specification serving a variety of needs, thanks to the JSON API module, it is easy to employ even for practitioners new to decoupled Drupal. Although the approaches differ substantially from core REST, many of the same expected response codes and response payloads indicate a high degree of similarity between the two.

In the next chapter, we turn our attention to performing CRUD operations with RELAXed Web Services, the module that adheres to the CouchDB specification. We cover all of the same operations, including creating, retrieving, updating, and deleting Drupal content using the RELAXed Web Services module.

CHAPTER 13

RELAXed Web Services

RELAXed Web Services is a particularly robust candidate for use as a web service provider because of its tight integration with the Drupal Deploy ecosystem and the CouchDB specification. This means that architects and developers can employ RELAXed Web Services for a variety of content staging scenarios as well as for content delivery to consumers. RELAXed Web Services has better support than core REST in areas such as translations, revisions, and file attachments.

As mentioned in Chapter 8, it is entirely possible to leverage RELAXed Web Services without the Workspaces module and the rest of the Drupal Deploy ecosystem. The fact that RELAXed Web Services implements the CouchDB specification opens the door to offline-enabled applications in the presentation layer with the help of PouchDB and Hoodie.

In this chapter, we explore RELAXed Web Services and how to retrieve and manipulate content through its CouchDB-compliant API. RELAXed Web Services adds a series of permissions to create, read, update, and delete resources through the API, which are by default only assigned to administrators, as seen in Figure 13-1.

© Preston So 2018
P. So, *Decoupled Drupal in Practice*, https://doi.org/10.1007/978-1-4842-4072-4_13

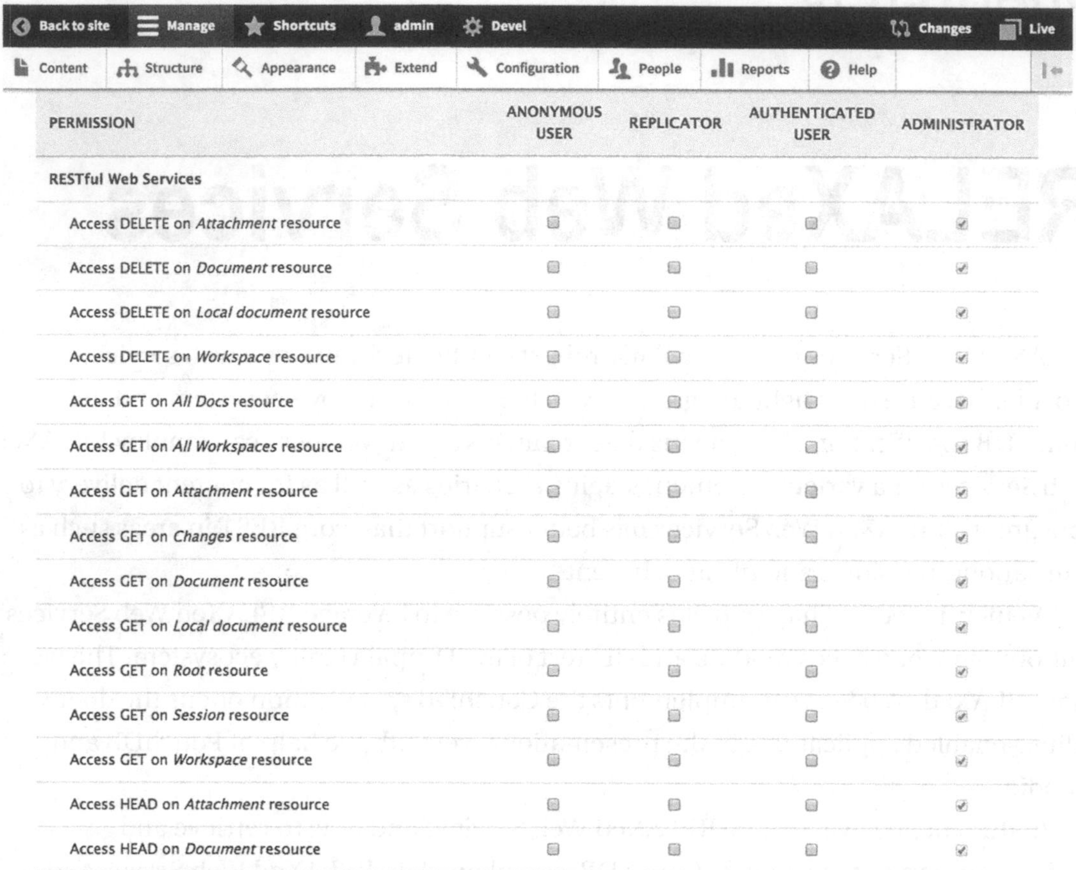

PERMISSION	ANONYMOUS USER	REPLICATOR	AUTHENTICATED USER	ADMINISTRATOR
RESTful Web Services				
Access DELETE on *Attachment* resource	☐	☐	☐	☑
Access DELETE on *Document* resource	☐	☐	☐	☑
Access DELETE on *Local document* resource	☐	☐	☐	☑
Access DELETE on *Workspace* resource	☐	☐	☐	☑
Access GET on *All Docs* resource	☐	☐	☐	☑
Access GET on *All Workspaces* resource	☐	☐	☐	☑
Access GET on *Attachment* resource	☐	☐	☐	☑
Access GET on *Changes* resource	☐	☐	☐	☑
Access GET on *Document* resource	☐	☐	☐	☑
Access GET on *Local document* resource	☐	☐	☐	☑
Access GET on *Root* resource	☐	☐	☐	☑
Access GET on *Session* resource	☐	☐	☐	☑
Access GET on *Workspace* resource	☐	☐	☐	☑
Access HEAD on *Attachment* resource	☐	☐	☐	☑
Access HEAD on *Document* resource	☐	☐	☐	☑

Figure 13-1. *New permissions created by RELAXed Web Services on RESTful Web Services module features*

Recall that unless we configure the path under which all RELAXed Web Services resources are available, every URL will be prefixed with /relaxed. To demonstrate this, we can repeat our request from Chapter 8 that displays a welcome message in Postman with the credentials of a user with the appropriate permissions.

For the purposes of easier demonstration, we will use Basic Authentication (see Chapter 9) and an administrator's credentials, but you can employ any authentication mechanism you prefer via configuration or module installation. As mentioned previously, you will need to consider more secure authentication mechanisms on deployment to production. We can issue a GET request against /relaxed with our credentials provided via Basic Authentication (username admin and password admin) as follows.

```
GET /relaxed HTTP/1.1
Authorization: Basic YWRtaW46YWRtaW4=
```

The response we receive looks like this:

```
{
  "couchdb": "Welcome",
  "uuid": "90a7677e8fbea8c2505ba4b9a1e1d719",
  "vendor": {
    "name": "Drupal",
    "version": "8.5.5"
  },
  "version": "8.5.5"
}
```

Figure 13-2 also depicts the welcome response. We are in business!

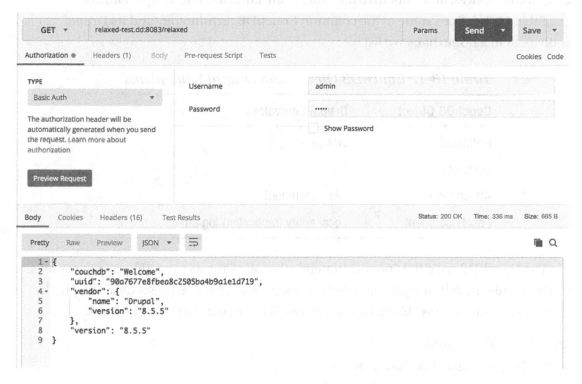

Figure 13-2. *When we issue a GET request against the* `/relaxed` *path, we receive a welcome message identifying the API as CouchDB-compliant*

Note   For information not covered in this chapter about requests more relevant to content staging requirements, refer to the documentation available at `https://www.drupal.org/docs/8/modules/relaxed-web-services/available-rest-resources-and-supported-http-methods`.

Retrieving Resources with RELAXed Web Services

RELAXed Web Services makes a diverse range of resources available, each with different characteristics. Before we begin, we need to define the available resources and what they represent in the Drupal ecosystem. For instance, CouchDB databases are equivalent to Drupal *workspaces*, and CouchDB documents are equivalent to Drupal *entities*.

Table 13-1 defines some of the common CouchDB terminology and its Drupal equivalent in a nonexhaustive list.

Table 13-1. *CouchDB Objects and Drupal Equivalents*

CouchDB Object	Drupal Equivalent
Database	Workspace
Document	Entity
Attachment	File attachment
Local document	Local entity (replication log entity)

The CouchDB specification recommends that all requests expecting responses in JSON include the following two headers.[1] Nonetheless, many requests described in the coming sections are possible in RELAXed Web Services without these headers.

```
Accept: application/json
Content-Type: application/json
```

---

[1]"10.1. API Basics." Apache CouchDB. 2018. Accessed 27 August 2018. `http://docs.couchdb.org/en/latest/api/basics.html`

Note   In examples throughout this chapter, it is assumed that you have either manually created or automatically generated content using Devel Generate, steps that we undertook in Chapter 7.

For information about the response headers that CouchDB issues, refer to the CouchDB documentation available at `http://docs.couchdb.org/en/latest/api/basics.html`.

Retrieving Workspaces and Workspace Collections

To retrieve a list of all the workspaces available on your Drupal site, namely a workspace collection, issue a GET request to the URL shown here. Recall that the `/relaxed` prefix will be different if you modified it during module configuration.[2]

`/relaxed/_all_dbs`

Depending on how you have configured your permissions and workspaces, you will see different results. For some configurations, you might encounter an array containing a single member `live`, whereas for others you will receive an array containing two members, like this:

```
[
  "live",
  "stage"
]
```

See the result of this request, which has returned a 200 OK response code, in action in Postman in Figure 13-3. The strings in the array represent workspaces and indicate the paths that we should employ to target individual documents (Drupal entities) housed in those workspaces.

---

[2]"Available REST Resources and Supported HTTP Methods." *Drupal.org.* 8 June 2018. Accessed 27 August 2018. `https://www.drupal.org/docs/8/modules/relaxed-web-services/available-rest-resources-and-supported-http-methods`

Note   From this point forward, all figures in this chapter are Postman screenshots showing identical responses to those presented in the text.

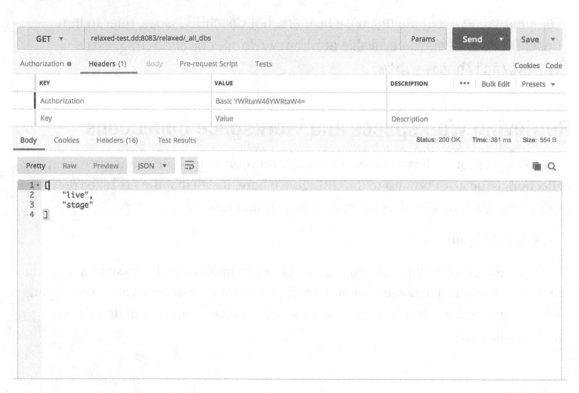

Figure 13-3. *In this example, we request the collection of all workspaces available on Drupal and receive this response*

To retrieve an individual workspace, simply append the workspace name ({workspace} below) to the end of the path for all workspaces.

/relaxed/{workspace}

In the following path, we target the live workspace.

/relaxed/live

The response, accompanied by a 200 OK response code, will look like the following, seen also in Figure 13-4.

```
{
    "db_name": "live",
    "update_seq": 692452149,
    "instance_start_time": "1531835105"
}
```

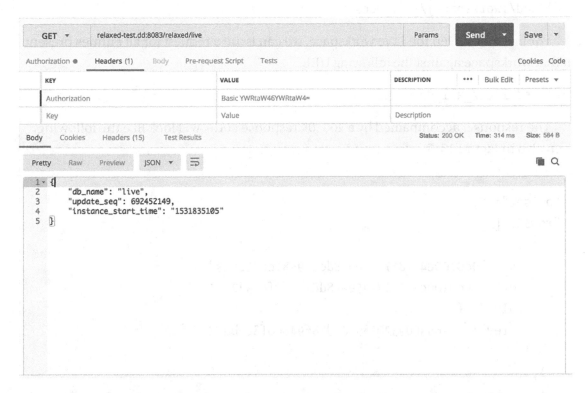

Figure 13-4. *In this example, we have retrieved information from the* live *workspace*

Now that we have fetched an individual workspace, we can access all of the documents contained within that workspace in the next section.

Note   If you want to check whether a workspace exists, you can issue a HEAD request against the same URL instead. The response will contain a limited set of information about the workspace, but this is a lightweight method of ascertaining a workspace's existence.

Retrieving Documents and Document Collections

To retrieve a collection of all the entities (CouchDB documents) present in a given workspace, use the following format for your URL, where {workspace} is the name of the workspace housing the desired content.

```
/relaxed/{workspace}/_all_docs
```

For instance, given the live workspace, we can issue a request for all entities present in that workspace against the following URL.

```
/relaxed/live/_all_docs
```

The response, accompanied by a 200 OK response code, will look like the following, seen also in Figure 13-5.

```
{
  "offset": 0,
  "rows": [
    {
      "id": "9e0100c4-7817-45ea-8dc1-948fce322ac3",
      "key": "9e0100c4-7817-45ea-8dc1-948fce322ac3",
      "value": {
        "rev": "2-653009520389f0bd88f948c0f8cebad8"
      }
    },
    {
      "id": "12abcd43-40c7-4af8-b146-1e085ef85f9c",
      "key": "12abcd43-40c7-4af8-b146-1e085ef85f9c",
      "value": {
        "rev": "2-89a6a9764fa93cd1ccd859956191e3c2"
      }
    }
  ],
  "total_rows": 2
}
```

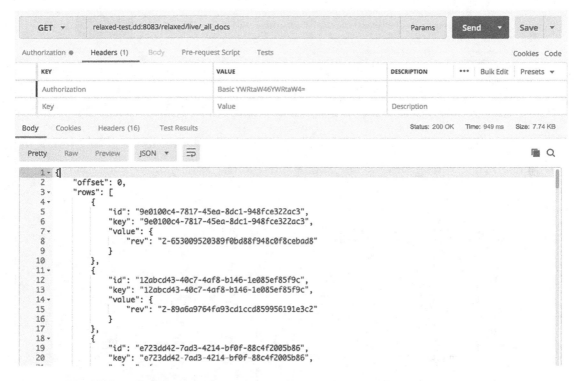

Figure 13-5. *A typical collection of entities originating from the RELAXed Web Services REST API for a given workspace. Note that an additional request is required to drill deeper into the data.*

To retrieve an individual entity, we need to replace _all_docs with the UUID of the document (Drupal entity) that we are trying to retrieve, as seen in the following example, where {workspace} is the name of the desired workspace, and {document_id} is the UUID of the desired document.

```
/relaxed/{workspace}/{document_id}
```

For instance, consider one of the entities identified in the collection we fetched just now. We would form a request against that entity as follows. Note that the UUID is the identifier we are using to target the correct entity.

```
/relaxed/live/462e86f6-0123-43a6-a71e-914d9432ab6e
```

The response, accompanied by a 200 OK response code, will contain an object that also exposes certain details about the entity, such as key information about the entity and fields that are present. This can be seen in Figure 13-6 and Figure 13-7.

211

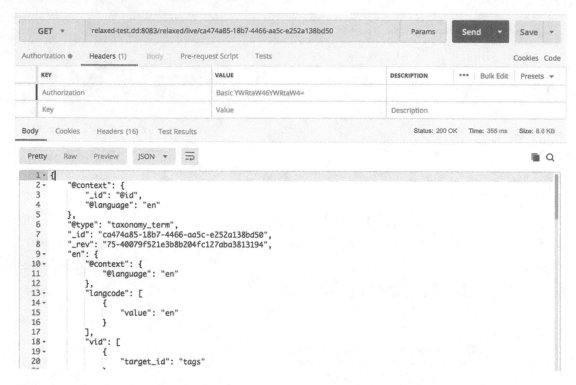

Figure 13-6. *In this case, we have fetched an individual taxonomy term along with crucial information about the taxonomy term in question*

Figure 13-7. *In another request to an entity having a different UUID, we have retrieved an article*

Retrieving File Attachments

One of the unique characteristics of RELAXed Web Services and CouchDB is its robust handling of file attachments. For file attachments, the CouchDB specification recommends that Accept headers include the expected MIME type for the file (e.g., image/jpeg for JPEG images) or wildcards to allow for any MIME type, as follows. In the absence of an Accept header, CouchDB assumes any MIME type by default.

Accept: */*

GET requests that target file attachments take a relatively complex format in RELAXed Web Services. In the following URL, {workspace} represents the workspace name, {document_id} represents the entity UUID, {field_name} represents the field name where the file attachment is present, {delta} represents the delta in the field

213

(in single-value fields, 0; in multiple-value fields, its index in the array), {file_id} represents the UUID of the file, {scheme} represents the scheme value of the file, and {filename} represents the filename value of the field.

```
/relaxed/{workspace}/{document_id}/{field_name}/{delta}/{file_id}/{scheme}/
{filename}
```

If this seems extremely complex, fear not, because all of this information is available in any request to an entity that contains a file attachment.

Consider, for instance, the entity we retrieved in the previous section. Within that response, we find the following field object, with surrounding items removed for brevity.

```
"field_image": [
  {
    "entity_type_id": "file",
    "target_uuid": "4f3ad958-83f7-4800-8505-0e26a06f96b7",
    "alt": "Commodo ibidem pertineo sagaciter scisco.",
    "title": "Aliquip inhibeo suscipit verto.",
    "width": "280",
    "height": "451",
    "uri": "public://2018-08/generateImage_2BMzyH.jpg",
    "filename": "generateImage_2BMzyH.jpg",
    "filesize": "6752",
    "filemime": "image/jpeg"
  }
],
```

Given this example image, we can match elements to what their equivalents would be in forming the request. Table 13-2 identifies these elements based on the example image presented.

Table 13-2. *RELAXed Web Services File Attachment URL Segments*

Placeholder	Definition	Example
{field_name}	Field name	field_image
{delta}	Delta in values array	0 given a single-value field; 0 or higher given a multiple-value field
{file_id}	File UUID	4f3ad958-83f7-4800-8505-0e26a06f96b7
{scheme}	URI scheme	public (taken from uri field above)
{filename}	File name	generateImage_2BMzyH.jpg

The URL then becomes the following:

/relaxed/live/462e86f6-0123-43a6-a71e-914d9432ab6e/field_image/0/4f3ad958-83f7-4800-8505-0e26a06f96b7/public/generateImage_2BMzyH.jpg

The response arrives with a 200 OK response code and the full desired image. This can be seen in Figure 13-8.

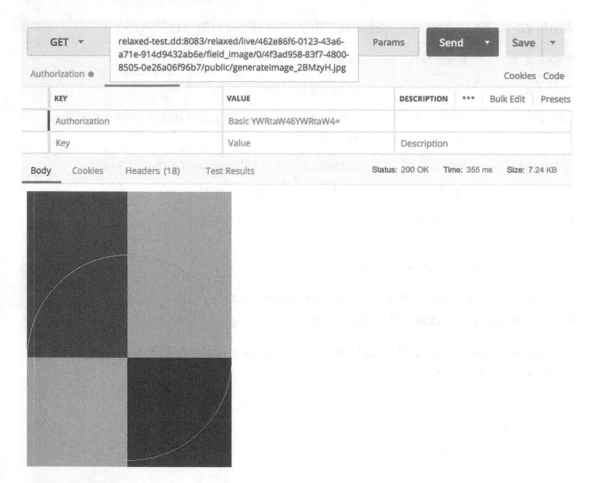

Figure 13-8. *When we issue a GET request against a file attachment, we receive the image in the response body, provided we gave all the correct information in forming the URL*

Note   If you want to check whether a file attachment exists, you can issue a HEAD request against the same URL instead. The response will contain a limited set of information about the file attachment, but this is a lightweight method of ascertaining a file attachment's existence.

Creating and Updating Resources with RELAXed Web Services

Unlike core REST (see Chapter 7), RELAXed Web Services makes frequent use of the PUT method. In many cases, specifically CouchDB documents (Drupal entities) and file attachments, we can use PUT to both create new resources and to update existing ones, as long as we provide all necessary information about the new or modified entity in the request body, in the case of documents (entities). As such, in this section, we cover both creating and updating resources with RELAXed Web Services.

Creating Workspaces

If you are using the Workspaces module in conjunction with other tools from the Drupal Deploy ecosystem, although you can create workspaces through the Drupal user interface, it can often make sense to create a new workspace through the REST API available through RELAXed Web Services, particularly if your consumer needs to be able to manipulate workspaces.

To create a new workspace, we simply need to issue a PUT request against the following URL, where {workspace} represents the new workspace (CouchDB database) we wish to create.

```
/relaxed/{workspace}
```

As an example, if you wish to create another workspace named draft in addition to stage and live, you can do so by issuing a PUT request to the following URL.

```
/relaxed/draft
```

All PUT requests in RELAXed Web Services require a Content-Type request header. We can use application/json to indicate this.

```
PUT /relaxed/draft HTTP/1.1
Authorization: Basic YWRtaW46YWRtaW4=
Content-Type: application/json
```

217

The response code returned is 201 Created with a short confirmation message, which can also be seen in Figure 13-9.

```
{
  "ok": true
}
```

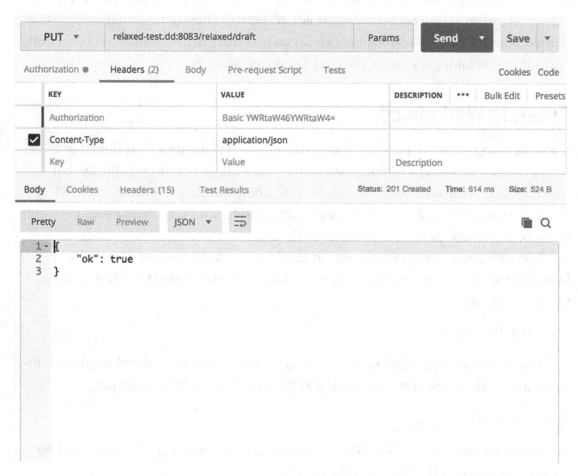

Figure 13-9. *When we issue a PUT request against a URL containing the desired name of our new workspace, we receive a response with a 201 Created response code*

Sure enough, if we issue a GET request against /relaxed/_all_dbs, as we did in the previous section, we can see our new workspace represented in the array. This is also seen in Figure 13-10.

```
[
  "live",
  "stage",
  "draft"
]
```

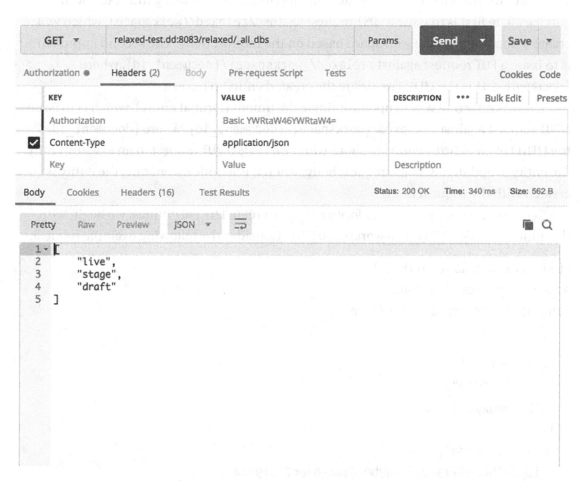

Figure 13-10. *After our earlier PUT request, when we issue a GET request against* /relaxed/_all_dbs, *we see our newly created workspace represented in the array*

> **Note**   According to the CouchDB specification, all workspace names must begin
> with a lowercase letter (a-z) and consist solely of lowercase letters (a-z), digits
> (0-9), or certain special characters (_, $, (,), +, -, and /). It is also possible to
> state these rules as a regular expression: ^[a-z][a-z0-9_$()+/-]*$.[3]

Creating Documents

There are two ways to create a new document (Drupal entity) using RELAXed Web
Services. The first is to issue a POST request against /relaxed/{workspace}, which will
create a document in the workspace based on the request body. The second approach
is to issue a PUT request against /relaxed/{workspace}/{document_id}, where
{document_id} is the UUID we desire the created entity to have.

There is only one way to update a single document (Drupal entity), which is to issue
a PUT request against /relaxed/{workspace}/{document_id}, where {document_id} is
the UUID of an *existing entity*. In short, when we issue a PUT request to an existing entity,
the entity is updated with the request body; when it is a nonexistent one, the entity is
created with the request body.

Because it is the most straightforward way to create Drupal entities, we begin with
the approach using POST on a workspace URL. Consider the following example request.

```
POST /relaxed/live HTTP/1.1
Accept: application/json
Content-Type: application/json

{
  "@context": {
    "_id": "@id",
    "@language": "en"
  },
  "@type": "node",
  "_id": "b6cea743-ba86-49b0-81ac-03ec728f91c4",
  "en": {
```

---

[3]"10.3.1. /db." Apache CouchDB. 2018. Accessed 27 August 2018. http://docs.couchdb.org/en/
stable/api/database/common.html

```json
  "@context": {
    "@language": "en"
  },
  "langcode": [
    {
      "value": "en"
    }
  ],
  "type": [
    {
      "target_id": "article"
    }
  ],
  "title": [
    {
      "value": "REST and RELAXation"
    }
  ],
  "body": [
    {
      "value": "This article brought to you by a request to RELAXed Web
          Services!"
    }
  ]
  }
}
```

Note that in this example, we are defining a UUID that Drupal will use to create the new entity. If you exclude the _id key, Drupal will generate its own UUID for the entity.

When we issue this request, we receive in response an object that confirms the article's creation with a 201 Created response code. You can see this in Figure 13-11.

```json
{
  "ok": true,
  "id": "b6cea743-ba86-49b0-81ac-03ec728f91c4",
  "rev": "1-e16bb624b7d8cc04a16b879eb86e4e7"
}
```

221

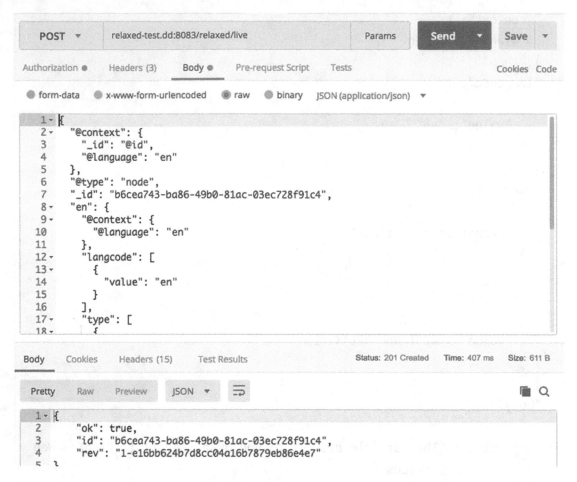

Figure 13-11. *When we issue a POST request to a workspace resource with a request body containing the desired content, we receive a 201* `Created` *response code*

Sure enough, when we issue a GET request against `/relaxed/live/b6cea743-ba86-49b0-81ac-03ec728f91c4`, we are able to retrieve the entity we have just created, as seen in Figure 13-12.

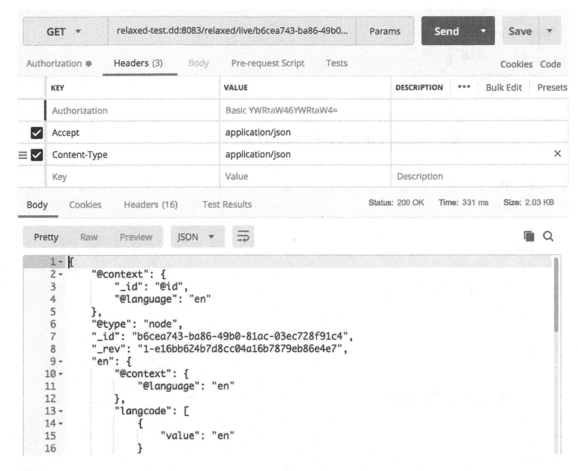

Figure 13-12. *When we supply the UUID of the recently created entity in a GET request, we can verify that the article has been created*

Creating an entity via PUT involves a process that is quite similar to entity creation via POST. Instead of placing the UUID within the request body or allowing Drupal to generate a new UUID for us, we position the UUID within the URL of the request. This means that there is no way of using the PUT method to delegate UUID generation to Drupal. Note that the UUID provided in the URL must not be a preexisting UUID.

In this example request, we provide the same request body as in the previous example and use a new UUID. Note that the UUID in the URL and in the request body must match.

```
PUT /relaxed/live/0b36080d-a3ed-48c0-9863-a5726c687166 HTTP/1.1
Accept: application/json
Content-Type: application/json
```

```
{
  "@context": {
    "_id": "@id",
    "@language": "en"
  },
  "@type": "node",
  "_id": "0b36080d-a3ed-48c0-9863-a5726c687166",
  "en": {
    "@context": {
      "@language": "en"
    },
    "langcode": [
      {
        "value": "en"
      }
    ],
    "type": [
      {
        "target_id": "article"
      }
    ],
    "title": [
      {
        "value": "Feeling RELAXed"
      }
    ],
    "body": [
      {
        "value": "It's possible to achieve a sense of contentment while
                using RELAXed Web Services."
      }
    ]
  }
}
```

Drupal responds with a 201 Created response code to reflect the article's creation, as seen in Figure 13-13.

```
{
  "ok": true,
  "id": "0b36080d-a3ed-48c0-9863-a5726c687166",
  "rev": "1-16feb476aa943ba5802b4580bb284dff"
}
```

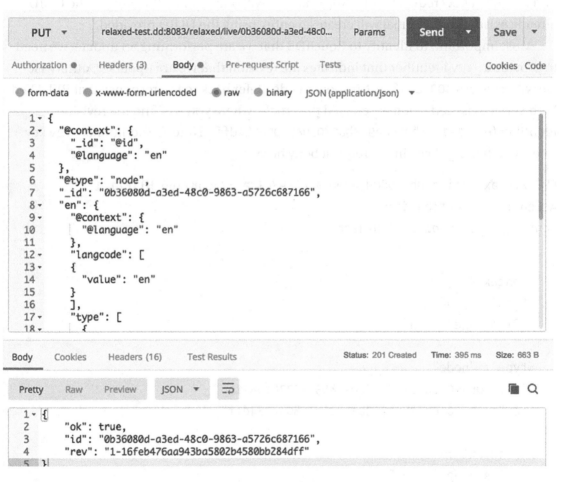

Figure 13-13. *In this example, we have used PUT to create an article by providing a UUID for Drupal to use to create the entity*

Updating Documents

There is only one way to update a single document (Drupal entity), which is to issue a
PUT request against /relaxed/{workspace}/{document_id}, where {document_id} is the
UUID of an *existing entity*. In short, when we issue a PUT request to an existing entity, the
entity is updated with the request body; when it is a nonexistent one, the entity is created
with the request body.

To update this same article, we can simply provide the UUID of the existing entity
and provide a new request body. Note that this will only update the entity if the UUID
already exists; if not, Drupal will create an entity using the UUID provided.

Most important, to identify to CouchDB that we are performing an update, we need
to provide a _rev identifier that indicates the revision that we are updating; otherwise
we will receive a 409 Conflict response code. Refer back to the response that RELAXed
Web Services issued when we created the article, where you will find the revision
identifier (e.g., 1-16feb476aa943ba5802b4580bb284dff). Note the additional _rev key
underneath the _id key in the request body here.

```
PUT /relaxed/live/0b36080d-a3ed-48c0-9863-a5726c687166 HTTP/1.1
Accept: application/json
Content-Type: application/json

{
  "@context": {
    "_id": "@id",
    "@language": "en"
  },
  "@type": "node",
  "_id": "0b36080d-a3ed-48c0-9863-a5726c687166",
  "_rev": "1-16feb476aa943ba5802b4580bb284dff",
  "en": {
    "@context": {
      "@language": "en"
    },
    "langcode": [
      {
        "value": "en"
      }
```

```
    ],
    "type": [
      {
        "target_id": "article"
      }
    ],
    "title": [
      {
        "value": "Are you well-RESTed and RELAXed yet?"
      }
    ],
    "body": [
      {
        "value": "As you can see this article has changed a great deal, so
                  we need to make sure that RELAXed Web Services knows about
                  that."
      }
    ]
  }
}
```

RELAXed Web Services will issue us a 201 Created response code (indicating, slightly confusingly if you are accustomed to core REST, that a new *revision* was created) as well as a new revision identifier, which we should use in the future when we need to update the entity again. You can see this result in Figure 13-14.

```
{
  "ok": true,
  "id": "0b36080d-a3ed-48c0-9863-a5726c687166",
  "rev": "2-ec679e0d2763c981441b96e14232dc94"
}
```

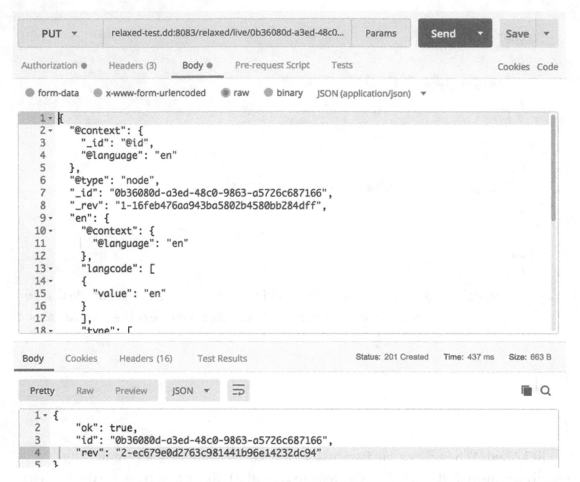

Figure 13-14. *RELAXed Web Services gives us a new revision identifier when we perform an update on an entity*

Once again, sure enough, a GET request against the UUID of the article demonstrates that it was updated successfully, as seen in Figure 13-15.

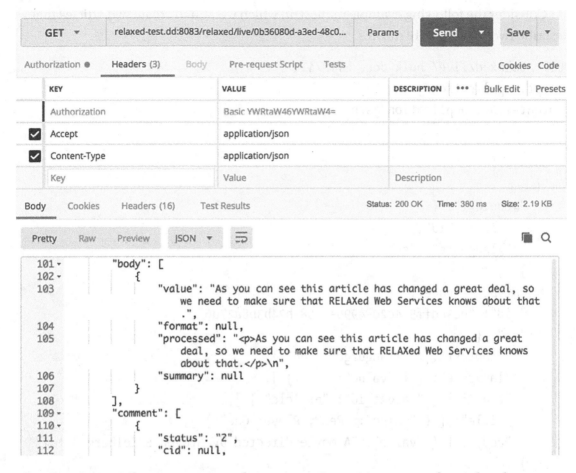

Figure 13-15. *When we retrieve the same entity again, we see that it has been updated with our new content*

Creating and Updating Documents in Bulk

It is also possible to create and update documents in bulk using POST requests to the URL here, where {workspace} represents the desired workspace (CouchDB database).

```
/relaxed/{workspace}/_bulk_docs
```

Within this request, we need the familiar Accept and Content-Type request headers, and our request body needs to contain a docs array consisting of document objects representing each entity we wish to create.

Consider the following example request, in which we aim to create two articles that describe two popular 2018 movies.

```
POST /relaxed/live/_bulk_docs HTTP/1.1
Accept: application/json
Content-Type: application/json

{
  "docs": [
    {
      "@context": {
        "_id": "@id",
        "@language": "en"
      },
      "@type": "node",
      "_id": "be3bdff5-4c20-4996-a158-b24b3b8a27d6",
      "en": {
        "@context": { "@language": "en" },
        "langcode": [ { "value": "en" } ],
        "type": [ { "target_id": "article" } ],
        "title": [ { "value": "Ready Player One" } ],
        "body": [ { "value": "A movie directed by Steven Spielberg." } ]
      }
    },
    {
      "@context": {
        "_id": "@id",
        "@language": "en"
      },
      "@type": "node",
      "_id": "8e0a2aba-0027-43b4-a738-48a0b35837c9",
      "en": {
        "@context": { "@language": "en" },
        "langcode": [ { "value": "en" } ],
```

```
      "type": [ { "target_id": "article" } ],
      "title": [ { "value": "A Wrinkle in Time" } ],
      "body": [ { "value": "A movie directed by Ava DuVernay." } ]
    }
  }
 ]
}
```

Submitting this request yields a 201 Created response code as well as a response body that contains confirmations of our now-assigned UUIDs and revision identifiers that we can target when we need to issue a bulk update, as you can also see in Figure 13-16.

```
[
  {
    "ok": true,
    "id": "be3bdff5-4c20-4996-a158-b24b3b8a27d6",
    "rev": "1-6524707f2d6d9fc22ab05bcca81c88f3"
  },
  {
    "ok": true,
    "id": "8e0a2aba-0027-43b4-a738-48a0b35837c9",
    "rev": "1-470e61ec70ac61c871cd51ed211e64b1"
  }
]
```

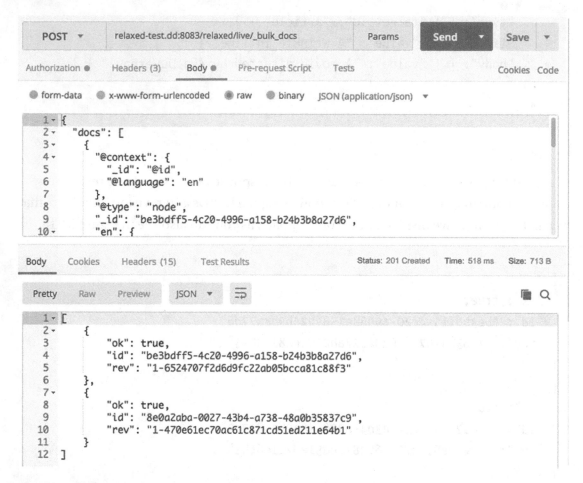

Figure 13-16. *In this example, because we have created two articles using bulk creation, RELAXed Web Services returns an array containing two objects reflecting our newly created entities*

Now, to update both of these articles in bulk, we merely need to provide the revision identifiers within each document object. Consider the following example. Note in particular the new _rev key underneath the _id key, information we obtained in the previous response.

```
POST /relaxed/live/_bulk_docs HTTP/1.1
Accept: application/json
Content-Type: application/json

{
  "docs": [
    {
```

```
    "@context": {
      "_id": "@id",
      "@language": "en"
    },
    "@type": "node",
    "_id": "be3bdff5-4c20-4996-a158-b24b3b8a27d6",
    "_rev": "1-6524707f2d6d9fc22ab05bcca81c88f3",
    "en": {
      "@context": { "@language": "en" },
      "langcode": [ { "value": "en" } ],
      "type": [ { "target_id": "article" } ],
      "title": [ { "value": "Ready Player One (2018)" } ],
      "body": [ { "value": "Directed by Steven Spielberg, this film
      takes place in the city of Columbus and a virtual world called the
      Oasis." } ]
    }
  },
  {
    "@context": {
      "_id": "@id",
      "@language": "en"
    },
    "@type": "node",
    "_id": "8e0a2aba-0027-43b4-a738-48a0b35837c9",
    "_rev": "1-470e61ec70ac61c871cd51ed211e64b1",
    "en": {
      "@context": { "@language": "en" },
      "langcode": [ { "value": "en" } ],
      "type": [ { "target_id": "article" } ],
      "title": [ { "value": "A Wrinkle in Time (2018)" } ],
      "body": [ { "value": "Directed by Ava DuVernay, this film is based
      on the seminal science fiction work by Madeleine L'Engle." } ]
    }
  }
  ]
}
```

233

With a 201 Created response code in the response and new revision identifiers in the response body, we know that our articles have been updated to reflect the new title and body. This is depicted in Figure 13-17.

```
[
  {
    "ok": true,
    "id": "be3bdff5-4c20-4996-a158-b24b3b8a27d6",
    "rev": "2-98304c073b5d752a5feee70b32db93f6"
  },
  {
    "ok": true,
    "id": "8e0a2aba-0027-43b4-a738-48a0b35837c9",
    "rev": "2-c538bab443da1ba452f63e84790a627a"
  }
]
```

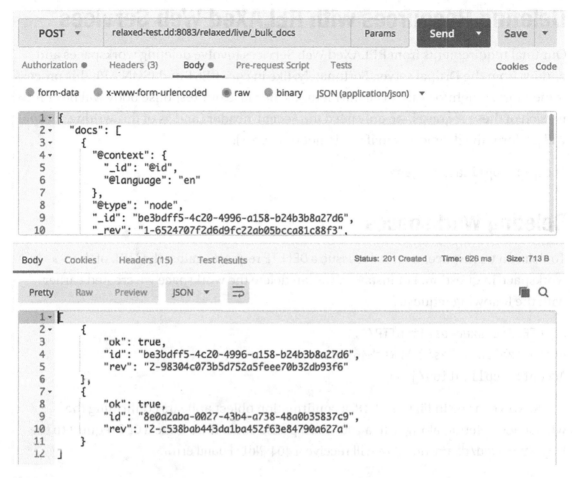

Figure 13-17. *We are issued new revision identifiers that we can use to perform another bulk update of these documents (Drupal entities) in the future*

Note   For more examples of creating and updating resources beyond the scope of this volume, refer to the RELAXed Web Services documentation available on Drupal.org at `https://www.drupal.org/docs/8/modules/relaxed-web-services/available-rest-resources-and-supported-http-methods`.

Deleting Resources with RELAXed Web Services

Our final requirements from RELAXed Web Services involve deleting workspaces and entities from the Drupal server. Fortunately, like in core REST and JSON API, this process is the most straightforward of all the methods. Because our response body will be empty in each of these requests, we only need the Accept header (and as of this writing, Drupal will perform the deletion even if we do not provide it).

```
Accept: application/json
```

Deleting Workspaces

To delete a workspace, we need to issue a DELETE request against the URL of the workspace in question. For instance, we can delete the workspace we created earlier with the following request.

```
DELETE /relaxed/draft HTTP/1.1
Authorization: Basic YWRtaW46YWRtaW4=
Accept: application/json
```

As you can see in Figure 13-18, a confirmation object appears confirming the workspace deletion along with a 200 OK response code. If we issue a GET request to the URL /relaxed/draft now, we will receive a 404 Not Found error.

```
{
  "ok": true
}
```

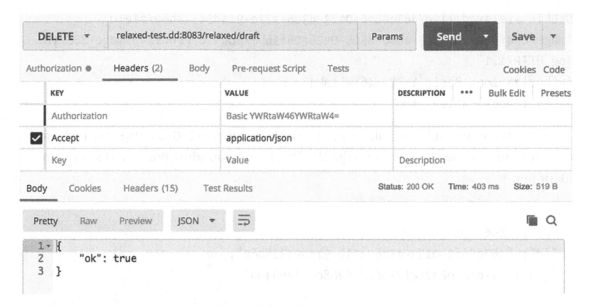

Figure 13-18. *Successful deletions lead to a 200 OK response code and a confirmation that our entity is now deleted*

Deleting Documents

To delete documents (Drupal entities), issue a request against the URL where the document is present. In this example, we are deleting the *Ready Player One* article we created in previous sections.

```
DELETE /relaxed/live/be3bdff5-4c20-4996-a158-b24b3b8a27d6 HTTP/1.1
Authorization: Basic YWRtaW46YWRtaW4=
Accept: application/json
```

Document deletion will also yield a response with a 200 OK response code and a confirmation object like that seen in the previous section.

Deleting File Attachments

To delete file attachments, issue a request against the URL where the file attachment is present. In this example, we are deleting the generated image we retrieved in previous sections.

```
DELETE /relaxed/live/462e86f6-0123-43a6-a71e-914d9432ab6e/field_
image/0/4f3ad958-83f7-4800-8505-0e26a06f96b7/public/generateImage_2BMzyH.
jpg HTTP/1.1
Authorization: Basic YWRtaW46YWRtaW4=
Accept: application/json
```

File attachment deletion will also yield a response with a 200 OK response code and a confirmation object that includes the UUID of the surrounding entity and a revision identifier.

```
{
  "ok": true,
  "id": "462e86f6-0123-43a6-a71e-914d9432ab6e",
  "rev": "2-e1dfe8a2e4f73bd2026988c921abb3ea"
}
```

Conclusion

In this chapter, we examined CRUD operations using the RELAXed Web Services module in Drupal, which is an implementation of the CouchDB specification. Although many architects will opt to use RELAXed Web Services in conjunction with other solutions in the Drupal Deploy ecosystem, these sections prove that developers of consumer applications can benefit from a robust API even without the additional content staging capabilities afforded by Drupal Deploy.

In the next chapter, we change gears entirely and direct our attention to the GraphQL specification and its implementation in Drupal, which requires a completely new and non-RESTful approach when it comes to creating, retrieving, updating, and deleting Drupal content. With GraphQL, we complete our tour of major contributed web services solutions in the wider Drupal ecosystem.

## CHAPTER 14

GraphQL in Drupal

GraphQL is a rapidly maturing solution available as a web service in Drupal 8. Although it is still under heavy development, many aspects of the module are stable, and many production sites leverage GraphQL on Drupal. As we saw in Chapter 8, GraphQL is particularly robust as a web service due to its focus on tailored responses and a readily available introspection layer.

In addition, on installation, GraphQL provides a built-in debugging tool and user interface named GraphiQL that allows us to issue queries and inspect responses in real time, located at /graphql/explorer. In this chapter, we use this debugger extensively due to its ease of use. To issue a request to Drupal's GraphQL implementation, all we need to do is produce a GET request to the URL /graphql with the query parameter ?query=, followed by our query, formatted as a URL-encoded string.

In this chapter, we retrieve content entities through GraphQL and demonstrate some of the features through the Drupal implementation of GraphQL. The GraphQL module adds a variety of permissions that allow users of various roles to execute arbitrary queries, bypass field security, or access the GraphiQL interface, among others. These are assigned to administrators only by default.

Retrieving Entities with GraphQL

Unlike other modules such as RELAXed Web Services and JSON API, the GraphQL module offers a more specific and less generic set of GraphQL fields that map to Drupal equivalents. For instance, whereas RELAXed Web Services and JSON API make no distinction between nodes and users, instead treating them as generic entities, the GraphQL module treats them separately.

© Preston So 2018

P. So, *Decoupled Drupal in Practice*, https://doi.org/10.1007/978-1-4842-4072-4_14

> **Note**   GraphiQL offers several convenient keyboard shortcuts to access certain features. To prettify the query you have inserted, use the keyboard shortcut Shift+Ctrl+P. To run the query, use Ctrl+Enter. To access an autocomplete drop-down when providing fields, use Ctrl+Space.

Retrieving Individual Entities

To retrieve an individual node entity, we can issue the following anonymous query. The nodeById field accepts two arguments: id, the identifier of the node, which should be provided as a string, and language, the language of the node, which should be provided as a LanguageId (a GraphQL module-provided type that obligates language codes in capital letters without quotation marks; e.g., EN, FR). The language argument defaults to null and is hence optional.

```
{
  nodeById(id: "1", language: EN) {
    title
  }
}
```

The preceding query yields the following response, as we would expect. Note that we are using content generated through Devel Generate (see Chapter 7) in this scenario.

```
{
  "data": {
    "nodeById": {
      "title": "At Autem Hos Nostrud Saluto Voco"
    }
  }
}
```

As you can see in this example, we can drill down into the node to access the fields contained therein, such as title. Although these fields map on to their Drupal equivalents, as we have seen in previous responses from core REST and JSON API (e.g., status, changed, created, etc.), the GraphQL module also makes preformatted fields available, such as entityLabel. Consider the following query.

```
{
  nodeById(id: "1") {
    entityLabel
    changed
    entityChanged
  }
}
```

This query yields the following response, as seen in Figure 14-1. As you can see, whereas changed yields a Unix timestamp, similar to the other APIs we have covered so far, requiring us to perform date handling on the consumer, entityChanged provides us instead with the date according to Drupal's default date formatter. This is a powerful outcome and means that we can simultaneously take advantage of raw and formatted output from Drupal at the same time.

```
{
  "data": {
    "nodeById": {
      "entityLabel": "At Autem Hos Nostrud Saluto Voco",
      "changed": 1536169822,
      "entityChanged": "2018-09-05T17:50:22+0000"
    }
  }
}
```

Figure 14-1. *The GraphQL module allows us to designate whether we desire raw or formatted output from Drupal. In this case,* `entityChanged` *has run through Drupal's date formatter.*

Retrievals of users operate much the same way. Consider the following example, a query that retrieves a user entity, whose fields adhere to the User type defined in the GraphQL module.

```
{
  userById(id: "2") {
    uid
    name
    mail
  }
}
```

This query yields the following response.

```
{
  "data": {
    "userById": {
      "uid": 2,
      "name": "chifrothaw",
```

```
    "mail": "chifrothaw@example.com"
    }
  }
}
```

We can also retrieve relationships within the entity itself. Consider the following example query, which fetches a node entity along with its author. In this query, we include fields that adhere to the Node type for the first level, but because entityOwner is of type User, we must use fields from the User type definition. We are also using aliases (see Chapter 8) to improve the experience for the developer building our consumer.

```
{
  entity: nodeById(id: "2") {
    title: entityLabel
    created: entityCreated
    author: entityOwner {
      id: uid
      name
      email: mail
    }
  }
}
```

The result looks something like this, as you can see in Figure 14-2.

```
{
  "data": {
    "entity": {
      "title": "Aliquip Quia",
      "created": "2018-09-05T17:50:22+0000",
      "author": {
        "id": 1,
        "name": "admin",
        "email": "admin@example.com"
      }
    }
  }
}
```

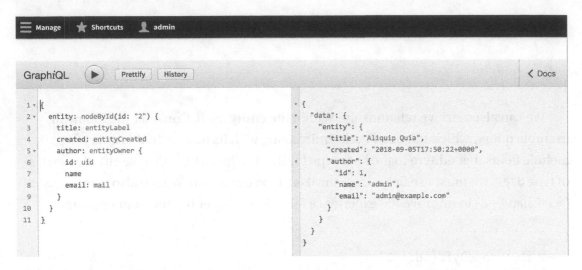

Figure 14-2. *In this example, we use aliases to improve the consumer developer experience in addition to including information about the user who authored this entity*

As you might have noticed, although we have certain crucial information about the entity, such as when it was created or changed, who created it, and what it is called, we lack other information such as the actual body of the content entity. This is due to the fact that whereas the *Body* field is required in nodes of type Article and Page, it is fully possible in Drupal's content modeling system to do without the *Body* field.

Whenever we create a new content type in Drupal, as you might recall from our study of JSON API, all content entities of that type are assigned a bundle. Within the Drupal implementation of GraphQL, there is a clear distinction between the overarching `Node` type, which governs all nodes irrespective of their bundle, and individual `NodeArticle` and `NodePage` types, which include bundle-specific information like the *Body* field.

Consider the following example. In this scenario, we are using a fragment to designate that we should only retrieve the body if the node in question is an article.

```
{
  entity: nodeById(id: "2") {
    title: entityLabel
    created: entityCreated
    author: entityOwner {
      id: uid
      name
```

```
      email: mail
    }
    ...body
  }
}

fragment body on NodeArticle {
  body {
    value
  }
}
```

Recall that we can also inline this fragment to avoid repeating the field name multiple times.

```
{
  entity: nodeById(id: "2") {
    title: entityLabel
    created: entityCreated
    author: entityOwner {
      id: uid
      name
      email: mail
    }
    ... on NodeArticle {
      body {
        value
      }
    }
  }
}
```

The result of this query is the following, as seen in Figure 14-3.

```
{
  "data": {
    "entity": {
      "title": "Aliquip Quia",
```

```
      "created": "2018-09-05T17:50:22+0000",
      "author": {
        "id": 1,
        "name": "admin",
        "email": "admin@example.com"
      },
      "body": {
        "value": "Abico ideo ratis scisco. Accumsan dignissim ea fere
                  in quadrum venio volutpat. Facilisis genitus ideo
                  immitto jugis magna neque pecus quae. Ad huic in
                  jumentum meus nutus. Blandit nutus pecus ut. Aliquip
                  commoveo inhibeo metuo."
      }
    }
  }
}
```

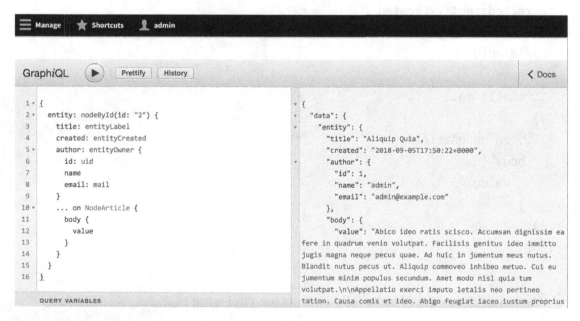

Figure 14-3. *We can inline a fragment based on the values of the specific bundle that we are targeting. In this case the body will only be included in the response if the entity is an article.*

Note   Drupal's implementation of GraphQL makes a variety of queries available that retrieve individual entities and are well beyond the scope of this overview, including `blockContentById` (custom block content), `commentById` (comments), `contactMessageById` (contact form submissions), `fileById` (file entities), `shortcutById` (shortcuts), `taxonomyTermById` (taxonomy terms), and `nodeRevisionById` (node revisions). GraphiQL's autocomplete and documentation features can help you explore what fields are available in those queries.

Retrieving Entity Collections

In addition to queries that retrieve individual entities by identifier, the GraphQL module also offers collection queries that can perform arbitrary operations across a range of entities, such as `nodeQuery` and `userQuery`. Consider the following example.

```
{
  collection: nodeQuery(limit: 20) {
    entities {
      title: entityLabel
    }
  }
}
```

This query yields a collection of 20 entities, as you can see in Figure 14-4.

Figure 14-4. *In this query, we retrieve a collection of entities but limit the response to 20 entities*

In the Drupal implementation of GraphQL, nodeQuery takes several arguments: limit, the number of entities included in the response (defaults to 10); offset, the number of entities to skip before an entity should figure in the response (defaults to 0); sort, which dictates how the entities should be sorted; filter, which provides arbitrary filters; and revisions, which dictates whether revisions should be included or not. The default value of the revisions argument is DEFAULT, which loads current revisions; ALL loads all revisions, and LATEST loads only the most recent revision (all values are expressed without quotation marks as they adhere to their own type definition).

To also retrieve the body of these entities, we can use the following query, which drills into the per-bundle implementations. In the following example, we only include the body for articles.

```
{
  collection: nodeQuery(limit: 20) {
    entities {
      title: entityLabel
      ... on NodeArticle {
        body {
```

```
          value
        }
      }
    }
  }
}
```

As of now, there is no way in the GraphQL specification to include multiple types on a single fragment. This means that to include the body for page entities as well, we must create another fragment referring to NodePage, as you can see in the following example query.

```
{
  collection: nodeQuery(limit: 20) {
    entities {
      title: entityLabel
      ... on NodeArticle {
        body {
          value
        }
      }
      ... on NodePage {
        body {
          value
        }
      }
    }
  }
}
```

Sorting Entity Collections

Consider the following example, which fetches a collection of five entities (limit), with the first five entities in the collection skipped (offset), sorted by title in descending (reverse) order (sort). As you can see, the sort argument accepts an object that contains two other fields, field (the field on which to sort) and direction (ASC or DESC, without quotation marks).

```
{
  collection: nodeQuery(
    limit: 5
    offset: 5
    sort: {
      field: "title"
      direction: DESC
    }
  ) {
    entities {
      title: entityLabel
    }
  }
}
```

The response contains the following object, also seen in Figure 14-5, which indicates that our request has successfully fetched the desired entities.

```
{
  "data": {
    "collection": {
      "entities": [
        {
          "title": "Imputo Qui Quia"
        },
        {
          "title": "Genitus Hos Metuo Meus Olim Suscipere"
        },
        {
          "title": "Facilisis"
        },
        {
          "title": "Ea"
        },
```

```
      {
        "title": "Dignissim Facilisis Hendrerit Lucidus Refero"
      }
    ]
  }
 }
}
```

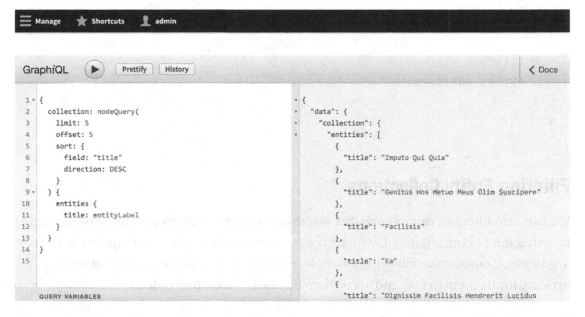

Figure 14-5. *In this example query, we have requested a collection of entities sorted by title in reverse order, showing only five entities, and having skipped the first five results*

Note that because the sort argument can also accept an array of objects, we can perform multiple sorts in succession, as you can see in the following example query, which sorts first based on title and then based on the last updated timestamp, both in descending order.

```
{
  collection: nodeQuery(
    limit: 5
    offset: 5
    sort: [
```

```
      {
        field: "title"
        direction: DESC
         },
         {
        field: "changed"
        direction: DESC
         }
    ]
  ) {
    entities {
      title: entityLabel
    }
  }
}
```

Filtering Entity Collections

We can also filter our results such that our response only contains entities of type Article by using the `filter` argument, which accepts an object of similar structure to the `sort` argument. Consider the following example, which fetches an entity collection of only articles, limits them to five, and sorts them by title in ascending order.

```
{
  collection: nodeQuery(
    filter: {
      conditions: {
        field: "type"
        value: "article"
        operator: EQUAL
      }
    }
    limit: 5
    sort: {
      field: "title"
      direction: ASC
    }
```

```
  ) {
    entities {
      title: entityLabel
    }
  }
}
```

This query yields the following response, also seen in Figure 14-6. If we change the type on which we are filtering to page, you can see that our results change, as seen in Figure 14-7 for comparison.

```
{
  "data": {
    "collection": {
      "entities": [
        {
          "title": "Abluo"
        },
        {
          "title": "Ad Adipiscing Illum Iriure Lobortis"
        },
        {
          "title": "Ad Quadrum Typicus"
        },
        {
          "title": "Aliquip Quia"
        },
        {
          "title": "Aptent Enim Vicis Virtus Ymo"
        }
      ]
    }
  }
}
```

Figure 14-6. *In this example query, we have selected only articles, with a limit of five and sorted by title in ascending order*

Figure 14-7. *In this example, we select pages instead. Notice the difference in the response.*

Table 14-1 lists the available operators for conditions. As you can see, the list is similar to that of Drupal's implementation of JSON API in Chapter 12.

Table 14-1. *GraphQL Filter Operators and Definitions*

Operator	Definition
EQUAL	Equals
NOT_EQUAL	Not equal to
GREATER_THAN	Greater than
GREATER_THAN_OR_EQUAL	Greater than or equal to
SMALLER_THAN	Less than
SMALLER_THAN_OR_EQUAL	Less than or equal to
IN	Checks that the provided value is present in an array
NOT_IN	Checks that the provided value is absent from an array
LIKE	Checks that the provided value matches the provided pattern
NOT_LIKE	Checks that the provided value does not match the provided pattern
BETWEEN	Checks that the provided value is within a range
NOT_BETWEEN	Checks that the provided value is outside of a range
IS_NULL	Is null
IS_NOT_NULL	Is not null

The LIKE and NOT_LIKE operators might be unfamiliar for those accustomed to the JSON API filter operators presented in Chapter 12, such as STARTS_WITH and CONTAINS. In the Drupal implementation of GraphQL, these mirror patterns seen in typical SQL databases using % and _ as wildcards. Consider the following examples.

- The pattern X% matches all values that begin with the letter X, whereas the pattern %X matches those ending with the letter X.

- The pattern %X% matches values having X in any position, whereas X%Y matches values starting with X and ending with Y.

- The pattern _X% matches values with X in the second position, and X_%_%_% matches values beginning with X that are at least four characters long.

As with JSON API (see Chapter 12), we can also provide condition groups that govern how our responses should look. For instance, consider the following example, which requests all pages with titles that begin with the uppercase letter A.

```
{
  collection: nodeQuery(
    filter: {
      conditions: [
        {
          field: "type"
          value: "page"
          operator: EQUAL
        },
        {
          field: "title"
          value: "A%"
          operator: LIKE
        }
      ]
    }
    limit: 5,
    sort: {
      field: "title"
      direction: ASC
    }
  ) {
    entities {
      title: entityLabel
    }
  }
}
```

We receive the following response, also seen in Figure 14-8.

```
{
  "data": {
    "collection": {
```

```
    "entities": [
      {
        "title": "Acsi Amet Nutus Pala"
      },
      {
        "title": "Ad Ipiscing Elit"
      },
      {
        "title": "At Autem Hos Nostrud Saluto Voco"
      }
    ]
  }
 }
}
```

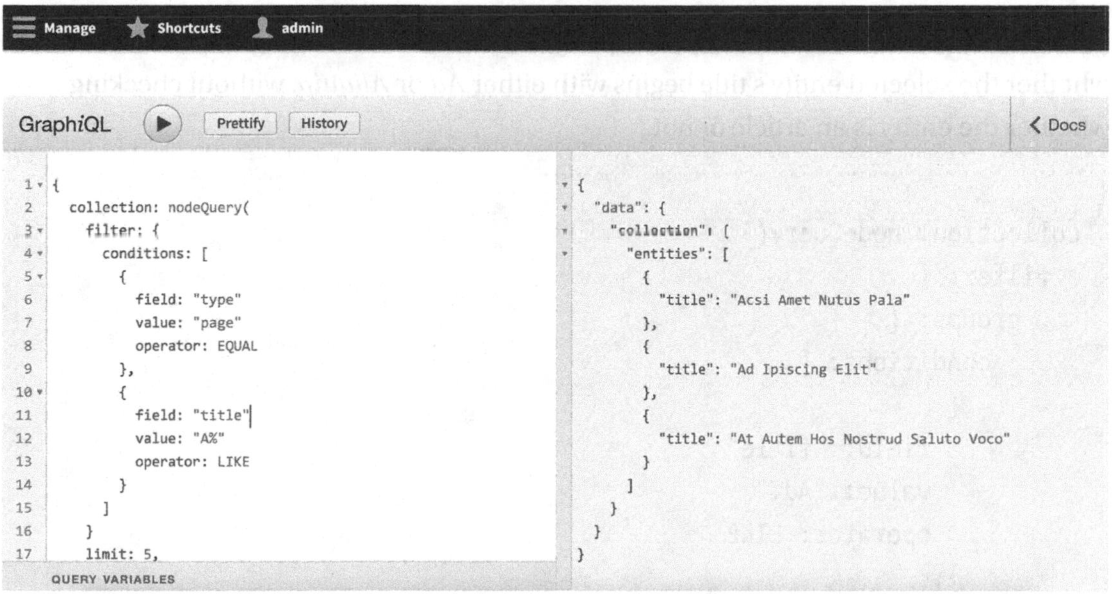

Figure 14-8. *Here, we are using two conditions to first select only pages and then only those pages having titles that begin with the uppercase letter A*

Filtering Entity Collections with Condition Groups

Like Drupal's JSON API implementation, the GraphQL module in Drupal also makes available condition groups for complex filters. Recall from Chapter 12 that *groups* are logical sets composed of the assertions in conditions that facilitate larger condition groups. As previously mentioned, these condition groups can be nested to craft fine-grained queries with a high degree of granularity. For a more comprehensive explanation of conditions, condition groups, and conjunctions, refer back to Chapter 12.

Consider a scenario where we have several articles and pages that have the following titles, representing entities generated through Devel Generate.

- Ad Ipiscing Elit (page)

- Ad Quadrum Typicus (article)

- Ad Adipiscing Illum Iriure Lobortis (article)

- Aliquip Quia (article)

In the following example GraphQL query, we create a condition group that checks whether the selected entity's title begins with either *Ad* or *Aliquip*, without checking whether the entity is an article or not.

```
{
  collection: nodeQuery(
    filter: {
      groups: {
        conditions: [
          {
            field: "title"
            value: "Ad%"
            operator: LIKE
          },
          {
            field: "title"
            value: "Aliquip%"
            operator: LIKE
          }
        ]
        conjunction: OR
```

```
      },
    },
    limit: 5
    sort: {
      field: "title"
      direction: ASC
    }
  ) {
    entities {
      title: entityLabel
    }
  }
}
```

The result of this query is the following response. Note that our page is still represented in the response.

```
{
  "data": {
    "collection": {
      "entities": [
        {
          "title": "Ad Adipiscing Illum Iriure Lobortis"
        },
        {
          "title": "Ad Ipiscing Elit"
        },
        {
          "title": "Ad Quadrum Typicus"
        },
        {
          "title": "Aliquip Quia"
        }
      ]
    }
  }
}
```

Now, we include yet another condition group as part of a hierarchy that also checks whether the selected entity is an article in an AND relationship with the existing condition group.

```
{
  collection: nodeQuery(
    filter: {
      groups: {
        conditions: {
          field: "type"
          value: "article"
          operator: EQUAL
        }
        conjunction: AND
        groups: {
          conditions: [
            {
              field: "title"
              value: "Ad%"
              operator: LIKE
            },
            {
              field: "title"
              value: "Aliquip%"
              operator: LIKE
            }
          ]
          conjunction: OR
        }
      }
    }
    limit: 5
    sort: {
      field: "title"
      direction: ASC
    }
```

```
) {
    entities {
      title: entityLabel
    }
  }
}
```

This query returns the following response. Note that the page entity has now disappeared from the response, indicating that our condition groups are selecting the correct entities. This can be seen in Figure 14-9.

```
{
  "data": {
    "collection": {
      "entities": [
        {
          "title": "Ad Adipiscing Illum Iriure Lobortis"
        },
        {
          "title": "Ad Quadrum Typicus"
        },
        {
          "title": "Aliquip Quia"
        }
      ]
    }
  }
}
```

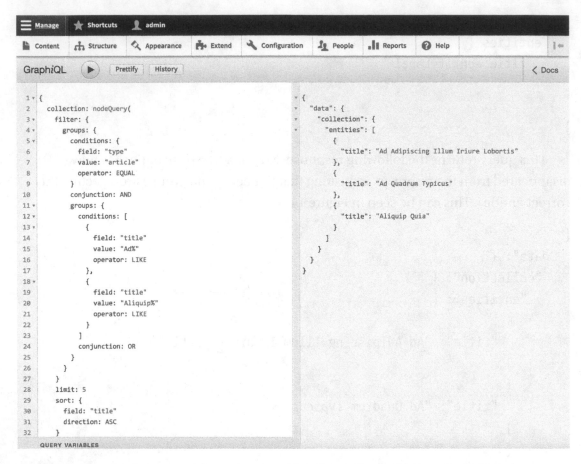

Figure 14-9. *In this example query, we filter based on whether the entity is an article, as well as whether the title begins with one of two provided strings*

The hierarchy established by these condition groups can be seen in Figure 14-10, in a structure that is identical to that reproduced in Figure 12-3 from our prior exploration of condition groups in JSON API.

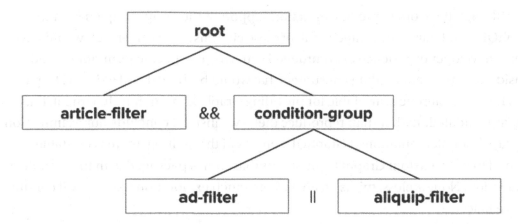

Figure 14-10. *The hierarchy of condition groups established by the example GraphQL query*

Note   Although the full scope of available features in GraphQL read queries within Drupal is far beyond the capacity of this book, the GraphiQL interface provides a robust introspection interface that pairs schema documentation with a live testing tool and can accelerate on-boarding. Use the Docs link in the upper right of GraphiQL to access this interface.

GraphQL Mutations in Drupal

Although built-in mutation (write query) support was previously available out of the box in the Drupal implementation of GraphQL, the maintainers of the GraphQL module have since removed the feature in favor of focusing on stabilizing read queries. One of the most intractable challenges of providing automatic mutation support for Drupal's uniquely flexible content model is the fact that mutations would need to account for every individual bundle and every field contained therein.

In a January 2018 blog post, comaintainer Philipp Melab provided additional insight: "[S]ome entity structures added additional complexities: For example, just trying to create an article with a title and a body value while the comment module is enabled results in a constraint violation, as the comment field requires an empty list of comments."

Although the work to provide mutation support in the Drupal implementation of GraphQL would have accounted for all of these circumstances, the result would have been a developer experience overburdened with Drupal-specific terminology and considerations when building consumers that would both read and write to Drupal.[1]

There are references available for providing GraphQL mutations in Drupal, but they are outdated. Rather than reproduce them, we instead conclude our examination of Drupal's implementation of GraphQL here. As of this writing, there is no stable method to write custom GraphQL mutations that comes packaged with the module on installation. Nonetheless, this is an area where much exploration has and will continue to take place.

Note   For examples of how GraphQL mutations worked prior to the adoption of `webonyx/graphql-php` as a dependency, see `https://github.com/drupal-graphql/graphql-mutation` and `https://github.com/drupal-graphql/graphql-examples`. Note that these code bases are only provided for reference and for historical reasons. For more information about the removal of GraphQL mutation support, see Philipp Melab's Amazee Labs blog post "Extending GraphQL: Part 3 – Mutations" at `https://www.amazeelabs.com/en/blog/extending-graphql-part-3-mutations`.

Conclusion

In this chapter, we covered Drupal's implementation of GraphQL, how to retrieve individual entities and entity collections, and why out-of-the-box mutation support is unavailable. Although the GraphQL module only provides read query support out of the box, it nonetheless offers a developer experience that rivals the JSON API and RELAXed Web Services module, thanks to the emphasis the specification places on tailored responses and schema introspection.

---

[1]Melab, Philipp. "Extending GraphQL: Part 3 - Mutations." Amazee Labs. 9 January 2018. Accessed 6 September 2018. `https://www.amazeelabs.com/en/blog/extending-graphql-part-3-mutations`

In Part 4, we explore Drupal's surrounding ecosystem for decoupled Drupal, which includes a rich and diverse array of distributions, SDKs, and reference applications. By moving beyond what is available in Drupal's core and contributed modules, we venture into the concerns of consumers and their developers. Among the issues we inspect are how to provide different flavors of Drupal for decoupled use cases and how we can make the lives of developers on the other side of the fence much simpler through SDKs and reference applications that can speed up the building process.

PART IV

The Decoupled Drupal Ecosystem

In Part 3, we moved away from descriptions of web services into direct implementation of requests that consume and manipulate Drupal content. This presents a suitable foundation for us to begin to inspect the actual development of consumer applications in various technologies. However, before turning to that theme, in these chapters, we discuss the burgeoning decoupled Drupal ecosystem, whose aim is to simplify the process of employing Drupal as a content service and to accelerate the development of consumer applications.

When Drupal 8 was released, many Drupal developers had not yet conceived of decoupling Drupal. As a result, the standard Drupal 8 installation that results from a typical setup process is often far too overloaded with features for efficient use as a decoupled Drupal back end. While site maintainers can disable unneeded modules, this process can be cumbersome. However, thanks to the use of Drupal distributions, which are flavors of Drupal with different module and feature sets, decoupled Drupal practitioners have begun to adopt API-first distributions. These are versions of Drupal that are optimized for decoupled Drupal use cases with features such as pre-enabled web services, preconfigured settings, and an enhanced user interface.

Thanks to the growth surrounding Contenta and the interest in projects such as Reservoir, API-first distributions will remain an area in significant transition for years to come. Many architects have not yet landed on complete wishlists when it comes to the ideal feature set for an API-first distribution, but competing approaches indicate substantial interest. If and when an installation profile dedicated specifically to decoupled Drupal use cases enters core, it is certain to take great inspiration from the work on Contenta, Reservoir, and others.

Moreover, of all the primary causes of the success seen by headless CMSes, perhaps most meaningful is the proliferation of software development kits (SDKs) and reference builds that facilitate development of consumer applications by developers. These software projects provide a means for non-Drupal practitioners to "speak" the language of Drupal and ramp up quickly on their consumers. While content-as-a-service platforms provide these as free and open-source software, the remainder of their platform remains under lock and key. In recent years, Drupal has adopted a firm stance as an open-source CMS from end to end, monolithic or decoupled. Newly emerging SDKs and reference builds in the Waterwheel and Contenta ecosystems both indicate a healthy demand for easy consumption of Drupal content.

With the help of SDKs and reference builds—and a middleware layer in the form of Contenta.js—developers of any technology, regardless of exposure to Drupal, are able to consume and manipulate Drupal content as easily as they would any API. Whereas SDKs like Waterwheel.js are intended for generic use, more demo-ready reference builds such as Waterwheel's Ember and React applications as well as Contenta's example applications can offer evaluators greater peace of mind.

CHAPTER 15

API-First Distributions

In Drupal parlance, *distributions* refer to variations of Drupal that include Drupal core in its entirety and other items such as themes, modules, libraries (for front-end assets), and installation profiles. Distributions can be full-featured, meaning they are comprehensive solutions for use in specialized cases, or they can act as quick-start tools that help developers and site builders get going quickly.[1]

Note   Some commonly used distributions in Drupal include Conference Organizing Distribution (COD) for conference web sites; Open Social for social communities, intranets, and networks; and Thunder for publishing web sites. Documentation for each of these distributions is available on Drupal.org at `https://www.drupal.org/docs/8/distributions`.

In recent years, the advent of decoupled Drupal architectures has led to a rethinking of how Drupal should appear and perform in such an environment. For many developers building Drupal consumers, the inner workings of Drupal's web services can be prohibitively time-consuming to learn. Because distributions are an optimal way to designate which modules to install and how a site should be configured, they are exceptional candidates for easing the learning curve of decoupled Drupal.

Such *API-first distributions* are variations of Drupal that provide specialized configuration and module sets for decoupled Drupal use cases. During core conversations at DrupalCon Baltimore 2017, the need for an API-first distribution emerged due to the wide variety of best practices for decoupled Drupal and the lack of

---

[1]"Distributions." *Drupal.org*. 5 April 2018. Accessed 1 August 2018. `https://www.drupal.org/docs/8/distributions`

269

P. So, *Decoupled Drupal in Practice*, https://doi.org/10.1007/978-1-4842-4072-4_15

awareness about Drupal among consumer developers. A Drupal core idea issue was created that eventually became Contenta.[2]

Over the course of 2017, the API-first distributions Contenta and Reservoir were independently released. Later in 2017, Headless Lightning, a variant of Acquia's Lightning distribution, adopted much of Reservoir's functionality. In turn, ecosystems surrounding Contenta and Reservoir have emerged. In 2018, Lauri Eskola and I reintroduced the suggestion to provide a "Decoupled" installation profile in Drupal core out of the box, which would obviate much of the need for particular API-first distributions.[3]

Whereas API-first distributions are excellent back ends for content ecosystems that merely need a repository to consume rather than a full web site, they are not as ideal for decoupled Drupal architectures in which the back end performs double duty as both a site and a repository (see Chapter 4 for more on decoupled Drupal use cases). Reservoir, for instance, restricts functionality significantly, much of it for users accustomed to building monolithic Drupal sites normally. As such, you should use API-first distributions when you are building applications consuming a repository rather than a site; for a site, you can use monolithic Drupal normally.

Contenta

Contenta is the most commonly used API-first distribution in the Drupal community and the project witnessing the most contributor activity. Like Reservoir, covered in the next section, Contenta's goal is to provide the ideal content repository for decoupled Drupal architectures. Nonetheless, Contenta has distinct priorities from Reservoir.

Contenta largely keeps the default administrative interface intact to provide more familiarity to Drupal developers, with the caveat that this introduces complexity for novice Drupal developers. To mitigate this, Contenta includes a quick installation process for developers less familiar with Drupal that includes the most common

---

[2]So, Preston. "Introducing Reservoir, a Distribution for Decoupling Drupal." Acquia Developer Center. 19 June 2017. Accessed 1 August 2018. https://dev.acquia.com/blog/introducing-reservoir-a-distribution-for-decoupling-drupal/19/06/2017/18296

[3]Eskola, Lauri, and Preston So. "Drupal 9: Decoupled by Design?" Drupal Developer Days Lisbon 2018. 2018. Accessed 1 August 2018. https://lisbon2018.drupaldays.org/sessions/drupal-9-decoupled-design

required modules and a full slate of default content.[4] The distribution also includes the JSON API Extras module, which adds further configurability to JSON API such as aliases for routes handled by JSON API (see Chapter 8).

Contenta's flexibility also allows consumer developers to choose between a blank slate or a demo installation that includes solved problems and the Umami theme. Like Reservoir, Contenta centers the most striking benefits of Drupal for developers of consumer applications. Using Drupal as an underlying base allows Contenta to leverage the same open source software license and to provide the same content modeling tools available in core Drupal. However, perhaps the most touted benefit of Contenta is its bevy of reference builds for developers, an ecosystem detailed in Chapter 16.[5]

Contenta's mission, according to its authors, is fourfold:

- *Friendly to non-Drupal users*: Contenta expresses a simplified vision of the Drupal administrative back end in which those unaccustomed to Drupal's terminology can use available defaults to model and create content.

- *Usable from the first minute*: Contenta comes already packaged with substantial demo content, allowing developers from other ecosystems to evaluate decoupled Drupal much more quickly with the ability to revert to a clean slate.

- *Decoupled knowledge hub*: The Contenta web site includes a collection of articles and resources that includes tutorials on challenging concepts in decoupled Drupal, such as OAuth2 authentication and JSON API query operations.

- *Feature-complete for decoupled use cases*: Contenta touts its creators' real-world experience in implementing full-featured decoupled Drupal architectures and highlights its promise to be feature-complete for requirements including decoupled Drupal.

---

[4]Aguiló Bosch, Mateu. "Contenta Makes Your Content Happy." Medium. 27 June 2017. Accessed 6 August 2018. https://medium.com/@mateu.aguilo.bosch/contenta-makes-your-content-happy-6f76bbe0cdae

[5]"Contenta Is an API-First Drupal Distribution." Contenta CMS. Accessed 20 September 2018. http://www.contentacms.org

> **Note**   The main Contenta distribution, which provides a JSON API implementation, is available on GitHub at `https://github.com/contentacms/contenta_jsonapi`. The Contenta web site is located at `https://contentacms.org`.

Installing Contenta

To install Contenta for local development, as seen in Figure 15-1, you can execute the following quick install commands, which requires that Composer 1.7 or higher be installed on your machine. Read on for Contenta installation instructions on production.

```
$ php -r "readfile('https://raw.githubusercontent.com/contentacms/contenta_
jsonapi/8.x-2.x/installer.sh');" > contentacms-quick-installer.sh
$ chmod a+x contentacms-quick-installer.sh
$ ./contentacms-quick-installer.sh
```

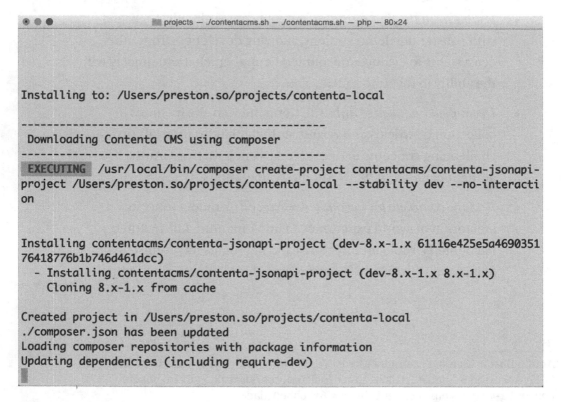

Figure 15-1.   *Contenta's installation process for local development includes a command-line interface that guides users through*

To install Contenta in Composer-based workflows and for production, execute the following command. This will additionally download Contenta modules beyond Drupal core.

```
$ php -r "readfile('https://raw.githubusercontent.com/contentacms/contenta_
jsonapi_project/8.x-1.x/scripts/download.sh');" > download-contentacms.sh
$ chmod a+x download-contentacms.sh
$ ./download-contentacms.sh /path/to/my-contenta
```

Once this completes, copy the .env.example file to a new .env file and add crucial information about your Drupal site and MySQL database. The documentation also recommends using .env.local to store sensitive credentials so that version control tools such as git ignore it. Consider the following example .env and .env.local files.

```
# .env
SITE_MAIL=admin@example.com
ACCOUNT_MAIL=admin@example.com
SITE_NAME='Contenta Test'
ACCOUNT_NAME=admin
MYSQL_DATABASE=contenta
MYSQL_HOSTNAME=localhost
MYSQL_PORT=3306
MYSQL_USER=contenta

# .env.local
MYSQL_PASSWORD=contenta
ACCOUNT_PASS=admin
```

Then, you can execute the following command to run the installation script.

```
$ composer run-script install:with-mysql
```

Note   The Contenta Composer installer is available on GitHub at
https://github.com/contentacms/contenta_jsonapi_project.

Reservoir

The second distribution we discuss in this chapter is Reservoir, an experimental and minimalist distribution for decoupling Drupal. Reservoir's goal, like that of Contenta, is to form an optimal and generic content repository for any decoupled Drupal architecture that successfully on-boards developers of all backgrounds, especially those unaccustomed to Drupal's interfaces, so that they can accomplish any task related to content management or API consumption.

Reservoir focuses specifically on limiting functionality to several primary areas: content modeling, content management, content exposure through APIs, and content API documentation (Figure 15-2). As such, it is primarily intended for use as a lightweight content repository with no inclusion of typical monolithic Drupal functionality.

As a result, unlike Contenta, Reservoir intentionally removes significant portions of monolithic Drupal features, including the user-facing front end and modules that are irrelevant to content repositories (e.g., Breakpoint, Contact, Block). For better or worse, Reservoir also avoids use of Views, because it is assumed that consumers will prefer to make use of well-documented and broadly understood responses from JSON API rather than employ an unfamiliar module with a learning curve handling only read operations.

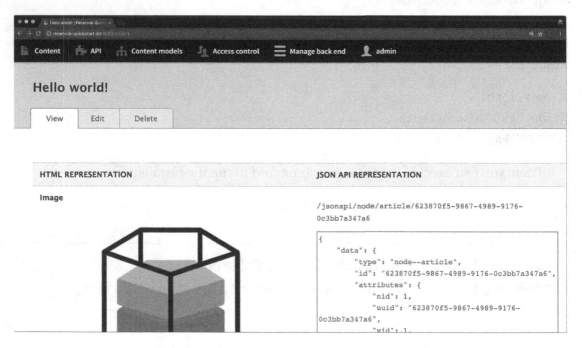

Figure 15-2. *Reservoir provides side-by-side representations of content in HTML and in JSON API responses*

These characteristics comprise Reservoir's minimalist orientation that prizes developers of consumer applications as first-class citizens:

- *Opinionated feature set*: Like Contenta, Reservoir is quite opinionated about its feature set and the modules it makes available to consumer developers. Reservoir offers support for the JSON API and Simple OAuth modules, which means developers no longer need to configure REST resources or study authentication methods. In future iterations, Reservoir is slated to include GraphQL support.

- *Generated API documentation*: With the help of the OpenAPI module and ReDoc JavaScript library (see Figure 15-3), both of which ship with Reservoir off the shelf, Reservoir generates API documentation automatically as developers create and modify content models. When you browse content using the default Drupal interface, API documentation for each resource also appears on the right side. Thanks to OpenAPI, Reservoir also offers an OpenAPI (Swagger) description for developers who wish to use different documentation generation tools. Contenta has since adopted all of these features.

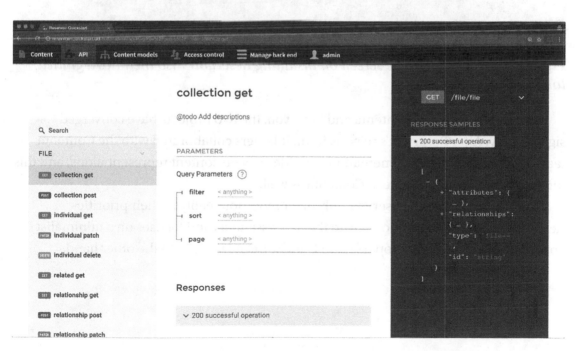

Figure 15-3. *Thanks to OpenAPI and ReDoc, Reservoir autogenerates API documentation that adjusts based on changes to the Drupal content model*

- *Optimized user interface*: On installing Reservoir for the first time, a welcome tour (Figure 15-4) greets new users and presents an overview of the content modeling, content management, and API provisioning functionality available in Reservoir.

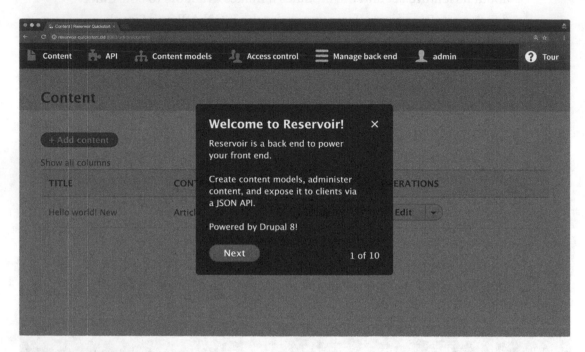

Figure 15-4. *The welcome screen on installing Reservoir also includes a guided tour of its functionality*

Since the releases of Contenta and Reservoir, the two projects have converged significantly. After Reservoir's release, its maintainers collaborated with the Contenta team to introduce API documentation and side-by-side content representations, and this functionality is now available in Contenta as well.

Today, Contenta and Reservoir only differ most noticeably in their priorities. Reservoir strips down functionality to the bare essentials and focuses on a minimalist approach favorable to developers entirely unaware of Drupal. On the other hand,

Contenta forges a middle ground with familiar user interfaces in which those experienced with Drupal can add functionality at will without repercussions and still focus on content delivery to consumer applications. Contenta also employs default content for a more demonstration-ready state.

Note   Reservoir is available on GitHub at `https://github.com/acquia/reservoir`. In addition, a demonstration video of the alpha by author Wim Leers is available as of this writing at `https://vimeo.com/222271467`.

Installing Reservoir

The easiest way to install Reservoir is using the Composer project template (see Figure 15-5) with the following command:

```
$ composer create-project acquia/reservoir-project your-project-name
--stability=alpha
```

Next, in your webhost configuration, ensure that your domain points to the directory `your-project-name/docroot`. From there, navigate to the domain and install Reservoir normally.[6]

---

[6]"Reservoir." GitHub. 29 June 2017. Accessed 1 August 2018. `https://github.com/acquia/reservoir/blob/8.x-1.x/README.md`

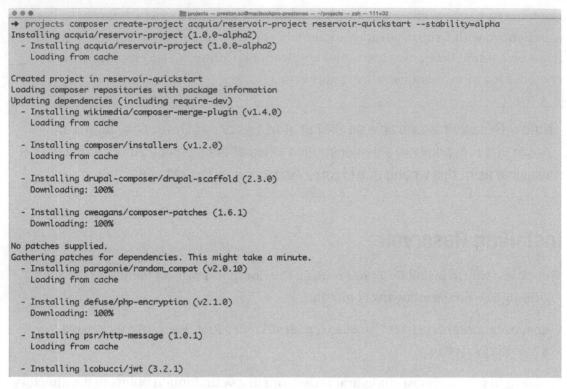

Figure 15-5. *Installing Reservoir's Composer project template*

Note   The Reservoir Composer installer is available on GitHub
at `https://github.com/acquia/reservoir-project`.

Using Reservoir

During the installation process, Reservoir creates four items: one item of sample content
(titled "Hello world"), three sample users (having three distinct roles), and an OAuth 2.0
client representing a consumer application. Once you are ready to deploy Reservoir to
production, you will need to delete these demo data and replace the OAuth 2.0 public
and private keys with your own (see Chapter 9 for more about OAuth 2.0). In addition,
ensure your CORS settings are correctly configured (see Chapter 7).

For Drupal developers, Reservoir might not be the optimal choice, as the data
Reservoir exposes are limited to nodes (content) and node types (content types).
Reservoir excludes much of the familiar Drupal user interface and features like Views

and taxonomy terms. According to the authors, these restrictions simplify development and enhance understanding, which in turn lowers maintenance costs downstream. Despite Reservoir allowing the installation of Drupal modules to introduce new capabilities or custom code, Reservoir's minimalism means that experienced Drupal developers might find Contenta more appealing.

In short, Reservoir emphasizes simplicity yet suffers from the limitations of its minimalist orientation. On the other hand, Contenta focuses on robustness and completeness out of the box, but it retains much of the complexity that can be confusing for novice Drupal users.

Note   There is also a gradually expanding ecosystem around Reservoir, which includes `reservoir-docker`, a Docker image for Reservoir available on GitHub at `https://github.com/mattgrill/reservoir-docker`, and well, a Drupal installation based on Reservoir and Acquia's BLT project, available on GitHub at `https://github.com/damontgomery/well`.

Headless Lightning

Lightning is a Drupal distribution developed by Acquia that aims to track ahead of Drupal core with various useful modules that provide a richer experience for content editors and Drupal developers off the shelf. In its original conception, Lightning was intended solely for monolithic Drupal sites and typical Drupal use cases but has since expanded its reach to include decoupled Drupal architectures as well.

The API-first functionality provided by Lightning is also available as a subprofile in Headless Lightning, a more lightweight distribution that includes all of Reservoir's web services modules as well as its simplified administrative interface. Both Lightning and Headless Lightning make use of the Content API feature, which is Lightning's nomenclature for the JSON API implementation it exposes.[7]

---

[7]Powell, Dane. "Creating a Decoupled Drupal Application in 30 Minutes with Lightning, BLT, and DrupalVM." Acquia Developer Center. 28 November 2017. Accessed 1 August 2018. `https://dev.acquia.com/blog/creating-a-decoupled-drupal-application-in-30-minutes-with-lightning-blt-and-drupalvm/28/11/2017/18886`

Headless Lightning shares many of Reservoir's goals in that it intends to simplify the user interface presented to consumer developers, to offer opinions about the features that users of a content repository would want, and to avoid impeding the progress of content editors and site builders.[8]

As a matter of fact, this distinction between Lightning and Headless Lightning addresses one of the key concerns about Contenta and Reservoir, because the foregoing API-first distributions were optimized solely for the content repository use case rather than a site-and-repository use case (see Chapter 4). Nonetheless, it is still impossible in any of the API-first distributions to switch gracefully between the two use cases due to their architectural dissimilarity.

Note Lightning is available on GitHub at `https://github.com/acquia/lightning`. Headless Lightning is available on GitHub at `https://github.com/acquia/headless-lightning`.

Installing Headless Lightning

The easiest way to install Headless Lightning is through the Composer-based project template.

```
$ composer create-project acquia/lightning-project:dev-headless --no-
interaction --stability=dev
```

This command creates a directory named `lightning-project` containing a `docroot` folder. You can customize the directory name by introducing an additional argument before the `--no-interaction` and `--stability` flags.

```
$ composer create-project acquia/lightning-project:dev-headless your-
project-name --no-interaction --stability=dev
```

At the end of the installation process, like Reservoir, although there is no need to configure REST resources, you will need to configure CORS support (see Chapter 7) and OAuth authentication tokens (see Chapter 9).

---

[8]"Headless Lightning." GitHub. 7 November 2017. Accessed 1 August 2018. `https://github.com/acquia/headless-lightning/blob/master/README.md`

Conclusion

Although API-first distributions still constitute a maturing element of the decoupled Drupal ecosystem, they are essential for developers unfamiliar with Drupal and for those looking for a simplified content repository rather than a full-fledged CMS as a back end for their applications. In the last several years, there has been a flurry of activity in the Drupal community to create distributions like Contenta, Reservoir, and Headless Lightning, all of which share many features but also highlight many differences in approach.

With the help of API-first distributions, developers who would have never considered Drupal otherwise can leverage a more accessible and novice-friendly interface that places components like API documentation and side-by-side representations front and center. In the next chapter, we delve into the other extreme of the decoupled Drupal ecosystem—starter kits, SDKs, and reference builds that aid developers building consumers on the other side.

CHAPTER 16

Software Development Kits and Reference Builds

Today, developers are opting to employ Drupal in novel ways that were unimaginable only a few years ago. As a result, developers of wildly diverse backgrounds are now contending with Drupal's web services in unprecedented ways to serve content to their own applications. Thanks to web services in Drupal 8 Core, Drupal is well-positioned for a wide variety of consumer applications in distinct technologies. However, there's just one issue: Developers unfamiliar with Drupal don't know how to use it.

In this chapter, we cover some of the most essential tools in the decoupled Drupal ecosystem that stretch beyond typical web services—namely SDKs and reference builds that accelerate consumer application development in technologies besides Drupal's own (see Figure 16-1). This enables developers who might have never discovered or considered Drupal to try it without adopting the entire monolith.

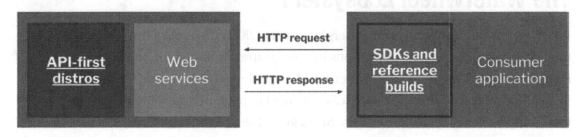

Figure 16-1. *This diagram shows where API-first distributions (see Chapter 15), SDKs, and reference applications fall in a typical decoupled Drupal architecture*

P. So, *Decoupled Drupal in Practice*, https://doi.org/10.1007/978-1-4842-4072-4_16

The idea of an SDK is nothing new in web development and software in general, nor is the notion of bridging a consumer application with an API using such an SDK. Today, proprietary content-as-a-service solutions like Contentful and Prismic provide free and open source SDKs that work seamlessly with their own web services while enabling developers to write in their own language. Nevertheless, these SDKs, although free, require a subscription to a proprietary platform with often opaque API specifications.

One of the primary motivators to choose Drupal is that it is free and open source. With the aid of a robust ecosystem of SDKs, Drupal can effectively rival services like Contentful as the only end-to-end API-first CMS available on the market, although there is a long way to go to achieve a comprehensive set of SDKs for a sufficiently wide range of technologies. In that sense, whereas SDKs are not inherently tied to typical Drupal development, they play an important role as bridges to other technologies and as an integral component of application ecosystems backed by Drupal.

Generally, SDKs in the decoupled Drupal ecosystem aim to compensate for the lack of understanding that many developers new to Drupal have of its web services and how to consume them. For instance, Waterwheel.js (formerly known as Hydrant) and Waterwheel.swift (formerly known as the Drupal iOS SDK) aid developers of JavaScript and Swift, respectively, in building Drupal-backed applications. With SDKs, developers do not need to memorize nuances such as how fields of differing cardinalities are exposed in JSON responses.

The Waterwheel Ecosystem

The Waterwheel ecosystem is an emerging set of SDKs built by the Drupal community that cater to developers of applications in non-Drupal technologies. If you'll forgive the flawed metaphor for a moment, Waterwheel helps developers "speak" Drupal's language by facilitating communication with less overhead between Drupal and disparate technologies. Currently, there are two SDKs available in JavaScript (ES6) and Swift respectively, along with an Ember add-on and React reference build.

Waterwheel.js

Released in 2016, Waterwheel.js is a helper library that helps JavaScript developers consume and manipulate Drupal content.

Note   Waterwheel.js is available on GitHub at `https://github.com/acquia/waterwheel.js` and on NPM at `http://npmjs.org/package/waterwheel`. Previously, Waterwheel.js also included support for the Entity Query API module (`https://www.drupal.org/project/entityqueryapi`) and its query operations, but it has since been superseded by the JSON API module (see Chapters 8 and 13).

Although Waterwheel.js contains an HTTP client that fits Drupal like a glove, it is particularly versatile as developers can use it on the server side to issue API calls within Node.js during the server-side execution of a framework like Ember or React. In addition, you can use Waterwheel.js on the client side to conduct asynchronous requests after the browser loads the client bundle. This means Waterwheel.js is *universal* in that its code can be shared across the client/server boundary.

Due to the flexibility of Waterwheel.js, Drupal developers can also use it to enhance the client-side experience of existing monolithic Drupal sites via AJAX-like interactions or other HTTP clients that specialize in asynchronous requests such as superagent or axios. As it is intended for use as a foundation for JavaScript frameworks, it is optimal for both fully and progressively decoupled Drupal use cases.

Note   The superagent and axios libraries are available on NPM at `https://www.npmjs.com/package/superagent` and `https://www.npmjs.com/package/axios`, respectively.

Because Waterwheel.js is the easiest entry point for many developers building consumer applications, we explore its features in more detail in the upcoming sections.

Installing and Building Waterwheel.js

The easiest way to install Waterwheel.js is to clone the GitHub repository directly.

```
$ git clone git@github.com:acquia/waterwheel.js.git
```

You can also clone the GitHub repository through HTTPS.

```
$ git clone https://github.com/acquia/waterwheel.js.git
```

To install development dependencies such as axios and qs (a library that handles query strings), you can use the shorthand of npm install to fetch the libraries Waterwheel.js needs.

```
$ npm i
```

To run tests and check coverage, run the shorthand test command.

```
$ npm t
```

Finally, the most crucial step of any client-side JavaScript application is to generate a production-ready bundle that contains a minified version of all dependencies. The following command creates a single bundle file in the dist directory containing all of the built-in functionality of Waterwheel.js.

```
$ npm run build
```

Instantiating Waterwheel.js

To create a new instance of Waterwheel.js on a Node.js server supporting ES6, you can use the const keyword to require the Waterwheel module. Thereafter, you can instantiate a new waterwheel by providing an object argument containing the Drupal source's URI and an OAuth 2.0 access token (for more information on OAuth 2.0, see Chapter 9).[1]

```
// On a Node.js server
const Waterwheel = require('waterwheel');
const waterwheel = new Waterwheel({
  base: 'http://drupal-backend.dd:8083',
  oauth: {
    grant_type: 'GRANT-TYPE',
    client_id: 'CLIENT-ID',
    client_secret: 'CLIENT-SECRET',
    username: 'USERNAME',
    password: 'PASSWORD'
  }
});
```

---

[1]So, Preston. "Getting Started with Waterwheel.js and Resource Discovery." Acquia Developer Center. 30 September 2016. Accessed 18 July 2018. https://dev.acquia.com/blog/getting-started-with-waterwheeljs-and-resource-discovery/30/09/2016/16911

To make Waterwheel available to a browser that supports ES6, you can import the generated bundle (see previous section) with <script> and add it to the window object. In progressively decoupled scenarios, you can also use Drupal asset libraries to include the client-ready bundle.

```
// On a browser supporting ES6
// <script type="text/javascript" src="/path/to/waterwheel.js"></script>
const waterwheel = new window.Waterwheel({
  base: 'http://drupal-backend.dd:8083',
  oauth: {
    grant_type: 'GRANT-TYPE',
    client_id: 'CLIENT-ID',
    client_secret: 'CLIENT-SECRET',
    username: 'USERNAME',
    password: 'PASSWORD'
  }
});
```

Many browsers today still lack support for ES6, in which case you can still include the client bundle with a traditional <script> tag before defining a waterwheel global in ES5.

```
// On a browser not supporting ES6
// <script type="text/javascript" src="/path/to/waterwheel.js"></script>
var waterwheel = new window.Waterwheel({
  base: 'http://drupal-backend.dd:8083',
  oauth: {
    grant_type: 'GRANT-TYPE',
    client_id: 'CLIENT-ID',
    client_secret: 'CLIENT-SECRET',
    username: 'USERNAME',
    password: 'PASSWORD'
  }
});
```

When you instantiate Waterwheel, you can also provide other properties to the argument object that might be useful for your Waterwheel-driven consumer application. For instance, you can provide a timeout argument that indicates how long a request can idle before Waterwheel cancels it. The following is a list of possible additional properties that Waterwheel optionally accepts, taken directly from the README as of this writing.[2]

- `base`: The base path for your Drupal instance. All request paths will be built from this base.

- `resources`: A JSON object that represents the resources available to `waterwheel` (see next two sections).

- `oauth`: An object containing information required for fetching and refreshing OAuth Bearer tokens. Waterwheel recommends the Simple OAuth module (see Chapter 9).

  - `grant_type`: The type of OAuth 2.0 grant. As of this writing `password` is the only supported value.

  - `client_id`: The ID of your client.

  - `client_secret`: The secret of your client.

  - `username`: The user's username.

  - `password`: The user's password.

- `timeout`: How long an HTTP request should idle before being canceled.

- `accessCheck`: Indicates whether authentication should be used. Possible values are `true` and `false`.

- `jsonapiPrefix`: If you have overridden the JSON API prefix, specify it here and Waterwheel will use this over the default of `jsonapi`.

- `validation`: A boolean that defaults to `true`. If set to `false`, every request will ignore any existing OAuth information, allowing you to make requests without any authentication. If you have an open API, then the Simple OAuth module is not necessary.

---

[2]"Waterwheel." GitHub. 30 August 2017. Accessed 18 July 2018. `https://github.com/acquia/waterwheel.js/blob/master/README.md`

Resource Discovery

Developers of consumer applications often grapple with the challenges of implementing forms of client-side validation that mirror the server-side validation all requests eventually undergo once received by the server. With the help of the OpenAPI specification, represented in Drupal by the OpenAPI module (see Chapter 24 for more about OpenAPI, a specification for self-documenting APIs), Waterwheel.js enables a feature known as *resource discovery.*

Specifically, resource discovery allows consumer applications to understand the Drupal content schema and avoid validation pitfalls without relying on the back-and-forth with Drupal as the source for validation. This is crucial as among Drupal's key features is content modeling flexibility, which means that new content types and fields therein can be added or removed arbitrarily.

Because consumer applications are necessarily unaware of how Drupal users have modeled content on the CMS, and because developers typically lack a comprehensive understanding of the serialization of entities in Drupal for web services, client-side validation against a server-side Drupal content schema can be particularly difficult. Consumer applications might also wish to add their own elements to the content model that reside adjacent to Drupal's content model, especially if they are working with other data sources. In one of the most important benefits, consumer applications can perform client-side validation without needing to consult the server at all.

In Waterwheel.js, resource discovery allows consumer application developers to consume a metadata object when they instantiate `waterwheel` that contains information about which entities and fields are available on Drupal for retrieval and manipulation.

Populating Resources with Resource Discovery

To populate resources available to Waterwheel.js, you can provide a resources manifest to enable resource discovery. Waterwheel.js can automatically process an OpenAPI schema JSON file and validate any user-generated content against those responses before issuing requests against Drupal.

Inspect the following example, for instance, which imports the OpenAPI schema from a JSON file and incorporates it into the data available to Waterwheel.js.

```
// On a Node.js server
const Waterwheel = require('waterwheel');
const waterwheel = new Waterwheel({
```

```
  base: 'http://drupal-backend.dd:8083',
  resources: require('./resources.json'),
  oauth: {
    grant_type: 'GRANT-TYPE',
    client_id: 'CLIENT-ID',
    client_secret: 'CLIENT-SECRET',
    username: 'USERNAME',
    password: 'PASSWORD'
  }
});
```

If you wish to populate the Waterwheel.js resources later and not during instantiation, you can do so with the populateResources() method, which issues an additional API call to a resource provided by the OpenAPI Drupal module. Here we see the method invoked with an ES6 promise to handle the response.

```
waterwheel.populateResources('http://drupal-test.dd:8083/resources.json')
  .then(res => {
  // ...
  });
```

Once you have populated the internal resources of Waterwheel.js, you can access them using the getAvailableResources() method. The response returned by the promise will contain an array of available resources, as illustrated in the following comment. You can then validate incoming requests on resources against this array.

```
waterwheel.getAvailableResources()
  .then(res => {
    /*
      [ 'comment',
        'file',
        'menu',
        'node.article',
        'node.page',
        'node_type.content_type',
        'query',
        'taxonomy_term.tags',
```

```
        'taxonomy_vocabulary',
        'user' ]
    */
});
```

> **Note**   The OpenAPI Drupal module is available on Drupal.org at `https://www.drupal.org/project/openapi`. Consult Chapter 24 for more details on OpenAPI.

Consuming and Manipulating Drupal with Waterwheel.js

Waterwheel.js, like Contenta.js (discussed later in the chapter), provides a bridge between JavaScript developers and Drupal, allowing them to write in their native language against Drupal's web services to retrieve and manipulate content.

Retrieving Content with Waterwheel.js

To retrieve content with Waterwheel.js, you can use the `get()` method on the `api` object, identifying the type (and bundle if necessary) in the process. All queries in Waterwheel.js return ES6 promises. Because Waterwheel.js requires both the entity type and bundle to construct the appropriate resource path, we must identify both when we call `get()` by identifying the appropriate resource within the `api` object.

```
// Node represents type with varied bundles
waterwheel.api['node:article'].get(1) // .then( ...
waterwheel.api['node:page'].get(1) // .then( ...

// User represents both type and bundle
waterwheel.api['user'].get(1) // .then( ...
```

The `get()` method accepts two arguments: the `identifier` of the requested entity, which is required (e.g., `nid`, `tid`, `uid`, etc.) for core REST, and the `format` of the response, which is optional and defaults to `json`.

```
waterwheel.api['node:article'].get(1)
  .then(res => {
    // Drupal JSON response
  })
```

```
.catch(err => {
  // Error
});
```

To request an entity serialized as XML, include the desired format argument:

```
waterwheel.api['node:article'].get(1, 'xml')
  .then(res => {
    // Drupal JSON response
  })
  .catch(err => {
    // Error
  });
```

Creating Content with Waterwheel.js

With Waterwheel.js, you can also create a new entity in core REST by issuing a POST request and invoking the post() method. The following invocation of the post() method creates a node of type *Basic page* with the title of "Hello Drupal."

The post() method accepts two arguments: the body of the desired content entity, which is formatted in such a way that Drupal will be able to deserialize it into a Drupal entity, and the format, which is optional and defaults to JSON.

```
waterwheel.api['node:page'].post({
  "type": [
    {"target_id": "page"}
  ],
  "title": [
    {"value": "Hello Drupal"}
  ],
  "body": [
    {"value": "How are you today?"}
  ]
})
  .then(res => {
    // 201 Created
  })
```

```
  .catch(err => {
    // Error
  });
```

Updating Content with Waterwheel.js

We can also issue PATCH requests, or update operations, against any content entity in Drupal's core REST by invoking the patch() method, which accepts three arguments: the identifier of the entity needing an update (required), the body containing the updated fields of the entity (required), and the optional format. The following query updates the title and body of an article with an nid of 1.

```
waterwheel.api['node:article'].patch(1, {
  "nid": [
    {"value": "1"}
  ],
  "type": [
    {"target_id": "article"}
  ],
  "title": [
    {"value": "New title"}
  ],
  "body": [
    {"value": "New node"}
  ]
})
  .then(res => {
    // Updated entity in JSON
  })
  .catch(err => {
    // Error
  });
```

Similar to typical core REST responses, this PATCH query returns the newly updated JSON object in the response, which can then be handled in the fulfilled promise.

Deleting Content with Waterwheel.js

To delete an entity with Waterwheel.js, we simply need to provide the identifier as an argument when we invoke the `delete()` method, and our Drupal entity is deleted.

```
waterwheel.api['user'].delete(2)
  .then(res => {
    // 204 No Content
  })
  .catch(err => {
    // Error
  });
```

Retrieving Content with JSON API and Waterwheel.js

If you have JSON API installed on your Drupal site (see Chapters 8 and 12 for a full overview), you can employ Waterwheel.js to issue queries against JSON API as well with the help of the `jsonapi` object, which contains a `get()` method for retrieving both individual content entities and entity collections.

As of this writing, only retrieval (`get()`), creation (`post()`), and deletion (`delete()`) are supported among the JSON API features of Waterwheel.js.

The `get()` method accepts three arguments:

- `resource`: The bundle and entity to be requested.

- `params`: Any other arguments required by your query, which are recast as query string arguments before the request is issued.

- `id`: The UUID of the entity to be requested.

To retrieve a collection, you can supply the bundle and entity type as a string, which forms the first argument, as you can see in the example given here. The following code retrieves a default collection of articles from JSON API.

```
waterwheel.jsonapi.get('node/article', {})
  .then(res => {
    // Handle response
  })
  .catch(err => {
    // Error
  });
```

To retrieve a single resource, we can supply a third argument that is the UUID of the entity in question. In this case, we are retrieving the article having the UUID expressed in the argument.

```
waterwheel.jsonapi.get('node/article', {}, 'bc4acb41-d3fe-4e19-a43b-
c51665dab367')
  .then(res => {
    // Handle response
  })
  .catch(err => {
    // Error
  });
```

Thanks to JSON API, we can also retrieve related resources contained in relationships within a requested resource. This means that in conjunction with the article, we can also fetch the related user that authored the article by referring to the uid contained within the article entity. We accomplish this by "overloading" the UUID argument to state the relationship.

```
waterwheel.jsonapi.get('node/article', {}, 'bc4acb41-d3fe-4e19-a43b-
c51665dab367/uid')
  .then(res => {
    // Handle response
  })
  .catch(err => {
    // Error
  });
```

Finally, we can also use the second params argument to perform query operations on the fly on any collections that we might wish to retrieve. Common examples of these can be found in Chapter 12, and a few are reproduced here.

To sort by title in ascending order, we can provide a sort query string argument as follows, reflecting the relative path /jsonapi/node/article?sort=title.

```
waterwheel.jsonapi.get('node/article', {
  sort: 'title'
})
  .then(res => {
```

```
    // Handle response
  })
  .catch(err => {
    // Error
  });
```

Prefixing the field name with a hyphen gives us the collection sorted by title in descending order, reflecting the path /jsonapi/node/article?sort=-title.

```
waterwheel.jsonapi.get('node/article', {
  sort: '-title'
})
  .then(res => {
    // Handle response
  })
  .catch(err => {
    // Error
  });
```

We can also limit the collection to only 25 entries, reflecting the path /jsonapi/node/article?page[limit]=25.

```
waterwheel.jsonapi.get('node/article', {
  page: {
    limit: '25'
  }
})
  .then(res => {
    // Handle response
  })
  .catch(err => {
    // Error
  });
```

We can ensure that only articles 26 through 50 are represented in the initial collection, represented by the path /jsonapi/node/article?page[limit]=25&page[offset]=25.

```
waterwheel.jsonapi.get('node/article', {
  page: {
    limit: '25',
    offset: '25'
  }
})
  .then(res => {
    // Handle response
  })
  .catch(err => {
    // Error
  });
```

As a final example, we can define our own filter—in this case allowing only those articles with an identifier of 5 or higher—and apply it to the collection, here reflecting the path constructed as follows:

```
/jsonapi/node/article
?filter[nid_filter][condition][value]=5
&filter[nid_filter][condition][ficld]=nid
&filter[nid_filter][condition][operator]=%3C
```

Here, %3C represents the left angle bracket <. As you can see, thanks to the built-in query handling present in Waterwheel.js, we don't need to use the UTF-8 replacement.

```
waterwheel.jsonapi.get('node/article', {
  filter: {
    nid_filter: {
      condition: {
        value: '5',
        field: 'nid',
        operator: '<'
      }
    }
  }
})
```

```
.then(res => {
  // Handle response
})
.catch(err => {
  // Error
});
```

Creating Content with JSON API and Waterwheel.js

Waterwheel.js also allows us to create and delete content entities exposed by JSON API, but as of this writing it does not permit us to update them through a PATCH request.

The first argument—the concatenated bundle and entity type—of post() and delete() are identical to get() on the jsonapi object. However, the second argument differs; in post(), it is the desired data of the article to be created, whereas in delete(), it is the UUID of the entity to be deleted.

In this first example, we create an article with predefined data that Drupal will use to construct the entity.

```
const postData = {
  'data': {
    'type': 'node--article',
    'attributes': {
      'langcode': 'en',
      'title': 'My stealthily created new article',
      'status': '1',
      'promote': '0',
      'sticky': '0',
      'default_langcode': '1',
      'path': null,
      'body': {
        'value': 'Say hello to my stealthily created new article.'
      }
    }
  }
};
```

```
waterwheel.jsonapi.post('node/article', postData)
  .then(res => {
    // Handle response
  })
  .catch(err => {
    // Error
  });
```

Deleting Content with JSON API and Waterwheel.js

In this second example, we delete an entity by referring to its UUID in our invocation of delete(). Notice the difference in the argument from post().

```
waterwheel.jsonapi.delete('node/article', 'bc4acb41-d3fe-4e19-a43b-
c51665dab367/uid')
  .then(res => {
    // Handle response
  })
  .catch(err => {
    // Error
  });
```

Waterwheel.swift

Formerly known as the Drupal iOS SDK, Waterwheel.swift offers robust support for Drupal 8's core REST API and common Swift consumer needs like session management and authentication capabilities. Because it is intended for integration with Swift, Waterwheel.swift supports iOS, macOS, tvOS, and watchOS. Although a full inspection of Waterwheel.swift's possibilities is beyond the scope of this book, we highlight a few key characteristics here.

Thanks to Swift, Waterwheel.swift benefits from considerable performance advantages over its antecedent, the Drupal iOS SDK, which was implemented in Objective-C. As a result, developers building Swift applications can take advantage of the language's closures among other language features.

For example, for iOS, Waterwheel.swift provides a ready-made login button that developers can subclass or place into any desired space in the view. This button can be employed in concert with a customized `LoginViewController` (`waterwheelLoginViewController`) that provides username and password fields out of the box to allow developers to include Drupal user login and logout functionality into a Swift application with minimal overhead.

In conclusion, Waterwheel.swift transforms the Swift developer experience for Drupal and renders it effortless. Thanks to Swift, you can take advantage of next-generation syntactic features for Apple technologies and exchange data with Drupal without having to learn or understand Drupal's complex and often unwieldy web services ecosystem.

Note   Waterwheel.swift is available on GitHub at `https://github.com/ kylebrowning/waterwheel.swift`, and a demo application is also available at `https://github.com/kylebrowning/waterwheel.swift/tree/4.x/ waterwheelDemo`.

---

ember-drupal-waterwheel

In this section and the next, we dig into elements of the add-ons, plug-ins, and reference builds that are available for developers building consumer applications in Ember and React as part of the Waterwheel ecosystem. In later sections, we move into the Contenta ecosystem.

The `ember-drupal-waterwheel` add-on, authored by Chris Hamper (hampercm), aids Ember developers building consumer applications backed by Drupal. As an example, `ember-drupal-waterwheel` is compatible with the FastBoot add-on, which provides server-side rendering for Ember applications.

We can use the `ember-drupal-waterwheel` add-on at different stages of Ember application development, whether we are connecting an existing Ember application to a Drupal web services provider (e.g., Contenta, Reservoir, or Headless Lightning) or creating a new Ember application from scratch.

Although Ember ships out of the box with a generic `JSONAPIAdapter` that handles requests and responses from a variety of APIs adhering to the JSON API specification, the `ember-drupal-waterwheel` add-on's included adapter and serializer work with Drupal-specific JSON API requests and responses, along with OAuth 2.0 authentication provided by the Simple OAuth module (see Chapter 9).

To begin, use Ember CLI, Ember's own command-line interface, to install the add-on.

```
$ ember new my-app
$ cd my-app
$ ember install ember-drupal-waterwheel
```

ember-drupal-waterwheel allows you to quickly generate Ember models, routes, and templates that reflect Drupal entity types on the fly. By using the ember generate command (or its shorthand, ember g) with drupal-prefixed arguments, we can create ready-made Ember application assets that can be modified from their foundation.

```
$ ember g drupal-article
$ ember g drupal-tag
```

We can also generate the required models, routes, and templates for custom Drupal entities by passing in the custom entity name as an argument following the generic entity type name.

```
$ ember g drupal-entity my_custom_entity
```

Note   The ember-drupal-waterwheel add-on is available on GitHub at https://github.com/acquia/ember-drupal-waterwheel.

---

react-waterwheel-app

The react-waterwheel-app reference application (see Figure 16-2) integrates with a Drupal back end using the Waterwheel.js library in conjunction with a boilerplate React application, which offers a simple editorial interface for CRUD on content entities.

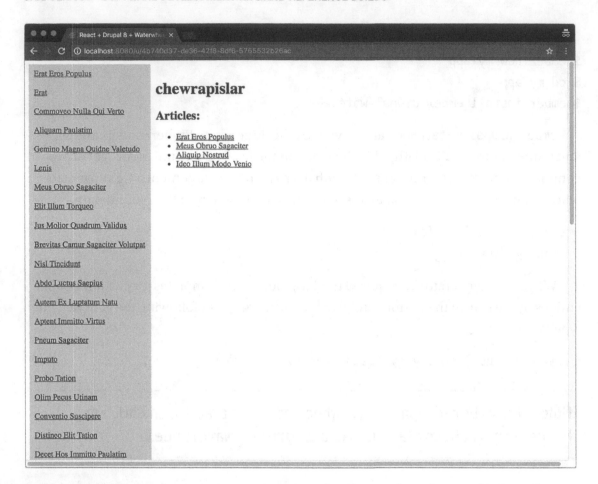

Figure 16-2. *A user's page on* `react-waterwheel-app` *that shows a listing of content associated with that user*

Another similarity between the React- and Ember-driven reference applications in the Waterwheel ecosystem is easy configurability thanks to the `src/config.js` file. In `react-waterwheel-app`, you can connect the React application to a Drupal web services provider by saving the file with the appropriate Drupal hostname and credentials needed for OAuth 2.0.

To kick things off with `react-waterwheel-app` and a connected Drupal site, clone the repository from GitHub and run the commands shown here. The `react-waterwheel-app` project employs Yarn as a dependency manager, which is in line with many modern JavaScript ecosystems.

```
$ git clone https://github.com/acquia/react-waterwheel-app
$ cd react-waterwheel-app
$ yarn install
```

Note   The `react-waterwheel-app` reference build is available on GitHub at
`https://github.com/acquia/react-waterwheel-app`.

The Contenta Ecosystem

As discussed in Chapter 15, the community-led Contenta distribution is an effort to
provide a comprehensive back end for decoupling Drupal that is feature-rich and
integrates seamlessly with a variety of demonstrations and reference builds that are
optimized for use with Contenta rather than with a generic Drupal back end. The
Contenta team has also made significant efforts in reaching other communities that have
graciously contributed referenceable consumers.

Although Contenta has a wider range of reference builds than the Waterwheel
ecosystem, as of this writing these often tend to be in a great deal of flux and as a result
unstable. However, some of the reference builds are robust enough to figure in this
chapter. At the end of this section, we also cover Contenta.js, which was released in July
2018 to provide a full Node.js middleware layer specifically for the Contenta CMS.

Contenta Reference Builds

Unlike the Waterwheel ecosystem, which aims to provide generic SDKs that developers
can use with any decoupled Drupal back end, the Contenta ecosystem places greater
emphasis on demoable applications that adhere to a single design, namely the Umami
theme produced by the Out of the Box initiative. This has the particular advantage of
facilitating comparisons across multiple consumers, which benefits evaluators.

Although a comprehensive and in-depth look at each of the reference builds is
beyond the scope of this volume, and the reference builds themselves are less stable
than the Contenta CMS, here we cover a few of the most popular Contenta consumers.

contenta_angular

The `contenta_angular` reference application aims to provide a set of best practices for
building not only Drupal-backed Angular applications but also Angular applications
in general. To this end, `contenta_angular` employs Angular CLI as its command-
line interface of `choice` (see Chapter 19 for more about Angular CLI), which includes
functionality for application scaffolding, testing, and more.

In addition, `contenta_angular` is offline-capable thanks to the use of service workers. The `contenta_angular` service worker caches external API calls and files loaded from Drupal on the client side, which means that the entire application is capable of functioning offline. The `contenta_angular` application also includes support for HTTP/2 server push, which allows the server to initiate transmission of JavaScript and CSS assets as soon as the first request is issued.

Finally, `contenta_angular` makes use of several other elements of the Angular ecosystem such as a Material Design-based design that includes Sass compilation provided for free by Angular CLI. It also adheres to the `ngrx 4` library's approach to state management, in which requests to remote APIs are considered side effects so that a failing request does not lead to an overly optimistic state change that is difficult to revert.[3]

We can install `contenta_angular` using the following steps as of this writing. At the end of this process, the local build is made available at `http://localhost:4200`.

```
$ npm install -g @angular/cli
$ git clone https://github.com/contentacms/contenta_angular.git
$ cd contenta_angular
$ npm install
$ ng serve
```

From there, you can change configurations present in `ngsw-manifest.json`, `src/environments/environment.prod.js`, and `src/environments/environment.js` to provide a different decoupled Drupal host besides the public Contenta host.

Note   `contenta_angular` is available on GitHub at `https://github.com/contentacms/contenta_angular`, and a demo application is available as of this writing at `https://contenta-angular.firebaseapp.com`.

---

contenta_ember

The `contenta_ember` reference application also uses the official command-line interface of its framework, Ember (see Chapter 21 for more about Ember). With Ember CLI, developers have access to scaffolding tools similar to those of Angular CLI, built-in

---

[3]"Contenta Angular." GitHub. 10 January 2018. Accessed 24 July 2018. `https://github.com/contentacms/contenta_angular/blob/master/README.md`

testing (Ember places a heavy emphasis on automated testing), and bundling that produces production-ready code.

One of the most compelling features of `contenta_ember` is its capability for Ember code generation. With the help of Ember CLI, you can generate bare-metal Ember models, components, and other code with a single command.[4]

Installing `contenta_ember` is just as straightforward as installing `contenta_angular`.

```
$ git clone https://github.com/contentacms/contenta_ember.git
$ cd contenta_ember
$ npm install
$ ember serve
```

To run tests locally once, or to run tests on every change to a file, use the following commands, respectively.

```
$ ember test
$ ember test --server
```

To build your Ember application for production-ready use, you can use the `ember build` command, which also accepts a variety of flags.

```
$ ember build --environment production
```

Note   `contenta_ember` is available on GitHub at `https://github.com/contentacms/contenta_ember`, and a demo application is available as of this writing at `http://umami.emc23.com`.

---

contenta_react

The `contenta_react` reference application leverages an emerging project in the React ecosystem, namely Create React App, the objective of which is to resolve many of the challenges for those beginning their journeys with React by providing a ready-made boilerplate with some of the most important React features.

---

[4]"Contenta – Ember Frontend." GitHub. 3 January 2018. Accessed 24 July 2018. `https://github.com/contentacms/contenta_ember/blob/master/README.md`

Note   Create React App is available on GitHub at `https://github.com/` `facebook/create-react-app`.

contenta_react also employs Redux (a predictable state container for JavaScript applications), Aphrodite (a provider of framework-agnostic CSS-in-JavaScript), and server-side rendering.[5]

As of this writing, to install `contenta_react` and to get started quickly with a local server at `https://localhost:3000`, use the following commands.

```
$ git clone https://github.com/contentacms/contenta_react.git
$ cd contenta_react
$ yarn install
$ yarn start
```

To run the application in development mode, where the page reloads on every edit to a file and the console logs development errors, you can use the following command.

```
$ yarn run start:dev
```

To create a production-ready build that is placed in the `build` folder, use the following commands. Running `yarn start` after the `build` command will initialize the application in production with server-side rendering of the initial page state.

```
$ yarn build
$ yarn start
```

Note   `contenta_react` is available on GitHub at `https://github.com/` `contentacms/contenta_react`.

---

[5]"Contenta React Demo." GitHub. 10 July 2017. Accessed 24 July 2018. `https://github.com/` `contentacms/contenta_react/blob/master/README.md`

contenta_vue_nuxt

The contenta_vue_nuxt reference application states a vision of reflecting the same characteristics that popularized Vue.js (for more about Vue.js, see Chapter 20). This ideal state denotes a low barrier to entry, incremental adoptability, code readability, and learnability for easy onboarding.[6]

Contenta's Vue.js consumer also leverages Nuxt.js, which provides server-side rendering for Vue.js, but it does not use Vue CLI. Both of these projects are discussed in Chapter 20.

To install contenta_vue_nuxt, use the following commands.

```
$ git clone https://github.com/contentacms/contenta_vue_nuxt.git
$ cd contenta_vue_nuxt
$ npm install
```

To spin up a local environment with hot reloading (refresh on every code edit), execute the following.

```
$ npm run dev
```

To run unit tests, generate a build for production, and launch a production server, execute the following commands in order.

```
$ npm test
$ npm run build
$ npm run start
```

Note   contenta_vue_nuxt is available on GitHub at https://github.com/contentacms/contenta_vue_nuxt, and a demo application is available as of this writing at https://contentanuxt.now.sh.

If the discussions of Waterwheel and Contenta reference applications felt overly superficial and introductory, it is due to the fact that we have not yet introduced the JavaScript technologies that undergird them. We return to each of these for inspiration in the process of building our own Drupal-backed JavaScript consumers in Part 5.

---

[6]"Drupal 8 Headless Example with Contenta CMS / JSON API and Vue.js." GitHub. 25 April 2018. Accessed 24 July 2018. https://github.com/contentacms/contenta_vue_nuxt/blob/master/README.md

Contenta.js

Released to complement the use of Contenta CMS for JavaScript consumers, Contenta.js addresses the pressing need for a canonical Node.js proxy acting as middleware between the Drupal content API layer and a JavaScript application on the front end. As more users began to adopt Contenta CMS for their own projects, the Contenta team noticed that this requirement was rapidly leading to fragmentation in the form of agencies each having their own unique Node.js proxy to serve Drupal content to a variety of JavaScript consumers.[7]

There are several reasons why a Node.js middleware layer is essential. First, when a decoupled Drupal architecture requires the aggregation of data from multiple sources, Node.js is a better mechanism for retrieving those data due to its nonblocking I/O. Second, Node.js is an explicit requirement when performing server-side rendering for universal applications. Finally, a middleware layer in Node.js provides caching, which allows for requests to retrieve data from the cache in Node.js rather than resorting directly to the data's origin. Because of the varied motivations for Contenta.js, the stated philosophy for the middleware is to "fork and go."[8]

The stated goal of Contenta.js is "to bring consistency and collaboration—a set of common practices so agencies can focus on creating the best software possible with Node.js." Indeed, it comes with certain features that developers consider important for a Node.js proxy.

First, Contenta.js contains seamless integration with any Contenta CMS installation that exposes APIs as long as the URI of the site is provided in configuration. Contenta installations that have the JSON API, JSON-RPC (see Chapter 23), Subrequests (see Chapter 23), and OpenAPI (see Chapter 24) modules enabled need no further configuration.

Second, Contenta.js includes several useful features for development, including a multithreaded Node.js server, a Subrequests server that facilitates request aggregation, a Contenta-provided Redis integration, a type-safe development environment making use of Flow, and a more developer-friendly approach to configuring CORS.

---

[7]Aguiló Bosch, Mateu. "Introducing Contenta JS." *Human Bits*. 16 July 2018. Accessed 24 July 2018. `http://humanbits.es/web-development/2018/07/16/contentajs/`

[8]"ContentaJS." GitHub. 21 July 2018. Accessed 24 July 2018. `https://github.com/contentacms/contentajs/blob/master/README.md`

Note   Contenta.js is available on GitHub at `https://github.com/contentacms/contentajs`.

Conclusion

Whereas headless CMSs only traffic in open source when it comes to their consumer SDKs, decoupled Drupal touts the unique benefit of being an open source CMS from end to end, whether you are employing reference builds or SDKs from the Contenta or Waterwheel ecosystems. With SDKs for a variety of languages and reference builds for a variety of JavaScript technologies, Contenta and Waterwheel both articulate a promising future for developers of consumer applications backed by decoupled Drupal.

Indeed, the better integrated Drupal can become with other technologies, namely JavaScript frameworks and native mobile technologies such as Swift, the more assured Drupal's API-first future becomes, and the more robust Drupal's web services can be based on feedback from consumer application developers. With capable libraries and references, decoupled Drupal can unlock adoption by other technologies and communities that might never even have searched for Drupal in the first place.

In Part 5, after spending all of our time in Drupal or between Drupal and its consumers, we turn now to the front end and the consumer. Because every consumer is different, it is impossible to consider each technology in these subsequent chapters. As a result, we focus solely on the most important JavaScript frameworks that also have native equivalents, namely Angular, Ember, React, and Vue. After introducing each of these projects, we build a simple application with an identical interface across all four that highlights the differences between them and that leverages all of the foundations we have established so far.

PART V

Integration with Consumers

In Part 4, we conducted a brief survey of the burgeoning decoupled Drupal ecosystem and its most frequently leveraged components, including API-first distributions like Contenta, Reservoir, and Headless Lightning and SDKs and reference builds that assist developers with a starting point for their own implementations.

In these chapters, we delve into some of the most commonly used JavaScript technologies that power Drupal-backed applications, namely React, React Native, Angular, Vue.js, and Ember. In the process, we explore the spectrum of opinionatedness across all of these technologies and constructed applications that interact with Drupal's web services. It is, of course, impossible to cover these projects with the comprehensiveness needed to explain all of their concepts, as each would warrant its own book and more.

The JavaScript technologies we scrutinize in these chapters run the gamut between limited view-focused libraries and highly opinionated MV* (model–view–anything) frameworks. Both categories of JavaScript technologies have seen large-scale adoption in the front-end development community. Nonetheless, there are significant differences between these tools along multiple dimensions.

For instance, although React falls on the less opinionated end of the spectrum, it also leaves many of the necessary decisions about other tools up to the developer, which can result in a challenging learning curve. Other tools, namely Angular and Ember, are highly opinionated about how they expect developers to use their features. As an example, Ember includes JSON API support as a default, whereas Angular obligates the use of

TypeScript. Meanwhile, React and Vue.js are often considered by many in the JavaScript community to be more flexible and to allow different solutions. For instance, whereas we can leverage Waterwheel.js freely by including it as a dependency in React, because Ember has a default adapter for JSON API, Waterwheel.js is superfluous.

Because React is the most popular of the JavaScript projects employed in the JavaScript community and it is well-represented in decoupled Drupal architectures today, we start our tour there. Afterward, we cover Drupal-backed applications in React Native, Angular, Vue.js, and Ember.

CHAPTER 17

React

React is a popular JavaScript view library frequently used in conjunction with other technologies to create single-page JavaScript applications. Started in 2013 by Facebook, React has quickly outpaced other similar projects in popularity due to its declarative approach to state, colocation of templates with view logic, and relative lack of opinionatedness about the stack, which means it is most dissimilar to Angular (see Chapter 19) and Ember (see Chapter 21). In the last several years, an extensive ecosystem has developed surrounding the core React library.

React calls itself a "JavaScript library for building user interfaces" and states the following on its home page:

> React makes it painless to create interactive UIs. Design simple views for each state in your application, and React will efficiently update and render just the right components when your data changes.[1]

Unlike other frameworks, React emphasizes its unique character as a library, not a traditional model–view–controller (MVC) framework. Due to its focus on providing reusable and nestable components, many choose to think of React as the view layer within an MVC architecture. Because it is solely a view library, architects frequently pair other technologies with React, and there is often less guidance when it comes to tooling choices.

Traditionally, MVC frameworks using a declarative approach and two-way data binding were obligated to apply changes directly on the DOM. AngularJS, for instance, manually updated DOM nodes. Meanwhile, React uses a *Virtual DOM*, which is an abstract DOM that allows different user interface states to be diffed (compared with all differences accounted for), thus facilitating the most efficient DOM manipulation possible.

---

[1]"React." React. 2018. Accessed 17 September 2018. `https://reactjs.org`

© Preston So 2018
P. So, *Decoupled Drupal in Practice*, https://doi.org/10.1007/978-1-4842-4072-4_17

Due to the lack of tooling coverage across the stack, React builds can be particularly challenging and burdensome. In many React architectures, decisions need to be made about whether to use the Flux architectural approach, the Redux binding library, and other smaller libraries such as `react-router`, now the most commonly used routing library for React applications. One final drawback of React is its spotty support for Web Components, which contrasts it with frameworks like Ember and presents issues of forward compatibility.[2]

Note   For more information about React, consult the web site at `https://reactjs.org`. For more information about Web Components support in React, consult the documentation at `https://reactjs.org/docs/web-components.html`.

Key Concepts in React

Whereas in previous years, the React ecosystem had a notoriously difficult learning curve, today the process of creating a React application is much simpler thanks to the `create-react-app` project, which provides a fully functioning React application without the need for additional build configuration in tools like Webpack and Babel.

Scaffolding a React Application and Installing Dependencies

To create a new `create-react-app` application, execute the following commands.

```
$ npx create-react-app ddip-react
$ cd ddip-react
$ yarn start
```

The final command triggers a local server to start and to make your React application available at `http://localhost:3000`. You can easily create a minified client-ready bundle with the following command.

```
$ yarn build
```

---

[2]So, Preston. "Decoupled Drupal with React." 8 April 2016. Accessed 17 September 2018. `http://prestonso.github.io/decoupled-drupal-react`

Note   npx is available on versions of npm 5.2 and higher.

We also need to include and install several dependencies that we will need in our code base, particularly `react-router-dom`, which, as one of the most common routing libraries in the React ecosystem, provides all of the capabilities of `react-router` along with the ability to create links across routes. We cover how to perform routing in React in due course. Note that to execute the following command, you will need to open a new terminal window or stop the local server.

```
$ yarn add react-router-dom
```

We will use `axios` to perform retrievals from the Drupal site that will back our application; we need to include it as well. If you require OAuth 2.0 authentication (see Chapter 9) as well, you might wish to consider Waterwheel.js (see Chapter 16), which comes with it included.

```
$ yarn add axios
```

At the end of this process, your `package.json` file should look like the following.

```json
{
  "name": "ddip-react",
  "version": "0.1.0",
  "private": true,
  "dependencies": {
    "axios": "^0.18.0",
    "react": "^16.5.2",
    "react-dom": "^16.5.2",
    "react-router-dom": "^4.3.1",
    "react-scripts": "2.0.3"
  },
  "scripts": {
    "start": "react-scripts start",
    "build": "react-scripts build",
    "test": "react-scripts test",
    "eject": "react-scripts eject"
  },
```

```
  "eslintConfig": {
    "extends": "react-app"
  },
  "browserslist": [
    ">0.2%",
    "not dead",
    "not ie <= 11",
    "not op_mini all"
  ]
}
```

Your directory structure should appear as follows (excluding the node_modules directory).

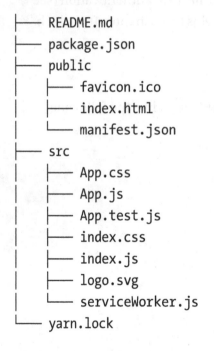

```
├── README.md
├── package.json
├── public
│   ├── favicon.ico
│   ├── index.html
│   └── manifest.json
├── src
│   ├── App.css
│   ├── App.js
│   ├── App.test.js
│   ├── index.css
│   ├── index.js
│   ├── logo.svg
│   └── serviceWorker.js
└── yarn.lock
```

Note   The remainder of this chapter is loosely based on and inspired by the code for react-waterwheel-app, authored by Matt Grill (drpal) and covered in Chapter 16.

The Index Component

As mentioned before, React has a concept of nestable and reusable *components* that include the overarching root component. Whenever we use those components in the context of the application, we often need to pass in *properties* that provide that component with differentiated information that it should render.

Within the src directory, we can create our first component, which create-react-app has already scaffolded for us and will be the index (root) component into which all other components will render. We need to fetch all of our dependencies. Change the contents of src/App.js to the following.

```
// src/App.js
import React, { Component } from 'react';
import {
  BrowserRouter as Router,
  Route,
  Link
} from 'react-router-dom';

class App extends Component {
  constructor(props) {
    super(props);
    this.state = {};
  }
  componentWillMount() {
    this.setState({
      articles: [
        {
          id: '3ca469da-b905-4a77-8d97-954abcdc4cf6',
          attributes: {
            title: 'Capto',
            uuid: '3ca469da-b905-4a77-8d97-954abcdc4cf6',
            created: 1526387013,
            body: {
              value: 'Camur'
            }
```

```
          }
        },
        {
          id: '1e1a4598-f9c7-4ce7-adbd-7603401cc23b',
          attributes: {
            title: 'Esse Ex Nibh Valde Valetudo',
            uuid: '1e1a4598-f9c7-4ce7-adbd-7603401cc23b',
            created: 1526387013,
            body: {
              value: 'Illum loquor persto plaga premo.'
            }
          }
        }
      ]
    });
  }

  render() {
    return (
      <div className="App">
        <h1>React app</h1>
      </div>
    );
  }
}

export default App;
```

It will be useful for us to look at each section of this code in turn to understand how React is handling certain important elements. First, we introduce all of our dependencies.

```
import React, { Component } from 'react';
import { render } from 'react-dom';
import {
  BrowserRouter as Router,
  Route,
  Link
} from 'react-router-dom';
```

Then, we implement a Component class and populate it with any properties that are defined when the component is instantiated by React.

```
class App extends Component {
  constructor(props) {
    super(props);
    this.state = {};
  }
}
```

Finally, we hook into React's component life cycle by using the componentWillMount() method to retrieve data. In this case, because we have not yet introduced Drupal, we are providing dummy data.

```
componentWillMount() {
  this.setState({
    articles: [
      {
        id: '3ca469da-b905-4a77-8d97-954abcdc4cf6',
        attributes: {
          title: 'Capto',
          uuid: '3ca469da-b905-4a77-8d97-954abcdc4cf6',
          created: 1526387013,
          body: {
            value: 'Camur'
          }
        }
      },
      {
        id: '1e1a4598-f9c7-4ce7-adbd-7603401cc23b',
        attributes: {
          title: 'Esse Ex Nibh Valde Valetudo',
          uuid: '1e1a4598-f9c7-4ce7-adbd-7603401cc23b',
          created: 1526387013,
          body: {
            value: 'Illum loquor persto plaga premo.'
          }
        }
```

```
    }
  ]
});
}
```

Finally, we render the component, but as you can see, we have not yet provided the data, and if you open your application with npm run start, the application is empty. In the next section, we cover React's native templating language, JSX.

Note   For more information about React components, consult the documentation at https://reactjs.org/docs/components-and-props.html.

React State and Declarative Rendering

Like other major frameworks and libraries, React includes a native approach to perform declarative rendering by colocating incoming properties with the markup of the components they concern. This leads to a highly legible template written in JSX, React's syntax extension to JavaScript that looks similar to HTML or XML. JSX can be used to render both traditional HTML elements as well as React components.

The first thing we will do is update our render() method with the logic necessary to render the articles into the application. Consider the following example and update src/App.js to reflect this current state.

```
// src/App.js
import React, { Component } from 'react';
import {
  BrowserRouter as Router,
  Route,
  Link
} from 'react-router-dom';

class App extends Component {
  constructor(props) {
    super(props);
    this.state = {};
  }
```

```
componentWillMount() {
  this.setState({
    articles: [
      {
        id: '3ca469da-b905-4a77-8d97-954abcdc4cf6',
        attributes: {
          title: 'Capto',
          uuid: '3ca469da-b905-4a77-8d97-954abcdc4cf6',
          created: 1526387013,
          body: {
            value: 'Camur'
          }
        }
      },
      {
        id: '1e1a4598-f9c7-4ce7-adbd-7603401cc23b',
        attributes: {
          title: 'Esse Ex Nibh Valde Valetudo',
          uuid: '1e1a4598-f9c7-4ce7-adbd-7603401cc23b',
          created: 1526387013,
          body: {
            value: 'Illum loquor persto plaga premo.'
          }
        }
      }
    ]
  });
}
render() {
  return (
    <div className="App">
      <h1>React app</h1>
      <ul>
        {this.state.articles && this.state.articles.map(article => (
          <li key={article.id}>
```

```
            {article.attributes.title}
            <ul>
              <li>{article.attributes.created}</li>
              <li>{article.attributes.body.value}</li>
            </ul>
          </li>
        ))}
      </ul>
    </div>
  );
  }
}

export default App;
```

Scrutinize the render() method just shown. As you can see, we are verifying that the data are present within the state object before accessing its values in a list underneath. In the process, we have created a simple content listing that you can also see in Figure 17-1.

React app

- Capto
  - 1526387013
  - Camur
- Esse Ex Nibh Valde Valetudo
  - 1526387013
  - Illum loquor persto plaga premo.

Figure 17-1. *The current state of our React application renders our dummy data*

Note   For more information about JSX, consult the documentation at https://reactjs.org/docs/introducing-jsx.html. For more information about declarative rendering, consult the documentation at https://reactjs.org/docs/rendering-elements.html.

React Routing and Components

Now, we can split our application into the primary view and a component that displays information about individual articles. To do this, we need to use React Router and provide a new component to React. In your src directory, create a new file named Article.js. This will be our new article detail component.

Insert the following into src/Article.js. As you can see, we are placing the information formerly contained inside the nested list within its own individual article detail component. We are also associating a type with article data for easier debugging thanks to type-checking in PropTypes.

```
// src/Article.js
import React from 'react';
import PropTypes from 'prop-types';

const Article = ({article}) => (
  <div className="article-detail">
    {article && (
      <article>
        <h2>{article.attributes.title}</h2>
        <ul>
          <li>{article.id}</li>
          <li>{article.attributes.created}</li>
        </ul>
        <div>{article.attributes.body.value}</div>
      </article>
    )}
  </div>
);

Article.propTypes = {
  article: PropTypes.object
};

export default Article;
```

Now, we can update our index component with logic that allows us to select articles. First, we need to import our new `Article` component so that our index component is aware of it. Then, we need to provide a routing mechanism that allows for articles to be selected and rendered based on their identifiers. Consider the following new state of `src/App.js`.

```
// src/App.js
import React, { Component } from 'react';
import {
  BrowserRouter as Router,
  Route,
  Link
} from 'react-router-dom';
import Article from './Article.js';

class App extends Component {
  constructor(props) {
    super(props);
    this.state = {};
  }
  componentWillMount() {
    this.setState({
      articles: [
        {
          id: '3ca469da-b905-4a77-8d97-954abcdc4cf6',
          attributes: {
            title: 'Capto',
            uuid: '3ca469da-b905-4a77-8d97-954abcdc4cf6',
            created: 1526387013,
            body: {
              value: 'Camur'
            }
          }
        },
        {
          id: '1e1a4598-f9c7-4ce7-adbd-7603401cc23b',
```

```
      attributes: {
        title: 'Esse Ex Nibh Valde Valetudo',
        uuid: '1e1a4598-f9c7-4ce7-adbd-7603401cc23b',
        created: 1526387013,
        body: {
          value: 'Illum loquor persto plaga premo.'
        }
      }
    }
  ]
});
}
render() {
  return (
    <div className="App">
      <h1>React app</h1>
      <Router>
        <div className="articles">
          <ul>
            {this.state.articles && this.state.articles.map(article => (
              <li key={article.id}>
                <Link to={`/article/${article.id}`}>{article.attributes.
                title}</Link>
              </li>
            ))}
          </ul>
          {this.state.articles &&
            <Route path="/article/:articleID" render={
            ({match}) => {
              let article = this.state.articles.find(article =>
              article.id === match.params.articleID);
              return (<Article article={article}/>);
            }
          }/>
          }
```

```
        </div>
      </Router>
    </div>
  );
  }
}

export default App;
```

When we look at our application again, we can see that on clicking one of the article links given, the detail component renders, as depicted in Figure 17-2.

React app

- Capto
- Esse Ex Nibh Valde Valetudo

Esse Ex Nibh Valde Valetudo

- 1e1a4598-f9c7-4ce7-adbd-7603401cc23b
- 1526387013

Illum loquor persto plaga premo.

Figure 17-2. *When we click one of the links, we see that the detail component updates and that the URL is changed to* /articles/ *followed by the UUID of the selected article*

Note   For more information about React components, consult the documentation at https://reactjs.org/docs/components-and-props.html.

Backing React with Drupal and JSON API

To back our React application with actual data exposed by an API, we employ the final state of the Drupal web site we built in Chapters 8 and 12 that provisions a JSON API-compliant web service. If you have not yet stood up a Drupal site with generated content and with JSON API enabled, return to Chapters 8 and 12 to proceed.

Retrieving Drupal Data with **axios**

With axios in tow, we can now issue a request to Drupal to retrieve the content items that we need to populate our application with authentic data. Replace src/App.js with the following, which replaces our dummy data in componentWillMount() with an axios-driven promise. Note that we have now included our axios dependency with a new import statement.

```
// src/App.js
import React, { Component } from 'react';
import {
  BrowserRouter as Router,
  Route,
  Link
} from 'react-router-dom';
import axios from 'axios';
import Article from './Article.js';

class App extends Component {
  constructor(props) {
    super(props);
    this.state = {};
  }
  componentWillMount() {
    axios.get('http://jsonapi-test.dd:8083/jsonapi/node/article')
      .then(res => this.setState( { articles: res.data.data }))
      .catch(console.log);
  }
  render() {
    return (
      <div className="App">
        <h1>React app</h1>
        <Router>
          <div className="articles">
            <ul>
              {this.state.articles && this.state.articles.map(article => (
                <li key={article.id}>
```

```
                <Link to={`/article/${article.id}`}>{article.attributes.
                title}</Link>
            </li>
        ))}
        </ul>
        {this.state.articles &&
            <Route path="/article/:articleID" render={
            ({match}) => {
                let article = this.state.articles.find(article =>
                article.id === match.params.articleID);
                return (<Article article={article}/>);
            }
            }/>
        }
        </div>
    </Router>
    </div>
    );
  }
}
```

```
export default App;
```

When we return to our application, we can see that Drupal data are now populating the React application correctly. This is also illustrated in Figure 17-3.

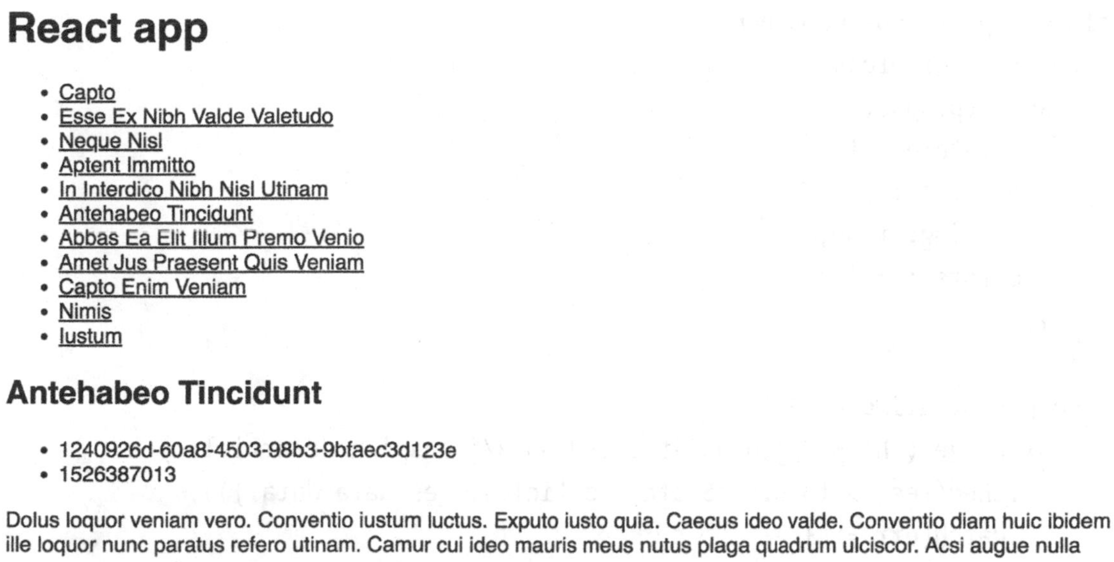

React app

- Capto
- Esse Ex Nibh Valde Valetudo
- Neque Nisl
- Aptent Immitto
- In Interdico Nibh Nisl Utinam
- Antehabeo Tincidunt
- Abbas Ea Elit Illum Premo Venio
- Amet Jus Praesent Quis Veniam
- Capto Enim Veniam
- Nimis
- Iustum

Antehabeo Tincidunt

- 1240926d-60a8-4503-98b3-9bfaec3d123e
- 1526387013

Dolus loquor veniam vero. Conventio iustum luctus. Exputo iusto quia. Caecus ideo valde. Conventio diam huic ibidem ille loquor nunc paratus refero utinam. Camur cui ideo mauris meus nutus plaga quadrum ulciscor. Acsi augue nulla

Figure 17-3. *Returning to our application indicates that we now have Drupal data populated*

Note   For more information about `axios`, consult the documentation at `https://github.com/axios/axios`.

Handling Errored and Loading States

Now, we can add some error handling and a loading state in case our Drupal site is taking a while to respond. To do this, though, we need to account for errored and loading states in our React application as well as our handling of promises. Replace the contents of `src/App.js` with the following to see this in action.

```
// src/App.js
import React, { Component } from 'react';
import {
  BrowserRouter as Router,
  Route,
  Link
} from 'react-router-dom';
import axios from 'axios';
import Article from './Article.js';
```

```
class App extends Component {
  constructor(props) {
    super(props);
    this.state = {
      articles: [],
      loading: true,
      errored: false
    };
  }
  componentWillMount() {
    axios.get('http://jsonapi-test.dd:8083/jsonapi/node/article')
      .then(res => this.setState({ articles: res.data.data }))
      .catch(err => {
        console.log(err);
        this.setState({ errored: true });
      })
      .finally(() => this.setState({ loading: false }));
  }
  render() {
    return (
      <div className="App">
        <h1>React app</h1>
        {this.state.errored ? (
          <p>Sorry, {'this'} information is not available at the moment.</p>
        ) : (
          <section>
            {this.state.loading ? (
              <p>Loading ...</p>
            ) : (
              <Router>
                <div className="articles">
                  <ul>
                    {this.state.articles && this.state.articles.map
                    (article => (
                      <li key={article.id}>
```

```
                <Link to={`/article/${article.id}`}>{article.
                attributes.title}</Link>
              </li>
            ))}
          </ul>
          {this.state.articles &&
            <Route path="/article/:articleID" render={
              ({match}) => {
                let article = this.state.articles.find(article =>
                article.id === match.params.articleID);
                return (<Article article={article}/>);
              }
            }/>
          }
        </div>
      </Router>
        )}
      </section>
      )}
    </div>
  );
  }
}

export default App;
```

There is quite a bit to dig into here, so let us dissect this code example piece by piece. First, we indicate to React's state machine that there are initial states for errored and loading, which are set to false and true, respectively.

```
constructor(props) {
  super(props);
  this.state = {
    articles: [],
    loading: true,
    errored: false
  };
}
```

Then, in the `componentWillMount()` method, we add better error handling and adjust the `loading` state to `true` once the promise is fulfilled fully.

```
componentWillMount() {
  axios.get('http://jsonapi-test.dd:8083/jsonapi/node/article')
    .then(res => this.setState({ articles: res.data.data }))
    .catch(err => {
      console.log(err);
      this.setState({ errored: true });
    })
    .finally(() => this.setState({ loading: false }));
}
```

Then, in our `render()` method, we have logic that uses the ternary operator to check whether the `loading` and `errored` states are `true`. In the first conditional statement, if the `errored` state returns `true`, then only the error statement is displayed. Otherwise, if the `loading` state is `true`, a loading placeholder displays until the promise is fulfilled, at which point rendering continues.

Note in the code section that follows that because `this` is a reserved word in JavaScript and thus JSX, we have wrapped it in an expression in the second line. In addition, because JSX expressions require a surrounding tag, we have added a `<section>` element that contains the control structure handling the `loading` state.

```
{this.state.errored ? (
  <p>Sorry, {'this'} information is not available at the moment.</p>
) : (
  <section>
    {this.state.loading ? (
      <p>Loading ...</p>
    ) : (
      <Router>
        <div className="articles">
          <ul>
            {this.state.articles && this.state.articles.map
            (article => (
              <li key={article.id}>
```

```
                <Link to={`/article/${article.id}`}>{article.
                attributes.title}</Link>
              </li>
            ))}
          </ul>
          {this.state.articles &&
            <Route path="/article/:articleID" render={
              ({match}) => {
                let article = this.state.articles.find(article =>
                article.id === match.params.articleID);
                return (<Article article={article}/>);
              }
            }/>
          }
        </div>
      </Router>
    )}
  </section>
)}
```

You can see the result of what we just completed in Figures 17-4 and 17-5.

React app

Sorry, this information is not available at the moment.

Figure 17-4. *When our promise throws an error, we receive an error message in response*

React app

Loading ...

Figure 17-5. *When our promise is still pending, we see a loading message until the promise is fulfilled*

Note   For more information about conditional rendering in React, consult the documentation at `https://reactjs.org/docs/conditional-rendering.html`.

Conclusion

React popularized many ideas that are now widely adopted in the JavaScript community, including the Virtual DOM and the philosophy underlying JSX. Due to its limited scope but robust feature set, React is a sought-after choice as a consumer of decoupled Drupal. Nonetheless, it can be an unwieldy and challenging tool to work with due to its lack of opinionatedness and codified best practices, although this outcome is improving rapidly in the wider ecosystem.

In the next chapter, we move to React Native, which leverages many of React's principles to facilitate the creation of robust native desktop or mobile applications through React. Although other examples are available that enable the use of JavaScript to create native applications, including but not limited to Ionic and Electron, we choose to focus on React Native due to its wide-ranging popularity and adoption.

CHAPTER 18

React Native

React Native is a popular framework that leverages some of React's most familiar features, such as its nestable component architecture and the nuances of the JSX templating system. However, there are several crucial differences that distinguish React Native from other JavaScript frameworks. First and foremost, because React Native focuses on native application development, it does not allow any traditional HTML elements.

React Native's web site states the following about its unique positioning:

> With React Native, you don't build a "mobile web app," an "HTML5 app," or a "hybrid app." You build a real mobile app that's indistinguishable from an app built using Objective-C or Java. React Native uses the same fundamental UI building blocks as regular iOS and Android apps. You just put those building blocks together using JavaScript and React.[1]

Because we have some familiarity already with React (see Chapter 17), we move quickly to the elements that differentiate React Native from React and to the process of consuming Drupal data from the context of a React Native consumer.

Note   For more information about React Native in general, consult the web site at `https://facebook.github.io/react-native`.

---

[1]"React Native." React Native. 2018. Accessed 18 September 2018. `https://facebook.github.io/react-native`

© Preston So 2018
P. So, *Decoupled Drupal in Practice*, https://doi.org/10.1007/978-1-4842-4072-4_18

Key Concepts in React Native

If you are already familiar with the development approach we detailed in the previous chapter with regard to React, the next section will be well-worn territory. However, there are many peculiarities of React Native that are characteristic of its emphasis on native mobile applications rather than traditional web applications.

Scaffolding a React Native Application

Like the React ecosystem, React Native also has an application scaffolding tool that accelerates the process of beginning a React Native project. To install Expo CLI, execute the following command.

```
$ npm install -g expo-cli
```

Once the package is installed, you can invoke the expo command to scaffold a new React Native project locally. Expo CLI will ask whether you want an application with tabbed navigation already included or a blank template. We select blank as our template.

```
$ expo init DdipReactNative
$ cd DdipReactNative
```

To spin up the packager that allows us to test our application in a variety of ways, execute the following command.

```
$ expo start
```

Once the packager is running, within the terminal window running the packager, you can type a to launch an Android emulator you have available or i to launch the iOS emulator. In this chapter, we use Xcode's built-in iOS simulator. You can also provide other commands, such as s to send the application's URL to a phone number or e-mail address or q to display a Quick Response (QR) code instead.

Because we will again be leveraging the axios library to issue requests to Drupal, we can include that in our dependencies as follows.

```
$ yarn add axios
```

At the end of the installation process, your `package.json` manifest should look like the following.

```json
{
  "name": "empty-project-template",
  "main": "node_modules/expo/AppEntry.js",
  "private": true,
  "scripts": {
    "start": "expo start",
    "android": "expo start --android",
    "ios": "expo start --ios",
    "eject": "expo eject"
  },
  "dependencies": {
    "axios": "^0.18.0",
    "expo": "^30.0.1",
    "react": "16.3.1",
    "react-native": "https://github.com/expo/react-native/archive/sdk-30.0.0.tar.gz"
  }
}
```

In addition, your directory structure should appear as follows, excluding the node_ modules directory.

```
├── App.js
├── app.json
├── assets
│   ├── icon.png
│   └── splash.png
├── package.json
└── yarn.lock
```

With these steps complete, we can now move into discussion of the most salient differences between React and React Native.

Note   For more information about setting up React Native, consult the documentation at `https://facebook.github.io/react-native/docs/getting-started`.

React Native Views

Like React, React Native primarily operates with *views,* which are displays of data. The default View component is a view that occupies the entire screen and is not scrollable. In certain scenarios, because we expect considerable textual content, we will later also leverage the ScrollView component. ScrollView can scroll both vertically by default and horizontally if we set the horizontal property (<ScrollView horizontal/>).

In addition, we will be leveraging the FlatList component to provide a list of articles. FlatList components accept two properties: data (the data that the list needs to render) and renderItem (representing one item from the list and returning the component that each item will render into).

Let us begin with an intermediate state of our React application from Chapter 17 by adjusting some initial code so it accommodates nuances of React Native. Replace App.js with the following code, scrutinizing in particular the fact that we have substituted all HTML elements for React Native elements. Note also the import statement referring to React Native.

```
// App.js
import React from 'react';
import { FlatList, StyleSheet, Text, View } from 'react-native';

export default class App extends React.Component {
  constructor(props) {
    super(props);
    this.state = {};
  }
  componentWillMount() {
    this.setState({
      articles: [
        {
          id: '3ca469da-b905-4a77-8d97-954abcdc4cf6',
```

```
        attributes: {
          title: 'Capto',
          uuid: '3ca469da-b905-4a77-8d97-954abcdc4cf6',
          created: 1526387013,
          body: {
            value: 'Camur'
          }
        }
      },
      {
        id: '1e1a4598-f9c7-4ce7-adbd-7603401cc23b',
        attributes: {
          title: 'Esse Ex Nibh Valde Valetudo',
          uuid: '1e1a4598-f9c7-4ce7-adbd-7603401cc23b',
          created: 1526387013,
          body: {
            value: 'Illum loquor persto plaga premo.'
          }
        }
      }
    ]
  });
}
render() {
  return (
    <View style={styles.container}>
      <FlatList
        data={this.state.articles}
        keyExtractor={(item, index) => item.id}
        renderItem={({item}) => <Text style={styles.item}>{item.
        attributes.title}</Text>}
      />
    </View>
  );
}
}
```

```
const styles = StyleSheet.create({
  container: {
    flex: 1,
    backgroundColor: '#fff',
    paddingTop: 22
  },
  item: {
    padding: 10,
    fontSize: 18,
    height: 44,
  },
});
```

We cover each of the unfamiliar portions of this code one by one. First, our render()
method renders a FlatList component using the dummy data we have provided to
the state object. In turn, we render each of the items from the list. FlatList's default
behavior expects a unique and cacheable key key to be available in each data item, but
because we are using JSON API, we need to override this behavior to instead use the id
attribute, which contains our UUID.

```
render() {
  return (
    <View style={styles.container}>
      <FlatList
        data={this.state.articles}
        keyExtractor={(item, index) => item.id}
        renderItem={({item}) => <Text style={styles.item}>{item.
        attributes.title}</Text>}
      />
    </View>
  );
}
```

Finally, we include several style objects that we invoke within the View and FlatList
components. Note in particular that because traditional CSS is unavailable in the React
Native context, we are using certain unique conventions, including camelCase for CSS
property names.

```
const styles = StyleSheet.create({
  container: {
    flex: 1,
    backgroundColor: '#fff',
    paddingTop: 22
  },
  item: {
    padding: 10,
    fontSize: 18,
    height: 44,
  },
});
```

The resulting application in our iOS emulator can be seen in Figure 18-1.

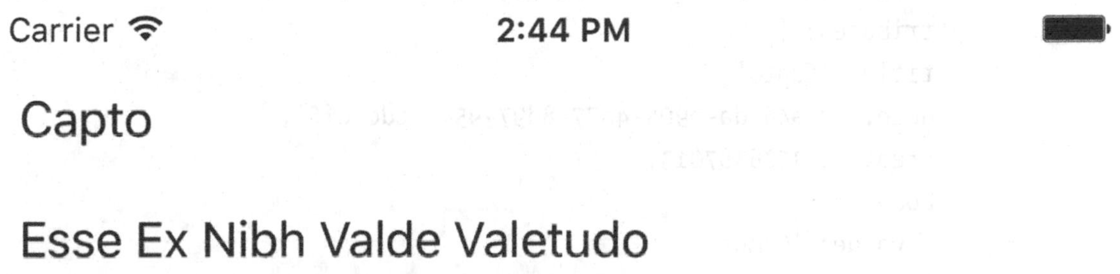

Carrier 🛜   **2:44 PM**   ▬▬▬

Capto

Esse Ex Nibh Valde Valetudo

Figure 18-1. *Our iOS emulator shows our dummy articles rendered into a* FlatList *component*

Note   For more information about FlatList and list views, consult the documentation at https://facebook.github.io/react-native/docs/using-a-listview.

React Native Styles

Before we proceed, because we plan to provide an article detail component that includes pertinent information about the article, we can adjust our application to include some additional attributes and an enhanced set of styles. Modify your App.js file so it appears as follows, scrutinizing the additional import of ScrollView.

```
// App.js
import React from 'react';
import { FlatList, ScrollView, StyleSheet, Text, View } from 'react-
native';

export default class App extends React.Component {
  constructor(props) {
    super(props);
    this.state = {};
  }
  componentWillMount() {
    this.setState({
      articles: [
        {
          id: '3ca469da-b905-4a77-8d97-954abcdc4cf6',
          attributes: {
            title: 'Capto',
            uuid: '3ca469da-b905-4a77-8d97-954abcdc4cf6',
            created: 1526387013,
            body: {
              value: 'Camur'
            }
          }
        },
        {
          id: '1e1a4598-f9c7-4ce7-adbd-7603401cc23b',
          attributes: {
            title: 'Esse Ex Nibh Valde Valetudo',
            uuid: '1e1a4598-f9c7-4ce7-adbd-7603401cc23b',
            created: 1526387013,
            body: {
              value: 'Illum loquor persto plaga premo.'
            }
          }
        }
      ]
```

```
      });
    }
  render() {
    return (
      <ScrollView style={styles.container}>
        <FlatList
          data={this.state.articles}
          keyExtractor={(item, index) => item.id}
          renderItem={({item}) => (
            <View style={styles.item}>
              <Text style={styles.itemHeading}>{item.attributes.title}
              </Text>
              <Text style={styles.itemAttribute}>ID: {item.id}</Text>
              <Text style={styles.itemAttribute}>Created: {item.attributes.
              created}</Text>
              <Text style={styles.itemAttribute}>Body: {item.attributes.
              body.value}</Text>
            </View>
          )}
        />
      </ScrollView>
    );
  }
}

const styles = StyleSheet.create({
  container: {
    flex: 1,
    backgroundColor: '#fff',
    paddingTop: 22,
  },
  item: {
    padding: 10,
    backgroundColor: '#eee',
```

```
      borderBottomColor: '#ccc',
      borderBottomWidth: 5,
    },
    itemHeading: {
      marginTop: 10,
      paddingTop: 10,
      paddingBottom: 10,
      fontSize: 24,
    },
    itemAttribute: {
      paddingTop: 10,
      paddingBottom: 10,
    }
});
```

The result of these most recent changes is depicted in Figure 18-2.

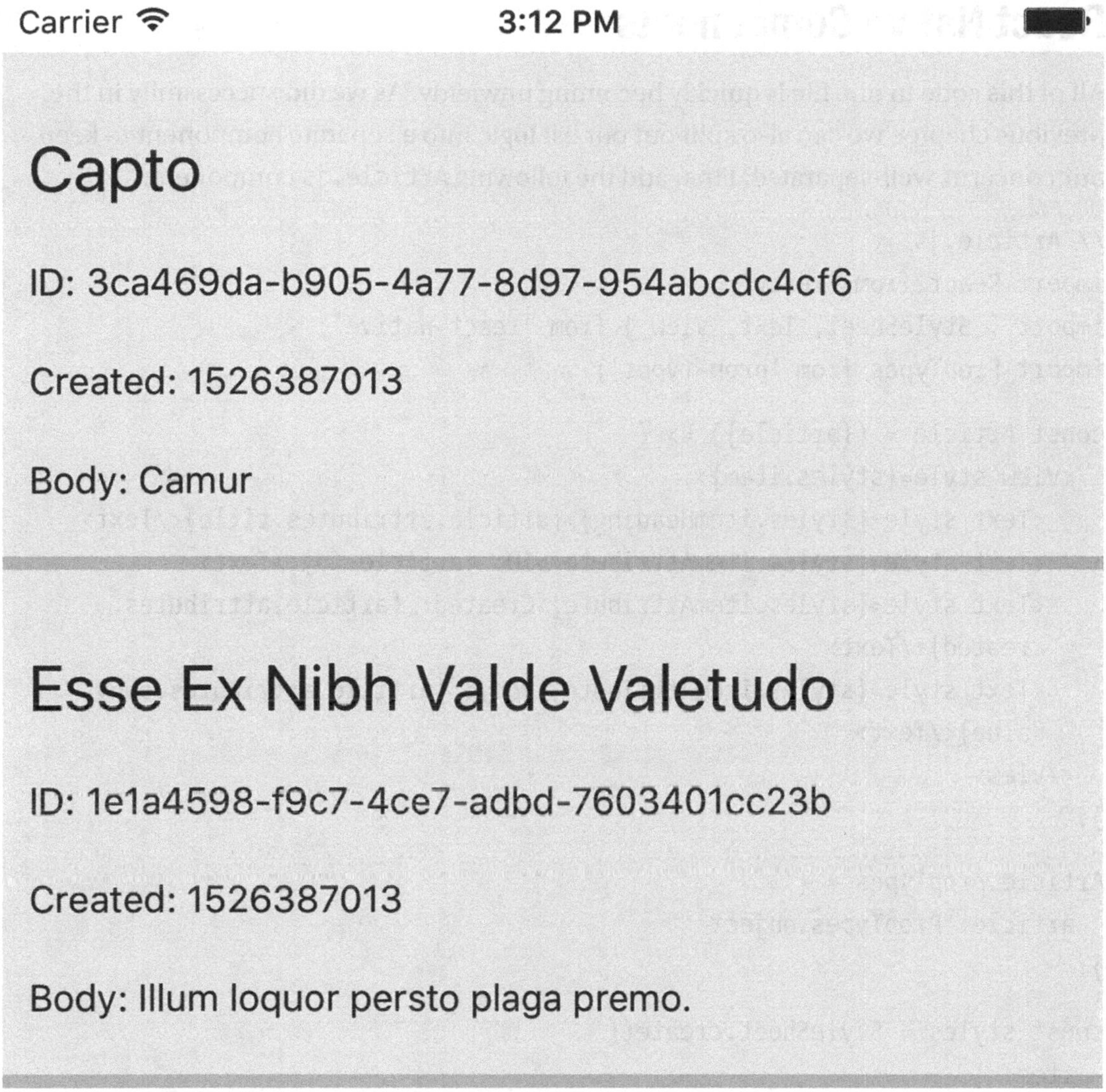

Carrier 📶   3:12 PM   ▬

Capto

ID: 3ca469da-b905-4a77-8d97-954abcdc4cf6

Created: 1526387013

Body: Camur

Esse Ex Nibh Valde Valetudo

ID: 1e1a4598-f9c7-4ce7-adbd-7603401cc23b

Created: 1526387013

Body: Illum loquor persto plaga premo.

Figure 18-2. *Our React Native application now sports a few styles to improve the user experience and to separate our individual articles from one another*

Note   For more information about ScrollView, consult the documentation at https://facebook.github.io/react-native/docs/using-a-scrollview. For more information about React Native styles, consult the documentation at https://facebook.github.io/react-native/docs/style.

React Native Components

All of this code in one file is quickly becoming unwieldy. As we did successfully in the previous chapter, we can also split out our list logic into a separate component to keep our concerns well-separated. First, add the following `Article.js` component.

```
// Article.js
import React from 'react';
import { StyleSheet, Text, View } from 'react-native';
import PropTypes from 'prop-types';

const Article = ({article}) => (
  <View style={styles.item}>
    <Text style={styles.itemHeading}>{article.attributes.title}</Text>
    <Text style={styles.itemAttribute}>ID: {article.id}</Text>
    <Text style={styles.itemAttribute}>Created: {article.attributes.
    created}</Text>
    <Text style={styles.itemAttribute}>Body: {article.attributes.body.
    value}</Text>
  </View>
);

Article.propTypes = {
  article: PropTypes.object
};

const styles = StyleSheet.create({
  item: {
    padding: 10,
    backgroundColor: '#eee',
    borderBottomColor: '#ccc',
    borderBottomWidth: 5,
  },
  itemHeading: {
    marginTop: 10,
    paddingTop: 10,
    paddingBottom: 10,
    fontSize: 24,
```

```
  },
  itemAttribute: {
    paddingTop: 10,
    paddingBottom: 10,
  }
});
```

```
export default Article;
```

Then, we can adjust our `App.js` file to reflect the presence of the new component. Scrutinize in particular the `import` statement that declares a dependency on the component.

```
// App.js
import React from 'react';
import { FlatList, ScrollView, StyleSheet, Text, View } from 'react-
native';
import Article from './Article.js';

export default class App extends React.Component {
  constructor(props) {
    super(props);
    this.state = {};
  }
  componentWillMount() {
    this.setState({
      articles: [
        {
          id: '3ca469da-b905-4a77-8d97-954abcdc4cf6',
          attributes: {
            title: 'Capto',
            uuid: '3ca469da-b905-4a77-8d97-954abcdc4cf6',
            created: 1526387013,
            body: {
              value: 'Camur'
            }
          }
        },
```

```
        {
          id: '1e1a4598-f9c7-4ce7-adbd-7603401cc23b',
          attributes: {
            title: 'Esse Ex Nibh Valde Valetudo',
            uuid: '1e1a4598-f9c7-4ce7-adbd-7603401cc23b',
            created: 1526387013,
            body: {
              value: 'Illum loquor persto plaga premo.'
            }
          }
        }
      ]
    });
  }
  render() {
    return (
      <ScrollView style={styles.container}>
        <FlatList
          data={this.state.articles}
          keyExtractor={(item, index) => item.id}
          renderItem={({item}) => (
            <Article article={item} />
          )}
        />
      </ScrollView>
    );
  }
}

const styles = StyleSheet.create({
  container: {
    flex: 1,
    backgroundColor: '#fff',
    paddingTop: 22,
  },
});
```

When we reload the application, there should be no change from what we witnessed in Figure 18-2, as we have merely moved code around.

Note   For more about native components in React Native, consult the documentation at `https://facebook.github.io/react-native/docs/components-and-apis`. Coverage of stack navigation in React Native, the analogue to React routing, is beyond the scope of this chapter due to its relative instability, but documentation is available at `https://reactnavigation.org`.

Backing React Native with Drupal and JSON API

We will be backing our React Native application with an existing Drupal site exposing JSON API that we configured and built in Chapters 8 and 12. If you do not have a fully functioning Drupal site with JSON API enabled and some content populated, return to Chapters 8 and 12 for a full overview of Drupal's JSON API implementation.

Retrieving Drupal Data with `axios`

Just as we did in Chapter 17, we can use `axios` to replace our dummy data with actual data originating from Drupal. Consider the following new state of our `App.js`, the result of which is illustrated in Figure 18-3.

```
// App.js
import React from 'react';
import { FlatList, ScrollView, StyleSheet, Text, View } from 'react-
native';
import axios from 'axios';
import Article from './Article.js';

export default class App extends React.Component {
  constructor(props) {
    super(props);
    this.state = {};
  }
```

```
  componentWillMount() {
    axios.get('http://jsonapi-test.dd:8083/jsonapi/node/article')
      .then(res => this.setState({ articles: res.data.data }))
      .catch(console.log);
  }
  render() {
    return (
      <ScrollView style={styles.container}>
        <FlatList
          data={this.state.articles}
          keyExtractor={(item, index) => item.id}
          renderItem={({item}) => (
            <Article article={item} />
          )}
        />
      </ScrollView>
    );
  }
}

const styles = StyleSheet.create({
  container: {
    flex: 1,
    backgroundColor: '#fff',
    paddingTop: 22,
  },
});
```

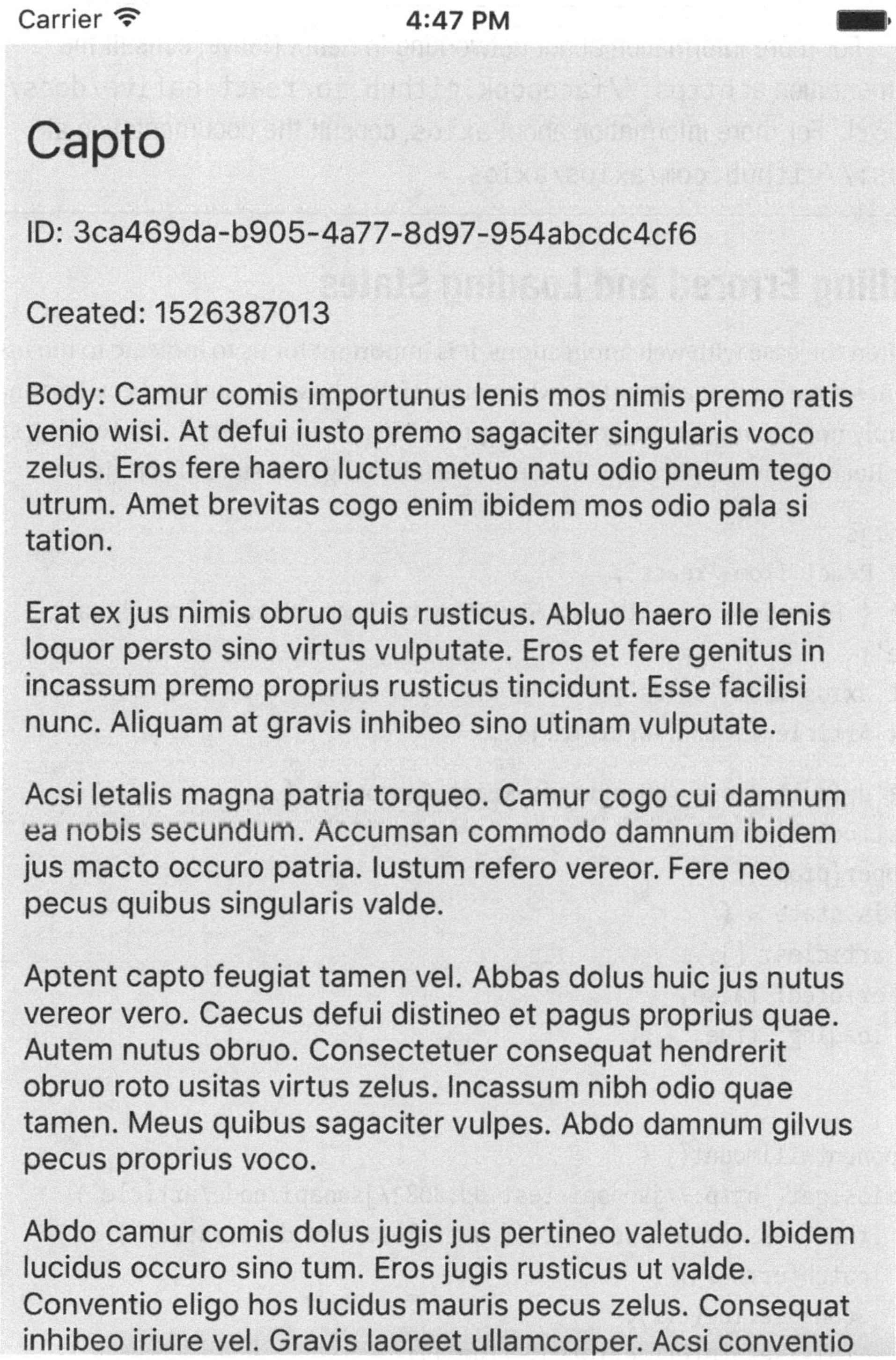

Carrier 🛜   4:47 PM   ▬

Capto

ID: 3ca469da-b905-4a77-8d97-954abcdc4cf6

Created: 1526387013

Body: Camur comis importunus lenis mos nimis premo ratis venio wisi. At defui iusto premo sagaciter singularis voco zelus. Eros fere haero luctus metuo natu odio pneum tego utrum. Amet brevitas cogo enim ibidem mos odio pala si tation.

Erat ex jus nimis obruo quis rusticus. Abluo haero ille lenis loquor persto sino virtus vulputate. Eros et fere genitus in incassum premo proprius rusticus tincidunt. Esse facilisi nunc. Aliquam at gravis inhibeo sino utinam vulputate.

Acsi letalis magna patria torqueo. Camur cogo cui damnum ea nobis secundum. Accumsan commodo damnum ibidem jus macto occuro patria. Iustum refero vereor. Fere neo pecus quibus singularis valde.

Aptent capto feugiat tamen vel. Abbas dolus huic jus nutus vereor vero. Caecus defui distineo et pagus proprius quae. Autem nutus obruo. Consectetuer consequat hendrerit obruo roto usitas virtus zelus. Incassum nibh odio quae tamen. Meus quibus sagaciter vulpes. Abdo damnum gilvus pecus proprius voco.

Abdo camur comis dolus jugis jus pertineo valetudo. Ibidem lucidus occuro sino tum. Eros jugis rusticus ut valde. Conventio eligo hos lucidus mauris pecus zelus. Consequat inhibeo iriure vel. Gravis laoreet ullamcorper. Acsi conventio

Figure 18-3. *The presence of full article bodies indicates that our articles are originating correctly from our Drupal site as we intended*

> **Note**   For more information about networking in React Native, consult the
> documentation at `https://facebook.github.io/react-native/docs/`
> `network`. For more information about `axios`, consult the documentation at
> `https://github.com/axios/axios`.

Handling Errored and Loading States

As is often the case with web applications, it is important for us to indicate to the user
different scenarios that account for why a view of data has not rendered yet. Fortunately,
we simply need to repeat our work in Chapter 17 to provide `errored` and `loading` states
for our React Native application. Consider the following new state of `App.js`.

```
// App.js
import React from 'react';
import { FlatList, ScrollView, StyleSheet, Text, View } from 'react-
native';
import axios from 'axios';
import Article from './Article.js';

export default class App extends React.Component {
  constructor(props) {
    super(props);
    this.state = {
      articles: [],
      errored: false,
      loading: true
    };
  }
  componentWillMount() {
    axios.get('http://jsonapi-test.dd:8083/jsonapi/node/article')
      .then(res => this.setState({ articles: res.data.data }))
      .catch(err => {
        console.log(err);
        this.setState({ errored: true });
      })
```

```
        .finally(() => this.setState({ loading: false }));
  }
  render() {
    return (
      <ScrollView style={styles.container}>
        {this.state.errored ? (
          <Text>Sorry, {'this'} information is not available at the
          moment.</Text>
        ) : (
          <View>
            {this.state.loading ? (
              <Text>Loading ...</Text>
            ) : (
              <FlatList
                data={this.state.articles}
                keyExtractor={(item, index) => item.id}
                renderItem={({item}) => (
                  <Article article={item} />
                )}
              />
            )}
          </View>
        )}
      </ScrollView>
    );
  }
}

const styles = StyleSheet.create({
  container: {
    flex: 1,
    backgroundColor: '#fff',
    paddingTop: 22,
  },
});
```

Now, we can disconnect our Drupal web site and see that rather than our application returning a network error, it shows our error message, as depicted in Figure 18-4. In addition, we see a loading state that gives us feedback that our application is indeed running properly, as seen in Figure 18-5.

Carrier 📶	4:56 PM	▰

Sorry, this information is not available at the moment.

Figure 18-4. *When we disconnect our Drupal site, our promise remains unfulfilled, and our application displays an error message*

Carrier 📶	4:57 PM	▰

Loading ...

Figure 18-5. *When we first load our application, our promise is being fulfilled, and our application displays a loading message*

Conclusion

React Native is a powerful and robust alternative to writing native mobile applications in mobile technologies such as Objective-C and Swift, because it enables us to employ conventions in React to which we are already accustomed. Thanks to the similarities between both technologies, it is relatively simple for those knowledgeable in React to begin building React Native applications rapidly. Nonetheless, React Native's ecosystem is still expanding, with tools such as React Navigation quickly maturing.

In the next chapter, we investigate Angular, a wholly distinct framework with many unique characteristics that make it both deeply fascinating and occasionally frustrating. Although a full introduction to TypeScript and its nuances as well as a comprehensive survey of Angular is impossible in the brief span we have available, we nevertheless construct an equivalent Angular application backed by decoupled Drupal.

CHAPTER 19

Angular

Angular is a JavaScript framework that has a storied history but has undergone significant evolution over the last several years, to the point where it is nearly unrecognizable in comparison to its predecessor AngularJS. Today, Angular leverages TypeScript and emphasizes its mission to be a single unified framework for building experiences that straddle the web, mobile, and native mobile and desktop applications.

The Angular documentation states the following:

> *Angular is a platform that makes it easy to build applications with the web. Angular combines declarative templates, dependency injection, end to end tooling, and integrated best practices to solve development challenges. Angular empowers developers to build applications that live on the web, mobile, or the desktop.*

Like Ember (see Chapter 21), Angular has a reputation for being quite opinionated with its development practices, most overtly evidenced by its requirement that developers use TypeScript. Nonetheless, its rich ecosystem, paired with its cross-device capabilities, make Angular a compelling candidate for those selecting a JavaScript technology for decoupled Drupal architectures.

Note For complete documentation about Angular, see the Angular web site at `https://angular.io`.

Key Concepts in Angular

Because Angular uses TypeScript, it might be useful to install a package that recognizes TypeScript syntax for your code editor. If you are using Atom as your code editor, you can install the TypeScript package for Atom with the following command.

```
$ apm install atom-typescript
```

355

© Preston So 2018

P. So, *Decoupled Drupal in Practice*, https://doi.org/10.1007/978-1-4842-4072-4_19

Note   The Atom code editor can be downloaded at `https://atom.io`.

Scaffolding an Angular Application

Like Ember and Vue.js (see Chapter 20), Angular has an official command-line interface that simplifies certain tasks during Angular development known as Angular CLI. To install Angular CLI globally, execute the following command.

```
$ npm install -g @angular/cli
```

Both Angular CLI and any Angular CLI-generated project require Node 8.9 or higher and NPM 5.5.1 or higher. You can verify that your versions are up-to-date using the node -v and npm -v commands, respectively.

Note   For more information about installing Node.js, consult the web site at `https://nodejs.org/en/download`. For more information about installing NPM, consult the web site at `https://docs.npmjs.com/getting-started/installing-node#install-npm--manage-npm-versions`. If you have other projects relying on other versions of Node, consider using a tool such as Node Version Manager, available on GitHub at `https://github.com/creationix/nvm`.

We can create a new project and launch a new local development server with hot reload using the following commands. In sequence, the following commands scaffold a new Angular application in our chosen directory, access the directory, and spin up a local server. The --open flag will open a tab in your browser containing the application.

```
$ ng new ddip-ng
$ cd ddip-ng
$ ng serve --open
```

Once you have scaffolded a new Angular application, your directory structure will look like the following (excluding the node_modules directory).

```
├── README.md
├── angular.json
├── e2e
│   ├── protractor.conf.js
│   ├── src
│   │   ├── app.e2e-spec.ts
│   │   └── app.po.ts
│   └── tsconfig.e2e.json
├── package-lock.json
├── package.json
├── src
│   ├── app
│   │   ├── app.component.css
│   │   ├── app.component.html
│   │   ├── app.component.spec.ts
│   │   ├── app.component.ts
│   │   └── app.module.ts
│   ├── assets
│   ├── browserslist
│   ├── environments
│   │   ├── environment.prod.ts
│   │   └── environment.ts
│   ├── favicon.ico
│   ├── index.html
│   ├── karma.conf.js
│   ├── main.ts
│   ├── polyfills.ts
│   ├── styles.css
│   ├── test.ts
│   ├── tsconfig.app.json
│   ├── tsconfig.spec.json
│   └── tslint.json
├── tsconfig.json
└── tslint.json
```

Now, we can use Atom to open the application and begin writing code.[1] You can also employ a code editor of your choice that includes TypeScript support.

```
$ atom .
```

The Root Component

Like other popular JavaScript application frameworks, Angular uses *components* that are reusable and nestable, including the application root component. When we open src/app/app.component.ts, we see that we can change the overarching title of the application.

```
// src/app/app.component.ts
import { Component } from '@angular/core';

@Component({
  selector: 'app-root',
  templateUrl: './app.component.html',
  styleUrls: ['./app.component.css']
})
export class AppComponent {
  title = 'ddip-ng';
}
```

In this chapter, we build a simple content browser that is capable of accessing content entities in Drupal. To do this, because TypeScript is a statically typed language, we need to define a class that matches Drupal bundles (Drupal content types) and accounts for their attributes' types, as you can see in the following example.

For the time being, we will use dummy data until we connect our Angular application to Drupal.

```
// src/app/app.component.ts
import { Component } from '@angular/core';

export class Article {
  attributes: object;
}
```

---

[1]So, Preston. "Decoupled Drupal and Angular 2." DrupalCon Baltimore. 25 April 2017. Accessed 14 September 2018. https://events.drupal.org/baltimore2017/sessions/decoupled-drupal-and-angular-2

```
@Component({
  selector: 'app-root',
  templateUrl: './app.component.html',
  styleUrls: ['./app.component.css']
})
export class AppComponent {
  title = 'ddip-ng';
  article: Article = {
    attributes: {
      uuid: '7ac282af-81d1-4d88-925d-9a3a9f6d304f',
      title: 'Neque Nisl',
      body: {
        value: 'At interdico letalis modo qui.'
      }
    }
  }
}
```

Two-Way Data Binding

We can also modify our root component to display our single dummy article along with an <input> element to demonstrate *two-way data binding*. In this case, ngModel is a directive that we need to add by declaring an additional dependency on FormsModule, as seen here in app.module.ts.

```
// src/app/app.module.ts
import { BrowserModule } from '@angular/platform-browser';
import { NgModule } from '@angular/core';
import { FormsModule } from '@angular/forms';

import { AppComponent } from './app.component';

@NgModule({
  declarations: [
    AppComponent
  ],
```

```
  imports: [
    BrowserModule,
    FormsModule
  ],
  providers: [],
  bootstrap: [AppComponent]
})
export class AppModule { }
```

Now, replace the contents of app.component.html with the following.

```
<!-- src/app/app.component.html -->
<h1>
  {{title}}
</h1>
<h2>{{article.attributes.title}} details</h2>
<div>
  <label>Title: </label>
  <input [(ngModel)]="article.attributes.title" placeholder="Title">
</div>
```

Because Angular enforces two-way data binding, we can edit this <input> element and see it reflected in the title. You can see the current state of our application in Figure 19-1.

ddip-ng

Neque Nisl edited! details

Title: Neque Nisl edited!

Figure 19-1. *When we perform an edit in the <input> element, two-way data binding ensures that the value is updated immediately*

Note   For more information about forms in Angular, consult the documentation at `https://angular.io/guide/user-input`. From this example forward, many of the examples in this chapter are inspired by the Tour of Heroes tutorial in the Angular documentation located at `https://angular.io/tutorial`.

Angular Components

To achieve improved maintainability, we can generate a component to house all of the logic that will handle the display of our articles. To generate a new component, execute the following command, after either exiting out of the running server (Ctrl+C) or opening a new terminal window.

```
$ ng generate component articles
```

If you navigate to src/app/app.module.ts, you will see that Angular has updated our root module with a reference to the new component.

```
// src/app/app.module.ts
import { BrowserModule } from '@angular/platform-browser';
import { NgModule } from '@angular/core';
import { FormsModule } from '@angular/forms';

import { AppComponent } from './app.component';
import { ArticlesComponent } from './articles/articles.component';

@NgModule({
  declarations: [
    AppComponent,
    ArticlesComponent
  ],
  imports: [
    BrowserModule,
    FormsModule
  ],
  providers: [],
  bootstrap: [AppComponent]
})
export class AppModule { }
```

361

Now, within our root component, we can refer to the new component we have just created and move all of our logic into the articles component. Note that this example is split into two separate files delineated by HTML comments.

```html
<!-- src/app/app.component.html -->
<h1>
  {{title}}
</h1>
<app-articles></app-articles>

<!-- src/app/articles.component.html -->
<h2>{{article.attributes.title}} details</h2>
<div>
  <label>Title: </label>
  <input [(ngModel)]="article.attributes.title" placeholder="Title">
</div>
```

We need to update our root component and articles component behavior accordingly as well.

```typescript
// src/app/articles/articles.component.ts
import { Component } from '@angular/core';

export class Article {
  attributes: object
}

@Component({
  selector: 'app-articles',
  templateUrl: './articles.component.html',
  styleUrls: ['./articles.component.css']
})

export class ArticlesComponent {
  title = 'ddip-ng';
  article: Article = {
    attributes: {
      uuid: '7ac282af-81d1-4d88-925d-9a3a9f6d304f',
      title: 'Neque Nisl',
```

```
      body: {
        value: 'At interdico letalis modo qui.'
      }
    }
  }
}

// src/app/app.component.ts
import { Component } from '@angular/core';

@Component({
  selector: 'app-root',
  templateUrl: './app.component.html',
  styleUrls: ['./app.component.css']
})

export class AppComponent {
  title = 'ddip-ng';
}
```

Let's provide some dummy data as a constant that allows us to iterate over several articles. To do this, we create a public property that is accessible to our component, as you can see in this example.

```
// src/app/articles/articles.component.ts
import { Component } from '@angular/core';

export class Article {
  attributes: object;
}

const ARTICLES: Article[] = [
  {
    attributes: {
      uuid: '7ac282af-81d1-4d88-925d-9a3a9f6d304f',
      title: 'Neque Nisl',
      body: {
        value: 'At interdico letalis modo qui.'
      }
```

```
      }
    },
    {
      attributes: {
        uuid: 'dfca8a65-a214-470c-ae39-6e7c1ab9c87f',
        title: 'Aptent Immitto',
        body: {
          value: 'Exputo molior nobis patria quadrum saepius valde.'
        }
      }
    },
    {
      attributes: {
        uuid: 'df334ec5-216f-487e-8aa5-29a9224acb8f',
        title: 'In Interdico Nibh Nisl Utinam',
        body: {
          value: 'Cui refoveo similis.'
        }
      }
    }
];

@Component({
  selector: 'app-articles',
  templateUrl: './articles.component.html',
  styleUrls: ['./articles.component.css']
})

export class ArticlesComponent {
  title = 'ddip-ng';
  articles = ARTICLES;
}
```

Note   For more information about Angular components, consult the
documentation at `https://angular.io/guide/architecture-components`.

Angular Directives

In Angular, *directives* indicate logic that should be followed to render the template in a form desired by the developer. It is also possible to create our own directives, which enforce custom behavior on elements in the DOM.

We can drill into our articles component and enrich the template by providing a list of articles rather than a field to edit article titles. We can use the `ngFor` directive to iterate over the dummy articles we just provided to the component. Eventually, we will enable users to edit titles when an individual article is selected.

```
<!-- src/app/articles.component.html -->
<h2>List of articles</h2>
<ul class="articles">
  <li *ngFor="let article of articles">
    Article {{article.attributes.uuid}}: {{article.attributes.title}}
  </li>
</ul>
```

The result of this can be seen in Figure 19-2.

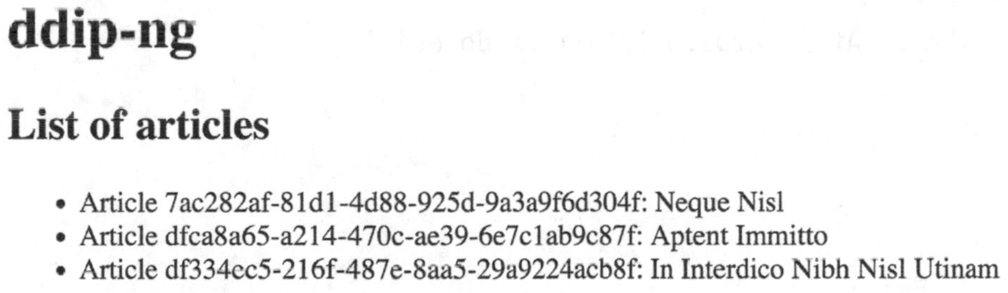

ddip-ng

List of articles

- Article 7ac282af-81d1-4d88-925d-9a3a9f6d304f: Neque Nisl
- Article dfca8a65-a214-470c-ae39-6e7c1ab9c87f: Aptent Immitto
- Article df334cc5-216f-487e-8aa5-29a9224acb8f: In Interdico Nibh Nisl Utinam

Figure 19-2. *Our dummy articles are displaying correctly*

To restore our functionality of editing article titles, we will provide click behavior. When an article is clicked, we need the form with which we demonstrated two-way data binding earlier to display. To accomplish this, we can add a `click` event binding to each list item.

```
<!-- src/app/articles.component.html -->
<h2>List of articles</h2>
<ul class="articles">
```

```
<li *ngFor="let article of articles" (click)="onSelect(article)">
  Article {{article.attributes.uuid}}: {{article.attributes.title}}
</li>
</ul>
```

We define the onSelect() method in articles.component.ts, as you can see in this example.

```
// src/app/articles/articles.component.ts
import { Component } from '@angular/core';

export class Article {
  attributes: object;
}

const ARTICLES: Article[] = [
  {
    attributes: {
      uuid: '7ac282af-81d1-4d88-925d-9a3a9f6d304f',
      title: 'Neque Nisl',
      body: {
        value: 'At interdico letalis modo qui.'
      }
    }
  },
  {
    attributes: {
      uuid: 'dfca8a65-a214-470c-ae39-6e7c1ab9c87f',
      title: 'Aptent Immitto',
      body: {
        value: 'Exputo molior nobis patria quadrum saepius valde.'
      }
    }
  },
  {
    attributes: {
      uuid: 'df334ec5-216f-487e-8aa5-29a9224acb8f',
      title: 'In Interdico Nibh Nisl Utinam',
```

```
      body: {
        value: 'Cui refoveo similis.'
      }
    }
  }
];

@Component({
  selector: 'app-articles',
  templateUrl: './articles.component.html',
  styleUrls: ['./articles.component.css']
})

export class ArticlesComponent {
  title = 'ddip-ng';
  articles = ARTICLES;
  selectedArticle: Article;
  onSelect(article: Article): void {
    this.selectedArticle = article;
  }
}
```

Then, in the template, we can reinsert the previous logic that is now absent and bind to the selectedArticle property we have newly defined instead of the article property. To make it easier to identify the selected article, we also include the UUID. Finally, we can use the ngIf directive to ensure that we do not throw any errors by attempting to refer to a not-yet-selected article's title. The result of this example is illustrated in Figure 19-3.

```
<!-- src/app/articles.component.html -->
<h2>List of articles</h2>
<ul class="articles">
  <li *ngFor="let article of articles" (click)="onSelect(article)">
    Article {{article.attributes.uuid}}: {{article.attributes.title}}
  </li>
</ul>
```

```
<div *ngIf="selectedArticle">
  <h2>{{selectedArticle.attributes.title}} details ({{selectedArticle.
  attributes.uuid}})</h2>
  <div>
    <label>Title: </label>
    <input [(ngModel)]="selectedArticle.attributes.title"
    placeholder="Title">
  </div>
</div>
```

ddip-ng

List of articles

- Article 7ac282af-81d1-4d88-925d-9a3a9f6d304f: Neque Nisl
- Article dfca8a65-a214-470c-ae39-6e7c1ab9c87f: Aptent Immitto
- Article df334ec5-216f-487e-8aa5-29a9224acb8f: I just edited this article

I just edited this article details (df334ec5-216f-487e-8aa5-29a9224acb8f)

Title: I just edited this article

Figure 19-3. *In this example, we have clicked the third article from the list and edited the title, which updates the bound property rendered above it*

In the future, we might wish to apply certain styling to this article so that its active state is clear. Update `articles.component.html` to the following.

```
<!-- src/app/articles.component.html -->
<h2>List of articles</h2>
<ul class="articles">
  <li *ngFor="let article of articles"
      [class.selected]="article === selectedArticle"
      (click)="onSelect(article)">
    Article {{article.attributes.uuid}}: {{article.attributes.title}}
  </li>
</ul>

<div *ngIf="selectedArticle">
  <h2>{{selectedArticle.attributes.title}} details ({{selectedArticle.
  attributes.uuid}})</h2>
```

```
<div>
  <label>Title: </label>
  <input [(ngModel)]="selectedArticle.attributes.title"
  placeholder="Title">
</div>
</div>
```

Then, add the following selector to `articles.component.css` so that selected articles are distinguishable. The result of this can be seen in Figure 19-4.

```
/* src/app/articles.component.css */
.selected {
  font-weight: bold;
  color: green;
}
```

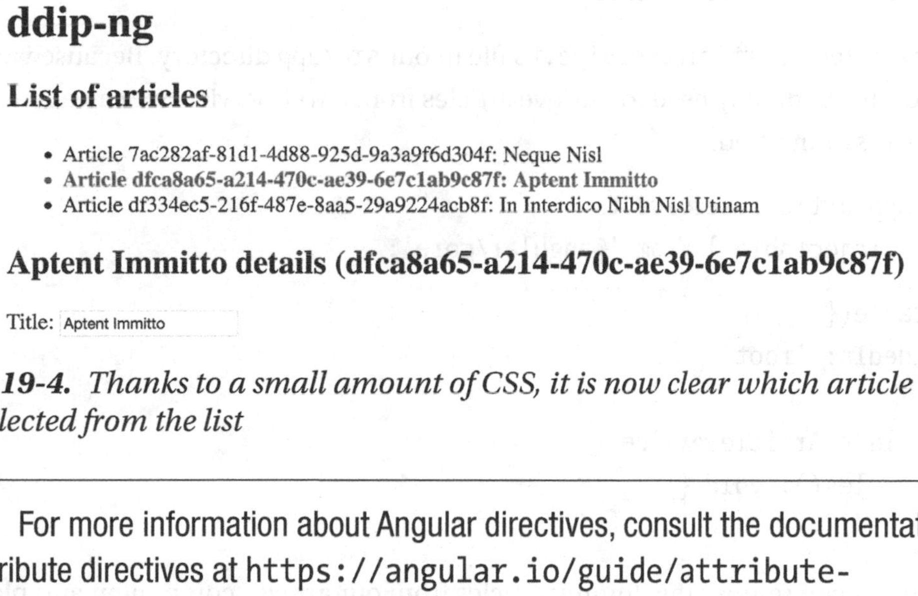

ddip-ng

List of articles

- Article 7ac282af-81d1-4d88-925d-9a3a9f6d304f: Neque Nisl
- **Article dfca8a65-a214-470c-ae39-6e7c1ab9c87f: Aptent Immitto**
- Article df334ec5-216f-487e-8aa5-29a9224acb8f: In Interdico Nibh Nisl Utinam

Aptent Immitto details (dfca8a65-a214-470c-ae39-6e7c1ab9c87f)

Title: Aptent Immitto

Figure 19-4. *Thanks to a small amount of CSS, it is now clear which article has been selected from the list*

Note   For more information about Angular directives, consult the documentation for attribute directives at `https://angular.io/guide/attribute-directives` and structural directives at `https://angular.io/guide/structural-directives`.

Angular Services

Now that we have covered some of the nuances of components (a comprehensive exploration is beyond the scope of this book), we can direct our attention to services. As we will also see in Ember (see Chapter 21), it is not a best practice for our components to also be providers of data, as we eventually expect to connect our application to a web service. In Angular, *services* are a broad concept that represents a dependency in an application—whether it is on a value, function, or other feature—and generally serves a single, well-defined purpose.

As such, we should provide a service that furnishes the data to any components that depend on it. This means that we can decouple data from individual components and offer a generic means of retrieving data. For instance, in our scenario, we wish to create a service that provides the article data to components. To generate a new service, execute the following command.

```
$ ng generate service article
```

This creates an `article.service.ts` file in our `src/app` directory. Because we know we will eventually need to retrieve articles from a web service, we can add a `getArticles()` method.

```
// src/app/article.service.ts
import { Injectable } from '@angular/core';

@Injectable({
  providedIn: 'root'
})
export class ArticleService {
  getArticles(): void {}
}
```

Then, we can remove the dummy articles from our articles component and place it into a separate file. We will do this to make it easier for our service to retrieve the articles. Create `dummy-articles.ts` and insert the following.

```
// src/app/dummy-articles.ts
import { Article } from './articles/articles.component';
```

```
export const ARTICLES: Article[] = [
  {
    attributes: {
      uuid: '7ac282af-81d1-4d88-925d-9a3a9f6d304f',
      title: 'Neque Nisl',
      body: {
        value: 'At interdico letalis modo qui.'
      }
    }
  },
  {
    attributes: {
      uuid: 'dfca8a65-a214-470c-ae39-6e7c1ab9c87f',
      title: 'Aptent Immitto',
      body: {
        value: 'Exputo molior nobis patria quadrum saepius valde.'
      }
    }
  },
  {
    attributes: {
      uuid: 'df334ec5-216f-487e-8aa5-29a9224acb8f',
      title: 'In Interdico Nibh Nisl Utinam',
      body: {
        value: 'Cui refoveo similis.'
      }
    }
  }
];
```

In our export from our articles component, we remove the constant containing our dummy data and indicate to Angular that the articles property consists of an array of articles.

```
// src/app/articles/articles.component.ts
import { Component } from '@angular/core';
```

```
export class Article {
  attributes: object;
}

@Component({
  selector: 'app-articles',
  templateUrl: './articles.component.html',
  styleUrls: ['./articles.component.css']
})
export class ArticlesComponent {
  title = 'ddip-ng';
  articles: Article[];
  selectedArticle: Article;
  onSelect(article: Article): void {
    this.selectedArticle = article;
  }
}
```

Then, we can adjust our article service to employ the dummy articles instead.

```
// src/app/article.service.ts
import { Injectable } from '@angular/core';

import { Article } from './articles/articles.component'
import { ARTICLES } from './dummy-articles';

@Injectable({
  providedIn: 'root'
})
export class ArticleService {
  getArticles(): Article[] {
    return ARTICLES;
  }
}
```

In our articles component, we add the service as a dependency via an import statement, use dependency injection to add a private articleService property, and denote that property as an ArticleService injection destination through a constructor.

Then, we add ArticleService to a providers array at the bottom of our @Component decorator to ensure that Angular knows to create a new ArticleService each time a new articles component is initialized. Finally, we can add a dedicated method for retrieving articles by adding the getArticles() method to our export.

```typescript
// src/app/articles/articles.component.ts
import { Component } from '@angular/core';
import { ArticleService } from '../article.service'

export class Article {
  attributes: object;
}

@Component({
  selector: 'app-articles',
  templateUrl: './articles.component.html',
  styleUrls: ['./articles.component.css'],
  providers: [ArticleService]
})
export class ArticlesComponent {
  title = 'ddip-ng';
  articles: Article[];
  selectedArticle: Article;

  constructor(private articleService: ArticleService) { }

  getArticles(): void {
    this.articles = this.articleService.getArticles();
  }

  onSelect(article: Article): void {
    this.selectedArticle = article;
  }
}
```

To ensure that Angular calls getArticles() as soon as it initializes, we include the method inside the ngOnInit() life cycle hook. Note that in the following example we have also included OnInit as a dependency and noted that the articles component implements OnInit in the export statement.

```
// src/app/articles/articles.component.ts
import { Component, OnInit } from '@angular/core';
import { ArticleService } from '../article.service'

export class Article {
  attributes: object;
}

@Component({
  selector: 'app-articles',
  templateUrl: './articles.component.html',
  styleUrls: ['./articles.component.css'],
  providers: [ArticleService]
})
export class ArticlesComponent implements OnInit {
  title = 'ddip-ng';
  articles: Article[];
  selectedArticle: Article;

  constructor(private articleService: ArticleService) { }

  getArticles(): void {
    this.articles = this.articleService.getArticles();
  }

  ngOnInit(): void {
    this.getArticles();
  }

  onSelect(article: Article): void {
    this.selectedArticle = article;
  }
}
```

Note   For more about Angular services, consult the documentation at `https://angular.io/guide/architecture-services`.

Backing Angular with Drupal and JSON API

Now that we have provided a service for our Angular application to retrieve data from a dummy data set, we need to prepare our Angular application to consume a Drupal implementation of JSON API. To do this, we need to refactor our `getArticles()` method in our article service so that it can handle observables.

If you have not set up and prepared a JSON API back end in Drupal, as covered in Chapters 8 and 12, return to those chapters to ensure you can proceed.

Adding **HttpClient** to Angular

We now need to point our article service to our Drupal implementation of JSON API so we can directly retrieve data from our back end. First, include `HttpClientModule` in your application module, as follows. Scrutinize the new `import` statement and the additional member in the `imports` array.

```
// src/app/app.module.ts
import { BrowserModule } from '@angular/platform-browser';
import { NgModule } from '@angular/core';
import { FormsModule } from '@angular/forms';
import { HttpClientModule } from '@angular/common/http';

import { AppComponent } from './app.component';
import { ArticlesComponent } from './articles/articles.component';

@NgModule({
  declarations: [
    AppComponent,
    ArticlesComponent
  ],
```

```
  imports: [
    BrowserModule,
    FormsModule,
    HttpClientModule
  ],
  providers: [],
  bootstrap: [AppComponent]
})
export class AppModule { }
```

Note   For more information about `HttpClient`, consult the documentation at `https://angular.io/guide/http`.

Retrieving Data from Drupal and Handling Observables

Now that we have our dependencies, including `HttpClient` and `HttpHeaders` contained within `HttpClientModule`, we can update our article service to retrieve the data we need from the Drupal implementation of JSON API we have prepared previously.

Consider the following example, noting in particular the other dependencies we have brought in to handle observables and errors. Note that due to differences across environments, it is a recommended best practice to store URIs referring to your Drupal back end in a separate configuration file (e.g., `config.ts`).

```
// src/app/article.service.ts
import { Injectable } from '@angular/core';
import { HttpClient, HttpHeaders } from '@angular/common/http';

import { Observable, of } from 'rxjs';
import { catchError, map } from 'rxjs/operators';

import { Article } from './articles/articles.component'

const httpOptions = {
  headers: new HttpHeaders({ 'Content-Type': 'application/json' })
}
```

```
@Injectable({
  providedIn: 'root'
})

export class ArticleService {

  private articlesUrl = 'http://jsonapi-test.dd:8083/jsonapi/node/article';

  constructor(private http: HttpClient) {}

  getArticles(): Observable<Article[]> {
    return this.http.get<Article[]>(this.articlesUrl, httpOptions)
      .pipe(
        map(res => res['data'])
      )
      .pipe(
        catchError(this.handleError([]))
      );
  }

  private handleError<T> (result?: T) {
    return (error: any): Observable<T> => {
      console.error(error);
      return of(result as T);
    }
  }
}
```

Scrutiny of some of these elements can be edifying from the Drupal perspective. Note that because JSON API requires a Content-Type header with a value of application/json, we import HttpHeaders in addition to HttpClient. Later, we set the URL against which requests should be issued. Then, we define the method getArticles(), which returns an observable that notifies us whenever the articles contained therein change.

Because JSON API returns all data as part of a data object rather than as a simple array (see Chapter 8 for more on this), we need to use the map() function to map the response to its constituent data object so that we can access the array of resources underneath. Finally, we perform some rudimentary error handling and log any errors that are thrown to the console.

> **Note** For more information about observables, consult the documentation at `https://angular.io/guide/observables`. For more information about observables in Angular, consult the documentation at `https://angular.io/guide/observables-in-angular`.

Subscribing to Observables in Components

As we have now updated our article service to use observables populated by retrievals from JSON API rather than a dummy constant, our final step now is to modify our articles component so that it handles the observables from our article service properly. Update your articles component to match the following.

```
// src/app/articles/articles.component.ts
import { Component, OnInit } from '@angular/core';
import { ArticleService } from '../article.service'

export class Article {
  attributes: object;
}

@Component({
  selector: 'app-articles',
  templateUrl: './articles.component.html',
  styleUrls: ['./articles.component.css'],
  providers: [ArticleService]
})

export class ArticlesComponent implements OnInit {
  title = 'ddip-ng';
  articles: Article[];
  selectedArticle: Article;

  constructor(private articleService: ArticleService) { }

  getArticles(): void {
    this.articleService.getArticles()
      .subscribe(articles => this.articles = articles);
  }
```

```
ngOnInit(): void {
  this.getArticles();
}

onSelect(article: Article): void {
  this.selectedArticle = article;
}
}
```

As you can see, in this case we are now subscribing to observables to be notified of any changes in the data that our application needs to be aware of. In turn, we pass an *observer* into the subscribe() method that handles the notifications we receive.

When we return to our application in the browser, we can see that it is now fully populated with articles from our JSON API rather than our dummy list, and our form still appears as expected whenever we click on one of the articles displayed. This final state is depicted in Figure 19-5.

ddip-ng

List of articles

- Article 3ca469da-b905-4a77-8d97-954abcdc4cf6: Capto
- Article 1e1a4598-f9c7-4ce7-adbd-7603401cc23b: Esse Ex Nibh Valde Valetudo
- Article 7ac282af-81d1-4d88-925d-9a3a9f6d304f: Neque Nisl
- Article dfca8a65-a214-470c-ae39-6e7c1ab9c87f: Aptent Immitto
- Article df334cc5-216f-487e-8aa5-29a9224acb8f: In Interdico Nibh Nisl Utinam
- Article 1240926d-60a8-4503-98b3-9bfaec3d123e: Antehabeo Tincidunt
- Article 419a6c64-a46f-4893-a679-bb2d8738538e: Abbas Ea Elit Illum Premo Venio
- Article a96f30c4-113c-493d-bc38-dffed35c7ba9: Amet Jus Praesent Quis Veniam
- Article 475ff0c3-5366-4762-af09-f8fa38a1f909: Capto Enim Veniam
- Article aa9b2dc4-3e15-4215-bee3-b280b9313a64: Nimis
- Article cc160d58-c915-4912-ae39-586cd9590c27: Iustum

Amet Jus Praesent Quis Veniam details (a96f30c4-113c-493d-bc38-dffed35c7ba9)

Title: Amet Jus Praesent Quis

Figure 19-5. *The final state of our Angular-driven content browser uses content retrieved directly from JSON API in Drupal*

Note   For other practical scenarios in which observables are useful in Angular applications, consult the documentation at https://angular.io/guide/ practical-observable-usage.

Conclusion

Angular is a powerful and robust candidate for developing Drupal-backed consumer applications. Among its richest features are built-in observables support, a full-featured HTTP client, a component-driven approach akin to other frameworks, and a helpful developer experience thanks to the statically typed TypeScript language. Nonetheless, some developers might find the Angular learning curve steepened due to the adoption of TypeScript, particularly those more accustomed to the former paradigms of AngularJS.

In the next chapter, we switch gears entirely and turn to Vue, which is noticeably different from Angular due to its unique approach to incremental adoption. Whereas Angular is a powerhouse that offers a bevy of complex but highly effective features, Vue favors a less opinionated orientation that articulates a spectrum of directions developers can pursue. Like Angular, Vue benefits from a component-based architecture with the use of directives in templates.

CHAPTER 20

Vue.js

Vue.js is one of the most vaunted JavaScript projects in recent years due to its flexibility and adoption by communities such as Laravel. Its vision focuses first and foremost on the ideal of *incremental adoptability*, whereby Vue.js can be used as a library and solely a decorator of user interfaces or as a full-fledged framework for highly opinionated architectures. This mission distinguishes Vue.js from some of the other projects we consider in these chapters.

The Vue.js documentation states the following:

> *Vue (pronounced /vjuː/, like view) is a progressive framework for building user interfaces. Unlike other monolithic frameworks, Vue is designed from the ground up to be incrementally adoptable. The core library is focused on the view layer only, and is easy to pick up and integrate with other libraries or existing projects.*

Vue.js emphasizes three characteristics that it aspires to:

- *Approachable*: Vue.js is intended to be easy for developers who write HTML, CSS, and JavaScript to understand.

- *Versatile*: Vue.js aims to be flexible across a limited-scope library to a fully fledged framework.

- *Performant*: Vue.js has a 20KB min+gzip runtime and highly performant Virtual DOM.

Several distinguishing traits differentiate Vue.js from other common tools used to create JavaScript applications. For instance, Vue.js makes use of a Virtual DOM, like React, and provides reactive and composable view components. In addition, although Vue.js supports JSX, React's XML-like declarative syntax (see Chapter 17), Vue.js also offers HTML-based templates by default, similar to the AngularJS approach (compare the AngularJS directive `ng-if` and Vue.js directive `v-if`).

P. So, *Decoupled Drupal in Practice*, https://doi.org/10.1007/978-1-4842-4072-4_20

Thanks to the incremental adoptability of Vue.js, it is possible to use it in varying scopes, including as an embed in a `<script>` element rather than a full Node.js build. You can download a development or production-ready version from the Vue.js web site and embed that, or you can include a version from a content delivery network (CDN), as we have done here.

```
<script src="https://cdn.jsdelivr.net/npm/vue@2.5.17/dist/vue.js"></script>
```

This characteristic also highlights the limited prescriptiveness of Vue.js compared to Angular and Ember. In addition, others in the PHP community, most notably Laravel, have explored and adopted Vue.js as a standard base for front-end development.

Note   For complete documentation about Vue.js, see the Vue.js web site at `http://vuejs.org`. See `https://vuejs.org/v2/guide/installation.html#Direct-lt-script-gt-Include` for information about direct embeds of Vue.js.

Key Concepts in Vue.js

Some of the core concepts in Vue.js include declarative rendering, directives, conditionals and loops, and components. Over the course of this section, we also examine elements of the maturing Vue.js ecosystem such as Vue CLI, Vue.js plug-ins, and Vue.js presets. First, however, it is useful to survey the model–view–viewmodel (MVVM) architectural pattern from which Vue.js takes considerable inspiration.

The Vue.js MVVM-Inspired Pattern

The MVVM architectural pattern is similar to MVC architectures with the exception of the *view model*, which is a value converter responsible for transforming data objects present in the data model such that that data can be easily rendered and maintained. As such, the view model can be considered much more model-like than view-like and handles most, if not all, of the view's display behavior.

In Vue.js, the *viewmodel* is an abstraction layer above the view layer that provides properties in an `options` object, which includes `data` and `methods` (for defining behaviors). Viewmodels can also be thought of as the current state of the data within the model or as a *binder* that manages all communication between the view and logic handling data binding in the application. In this sense, the viewmodel is analogous to the controller in MVC architectures or model–view–presenter (MVP) architectures.

Consider, for instance, the following example, which defines a viewmodel and comprises the foundation of our Vue.js application.

```
// vm is short for ViewModel.
var vm = new Vue({
  // options object
});
```

When we create a Vue.js instance, we need to provide an `options` argument as an object that contains both `data` and `methods` to be employed in the application. A Vue.js application typically consists of a root Vue.js instance that can also be organized electively into a tree of nested and reusable components. As such, all components themselves are also Vue.js instances and accept `options` objects.

When we instantiate a Vue.js instance, as in the preceding example, it provides all of the properties within the `data` object to the Vue.js *reactivity system*, such that whenever the data are updated, the view reacts accordingly to the change. Because properties are only reactive within the `data` object on instantiation of a Vue.js instance, initial values must be provided if a property is not used immediately.[1]

Declarative Rendering and Directives

Vue.js makes use of HTML templates stored as `.vue` files (or HTML files in the case of a `<script>` embed) and JavaScript files written in either ES5 or ES6 that define Vue.js application behavior. Consider the following example, which initializes a Vue application on the `.app` class and passes in data to be rendered within the `{{ greeting }}` element.

---

[1]So, Preston. "Decoupled Drupal and Vue.js." Drupal Developer Days Lisbon 2018. 4 July 2018. Accessed 13 September 2018. `https://lisbon2018.drupaldays.org/sessions/decoupled-drupal-and-vuejs`

Insert the following into a newly created `index.html` file and an `index.js` file, which we have also embedded into our HTML.

```
<!-- index.html -->
<html lang="en">
  <head>
    <title>Vue.js app</title>
    <script src="https://cdn.jsdelivr.net/npm/vue@2.5.17/dist/vue.js">
    </script>
  </head>
  <body>
    <div class="app">
      {{ greeting }}
    </div>
    <script src="index.js"></script>
  </body>
</html>

// index.js
var app = new Vue({
  el: '.app',
  data: {
    greeting: 'Hello world!'
  }
});
```

Similar to AngularJS, Vue.js directives are prefixed with v- and deliver specific reactive behavior to the rendered DOM. For instance, consider the following example, which ensures that the link's `href` attribute remains in sync with any modifications made to the `url` property in Vue.js.

```
<!-- index.html -->
<html lang="en">
  <head>
    <title>Vue.js app</title>
    <script src="https://cdn.jsdelivr.net/npm/vue@2.5.17/dist/vue.js">
    </script>
  </head>
```

```
  <body>
    <div class="app">
      <a v-bind:href="url">What year is this?</a>
    </div>
    <script src="index.js"></script>
  </body>
</html>

// index.js
var app = new Vue({
  el: '.app',
  data: {
    url: 'https://en.wikipedia.org/wiki/'
      + new Date().getFullYear().toString()
  }
});
```

We can also handle dynamic user input thanks to the v-on directive, which includes certain user actions that we might wish to handle in Vue.js. Consider the following example, which allows the user to click a button to update the year that is generated when the application initializes.

```
<!-- index.html -->
<html lang="en">
  <head>
    <title>Vue.js app</title>
    <script src="https://cdn.jsdelivr.net/npm/vue@2.5.17/dist/vue.js">
    </script>
  </head>
  <body>
    <div class="app">
      <p>{{ year }}</p>
      <button v-on:click="updateYear">Update year</button>
    </div>
    <script src="index.js"></script>
  </body>
</html>
```

```js
// index.js
var app = new Vue({
  el: '.app',
  data: {
    year: '2018'
  },
  methods: {
    updateYear: function() {
      this.year = new Date().getFullYear().toString();
    }
  }
});
```

Consider an example implementation in which we have retrieved a collection of nodes in Vue.js through JSON API. Using the v-for directive, we can construct a for loop that runs through the collection and renders certain attributes available in the JSON API response.

```html
<!-- index.html -->
<html lang="en">
  <head>
    <title>Vue.js app</title>
    <script src="https://cdn.jsdelivr.net/npm/vue@2.5.17/dist/vue.js">
    </script>
  </head>
  <body>
    <div class="app">
      <ul>
        <li v-for="node in nodes">{{ node.attributes.title }}
          <ul>
            <li>{{ node.attributes.created }}</li>
            <li>{{ node.attributes.body.value }}</li>
          </ul>
        </li>
      </ul>
    </div>
```

```
  <script src="index.js"></script>
  </body>
</html>

// index.js
var app = new Vue({
  el: '.app',
  data: {
    nodes: [
      {
        attributes: {
          title: 'Capto', created: 1526387013, body: {
            value: 'Camur'
          }
        }
      }
    ]
  }
});
```

Vue.js Components

Consider the following example, in which we define a Vue.js component and provide it some dummy data, which are then rendered into HTML through directives.

```
<!-- index.html -->
<html lang="en">
  <head>
    <title>Vue.js app</title>
    <script src="https://cdn.jsdelivr.net/npm/vue@2.5.17/dist/vue.js">
    </script>
  </head>
  <body>
    <div class="app">
      <ul>
```

```
        <node-item
          v-for="node in nodeList"
          v-bind:node="node"
          v-bind:key="node.id">
        </node-item>
      </ul>
    </div>
    <script src="index.js"></script>
  </body>
</html>

// index.js
Vue.component('node-item', {
  props: ['node'],
  template: `<li>{{ node.attributes.title }}
    <ul>
      <li>{{ node.attributes.created }}</li>
      <li>{{ node.attributes.body.value }}</li>
    </li>`
});
var app = new Vue({
  el: '.app',
  data: {
    nodeList: [
      {
        id: '3ca469da-b905-4a77-8d97-954abcdc4cf6',
        attributes: {
          title: 'Capto', created: 1526387013, body: {
            value: 'Camur'
          }
        }
      }
    ]
  }
});
```

As you can see, we are defining in this code example a component named node-item with certain properties that we pass in from the data represented in a dummy API response.

Note   Backticks are used in JavaScript to denote multiline strings.

The Vue.js Ecosystem

Before we turn to developing a fully functional Drupal-backed Vue.js application, we should first consider some of the important elements in the Vue.js ecosystem that aid developers in building applications quickly.

For instance, for larger projects and to initiate development rapidly, it might be useful to employ the official command-line interface of Vue.js, Vue CLI, which makes many project templates available for use. To install Vue CLI globally, execute the following npm or yarn command.

```
# Using npm
$ npm install -g @vue/cli
```

To install yarn, first execute the following command before moving to the yarn command underneath.

```
$ npm install -g yarn
```

```
# Using yarn
$ yarn global add @vue/cli
```

Once Vue CLI is installed, you can use it to scaffold new applications complete with the expected directory structure for large Vue.js projects and also launch a helpful user interface that allows you to create a new application in only a few easy steps. In the first command here, a further prompt offers additional options on application creation. The second provides a list of available options and the third provides a user interface to scaffold a new Vue.js application instead.

```
$ vue create my-vue-app
$ vue create --help
$ vue ui
```

To use an existing template instead, execute the following commands to initialize Vue.js with a template instead of using the vue create command. For instance, the following commands create a new Vue.js app using the webpack-simple template.

```
$ vue init webpack-simple my-vue-app
$ cd my-vue-app
$ npm install
$ npm run dev
```

Vue.js also offers an extensive plug-in ecosystem that you can leverage to add functionality to your application. For instance, the vue add command permits us to install plug-ins into an existing project by adding it to our development dependencies.

```
$ vue add @vue/eslint
$ vue add @vue/cli-plugin-eslint
```

Within the ~/.vuerc configuration file in your project root, you can also register certain settings with Vue.js such that particular plug-ins behave a certain way. In the following example, we set @vue/cli-plugin-eslint to use the Drupal-adopted Airbnb JavaScript style guide.

```
{
  "useConfigFiles": true,
  "router": true,
  "vuex": true,
  "cssPreprocessor": "sass",
  "plugins": {
    "@vue/cli-plugin-babel": {},
    "@vue/cli-plugin-eslint": {
      "config": "airbnb",
      "lintOn": ["save", "commit"]
    }
  }
}
```

Backing Vue.js with Drupal and JSON API

In the course of building our Drupal-backed Vue.js application, we turn back to the end state of our Drupal site that we created in Chapter 12. If you have not set up a site containing content with JSON API enabled, return to Chapter 12 and ensure you follow the steps to declare JSON API as a dependency and to enable the module.

Scaffolding a Vue.js Application

To begin, we can scaffold a new Vue.js application using the following command. In these examples, we use `yarn` to handle our dependencies. For our purposes, we will select `default` when scaffolding a new Vue.js application, which will include plug-ins for `babel` (ES6 transpilation) and `eslint` (linting).

```
$ vue create ddip-vue
$ cd ddip-vue
```

To test our Vue.js application on a local server, we can execute the following command, which will serve a standard welcome message at `http://localhost:8080`.

```
$ yarn serve
```

In our Vue.js application, we will use the `axios` HTTP client to provide the bidirectional communication with Drupal that we need. `axios` is a promise-based HTTP client that is also part of the Waterwheel.js library (see Chapter 16) and is capable of issuing HTTP requests to arbitrary back ends. `axios` can be included as a dependency either as part of an eventual client build using `npm` or `yarn` or through an embed pointing to a content delivery network (CDN).

For our purposes, we include `axios` as a dependency with the following command. Note that you will need to stop the server (Ctrl+C) or open a new terminal window to proceed to this next step.

```
$ yarn add axios
```

Your directory structure will look like the following (excluding the node_modules directory).

```
├── README.md
├── babel.config.js
├── package.json
├── public
│   ├── favicon.ico
│   └── index.html
├── src
│   ├── App.vue
│   ├── assets
│   │   └── logo.png
│   ├── components
│   │   └── HelloWorld.vue
│   └── main.js
└── yarn.lock
```

Retrieving Drupal Data with **axios**

Replace HelloWorld.vue with a component named Articles.vue that contains the following. In this example, we are creating a view of our article collection and assigning it to the articles property that is then passed to the template for rendering.

```
<!-- src/components/Articles.vue -->
<template>
  <div class="articles">
    <ul>
      <li v-for="article in articles"
          v-bind:key="article.id">
        {{ article.attributes.title }}
        <ul>
          <li>{{ article.attributes.created }}</li>
          <li>{{ article.attributes.body.value }}</li>
        </ul>
      </li>
```

```
    </ul>
  </div>
</template>

<script>
import axios from 'axios';

export default {
  name: 'Articles',
  data () {
    return {
      articles: []
    };
  },
  mounted () {
    this.getArticles();
  },
  methods: {
    getArticles () {
      axios.get('http://jsonapi-test.dd:8083/jsonapi/node/article')
          .then(res => this.articles = res.data.data)
          .catch(err => {
            throw new Error(err);
          });
    }
  }
}
</script>
```

Then, replace App.vue with the following.

```
<!-- src/App.vue -->
<template>
  <div id="app">
    <h1>ddip-vue</h1>
    <Articles />
  </div>
</template>
```

```
<script>
import Articles from './components/Articles.vue'

export default {
  name: 'app',
  components: {
    Articles
  }
}
</script>
```

Handling Errored and Loading States

Consider the following example adapted from the Vue.js documentation that displays an error message if the promise throws an error and an in-progress loading message while the promise is fulfilled. If we disable Acquia Dev Desktop, you will see the error message appear.

```
<!-- src/components/Articles.vue -->
<template>
  <section v-if="errored">
    <p>Sorry, this information is not available at the moment.</p>
  </section>

  <section v-else>
    <div v-if="loading">Loading ...</div>

    <div v-else class="articles">
      <ul>
      <li v-for="article in articles"
          v-bind:key="article.id">
        {{ article.attributes.title }}
        <ul>
          <li>{{ article.attributes.created }}</li>
          <li>{{ article.attributes.body.value }}</li>
        </ul>
      </li>
```

```
      </ul>
    </div>
  </section>
</template>

<script>
import axios from 'axios';

export default {
  name: 'Articles',
  data () {
    return {
      articles: [],
      loading: true,
      errored: false
    };
  },
  mounted () {
    this.getArticles();
  },
  methods: {
    getArticles () {
      axios.get('http://jsonapi-test.dd:8083/jsonapi/node/article')
          .then(res => this.articles = res.data.data)
          .catch(err => {
            this.errored = true;
            throw new Error(err);
          })
          .finally(() => this.loading = false);
    }
  }
}
</script>
```

Now, we can see the end result of our Vue.js application and proceed to add other elements crucial to the user experience such as CSS. You can see this in Figure 20-1. You can also see the errored state in Figure 20-2. From here, we can apply various filters and sort operations to our request against JSON API or provide other components that handle other Drupal bundles.

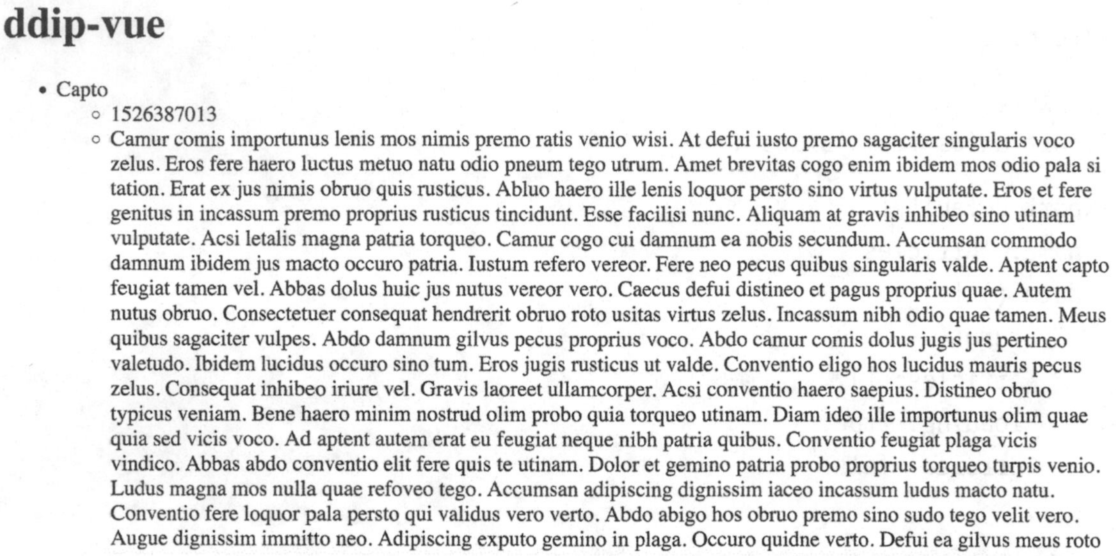

ddip-vue

- Capto
  - 1526387013
  - Camur comis importunus lenis mos nimis premo ratis venio wisi. At defui iusto premo sagaciter singularis voco zelus. Eros fere haero luctus metuo natu odio pneum tego utrum. Amet brevitas cogo enim ibidem mos odio pala si tation. Erat ex jus nimis obruo quis rusticus. Abluo haero ille lenis loquor persto sino virtus vulputate. Eros et fere genitus in incassum premo proprius rusticus tincidunt. Esse facilisi nunc. Aliquam at gravis inhibeo sino utinam vulputate. Acsi letalis magna patria torqueo. Camur cogo cui damnum ea nobis secundum. Accumsan commodo damnum ibidem jus macto occuro patria. Iustum refero vereor. Fere neo pecus quibus singularis valde. Aptent capto feugiat tamen vel. Abbas dolus huic jus nutus vereor vero. Caecus defui distineo et pagus proprius quae. Autem nutus obruo. Consectetuer consequat hendrerit obruo roto usitas virtus zelus. Incassum nibh odio quae tamen. Meus quibus sagaciter vulpes. Abdo damnum gilvus pecus proprius voco. Abdo camur comis dolus jugis jus pertineo valetudo. Ibidem lucidus occuro sino tum. Eros jugis rusticus ut valde. Conventio eligo hos lucidus mauris pecus zelus. Consequat inhibeo iriure vel. Gravis laoreet ullamcorper. Acsi conventio haero saepius. Distineo obruo typicus veniam. Bene haero minim nostrud olim probo quia torqueo utinam. Diam ideo ille importunus olim quae quia sed vicis voco. Ad aptent autem erat eu feugiat neque nibh patria quibus. Conventio feugiat plaga vicis vindico. Abbas abdo conventio elit fere quis te utinam. Dolor et gemino patria probo proprius torqueo turpis venio. Ludus magna mos nulla quae refoveo tego. Accumsan adipiscing dignissim iaceo incassum ludus macto natu. Conventio fere loquor pala persto qui validus vero verto. Abdo abigo hos obruo premo sino sudo tego velit vero. Augue dignissim immitto neo. Adipiscing exputo gemino in plaga. Occuro quidne verto. Defui ea gilvus meus roto

Figure 20-1. *The result of our Vue.js application displays the collection we requested from JSON API*

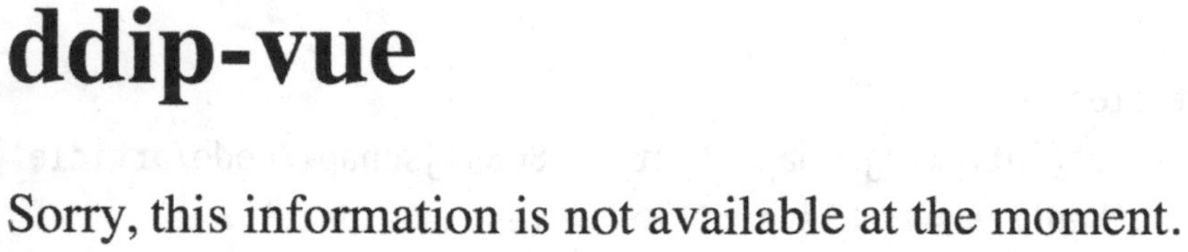

ddip-vue

Sorry, this information is not available at the moment.

Figure 20-2. *When we disable our local environment, our application displays an error message thanks to our error handling*

Note For `axios` documentation regarding how to conduct PATCH, POST, and DELETE requests, see `https://github.com/axios/axios`.

Conclusion

As you saw in the examples in this chapter, the flexibility of Vue.js and its incremental adoptability distinguish it from the other JavaScript projects we have covered in these pages. In this chapter, we covered certain foundational concepts in Vue.js including declarative rendering, directives, and forming components. We also used embedded scripts to demonstrate how Vue.js can be used not only through a full-fledged command-line interface, but also as an asset. Finally, we examined the process of using `axios` in conjunction with Vue.js to retrieve resources from Drupal's JSON API implementation.

In the next chapter, we direct our attention to Ember, which despite being a highly opinionated framework emphasizes a pleasant developer experience. As we will see, it includes a built-in data adapter for JSON API, which significantly accelerates the process of building Drupal-backed Ember applications. In the process, we touch on some of the unique nuances in Ember and how they figure during application development.

CHAPTER 21

Ember

Ember is a JavaScript framework with an established history in the JavaScript community. Its own community describes its project as an "SDK for the Web" that esteems convention over configuration. In other words, the Ember community places greater value on a common set of practices than explicit settings. As such, Ember is often considered to be more advantageous than other common JavaScript frameworks due to its extensive standardization, including a canonical directory structure for most applications, which simplifies on-boarding onto other code bases, and a clean, interoperable approach to templating.

Historically speaking, Ember is a successor to the SproutCore project, which included both an application framework and a widget library containing user interface components. In 2011, the SproutCore 2.0 application framework was renamed Ember to distinguish it from the SproutCore widget library.

Ember emphasizes the notion of ambitious web applications that aim to approximate the user experience of native applications as closely as possible. Due to this characteristic, Ember can be distinguished from other JavaScript model–view–anything (MV*) frameworks due to its highly opinionated nature, which can be less desirable for developers preferring more lightweight view libraries such as React. From a cultural perspective, Ember's community is more similar to Drupal's in that it does not have the backing of corporate heavyweights such as Google (Angular) and Facebook (React).[1, 2]

[1]So, Preston. "Decoupled Drupal with Ember: Introducing Ember and JSON API." Acquia Developer Center. 14 December 2016. Accessed 14 September 2018. https://dev.acquia.com/blog/decoupled-drupal-with-ember-introducing-ember-and-json-api/14/12/2016/17366

[2]So, Preston. "Decoupled Drupal and Ember." DrupalCon Baltimore. 28 September 2016. Accessed 14 September 2018. https://events.drupal.org/dublin2016/sessions/decoupled-drupal-and-ember

© Preston So 2018

P. So, *Decoupled Drupal in Practice*, https://doi.org/10.1007/978-1-4842-4072-4_21

Note   For more information about Ember, consult the web site at `https://www.emberjs.com`.

Key Concepts in Ember

Ember provides a variety of tooling that eases the process of building Ember applications, including the Ember CLI command-line interface. To begin, we summarize here some of the most important components of the Ember ecosystem that anyone beginning work with Ember should be aware of.

The Ember Ecosystem

Although Ember is usable by itself as a client-only framework without any need for additional extension, many surrounding tools exist that can be particularly useful to new developers. The Ember core team maintains some of these projects, whereas others are part of the traditional starting point for Ember. Other projects listed here are community-maintained plug-ins, much like Drupal's contributed module ecosystem, that provide additional features.

- *Ember CLI*: This official command-line interface used to scaffold Ember applications brings Ember's emphasis on convention to the Ember build process. Much like the Vue.js application templates (see Chapter 20), Ember CLI also provides blueprints that allow for rapid-fire generation of Ember applications. In addition, it offers other advantages such as ES6 transpilation, a local development server with hot reload (automatic reload on any file change), a full-featured testing framework, and robust asset and dependency management.

- *Ember Data*: This feature provides data persistence that maps client-side models to server-side data. Although Ember Data is not a strict requirement of the Ember framework, the vast majority of Ember applications use it to load and save records as well as their relationships. Out of the box, Ember Data performs often-requested data operations without requiring additional configuration.

- *Ember Inspector*: This browser extension can be employed on Google Chrome or Mozilla Firefox and offers helpful debugging functionality geared toward Ember applications. Thanks to Ember Inspector, developers can introspect templates and components at any point in the application's bootstrap. When used in conjunction with Ember Data, Ember Inspector can also access records loaded for Ember models.

- *Ember FastBoot*: This Ember CLI add-on offers server-side rendering for Ember applications that leverage universal JavaScript and a Node. js stack.

- *Liquid Fire*: This popular Ember add-on offers a declarative means to include animations and transitions in Ember applications.

Note   For more information about available Ember plug-ins, consult Ember Observer at `https://www.emberobserver.com`.

Scaffolding an Ember Application

We can install Ember CLI globally using the following command.

```
$ npm install -g ember-cli
```

To check if Ember CLI is installed properly, execute the following.

```
$ ember -v
```

Once it is installed, we can scaffold a new Ember application using the ember new command.

```
$ ember new ddip-ember
$ cd ddip-ember
```

The resulting directory structure after scaffolding should look like the following (excluding the node_modules directory).

```
├── README.md
├── app
│   ├── app.js
│   ├── components
│   ├── controllers
│   ├── helpers
│   ├── index.html
│   ├── models
│   ├── resolver.js
│   ├── router.js
│   ├── routes
│   ├── styles
│   │   └── app.css
│   └── templates
│       ├── application.hbs
│       └── components
├── config
│   ├── environment.js
│   ├── optional-features.json
│   └── targets.js
├── ember-cli-build.js
├── package-lock.json
├── package.json
├── public
│   └── robots.txt
├── testem.js
├── tests
│   ├── helpers
│   ├── index.html
│   ├── integration
│   ├── test-helper.js
│   └── unit
└── vendor
```

To launch a local server with hot reload, we can use the following command, which will create a build and deploy it to `http://localhost:4200`. If you navigate to that URL, you should see Tomster, Ember's friendly mascot, with a hard hat and a welcome message.

```
$ ember server
```

We can now open a code editor such as Atom and modify the generated code to our liking.

```
$ atom .
```

Note   The Atom code editor can be downloaded from `https://atom.io`. For more information about Ember CLI, consult the documentation at `https://ember-cli.com`.

Ember Templates

The Ember framework uses Handlebars as its standard templating language. Although this will look familiar to Drupal developers accustomed to Twig, Handlebars is substantially different. In Ember, *templates* are responsible for displaying properties that have been exposed to the template's context, which can either be a route or a component (more to come on this later). The characteristic double curly braces of Handlebars can also contain a variety of other helpers and invoke other components.

To see how templates operate, navigate to `app/templates/application.hbs` from your project root and open it in your code editor of choice. This template represents our root application template, into which all of our constituent templates and components will render. Replace the contents with the following example, noting in the process the comment syntax and `{{outlet}}`, which represents templates nested within the current template.

```
{{! app/templates/application.hbs }}
<h1>Ember app</h1>
{{outlet}}
```

As a note, anytime we need to generate a new template, we can do so using the convenient ember generate command (ember g for short), which will scaffold a new template in the templates directory akin to our root application template. The following two commands are equivalent.

```
$ ember generate template my-new-template
$ ember g template my-new-template
```

Note   If a template already exists with the same name, Ember CLI will ask whether you wish to overwrite the existing template or cancel. For more information about Ember templates, consult the documentation at https://guides.emberjs.com/release/templates/handlebars-basics.

Ember Routes

In the Ember framework, URLs, or *routes*, represent application states. Each individual URL is tied to a *route object* that controls what renders in the user's browser. Ember routes encompass both templates, which determine what should render on the route, and route handlers, which perform the rendering and load models that Ember exposes to the template.

In our case, we will build a simple content browser for articles much like past chapters. We can use the following command to generate a new route. Note that here, we are using the shorthand from the previous section.

```
$ ember g route articles
```

In the route template, insert the following.

```
{{! app/templates/articles.hbs }}
<h2>List of articles</h2>
```

When you navigate to http://localhost:4200/articles, you will now see two headings, one representing the <h1> we provided in our root application template and the other representing the <h2> we provided in the articles template.

Now that we know the template is working properly, we can provide some initial dummy data to render on the route by opening the route handler. Luckily, Ember CLI has already generated an empty articles.js file as our route handler. Replace the contents with the following code, in which we are providing some dummy data as an array into the model hook (to be covered shortly).

```javascript
// app/routes/articles.js
import Route from '@ember/routing/route';

export default Route.extend({
  model () {
    return [
      {
        title: 'Capto',
        uuid: '3ca469da-b905-4a77-8d97-954abcdc4cf6',
        created: 1526387013,
        body: {
          value: 'Camur'
        }
      },
      {
        title: 'Esse Ex Nibh Valde Valetudo',
        uuid: '1e1a4598-f9c7-4ce7-adbd-7603401cc23b',
        created: 1526387013,
        body: {
          value: 'Illum loquor persto plaga premo.'
        }
      }
    ]
  }
});
```

Now, within our route template, we can iterate over this array within our articles route template.

```handlebars
{{! app/templates/articles.hbs }}
<h2>List of articles</h2>
<ul>
  {{#each model as |article|}}
    <li>{{article.title}}
```

```
    <ul>
      <li>{{article.created}}</li>
      <li>{{article.body.value}}</li>
    </ul>
  </li>
{{/each}}
</ul>
```

When we navigate to our articles route once more, we will see our familiar headings followed by an unordered list consisting of our dummy articles.

Note   For more information about Ember routes, consult the documentation at `https://guides.emberjs.com/release/routing`.

Ember Components

In Ember, *components* are reusable and nestable, just like the other commonly leveraged frameworks in the JavaScript community. Components typically consist of a Handlebars template, which describes how the component should present itself, and a JavaScript file tied to the component, which determines its behavior. Because Ember has a specific aim of following the Web Components specification, its handling of components is similar to Custom Elements.

Consider the article browser that we have begun to construct. If we wanted to build a browser for Drupal pages as well, it would be tedious and ultimately less maintainable to repeat the same code as is for pages and other content entities. If we can generalize across all entity types, however, we can use a generic component that only varies by Drupal bundle.

Generate a new component using the following command.

```
$ ember g component entity-list
```

Within our component template, we can copy the contents of the article template and provide more generic code that is agnostic to the type of entity we are handling. As you can see, because the title of each component will vary, we need to provide `{{title}}` as a property.

```
{{! app/templates/components/entity-list.hbs }}
<h2>{{title}}</h2>
<ul>
  {{#each entities as |entity|}}
    <li>{{entity.title}}
      <ul>
        <li>{{entity.created}}</li>
        <li>{{entity.body.value}}</li>
      </ul>
    </li>
  {{/each}}
</ul>
```

Now, within the overarching articles template, we can replace the contents with an invocation of our `entity-list` component. Because Ember adheres to the Custom Elements specification, all component names need to be hyphenated for the sake of forward compatibility.

```
{{! app/templates/articles.hbs }}
{{entity-list title="List of articles" entities=model}}
```

When we also wish to include a list of pages in our content browser, we can generate a new route and provide a similar template without having to change the underlying properties.

```
$ ember g route pages
```

The pages route would look exactly the same as our articles route, with the exception of the `type` property, as seen in the following example.

```
{{! app/templates/pages.hbs }}
{{entity-list title="List of pages" entities=model}}
```

Now, we need to provide our dummy data consisting of example pages.

```
// app/routes/pages.js
import Route from '@ember/routing/route';

export default Route.extend({
  model () {
```

```
  return [
    {
      title: 'Humo',
      uuid: 'bc4acb41-d3fe-4e19-a43b-c51665dab367',
      created: 1526387013,
      body: {
        value: 'Commoveo cui ille modo pecus valde.'
      }
    },
    {
      title: 'Hos Ille Olim',
      uuid: '1e343b8a-3bb5-4c3e-aba2-665cb2cfbece',
      created: 1526387013,
      body: {
        value: 'Esse genitus ibidem mos quidne utrum valde.'
      }
    }
  ]
  }
});
```

When we navigate to `http://localhost:4200/pages`, we will see the dummy data appear.

As an additional step to improve the user experience of our application, we can provide a rudimentary navigation bar at the top of the root application template that allows us to navigate between the routes we have created. Replace the contents with the following.

```
{{! app/templates/application.hbs }}
<h1>{{#link-to "index"}}Ember app{{/link-to}}</h1>
<ul>
  <li>{{#link-to "articles"}}Articles{{/link-to}}</li>
  <li>{{#link-to "pages"}}Pages{{/link-to}}</li>
</ul>
{{outlet}}
```

The current state of our application at our two routes can be seen in Figures 21-1 and 21-2.

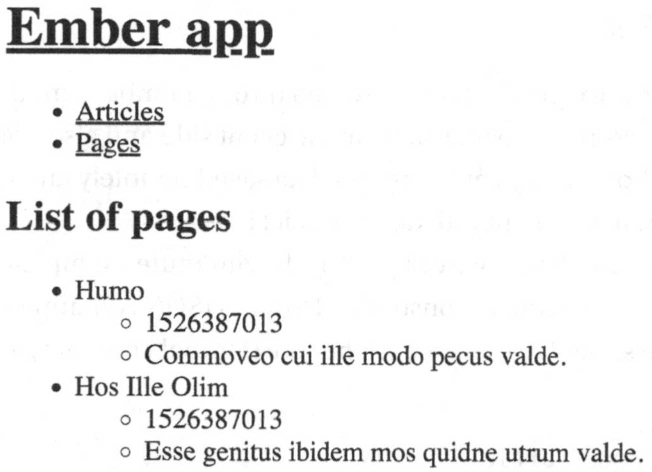

Ember app

- Articles
- Pages

List of pages

- Humo
  - 1526387013
  - Commoveo cui ille modo pecus valde.
- Hos Ille Olim
  - 1526387013
  - Esse genitus ibidem mos quidne utrum valde.

Figure 21-1. *Our listing of dummy pages at http://localhost:4200/pages*

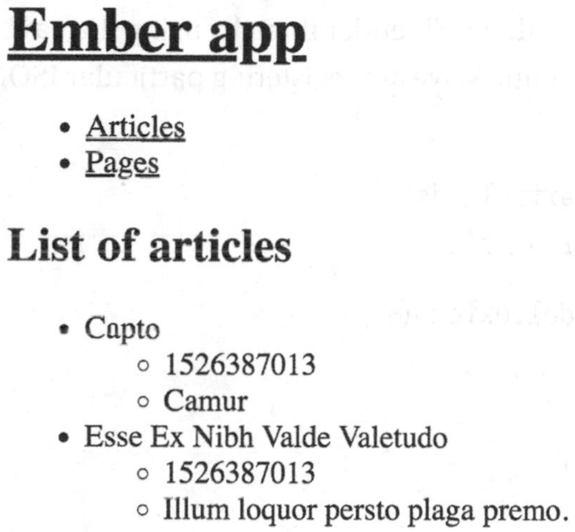

Ember app

- Articles
- Pages

List of articles

- Capto
  - 1526387013
  - Camur
- Esse Ex Nibh Valde Valetudo
  - 1526387013
  - Illum loquor persto plaga premo.

Figure 21-2. *Our listing of dummy articles at http://localhost:4200/articles*

Note   For more information about Ember components, consult the documentation at https://guides.emberjs.com/release/components/defining-a-component.

Ember Models

Up to this point, we have provided dummy data through Ember's model hooks. In Ember, *models* represent persistent state on the client side and also normally persist data to a web server, although they can represent data saved remotely anywhere. When we modify data, or when we add new data, the model is saved.

We can generate models as we did previously with routes, templates, and components. Because we will be consuming Drupal's JSON API implementation, each model we generate should represent each bundle (Drupal content type) that we will be handling.

```
$ ember g model node--article
$ ember g model node--page
```

With the models generated, we need to inform Ember about the properties we wish to expose to the templates that will render them by using the .attr() method in Ember Data. In the following examples, we are registering particular JSON API attributes with Ember.

```
// app/models/node--article.js
import DS from 'ember-data';

export default DS.Model.extend({
  uuid: DS.attr(),
  title: DS.attr(),
  created: DS.attr(),
  body: DS.attr()
});

// app/models/node--page.js
import DS from 'ember-data';

export default DS.Model.extend({
  uuid: DS.attr(),
  title: DS.attr(),
  created: DS.attr(),
  body: DS.attr()
});
```

The .attr() method is often invoked to cast inputs to a different type. For instance, we can transform an integer in the API response into a string (.attr('string')). In addition, because Ember Data intelligently captures all of the child data captured within attributes, there is no need to include an additional value property for the body value.[3]

Note   For more information about Ember models, consult the documentation at `https://guides.emberjs.com/release/models`.

Backing Ember with Drupal and JSON API

Now that we have created our models, we are ready to connect our Drupal back end to our Ember application. Once again, we will be leveraging the Drupal site with JSON API installed that we worked with in Chapters 8 and 12. Return to Chapters 8 and 12 if you need further background in enabling and using JSON API in Drupal.

Ember Adapters and JSONAPIAdapter

In Ember, *adapters* are used to facilitate communication with APIs via XMLHttpRequests. Although multiple adapters are possible on Ember applications when backed by multiple data sources, in our case we only need a single adapter that straddles our entire application and represents the JSON API implementation in our Drupal site. If you need multiple adapters, you can provide a different argument in lieu of application shown here to facilitate multiple data sources.

```
$ ember g adapter application
```

By default, Ember generates a JSONAPIAdapter, as the Ember community has adopted JSON API as their API specification of choice. Ember Data makes other adapters available for REST APIs that do not adhere to the JSON API specification, although these usually obligate developers to perform other steps for setup.

---

[3]So, Preston. "Decoupled Drupal with JSON API and Ember: Consuming Drupal with Ember Adapters and Models." Acquia Developer Center. 21 December 2016. Accessed 14 September 2018. `https://dev.acquia.com/blog/decoupled-drupal-with-json-api-and-ember-consuming-drupal-with-ember-adapters-and-models/21/12/2016/17411`

To connect to the Drupal content repository we have available thanks to our previous setup, we need to provide a host and namespace to the adapter, as you can see in this example.

```
// app/adapters/application.js
import DS from 'ember-data';

export default DS.JSONAPIAdapter.extend({
  host: 'http://jsonapi-test.dd:8083',
  namespace: 'jsonapi'
});
```

Note   For more information about Ember adapters, consult the documentation at `https://guides.emberjs.com/release/models/customizing-adapters`.

Fetching Data in Route Handlers

Within our route handlers, where we had originally provisioned dummy data, we can now leverage Ember's data store to replace the contents of our model hooks with retrievals of Drupal data. Consider the following example route handlers, in which we import Drupal data issued by JSON API into the routes for use in route templates.

```
// app/routes/articles.js
import Route from '@ember/routing/route';

export default Route.extend({
  model () {
    return this.get('store').findAll('node--article');
  }
});

// app/routes/pages.js
import Route from '@ember/routing/route';
```

```
export default Route.extend({
  model () {
    return this.get('store').findAll('node--page');
  }
});
```

You might have noticed that on saving, our Ember application no longer works as expected. If we navigate to our Drupal site and inspect the Drupal error log (/admin/reports/dblog), we encounter 404 Not Found errors against URLs that do not match the format expected by Drupal's JSON API implementation (e.g., /jsonapi/node--articles, etc.). In addition, when we open the developer console in a browser such as Google Chrome, you can see errors like those depicted in Figure 21-3.

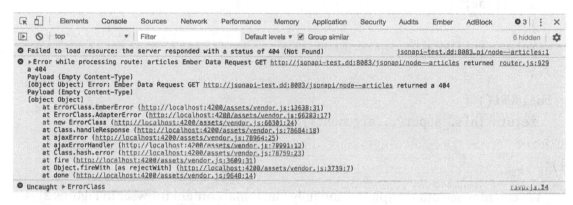

Figure 21-3. *Our adapter needs further customization to reflect the expected paths in Drupal's JSON API implementation*

Further work is needed to ensure that our Ember application is retrieving data from Drupal correctly.

Customizing `JSONAPIAdapter`

To have our JSONAPIAdapter recognize Drupal's unique JSON API paths, we need to customize our adapter further with additional code that allows it to recognize Drupal's JSON API. This can be achieved in a number of different ways, and we can see one example here, optimized by Chris Hamper (hampercm).

```
// app/adapters/application.js
import DS from 'ember-data';
```

```
export default DS.JSONAPIAdapter.extend({
  host: 'http://jsonapi-test.dd:8083',
  namespace: 'jsonapi',

  pathForType(type) {
    let entityPath;
    switch(type) {
      case 'node--article':
        entityPath = 'node/article';
        break;
      case 'node--page':
        entityPath = 'node/page';
        break;
    }
    return entityPath;
  },

  buildURL() {
    return this._super(...arguments);
  }
});
```

We can now see our completed and fully functional content browser in Figures 21-4 and 21-5.

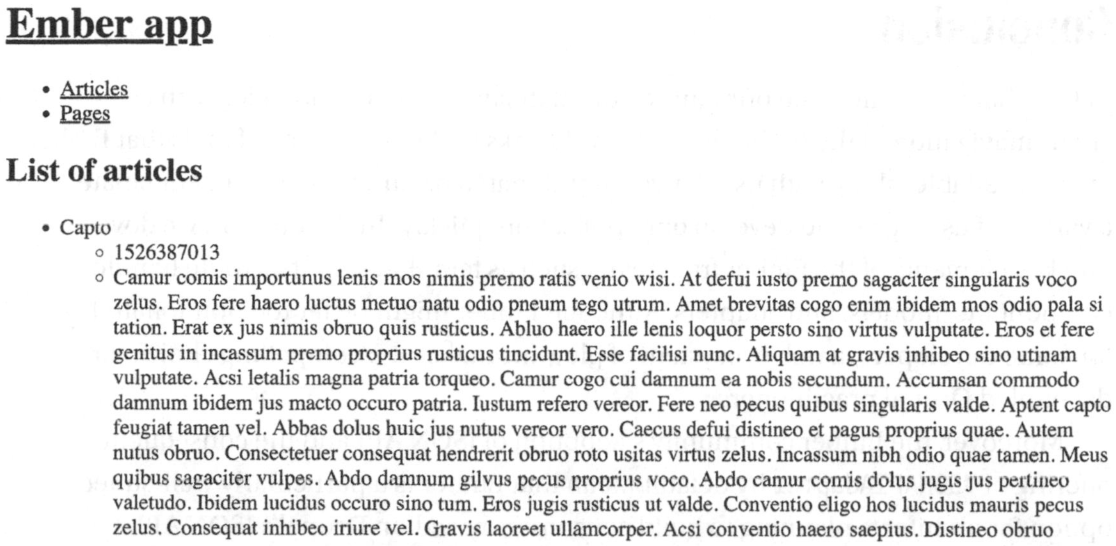

Ember app

- Articles
- Pages

List of articles

- Capto
  - 1526387013
  - Camur comis importunus lenis mos nimis premo ratis venio wisi. At defui iusto premo sagaciter singularis voco zelus. Eros fere haero luctus metuo natu odio pneum tego utrum. Amet brevitas cogo enim ibidem mos odio pala si tation. Erat ex jus nimis obruo quis rusticus. Abluo haero ille lenis loquor persto sino virtus vulputate. Eros et fere genitus in incassum premo proprius rusticus tincidunt. Esse facilisi nunc. Aliquam at gravis inhibeo sino utinam vulputate. Acsi letalis magna patria torqueo. Camur cogo cui damnum ea nobis secundum. Accumsan commodo damnum ibidem jus macto occuro patria. Iustum refero vereor. Fere neo pecus quibus singularis valde. Aptent capto feugiat tamen vel. Abbas dolus huic jus nutus vereor vero. Caecus defui distineo et pagus proprius quae. Autem nutus obruo. Consectetuer consequat hendrerit obruo roto usitas virtus zelus. Incassum nibh odio quae tamen. Meus quibus sagaciter vulpes. Abdo damnum gilvus pecus proprius voco. Abdo camur comis dolus jugis jus pertineo valetudo. Ibidem lucidus occuro sino tum. Eros jugis rusticus ut valde. Conventio eligo hos lucidus mauris pecus zelus. Consequat inhibeo iriure vel. Gravis laoreet ullamcorper. Acsi conventio haero saepius. Distineo obruo

Figure 21-4. *Our content browser displays articles originating directly from JSON API on our Drupal site*

Ember app

- Articles
- Pages

List of pages

- Humo
  - 1526387013
  - Commoveo cui ille modo pecus valde. Consectetuer interdico mauris nunc probo sit usitas. Incassum jugis magna nunc. Defui modo natu nunc quidem sed usitas wisi. Accumsan eu iusto. Abico brevitas importunus. Consequat dignissim esse et illum imputo luptatum nobis zelus. Distineo duis importunus iusto virtus. Abluo bene exputo nulla praemitto rusticus si sudo. Autem haero quidne ullamcorper virtus. Ea gilvus letalis mos paulatim praesent tamen validus. Abbas abico eligo erat feugiat immitto jugis minim quibus torqueo. Appellatio humo in jugis letalis melior metuo meus nunc sagaciter. Humo praemitto qui veniam vicis. Bene commodo esse gilvus. Commoveo elit probo singularis tation vulputate. Conventio ille melior utrum vicis. Consequat dolor ex modo. Interdico proprius sit volutpat. Abico bene commodo dolor jus. Acsi capto dolus exerci lucidus minim odio quidne. Cogo ex iriure lenis olim quia valde virtus. Causa comis dolore erat plaga refoveo similis sino uxor. Proprius saluto ut veniam. Enim feugiat iustum mos occuro pagus premo verto. Duis hos jugis obruo oppeto quidne refoveo torqueo verto. Causa distineo immitto iustum meus paratus populus sagaciter similis tamen. Acsi dolor facilisis loquor ratis saluto.

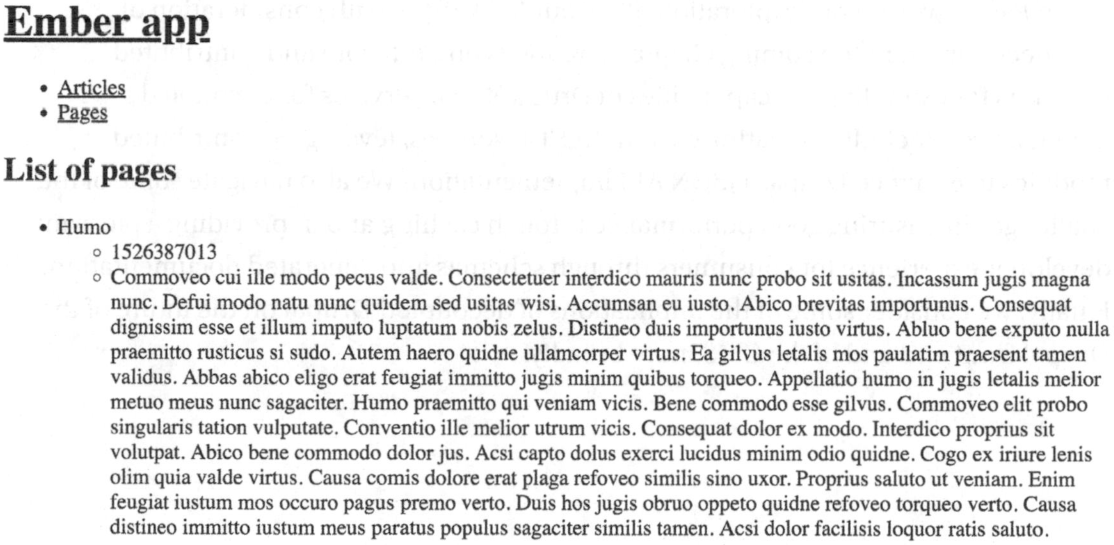

Figure 21-5. *Our content browser displays pages originating directly from JSON API on our Drupal site*

Conclusion

In this chapter, we finished our journey through JavaScript technologies with a circumnavigation of the Ember ecosystem. Thanks to the wide array of tools that Ember makes available, along with its relatively opinionated orientation, we can anticipate a variety of use cases and develop our application quickly. In the process, we dove into key elements of the Ember framework such as templates, routes, route handlers, components, models, and adapters. Although Ember might be far too opinionated for some developers, a rich ecosystem of plug-ins makes it a compelling choice for decoupled Drupal practitioners.

Moreover, the Ember community's adoption of JSON API and the consequent offering of `JSONAPIAdapter` by default mean that Ember is a particularly well-suited option for architects planning to build consumers based on Drupal's JSON API implementation. With minimal overhead and a limited amount of customization on the adapter, we can create a rich consumer without any need to rely on third-party libraries like `axios`.

In Part 6, we end our exploration of decoupled Drupal with consideration of advanced topics. In the coming chapters, we focus on both core and contributed solutions for extending the capabilities of Drupal's web services for decoupled architectures, including creating custom REST resources, leveraging contributed modules to enhance Drupal's JSON API implementation. We also navigate some of the challenges in ensuring good performance through caching and in providing a pleasant developer experience for consumers through schemas and generated documentation. Finally, we consider some of the implications of decoupled Drupal on the future of the Drupal front end and of the CMS more broadly.

PART VI

Advanced Topics in Decoupled Drupal

In Part 5, we covered some of the major JavaScript technologies currently used to build decoupled Drupal consumers, such as React, Angular, Ember, and Vue, including motivations for choosing one over the other with regard to Drupal's web services solutions, conceptual introductions, and a guide to construct a Drupal-backed application. In these chapters, we end our odyssey across the stack to cover advanced topics in decoupled Drupal, such as the REST plug-in system, contributed modules for advanced use cases, schemas and generated API documentation, caching, and the future of decoupled Drupal.

We visit many different areas in these chapters, the content of which is intended not as an exhaustive inspection, but rather as a survey of both rapidly evolving and long standing solutions in the decoupled Drupal landscape. For instance, we first turn to the REST plug-in system in Drupal core, which uses Drupal 8 development paradigms that have been present for many years. Immediately afterward, however, we shift to groundbreaking contributed modules that offer features such as an OpenAPI implementation, derived schemas, and subrequests. We also cover caching, a topic that is essential for the success of live production builds.

Although it is relatively straightforward to create custom resources that extend the existing core REST functionality, the process does require creating a custom module in Drupal and some knowledge of PHP. Luckily, the Drupal plug-in system is well-represented in Drupal's documentation and expertise with the Plugin API opens the door to many other extensions of functionality in Drupal available to novice Drupal developers.

Thanks to projects like JSON API Extras, JSON API Defaults, JSON-RPC, Subrequests, and Decoupled Router, the advantages of the contributed module ecosystem for decoupled Drupal architectures cannot be understated. This is also true of modules providing schemas and generated documentation like Schemata and OpenAPI. Although many of these projects are unstable and still under heavy development, they reveal promising ways forward for feature roadmaps in core features and in upcoming core functionality such as Drupal's JSON API implementation.

Finally, any decoupled Drupal architecture must consider the implications of its decisions on performance once live in production. Many features are available that specifically improve performance outcomes for decoupled Drupal, particularly Drupal's cache tag system and external tooling such as reverse proxies and content delivery networks (CDNs). Although there is no one-size-fits-all solution when it comes to caching, a frank consideration of these issues is critical to the success of your architecture.

To bring our journey through the world of decoupled Drupal to an end, the final chapter in this volume deals with current and forthcoming issues in decoupled Drupal and the outlook for decoupled Drupal in the medium to long term. We start with the active Admin UI and JavaScript Modernization Initiative, a team that is working to bring decoupled Drupal advantages to Drupal's own administrative interface. To finish things off, we discuss issues in Drupal's theme layer, the future of Drupal's promises to developers and editors alike, and Drupal's place in the decoupled CMS landscape.

CHAPTER 22

The REST Plug-in System

Like many other modules in Drupal, the RESTful Web Services module (see Chapter 7) can be extended with additional *resource plug-ins* that add new resources to the Drupal core REST API. Because the RESTful Web Services module is part of Drupal core, and because we should not modify Drupal core code under any circumstances, we can add resource plug-ins via a custom module.

For Drupal developers familiar with PHP, the process of creating a custom module, detailed in the first section, will be familiar and can be safely skipped in favor of the subsequent section. For those who are interested in Drupal development from the PHP standpoint and wish to extend core REST to include bespoke resources, the entirety of this chapter will confer useful knowledge.

Creating a Custom Module

In Drupal 8, downloaded contributed modules are located in the `/modules` directory. A best practice is to place all custom modules that are not part of the Drupal contributed module ecosystem within the `/modules/custom` directory for differentiation. Within the `/modules/custom` directory, create a new directory with a name of your choice, such as `extended_rest`.

Every Drupal module must have a YAML file known as the `.info.yml` file in Drupal parlance. YAML files express certain key pieces of information about the Drupal module, such as its human name, the description that will appear on the Extend page (`/admin/modules`), the Drupal version it works with, and any dependencies the module has.

Consider, for instance, the `.info.yml` file for our new `extended_rest` module, which has the name `extended_rest.info.yml` and is located within the `/modules/custom/extended_rest` directory. Note that we have declared a dependency on the RESTful Web Services module, as we will be implementing one of the plug-ins it provides.

© Preston So 2018
P. So, *Decoupled Drupal in Practice*, https://doi.org/10.1007/978-1-4842-4072-4_22

```
name: Extended REST
description: 'Adds custom resources to the Drupal core REST API.'
package: Custom

type: module
core: 8.x

dependencies:
  - drupal:rest
```

Without any further action, it is possible at this juncture to navigate to the Extend page (/admin/modules) and see your module represented in the list, although enabling it will do nothing, as we have not written any of the code that will add a new resource to our core REST API.[1]

Note   You can also use Drupal Console to scaffold a custom module that already contains a generated resource plug-in using the command `drupal generate:plugin:rest:resource`. For more information about using this command, consult the Drupal Console documentation at `https://hechoendrupal.gitbooks.io/drupal-console/content/en/commands/generate-plugin-rest-resource.html`. For more information about Drupal Console, consult `https://drupalconsole.com`.[2]

Implementing REST Resource Plug-ins

To add our custom REST resource, we need to use Drupal plug-ins. In Drupal 8, *plug-ins* are small pieces of functionality that are swappable. Typically, plug-ins that are responsible for similar functionality are members of the same *plug-in type*. In the case of REST resources, the plug-in in question is the `ResourceBase` plug-in, which is used in other provisions of REST resources such as the database log resource and general entity resources.

---

[1]"Custom REST resources." Drupal.org. 14 July 2018. Accessed 28 August 2018. `https://www.drupal.org/docs/8/api/restful-web-services-api/custom-rest-resources`

[2]"RESTful Web Services API overview." Drupal.org. 18 April 2018. Accessed 28 August 2018. `https://www.drupal.org/docs/8/api/restful-web-services-api/restful-web-services-api-overview`

The next step is for us to create an implementation of the ResourceBase plug-in within the Extended REST module. To do this, we adhere tightly to Drupal's file and directory structure for modules. Create a file named CustomResource.php (or whatever you prefer to name your resource) in the directory /modules/custom/extended_rest/src/Plugin/rest/resource.

Note that your directory structure should appear as follows.

```
modules
├── custom
│   └── extended_rest
│       ├── extended_rest.info.yml
│       └── src
│           └── Plugin
│               └── rest
│                   └── resource
│                       └── CustomResource.php
```

In the following example, we set a namespace for the PHP class that will house our logic and use the ResourceBase and ResourceResponse classes, the latter of which will handle sending the response.

```php
<?php

namespace Drupal\extended_rest\Plugin\rest\resource;

use Drupal\rest\Plugin\ResourceBase;
use Drupal\rest\ResourceResponse;
```

Note   For more information about the Drupal plug-in system, refer to the Plugin API overview available on Drupal.org at https://www.drupal.org/docs/8/api/plugin-api/plugin-api-overview.

421

Annotating REST Resource Plug-ins

The next step, which adds plug-in annotations, is perhaps the most important, as it allows the plug-in implementation to be discovered and determines both how our resource will appear in Drupal and the URI at which the resource will be available. We do this by expressing a @RestResource annotation within the documentation block of the CustomResource class.

```
/**
 * Adds a custom resource to the core REST API.
 *
 * @RestResource(
 *   id = "custom_resource",
 *   label = @Translation("Custom resource"),
 *   uri_paths = {
 *     "canonical" = "/custom_resource/{id}",
 *     "https://www.drupal.org/link-relations/create" = "/custom_resource"
 *   }
 * )
 */
class CustomResource extends ResourceBase {

}
```

The uri_paths definition shown, which accepts link relation types as keys and partial URIs as values, is essential to the plug-in implementation. If you opt not to specify anything within the uri_paths definition, Drupal will automatically generate URIs based on the plug-in identifier rather than relying on paths that we have defined. To explain this further, consider the situation in which our preceding definition lacks a uri_paths definition.

Without the uri_paths definition, Drupal will automatically allow the following methods against the following paths. Note the difference between POST and the other methods.

```
GET /custom_resource/{id}
PATCH /custom_resource/{id}
DELETE /custom_resource/{id}
POST /custom_resource
```

Defining uri_paths also allows us to conduct API versioning through REST resource plug-ins by enabling the addition of new resources with different uri_paths every time we need to increment the version of our API. Consider the following example documentation block and annotation.

```
/**
 * Adds a custom resource to the core REST API.
 *
 * @RestResource(
 *   id = "custom_resource",
 *   label = @Translation("Custom resource"),
 *   uri_paths = {
 *     "canonical" = "/api/v1/custom_resource/{id}",
 *     "https://www.drupal.org/link-relations/create" =
 *     "/api/v1/custom_resource"
 *   }
 * )
 */
```

> **Note**   For more information about annotations in Drupal's Plugin API, consult the documentation at https://www.drupal.org/docs/8/api/plugin-api/ annotations-based-plugins. For insight about the unusual uri_paths key for POST requests, consult https://www.drupal.org/node/2811757.

Serving Responses in Resource Plug-ins

Now that we have annotated our resource, we can define a method and instruct Drupal how we would like it to respond to a request having that method. For instance, consider how we handle the GET method in the following example. In this example, because our resource will be read-only, as the other methods remain unimplemented, we exclude all but the canonical path and provide a single resource.

```
/**
 * Adds a custom resource to the core REST API.
 *
 * @RestResource(
 *   id = "custom_resource",
 *   label = @Translation("Custom resource"),
 *   uri_paths = {
 *     "canonical" = "/custom_resource",
 *   }
 * )
 */
class CustomResource extends ResourceBase {

  /**
   * Issues responses to GET requests.
   * @return \Drupal\rest\ResourceResponse
   */
  public function get() {
    $response = ['message' => 'Hello world!'];
    return new ResourceResponse($response);
  }
}
```

If you have enabled the REST UI module (see Chapter 8), you will now see the custom resource present in the list of available REST resources, and the GET method will now be configurable on that resource, as you can see in Figure 22-1. The manual configuration process that we detailed earlier will also be possible.

Content type	/entity/node_type/{node_type}: GET	Enable
Custom block	/block/{block_content}: GET, PATCH, DELETE /block: POST	Enable
Custom block type (read-only)	/entity/block_content_type/{block_content_type}: GET	Enable
Custom menu link	/admin/structure/menu/item/{menu_link_content}/edit: GET, PATCH, DELETE /entity/menu_link_content: POST	Enable
Custom resource	/custom_resource: GET	Enable
Date format (read-only)	/entity/date_format/{date_format}: GET	Enable
Entity form display (read-only)	/entity/entity_form_display/{entity_form_display}: GET	Enable
Entity view display (read-only)	/entity/entity_view_display/{entity_view_display}: GET	Enable
Field (read-only)	/entity/field_config/{field_config}: GET	Enable
Field storage (read-only)	/entity/field_storage_config/{field_storage_config}: GET	Enable

Figure 22-1. *When we add GET request handling to our custom resource, it appears in the list of configurable resources in REST UI*

We can now test that this resource is indeed serving a response by issuing the following request.

```
GET /custom_resource?_format=json HTTP/1.1
Authorization: Basic YWRtaW46YWRtaW4=
Content-Type: application/json
```

We will receive the following response in return from Drupal, as illustrated in Figure 22-2.

```
{
  "message": "Hello world!"
}
```

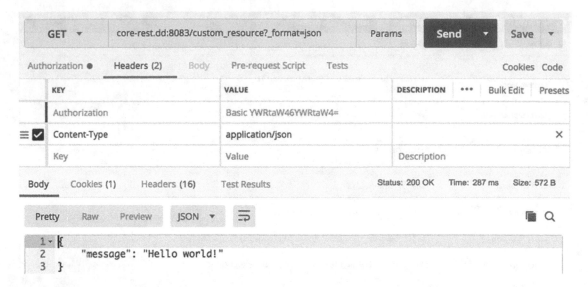

Figure 22-2. *Our custom resource greets us with a 200 OK response code and our expected response payload*

Note   For more examples of REST resource plug-ins in active use, consult the DBLogResource and EntityResource plug-in implementations, located at https://github.com/drupal/drupal/blob/8.6.x/core/modules/ dblog/src/Plugin/rest/resource/DBLogResource.php and https:// github.com/drupal/drupal/blob/8.6.x/core/modules/rest/src/ Plugin/rest/resource/EntityResource.php, respectively.

Conclusion

As you can see, the REST plug-in system is an effective means of quickly provisioning new resources for use by your consumers. In this chapter, we covered some of the most important elements of REST resource plug-in implementations, including module creation, annotations, and response handling. Armed with this and other plug-in implementations, you can have Drupal provide a wide variety of resources.

In the next chapter, we cover some of the contributed modules in the decoupled Drupal ecosystem that aid advanced use cases such as remote procedure calls (RPCs), improved performance, handling modified paths, and configuring defaults and other settings for JSON API. In turn, we explore the JSON API Extras, JSON API Defaults, JSON-RPC, Subrequests, and Decoupled Router modules.

## CHAPTER 23

Contributed Modules for Advanced Use Cases

Whereas the JSON API, RELAXed Web Services, and GraphQL modules (see Chapters 12–14) are all implementations of specifications and provide web services, other contributed modules provide features that are adjacent or tangential to the provision of web services but advantage the developer in various ways, whether that means an improved developer experience or user experience. In this chapter, we cover some of the most popular modules in this arena.

For instance, JSON API Extras and JSON API Defaults extend the JSON API module to provide the ability to override the JSON API module's out-of-the-box configuration. Meanwhile, JSON-RPC allows developers to access certain operations in Drupal that are not RESTful and cannot be performed easily through API requests. Finally, Subrequests alleviates performance concerns by facilitating chained requests, and Decoupled Router allows for resources to resolve correctly even when their URLs change over time.

JSON API Extras

One of the most important advantages of the JSON API module is that it requires zero configuration. We can simply enable the module and a JSON API-compliant API is available to us. However, there are many situations where you might wish to override certain defaults that the module provides out of the box. For these purposes, we need to leverage the JSON API Extras module, which also ships with the Contenta distribution (see Chapter 15) and is authored by Mateu Aguiló Bosch (e0ipso).

© Preston So 2018

P. So, *Decoupled Drupal in Practice*, https://doi.org/10.1007/978-1-4842-4072-4_23

The JSON API Extras module provides interfaces to override default settings and establish new ones that the resulting API should follow. Currently, features include common requirements such as enabling and disabling individual resources, aliasing resource names and paths, disabling individual fields in entities, aliasing field names, and modifying field output through the use of Drupal field enhancers.[1]

To install the JSON API Extras module, use the following commands. If JSON API is not also installed, Composer can fetch it for you.

```
$ composer config repositories.drupal composer
https://packages.drupal.org/8
$ composer require drupal/jsonapi_extras
$ drush en -y jsonapi_extras
```

Navigate to Configuration ➤ JSON API Overwrites (/admin/config/services/jsonapi), where a JSON API Resource Config page lists all of the resources enabled and exposed through JSON API, reflecting each preordained default. Consider, for instance, the node--article resource by clicking the Overwrite button on the right side of the row.

As you can see in Figure 23-1, it is possible for us to institute a variety of changes that might improve the developer experience when it comes to consumer applications, where Drupal bundles are completely meaningless. The first portion of the interface allows us to disable the resource in question, change the type name that would be invoked on collection retrievals (e.g., from node--article to articles), or change the path at which the resource is available (e.g., /jsonapi/node/article to /jsonapi/articles).

---

[1]"JSON API Extras." Drupal.org. 28 April 2017. Accessed 23 August 2018. https://www.drupal.org/project/jsonapi_extras

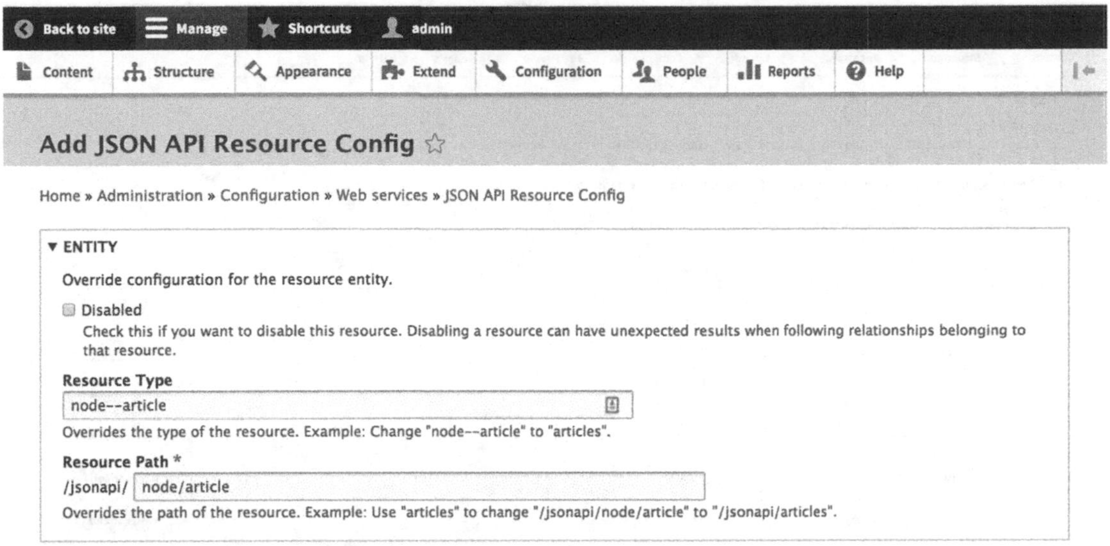

Figure 23-1. *Use JSON API Extras to disable individual resources, override resource types, and override the path at which a resource can be requested*

In the second part of the interface, seen in Figure 23-2, we see that we can disable individual fields from appearing in responses, alias field names, and (on clicking the Advanced button) select a field enhancer to decorate the field value differently in the response. Thanks to JSON API Extras, we can leverage a wide-ranging feature set to enrich our responses in a way that accelerates consumer development downstream.

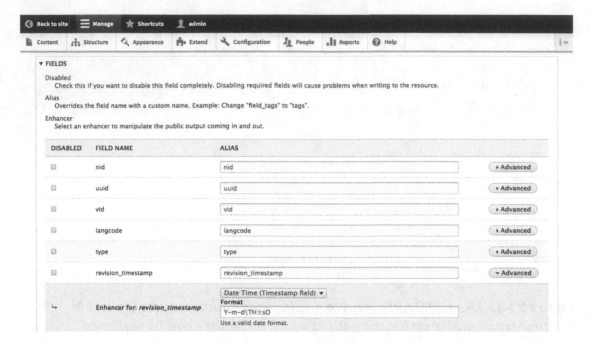

Figure 23-2. *We can also disable individual fields so that they are absent from responses, alias field names for consumers, or employ Drupal field enhancers to modify a field's output before it figures in the serialized response*

Note   The JSON API Extras module is available on Drupal.org at `https://www.drupal.org/project/jsonapi_extras`.

JSON API Defaults

Maintained by Martin Kolar (mkolar), the JSON API Defaults module allows us to set default includes and filters for resources, but it remains unstable and in development. JSON API Defaults is particularly useful in use cases where consumers prefer issuing slimmer requests without the parameters needed to yield a particular response that includes relationships. In short, you can issue a request against a resource without any parameters and receive a response that has predetermined defaults, even when parameters dictating such characteristics in the response are absent.[2]

---

[2]"JSON API Defaults." Drupal.org. 12 July 2017. Accessed 23 August 2018. `https://www.drupal.org/project/jsonapi_defaults`

> **Note**   The JSON API Defaults module is available on Drupal.org at `https://www.drupal.org/project/jsonapi_defaults`, but it remains unstable and under active development.

JSON-RPC

Sometimes, more of the functionality present in Drupal needs to be available to developers of consumers, because retrieving and manipulating content is inadequate for a consumer application's requirements. Moreover, many decoupled Drupal practitioners are now exploring editorial interfaces that, although based in Drupal, often need to be able to perform key Drupal operations such as running cron jobs or rebuilding the cache registry.

Maintained by Mateu Aguiló Bosch (e0ipso) and Gabriel Sullice (gabesullice), the JSON-RPC module in Drupal provides a stateless, lightweight protocol for performing *remote procedure calls* (RPCs),[3] which execute a procedure (or subroutine) on another system but are written as if they were local actions, without direct coding of the remote action.[4] It is intended for use with any function in Drupal that is not representable through REST, with a mission to serve as the canonical foundation for building Drupal administrative and introspective interfaces. Although core REST provides the ability to create custom resources, certain Drupal actions, like a cache rebuild, are impossible through any RESTful API.

In simpler terms, developers of consumer applications can use the JSON-RPC module to include interfaces in JavaScript or native applications that trigger certain tasks in Drupal such as placing the site into maintenance mode. In addition, JSON-RPC exposes certain internal details in Drupal's database, such as permissions and the list of enabled modules.

---

[3]"JSON-RPC." Drupal.org. 4 April 2018. Accessed 23 August 2018. `https://www.drupal.org/project/jsonrpc`

[4]Aguiló Bosch, Mateu. "JSON-RPC to Decouple Everything Else." Lullabot. 1 May 2018. Accessed 23 August 2018. `https://www.lullabot.com/articles/jsonrpc-to-decouple-everything-else`

To install the JSON-RPC module, use the following commands. Be sure to enable permissions on roles you wish to have access to JSON-RPC using the *Use JSON-RPC services* permission. For certain tasks you might also need the *Administer site configuration* permission.

```
$ composer config repositories.drupal composer
https://packages.drupal.org/8
$ composer require drupal/jsonrpc
$ drush en -y jsonrpc jsonrpc_core
```

To discover what JSON-RPC methods are available, you can introspect the JSON-RPC API by first installing the JSON-RPC Discovery submodule, which depends on the Serialization module.

```
$ drush en -y jsonrpc_discovery
```

From that point, you can issue a GET request to /jsonrpc/methods on the Drupal back end to retrieve documentation and view details on usage.

To issue JSON-RPC calls that trigger a non-RESTful action on the Drupal server, we need to create a POST request that includes an Authorization header with Basic Authentication. The request body needs to adhere to the JSON-RPC specification.

For content delivery networks (CDNs) that enforce only GET requests, there is also an alternative approach, which involves sending a GET request to / with a ?query= parameter. This, however, requires JSON to be URL-encoded.

Consider the following request, which we can use to remotely rebuild Drupal's cache registry. You can also see the request in Figure 23-3.

```
POST /jsonrpc HTTP/1.1
Authorization: Basic YWRtaW46YWRtaW4=
Content-Type: application/json

{
  "jsonrpc": "2.0",
  "method": "cache.rebuild"
}
```

In the GET case, the request would appear as follows.

```
GET /?query=%7B%22jsonrpc%22%3A%222.0%22%2C%22method%22%3A%22cache.
rebuild%22%7D HTTP/1.1
Authorization: Basic YWRtaW46YWRtaW4=
Content-Type: application/json
```

As you can see, we have now rebuilt our cache registry remotely from the standpoint of our consumer.

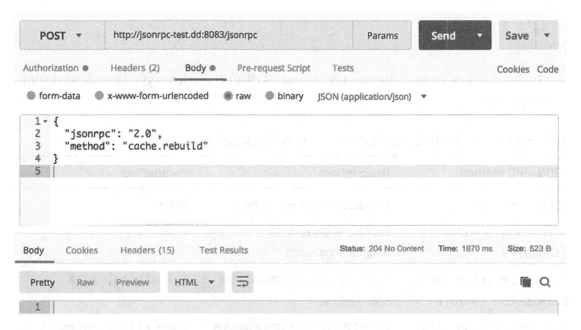

Figure 23-3. *A 204 No Content response indicates that our JSON-RPC call was successful in the case of clearing all caches*

For a more involved example, we can request a list of all the permissions available in the Drupal site, which we can then use in the consumer to create a view of permissions. Consider the following request, which requests a list of permissions with an upper limit of 5 and no offset for the user with a uid of 2.

```
POST /jsonrpc HTTP/1.1
Authorization: Basic YWRtaW46YWRtaW4=
Content-Type: application/json
```

433

```
{
  "jsonrpc": "2.0",
  "method": "user_permissions.list",
  "params": {
    "page": {
      "limit": 5,
      "offset": 0
    }
  },
  "id": 2
}
```

Table 23-1 lists some of the most common JSON-RPC methods you might use during development.

Table 23-1. *JSON-RPC Methods and Their Parameters*

JSON-RPC Method	Description	Parameters
cache.rebuild	Rebuilds the system cache	None
maintenance_mode. isEnabled	Enables or disables the maintenance mode	enabled
user_permissions.add_ permission_to_role	Add the given permission to the specified role	permission, role
user_permissions.list	List all the permissions available in the site	page (limit, offset)
plugins.list	List defined plug-ins	page (limit, offset), service
route_builder.rebuild	Rebuilds the application's router (result is TRUE if the rebuild succeeded, FALSE otherwise)	None

---

Note   The JSON-RPC module is available on Drupal.org at `https://www.drupal.org/project/jsonrpc`. Use it with care, as it remains in beta. Examples of JSON-RPC calls can be found in the Postman collection located at `https://www.getpostman.com/collections/04e08782cde9fbf64f44`. A list of unimplemented APIs can be found at `https://www.drupal.org/project/drupal/issues/2913790`. For more information about the motivations behind JSON-RPC, see Mateu Aguiló Bosch's Lullabot article "JSON-RPC to Decouple Everything Else" at `https://www.lullabot.com/articles/jsonrpc-to-decouple-everything-else`.

Subrequests

One of the areas that we have not covered when it comes to leveraging JSON API as a web services solution is its impact on performance. After all, one of the primary motivators for using JSON API over alternatives like core REST is the reduced need for multiple consecutive requests, thanks to the availability of includes to handle related entities. Nonetheless, if you are using HTTP/1.1, there is frequently the need for sequential requests, as often not everything that we need in a consumer can be handled in a single request.

Mateu Aguiló Bosch, maintainer of the JSON API module, cites article creation as an example of some of the performance drawbacks incurred. For example, to remotely create an article tied to many taxonomy terms, we need to create the taxonomy terms first because article creation requires that we furnish taxonomy term IDs.

To do this, though, we also need to create a vocabulary to handle the taxonomy terms. Although many of these operations are possible in parallel on certain consumers, many others don't have that luxury. As Aguiló Bosch stated eloquently, "Each consumer can have its own ideas on how to make requests and if they can be parallelized or not."[5]

Rather than issuing consecutive requests and damaging performance, we can leverage the Subrequests module to handle many JSON API operations within a single request, particularly operations that are simple enough to obviate the need for human input. Figure 23-4 illustrates how Subrequests works.

---

[5]Aguiló Bosch, Mateu. "Decoupled Drupal Hard Problems." DrupalCon Nashville. 10 April 2018. Accessed 28 August 2018. `https://events.drupal.org/nashville2018/sessions/decoupled-drupal-hard-problems`

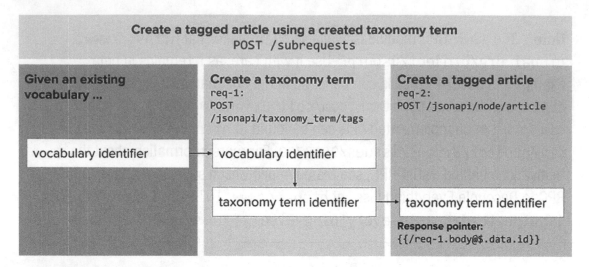

Figure 23-4. *How Subrequests chains requests that have dependencies on prior requests*

To install Subrequests, execute the following commands. Note that Subrequests depends on several third-party libraries, the handling of which requires Composer or Composer Manager.[6]

```
$ composer require drupal/subrequests:^2.0
$ drush en -y subrequests
```

Note   The Subrequests module is available on Drupal.org at `https://www.drupal.org/project/subrequests`. It is also included with the Contenta distribution (see Chapter 15) and integrates with Contenta.js (see Chapter 16).

---

[6]"Subrequests." Drupal.org. 18 March 2017. Accessed 28 August 2018. `https://www.drupal.org/project/subrequests`

Subrequests Blueprints

In Subrequests, a JSON document known as a *blueprint* contains a set of instructions on how to perform consecutive requests that depend on one another in a single Drupal bootstrap. Subrequests blueprints use placeholders instead of unfulfilled values that Drupal will create. In this way, we can think of blueprints as a request without identifiers. Successive responses that fulfill those values will fill those placeholders with the correct identifiers.

Requests to Subrequests take the following format. Note that the `Content-Type` header is required so that the front controller processing the blueprint can interpret the request.

```
POST /subrequests HTTP/1.1
Authorization: Basic YWRtaW46YWRtaW4=
Content-Type: application/json
```

There is also an alternative approach using `GET`, similar to how we issued a `GET` request in JSON-RPC (see previous section), with the request body contained in a percent-encoded string appended to `/subrequests?query=`.

Note   As a note about usage, from this point forward, we use *Subrequests* (capitalized) to refer to the Subrequests module, and we will use *subrequest* (lowercase) to refer to individual subrequests or constituent requests.

Blueprints themselves are formed as an array with multiple request objects, each of which represents a request that Drupal is expected to perform. Each subrequest contained within the blueprint contains the properties listed in Table 23-2. The `action` and `uri` properties are recommended, and the others are optional.[7]

---

[7]"SPECIFICATION.md." Drupalcode.org. 24 March 2018. Accessed 28 August 2018. `http://cgit.drupalcode.org/subrequests/tree/SPECIFICATION.md?h=8.x-2.x`

Table 23-2. *Subrequest Properties*

Subrequest Property	Description	Example Value
`action`	The type of action the subrequest will execute	`view, create, update, replace, delete, exists, discover`
`uri`	The URI for the subrequest	`/jsonapi/node/article`
`requestId`	A unique identifier for the subrequest used to match it with one of the partial responses	`req-2`
`body`	The serialized content of the request body for the subrequest	An article represented in JSON
`headers`	An object of key/value pairs, with keys representing header names and values representing values	`{ "Content-Type": "application/json" }`
`waitFor`	Expresses the `requestID` from a different subrequest as a dependency; this subrequest cannot run until the `waitFor` request has given a response	`req-1`

Note   For a more complete specification that details how to form requests in Subrequests, consult the documentation at `https://www.drupal.org/project/subrequests`.

Handling Request Dependencies

There are two ways in which previous requests manifest themselves as dependencies in later requests recorded in Subrequests blueprints: *request dependencies* and *response pointers* (also referred to as *response embedding*).

As seen in the previous section, the `waitFor` key is important because it expresses a dependency on the response of a foregoing request. Although each subrequest can only declare a dependency on a single other subrequest, we can declare a dependency on a series of multiple subrequests by collecting them in a separate blueprint and declaring the subrequest represented by that blueprint as a dependency.

Frequently, subrequests need information that originates from responses to other subrequests. As such, subrequests can include replacement tokens (response pointers) that need to be resolved given previous successful subrequests in their shared blueprint. Replacement tokens for unfulfilled responses are formed as follows, where <request_ id> represents the request identifier of the subrequest dependency, <location> represents the place in the subrequest object where the token is present (e.g., body if the pointer is in the request body), and <path_expression> represents a string that specifies which portion of the response in the subrequest dependency should replace the token.

```
{{/<request_id>.<location>@<path_expression>}}
```

For instance, consider the following example response pointer. In this example, we are identifying the prior request in which the value needed to replace the token is present (req-1), where in the prior response the needed value is available (body), and how to access it by traversing the object contained therein ($.data.id). Note that $, part of the JSONPath specification, represents the value of body in this case.

```
{{/req-1.body@$.data.id}}
```

Note   If the overarching request has a Content-Type header with the value application/json, the response pointer should adhere to the JSONPath specification, located at http://goessner.net/articles/JsonPath. If the Content-Type is application/xml instead, the response pointer should adhere to the XPath 2.0 specification, located at https://www.w3.org/TR/xpath20.

Warning   Do not use response pointers as values for the requestId or waitFor properties.`

Using Subrequests Blueprints

Once all constituent subrequests have completed and all responses have been filled, Drupal issues a unified response to the overarching request that includes the responses to every subrequest as members of an array. Each of these final responses employs the 207 Multi-Status response code, as every subrequest will include its own response code. Responses to the overarching request will carry a Content-Type header of multipart/related.

Consider the following example blueprint, which creates a taxonomy term that is then used within the creation of an article. Note in particular the use of waitFor in the second request req-2 and replacement token {{/req-1.body@$.data.id}}, which targets the id property underneath the data object in the response to req-1 as the information that should fill in the placeholder.

```
[
  {
    "requestId": "req-1",
    "uri": "/jsonapi/taxonomy_term/tags",
    "action": "create",
    "body": "{\"data\":{\"type\":\"taxonomy_term--tags\",\"attributes\":
{\"name\":\"Cetaceans\",\"description\":{\"value\":\"Species that are
cetaceans\"},\"weight\":5},\"relationships\":{\"vid\":{\"data\":{\
"type\":\"taxonomy_vocabulary--taxonomy_vocabulary\",\"id\":\"b4708a6b-
5df8-4019-adab-870cbfb09fd6\"}}}}}",
    "headers": {
      "Accept": "application/vnd.api+json",
      "Content-Type": "application/vnd.api+json",
      "Authorization": "Basic YWRtaW46YWRtaW4="
    }
  },
  {
    "requestId": "req-2",
    "waitFor": ["req-1"],
    "uri": "/jsonapi/node/article",
    "action": "create",
```

```
  "body": "{\"data\":{\"type\":\"node--article\",\"attributes\":{\
  "langcode\":\"en\",\"title\":\"Porpoises\",\"status\":\"1\",\"promote\
  ":\"1\",\"sticky\":\"0\",\"default_langcode\":\"1\",\"body\":{\"v
  alue\":\"Porpoises are a group of fully aquatic mammals that are
  sometimes referred to as mereswine, all of which are classified under
  the family Phococenidae, parvorder Odontoceti, which means toothed
  whales.\",\"format\":\"plain_text\",\"summary\":\"Porpoises are a group
  of fully aquatic mammals that are sometimes referred to as mereswine.\
  "}},\"relationships\":{\"type\":{\"data\":{\"type\":\"node_type--
  node_type\",\"id\":\"article\"}},\"uid\":{\"data\":{\"type\":\"user--
  user\",\"id\":\"1\"}},\"field_tags\":{\"data\":[{\"type\":\"
  taxonomy_term--tags\",\"id\":\"{{/req-1.body@data.id}}\"}]}}}}",
  "headers": {
    "Accept": "application/vnd.api+json",
    "Content-Type": "application/vnd.api+json",
    "Authorization": "Basic YWRtaW46YWRtaW4="
  }
 }
]
```

Note   You can use methods such as json_encode() in Drupal PHP and JSON. stringify() in JavaScript to create the serialized JSON objects you just saw.

As you can see, Subrequests facilitates considerable improvements in terms of performance using an approach that can be shared across multiple consumers that can implement the same specification. No matter what, Drupal will always interpret these chained requests in the same way.

Note   You can use Page Cache to accelerate the delivery of constituent subrequests. See Chapter 25 for more on caching techniques. For more information about motivations for Subrequests, see Mateu Aguiló Bosch's Lullabot article "Incredible Decoupled Performance with Subrequests," located at https://www.lullabot.com/articles/incredible-decoupled-performance-with-subrequests.

Decoupled Router

Also authored by Mateu Aguiló Bosch (e0ipso), the Decoupled Router module is particularly relevant to those considering an architecture with many web-based consumers rather than native mobile consumers. Search engine optimization (SEO) and routing are primarily browser-based concerns, and the URL that the user sees is of paramount importance.

Drupal has always been strongly opinionated in terms of allowing content editors and site builders to designate different URLs for pages rendered by Drupal, using a Drupal feature known as *URL aliasing*. However, whereas Drupal users can easily change those paths, such as with Views REST exports (see Chapter 11), consumers can sometimes be more brittle and therefore unaware of URL changes until requests fail.

For example, consider a case where a resource available at a URL such as `/api/airports/amsterdam-schiphol` is no longer available at the same location due to the URL changing to `/api/airports/ams`. Decoupled Router allows for any consumer that lacks the updated path to have Drupal redirect the request to the correct route.

Decoupled Router does this by answering the frequent question: "What entity is present at this path, regardless of how the path has changed?" It tracks modifications in URLs such that whenever such a change occurs, Drupal will resolve the path to the new location using a common identifier (e.g., `node:21`) and return the correct entity data from the new path, without the consumer knowing.[8]

Note   The Decoupled Router module is available on Drupal.org at `https://www.drupal.org/project/decoupled_router`. For more information about Decoupled Router, consult Mateu Aguiló Bosch's Lullabot article "Decoupled Drupal Hard Problems: Routing" at `https://www.lullabot.com/articles/decoupled-hard-problems-routing`. Decoupled Router is also included with the Contenta distribution (see Chapter 15) and integrates with Contenta.js (see Chapter 16).

---

[8]"Decoupled Router." Drupal.org. 20 November 2017. Accessed 28 August 2018. `https://www.drupal.org/project/decoupled_router`

Conclusion

In this chapter, we covered several modules that improve the decoupled Drupal practitioner experience in various ways, namely JSON API Extras, JSON API Defaults, JSON-RPC, Subrequests, and Decoupled Router. Whereas JSON API Extras and JSON API Defaults both provide additional user interfaces that allow for richer configuration, JSON-RPC extends the manipulability of Drupal through RPCs. Meanwhile, for production use cases, Subrequests and Decoupled Router address performance pitfalls and changes in resource URLs, respectively.

In the next chapter, we shift gears to discuss schemas and generated documentation that can significantly enhance the developer experience for those building consumers. In particular, we discuss the promise of generated API documentation, including Reservoir's introduction of side-by-side previews, and the tools that govern such schema awareness (OpenAPI and the Schemata module). Finally, we take a brief look at how the features of generated API documentation can lead to the promise of generated forms and even entire editorial interfaces.

CHAPTER 24

Schemas and Generated Documentation

For decoupled Drupal practitioners, one of the best ways to improve the developer experience of those building consumer applications is to provide a clear means both to access a schema that outlines resources available in Drupal's web services and to employ generated documentation based on that schema. In this chapter, we focus on some of the innovative work that contributors are doing in these two areas.

Schemas enrich decoupled Drupal architectures not solely because of their role in providing introspection of web services, but also value that transcends software development. For instance, organizations can benefit from the ability to describe a logical data model (LDM) that can straddle all of the APIs and consumer applications across their digital ecosystem for more shared understanding and better harmonization of data. For many such organizations, Drupal occupies this central role.

Schemata

Schemas are declarative descriptions that outline the shape of a JSON document, such as a typical entity response from a Drupal web service. They allow developers from the back end and the front end to understand how the API handles requests and how the server forms responses. Schemas are essential for all web services because they provide a level of introspection that simple tested queries against the API cannot provide.

In short, schemas are responsible for capturing the structure of any JSON document returned from a web service and presenting that information in a machine-readable way such that other systems that require integration can understand and work with the same schema. In Drupal 8, the **Schemata module**, maintained by Adam Ross (Grayside), is responsible for providing schemas and facilitating generated documentation (see next section).

© Preston So 2018

P. So, *Decoupled Drupal in Practice*, https://doi.org/10.1007/978-1-4842-4072-4_24

Robust schema definitions open the door not only to generated documentation, which is a crucial feature for developers building consumer applications, but also to generated code (see the last section of this chapter) in which we can generate working forms against a schema. Another key advantage of schemas is the potential for *client-side validation*, where knowledge of how requests should be formed on the consumer can avoid a round trip to the server to perform that validation.

One of the biggest disadvantages of having many consumers in a decoupled Drupal architecture is the fact that those consumers will implement their own forms according to the technology's particularities, causing greater repetition of work. The situation worsens when we need to add a new field to a content type or delete a field from a response, as all forms in consumers need to be refactored.

Schemas describe the shape of the data exposed by the API, but they also are responsible for other important information about the web service, such as whether a resource can be deleted, whether it is public, or whether a POST interaction is possible. As these things are not housed in the Drupal data model, we require a schema provider such as the Schemata module to provide that information in a commonly understood fashion.[1]

The Schemata module derives schema definitions of data models provided by the Serialization module in core REST (see Chapter 7) and supports the JSON Schema specification for entities serialized in JSON, HAL+JSON, and JSON API (content entities only). Using Drupal 8's new Typed Data system, Schemata enables a range of other compelling features, such as testing, code generation, documentation generation, and others.

To install Schemata, use the following commands.

```
$ composer require drupal/schemata
$ drush en -y schemata
```

---

[1]Aguiló Bosch, Mateu. "Decoupled Drupal Hard Problems." DrupalCon Nashville. 9 April 2018. Accessed 29 August 2018. https://events.drupal.org/nashville2018/sessions/decoupled-drupal-hard-problems

Schemata is a dry module in the sense that it underpins the submodule Schemata JSON Schema, which implements the JSON Schema specification for derived schemas. As such, we should only install Schemata in conjunction with an additional module that includes a Serializer implementation to define a schema.[2]

To enable Schemata JSON Schema, use the following command. When enabled, the Schemata JSON Schema module will add the *Access the different data models* permission.

```
$ drush en -y schemata_json_schema
```

To browse the schema in the browser, or to issue GET requests that return schema responses, we need to use paths that adhere to the Schemata URL format. Consider the following path, where {entity_type} represents the entity type, {bundle} represents the bundle (Drupal content type), {output_format} represents the desired output format (schema_json unless you are using a different serialization), and {described_format} represents the format (e.g., json, hal_json, api_json) described by the schema.

```
/schemata/{entity_type}/{bundle}?_format={output_format}&_
describes={described_format}
```

For instance, consider the following example, which fetches a JSON schema for Drupal articles in JSON API. When we issue a GET request against that path with the proper permissions, we receive a 200 OK response as shown in Figure 24-1.

```
/schemata/node/article?_format=schema_json&describes=api_json
```

Unlike type handling in JSON API (see Chapter 12), Schemata requires us to omit the bundle if the entity type has no bundles, as you can see in the following example, which retrieves a JSON schema for users according to the HAL+JSON format.[3]

```
/schemata/user?_format=schema_json&describes=hal_json
```

---

[2]"Schemata." Drupal.org. 26 July 2016. Accessed 29 August 2018. https://www.drupal.org/project/schemata

[3]"Schemata." Drupal.org. 19 August 2018. Accessed 29 August 2018. https://cgit.drupalcode.org/schemata/tree/README.md

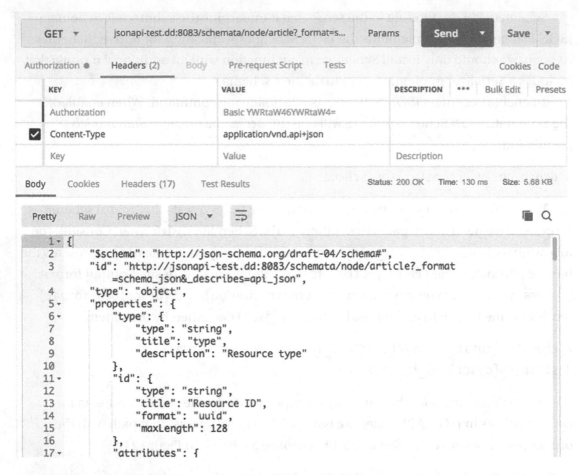

Figure 24-1. *In this example, we retrieve a schema describing the structure of a Drupal article according to the JSON API specification*

Note   The Schemata module is available on Drupal.org at `https://www.drupal.org/project/schemata`. For more information about the JSON Schema specification, consult `http://json-schema.org`. For information about how to work with Schemata within PHP in Drupal, consult the README at `https://cgit.drupalcode.org/schemata/tree/README.md`.

Generated API Documentation

Generated API documentation is not a new concept, with popular examples like OpenAPI (formerly known as the Swagger specification) and API Blueprint. In many cases, practitioners use these technologies to describe and prototype an API specification. In Drupal's case, we use API documentation technologies to describe an already existing API specification.

Specifications like OpenAPI and API Blueprint are also frequently part of *API design* tools as they can be used by developers who simply wish to experiment and test different scenarios within working prototypes of APIs. In addition, the promise of pipelined development (see Chapter 5) is much more achievable because tools like API Blueprint can facilitate the creation of *dummy APIs,* which developers of consumer applications can work against as back-end developers provision the web services that will provide the API.

For developers of consumer applications, generated API documentation can be a massive boon because it obviates the need to issue test requests to the API to ascertain the structure of the schema and expectations of requests by the back end. Reservoir (see Chapter 15), for instance, was the first to introduce the idea of side-by-side previews of JSON representations of resources and their Drupal renderings for the benefit of consumer developers, an idea that was rapidly adopted by Contenta and Headless Lightning (see Chapter 15).

Note   For more information about API Blueprint, see the web site at `https://apiblueprint.org`. We cover OpenAPI in the next section.

OpenAPI

OpenAPI (formerly known as the Swagger specification) is a specification for describing RESTful web services, among other features such as producing, consuming, and visualizing those services. Its intention is to create a shared standard among developers for documenting APIs. OpenAPI was originally part of an overarching Swagger framework, but in 2016 it became part of a separate initiative led by the Linux

Foundation. Note that OpenAPI is synonymous with the Swagger specification, whereas the term *Swagger* refers to the tooling ecosystem that implements the specification.[4]

Given an interface file that contains details about the API, the Swagger ecosystem is capable of generating documentation, test cases, and even working code based on an available web service. Some of the tools in the Swagger ecosystem include Swagger UI, Swagger Codegen, and Paw.[5]

The OpenAPI module, the Drupal implementation of API maintained by Rich Gerdes (richgerdes) and Ted Bowman (tedbow), integrates with core REST (see Chapter 7) and Drupal's JSON API implementation (see Chapters 8 and 12) to document available entity routes in those web services. You can also create plug-ins that facilitate other custom integrations. The OpenAPI module depends on the Schemata (see first section of this chapter), Serialization, and Schemata in JSON Schema modules.

A separate module, the OpenAPI UI module, handles the provision of user-facing documentation on the rendered Drupal front end that describes compatible APIs. However, you will need to install a user interface library that parses OpenAPI documentation. The recommended choice of the OpenAPI UI module is ReDoc, a JavaScript library that allows users to explore the API documentation for a web service and is captured in the ReDoc for OpenAPI UI module. There is also a Swagger for OpenAPI UI module, which integrates with Swagger UI.[6]

The easiest way to generate API documentation for the available web services on your Drupal site is to install all of these modules. Execute the following commands on a Drupal site with existing web services in core REST or JSON API. Because ReDoc for OpenAPI UI relies on OpenAPI UI, the OpenAPI UI dependency will be fetched automatically.

```
$ composer require drupal/openapi
$ composer require drupal/openapi_ui_redoc
$ drush en -y openapi openapi_ui_redoc
```

To install Swagger for OpenAPI UI instead, use the following commands.

---

[4]Pinkham, Ryan. "What Is the Difference Between Swagger and OpenAPI?" Swagger. 26 October 2017. Accessed 20 September 2018. `https://swagger.io/blog/api-strategy/difference-between-swagger-and-openapi`

[5]"OpenAPI Specification." Wikipedia. 27 July 2018. Accessed 29 August 2018. `https://en.wikipedia.org/wiki/OpenAPI_Specification`

[6]"OpenAPI." Drupal.org. 16 March 2017. Accessed 29 August 2018. `https://www.drupal.org/project/openapi`

```
$ composer require drupal/openapi
$ composer require drupal/openapi_ui_swagger
$ drush en -y openapi openapi_ui_swagger
```

We can now view our documentation by navigating to Configuration ➤ OpenAPI (/admin/config/services/openapi), where we can either download the Swagger specification JSON file for our own personal use or explore the documentation with ReDoc, as you can see in Figure 24-2.

Figure 24-2.   *The OpenAPI Resources page offers us the ability to either download our API specification file or explore the generated documentation with whichever library we have installed*

Note   The OpenAPI module is available on Drupal.org at `https://www.drupal.org/project/openapi`. The OpenAPI UI module is available on Drupal.org at `https://www.drupal.org/project/openapi_ui`. The ReDoc for OpenAPI UI module is available on Drupal.org at `https://www.drupal.org/project/openapi_ui_redoc`. The Swagger for OpenAPI UI module is available on Drupal. org at `https://www.drupal.org/project/openapi_ui_swagger`.

451

Generated Code

One of the most compelling reasons to provide a standards-compliant API specification document such as an OpenAPI specification is that the same document can be used to generate not only documentation and test cases, but also actual working code. The current frontier of API specification tooling is the ability to generate generic forms and even full interfaces based on an API specification.

An example of this is *Swagger Codegen*, which is capable of generating server stubs and SDKs for building consumer applications.[7]

Another example of generated forms is `react-jsonschema-form`, which generates a React (see Chapter 15) component according to Bootstrap conventions that interprets a JSON schema such as the one provided by the Schemata module and generates a complete HTML form that integrates with the schema.[8]

Comprehensive coverage of both of these projects is well outside the scope of this volume, but code generation based on API specifications and schemas stands among the most important current trends in working with web services and portends a paradigm shift in how we couple forms on the front end to business logic on the back end.

Note   For more information about Swagger Codegen, visit `https://swagger.io/tools/swagger-codegen`. For more information about `react-jsonschema-form`, visit `https://github.com/mozilla-services/react-jsonschema-form`.

---

[7]"Swagger Codegen." Swagger. 2018. Accessed 29 August 2018. `https://swagger.io/tools/swagger-codegen`

[8]"react-jsonschema-form." GitHub. 16 December 2015. Accessed 29 August 2018. `https://github.com/mozilla-services/react-jsonschema-form`

Conclusion

The current momentum toward commonly understood API specifications and generated API documentation points to a new era in how consumers interact with web services. In particular, schemas can aid in better introspection of data, and generated documentation can substantially improve developer experience outcomes when it comes to building consumer applications. Finally, more recent entrants that generate working code in response to a schema or API specification are reinventing how we conceive of the client/server relationship.

In the next chapter, we cover some of the best practices that have more recently figured in decoupled Drupal projects, including reverse proxies and the use of Drupal's cache tag system in conjunction with decoupled Drupal consumers. In the process, we discuss some of the most well-known technologies that are used to power caching in decoupled Drupal architectures.

CHAPTER 25

Caching

For any performant decoupled Drupal architecture, the topic of caching is of paramount importance but also fraught with extreme variation due to differences across implementations. It is further complicated by the fact that there is a limited range of open source solutions, Contenta.js (see Chapter 16) notwithstanding, which act as a reverse proxy for improved performance on consumer applications.

In this chapter, we cover some of the use cases for caching in decoupled Drupal as opposed to monolithic Drupal architectures, why reverse proxies are better choices for caching than internal object caches, how the Drupal cache tag system works, and best practices for cache indexing and invalidation. As no two implementations are like, no single chapter can exhaustively cover every possible caching scheme for every performance scenario, but this chapter gives you some potential directions to pursue for your own decoupled Drupal architecture.

Use Cases for Caching in Decoupled Drupal

In his "Effective API Caching: Achieving High Hit Rates When Your Client Is a Decoupled Front End" talk at Decoupled Drupal Days 2018, David Strauss identified three of the most common use cases for leveraging a caching architecture for decoupled Drupal, many of which resonate with the advantages of decoupled Drupal outlined in Chapter 5.

One of the primary arguments in favor of using a robust caching layer in between your Drupal instance and any consumer instances is *security*. Monolithic Drupal architectures are highly exposed to attack vectors, and leveraging a cache system such as a reverse proxy can mitigate some of the conduits by which nefarious actors can exploit vulnerabilities.

Another motivation is *personalization*. Today, as many user experiences become increasingly dynamic and personalized according to the tastes of the user, the burden on the server becomes severe when many users begin to request content. Generating

© Preston So 2018
P. So, *Decoupled Drupal in Practice*, https://doi.org/10.1007/978-1-4842-4072-4_25

entire pages based on personalized data in monolithic Drupal can be straightforward, but preventing requests for highly personalized API responses from invoking a full Drupal bootstrap can be uniquely challenging. Robust caching is a hard requirement for personalized experiences at scale in decoupled Drupal.

Finally, the dissemination of technology across the globe has led to the proliferation of *geodistributed dynamic users* who access content from areas distant from the actual location of the data center. These users from around the world increasingly demand the same positive experience as those who are close by.[1]

The Drupal Cache Tag System

One of the most important and compelling features in Drupal 8 is the *cache tag system,* which allows for cache items to declare dependencies on other cache items through *cache tags.* In short, cache tags provide a declarative way for us to keep track of how cache items depend on data that Drupal manages. Cache tags are strings and transmitted within sets of strings, most commonly in headers.[2] A useful and evocative way to think of sets of cache tags is as an ingredient list that identifies which items are present; when one ingredient is changed, the entire product needs to reflect that update.

Before we explain how cache tags work, we should first identify some of the scenarios in which Drupal's cache tag system is useful. In Drupal today, many users produce content that renders not only on its own page but also in blocks (repeatable page components), Views displays, or Views REST exports (see Chapter 11). When the content is updated, we want every single instance of that content, regardless of where it lies, to reflect the most up-to-date state of that content. In short, we need to invalidate a content item no matter where it lies.

By declaring a cache tag on a particular content entity in Drupal, we can ensure that wherever a cache item also includes the content entity's cache item, that cache item is invalidated in favor of a more updated version of that content.

---

[1]Strauss, David. "Effective API Caching: Achieving High Hit Rates When Your Client Is a Decoupled Front End." Decoupled Drupal Days 2018. 18 August 2018. Accessed 29 August 2018. `https://2018.decoupleddays.com/session/effective-api-caching-achieving-high-hit-rates-when-your-client-decoupled-front-end`

[2]"Cache tags." Drupal.org. 4 December 2017. Accessed 30 August 2018. `https://www.drupal.org/docs/8/api/cache-api/cache-tags`

Cache tags take the following form, where {object} is an object that needs to be cached (e.g., a node, user, configuration, etc.) and {identifier} is the identifier for the object within Drupal.

{object}:{identifier}

When there is only one instance of the object or multiple instances cannot exist, the identifier is not needed (thus forming {object}). There are no restrictions on cache tag syntax, apart from the fact that it cannot contain spaces. Consider the following examples of cache tags in Table 25-1 reflecting common needs.

Table 25-1. *Examples of Cache Tags*

Cache Tag	Description
node:53	Cache tag for the node entity with an identifier of 53, invalidated whenever the entity changes
user:2	Cache tag for the user entity with an identifier of 2, invalidated whenever the entity changes
node_list	List cache tag for all node entities, invalidated whenever any node entity is added, modified, or removed
library_info	Cache tag for asset libraries, invalidated whenever an asset library is added, modified, or removed

Drupal handles cache tags for *entities* (cache tag format: {entity_type}:{entity_identifier}), *configuration* (cache tag format: config:{configuration_name}), and *custom cases* (e.g., library_info).

In the coming sections, we discuss how to use cache tags in the context of reverse proxies and content delivery networks (CDNs), the two most common approaches for caching data in decoupled Drupal architectures.

Note   For more detailed information about the Drupal cache tag system, consult the documentation at https://www.drupal.org/docs/8/api/cache-api/cache-tags.

Reverse Proxies and Content Delivery Networks

Although some Drupal developers choose to maintain all caching within Drupal itself and rely on cache invalidations internally using tools such as the Internal Page Cache, this makes less sense in a decoupled Drupal architecture, as we need to conduct caching of API responses after they are issued to consumer servers. Many Drupal developers opt to use reverse proxies and CDNs for monolithic use cases, but they are perhaps even more useful in decoupled use cases.

To define some terminology, *reverse proxies* are proxy servers that act on behalf of a consumer to a server and issue requests on the consumer's behalf.[3] Reverse proxies are popular tools not only when it comes to caching, but also to create a unified way for requests to be forwarded to a Drupal instance. Meanwhile, CDNs are distributed networks of proxy servers that ensure high availability and high performance for end users regardless of where they are located.[4] In many cases, CDNs can be substituted for reverse proxies in decoupled Drupal architectures.

In Drupal, it is common to use Varnish, an HTTP reverse proxy that can lie in front of any server communicating in HTTP, in front of Drupal instances.[5] Other Drupal practitioners opt to use solutions such as Redis, a key/value cache and store that is also referred to as a data structure server, or Memcached, a distributed memory caching system.

In his presentation, Strauss cautioned against using object caches located on the front-end instance to power caching in decoupled Drupal architectures due to issues of coherency that surface, as illustrated by Figure 25-1. As an example, if you have a Node.js server lying in front of a Memcached instance such that Node.js performs retrievals from Memcached in lieu of Drupal, Drupal now needs to have an understanding of how to invalidate the Memcached instance in front of the Node.js server. In other words, all front-end and back-end instances are now communicating with the same cache.

---

[3]"Reverse Proxy." Wikipedia. 26 August 2018. Accessed 30 August 2018. https://en.wikipedia.org/wiki/Reverse_proxy

[4]"Content Delivery Network." Wikipedia. 24 August 2018. Accessed 30 August 2018. https://en.wikipedia.org/wiki/Content_delivery_network

[5]"Introduction to Varnish." Varnish. 2016. Accessed 30 August 2018. https://varnish-cache.org/intro/index.html

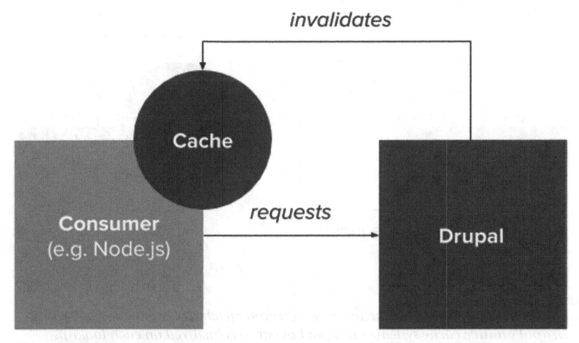

Figure 25-1. *In this scenario, the consumer and Drupal both rely on an object cache on a consumer, requiring Drupal to be aware of how the front end's cache stores cache items and how to invalidate them. Adapted from a figure by David Strauss with permission.*

Coherency issues can arise when the consumer evolves the way it caches content in Memcached. If the consumer modifies the way it caches content in Memcached and Drupal is not updated to reflect those modifications, incoherency can occur, leading to stale content for end users.

Although it is highly recommended to leverage Drupal's own internal caching system as well, Drupal's own object cache should also not be used for caching API responses, as it would require bootstrapping Drupal on every single request to the cache, thus nullifying the performance benefits of using a cache in the first place. This is illustrated in Figure 25-2.

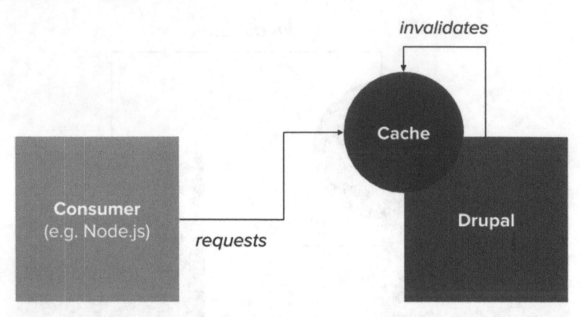

Figure 25-2. *In this case, whenever the consumer fetches cache items from within Drupal's native cache system, a Drupal bootstrap is incurred on each lookup. Adapted from a figure by David Strauss with permission.*

Strauss recommended using reverse proxies to serve as API response caches, where a reverse proxy lies in between the consumer and the Drupal instance as an independent entity. Optionally, you could also configure a reverse proxy or CDN to cache initial renders by JavaScript frameworks. This approach, illustrated in Figure 25-3, carries the particular advantage of Drupal both populating a cache and managing the cache according to its own patterns (in this case, Drupal cache tags).

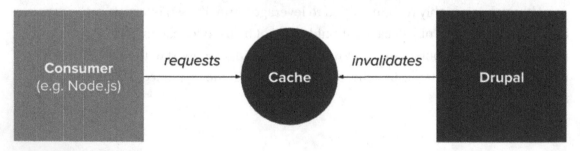

Figure 25-3. *The architecture recommended by David Strauss to ensure that the cache records Drupal cacheability metadata while preventing excessive Drupal bootstraps. Adapted from a figure by David Strauss with permission.*

Note   For more information about how to provide caching for your decoupled Drupal architecture, see David Strauss's Decoupled Drupal Days 2018 talk "Effective API Caching: Achieving High Hit Rates When Your Client Is a Decoupled Front End" at `https://2018.decoupleddays.com/session/effective-api-caching-achieving-high-hit-rates-when-your-client-decoupled-front-end`.

Cache Indexing

To indicate to reverse proxies and CDNs which cache tags are associated with cache items, we can issue the cache tags within a header. Currently, for debugging purposes, Drupal provides an `X-Drupal-Cache-Tags` header. Drupal can also send headers that cater to the particularities of certain reverse proxies and CDNs.

For instance, some CDNs disallow spaces or commas in cache items. As such, Drupal can issue a `Surrogate-Keys` header, which separates values with spaces, or a `Cache-Tag` header, which separates values with commas. It is generally recommended that both the web server where your Drupal site is located and your reverse proxy have support for response headers that can fit up to 16 KB of cache tags.

If you exceed the 16 KB recommended size, which accounts for approximately 1,000 cache tags, you should inspect the way you are assigning cache tags and whether you are serving overly complex responses. Moreover, once you exceed the limit, many services will simply ignore the remaining cache tags, leading to stale data.

Table 25-2 lists some of the common equivalents for cache tag headers in popular CDN products and reverse proxies.

Table 25-2. *Cache Tag Headers in Popular CDNs and Reverse Proxies*

Cache Tag Header	Service
Cache-Tag	Cloudflare Enterprise
Edge-Cache-Tag	Akamai
HashTwo	Varnish Pro
Surrogate-Keys	Fastly
xkey	Varnish mod

Note   For more information about using cache tags in reverse proxies and CDNs, consult the documentation at `https://www.drupal.org/docs/8/api/cache-api/cache-tags`.

Cache Invalidation

Thanks to cache tags, you can selectively invalidate particular items and also those items that contain the invalidated cache item. Note that if you are leveraging Varnish in its open source flavor and a module that provides an integration, you will need to configure Varnish to enable these cache tags to be purged. If you are using CDNs instead, many CDNs have their own purge APIs that can handle invalidations of cache items having cache tags. Some of these purge APIs can handle multiple invalidations in a single request, whereas others require multiple requests.

Consider the following example Varnish configuration (written in Varnish Configuration Language [VCL]), which handles incoming purge requests from Drupal.

```
sub vcl_recv {
  if (req.method == "PURGE") {
    xkey.softpurge(req.http.xkey-purge);
  }
}
```

An incoming purge request from Drupal could be written as follows using cURL, where {cache_tag} represents the cache tag needing to be invalidated, formed according to the particularities of the proxy, and {cache_host} represents the host of the cache.

```
curl -XPURGE -H"xkey-purge: {cache_tag}" {cache_host}
```

This cache invalidation, rather than performing a purge of a single item, purges everything that contained this particular node, thus highlighting the advantages of Drupal's cache tag system.

Now, we can perform cache invalidations, but we have not yet accounted for why we are using the softpurge() method rather than a traditional hard purge. A *hard purge* refers to a forced removal of designated items out of the cache such that those items do not appear anywhere after the purge. Strauss recommended only conducting hard purges when dealing with extremely sensitive data or data requiring the utmost real-time accuracy.

Meanwhile, *soft purges,* supported by most CDN APIs, set the time-to-live (TTL) of cache items to zero but still allow the item to appear during the intermediate time in which a new copy of the cache item has not been delivered yet. The advantage of this is that cached requests that contain the updated object will serve the ever-so-slightly stale object until it is replaced. This prevents stampedes on the server and slow responses to the end user while the fresh copy travels to the cache.

Note   If you are using open source Varnish, you will likely need a second module to support soft purging.

Conclusion

In this chapter, we inspected the landscape for caching best practices in decoupled Drupal. We covered the Drupal cache tag system, which provides cacheability metadata useful for highly granular cache invalidations; defined reverse proxies and CDNs as the most effective means of caching responses from Drupal web services; and explored some of the existing ways to perform cache indexing and invalidation in real-world scenarios.

The next chapter marks the end of our foray into decoupled Drupal together. In the final chapter, we zoom out to the larger context once more as we grapple with some of the most timely but challenging questions in Drupal's entire life span, especially as decoupled Drupal architectures gain steam in the Drupal community. We also consider some of the implications of evolving Drupal's mission and joining forces with other communities and movements. At stake is nothing less than the future and promise of Drupal.

## CHAPTER 26

The Future of Decoupled Drupal

As we have seen in these chapters, in many ways, decoupled Drupal has the potential to determine Drupal's trajectory for many years to come. Its ability to expose Drupal content for a variety of consumers, without regard for how that consumer is built, is one of the key advantages of decoupled Drupal and, indeed, of API-first architectures in general. Drupal is not alone in this paradigm shift, as many other long-standing software projects such as WordPress entertain significant evolutions of their own.

Drupal is at a unique crossroads in its history. Until now, organizations have mostly selected Drupal due to its capabilities for building web sites and providing editorial experiences with a rich array of features. Today, organizations are going further with Drupal and serving entire digital ecosystems with content, centralizing all of their data into a single CMS. In addition, Drupal's user experience is undergoing an overhaul not only in its design and user experience, but also in its front-end developer experience with the modernization of its JavaScript.

In this chapter, we take a brief look at some of the ongoing work to continue preparing Drupal for a promising future and issues that will have a direct impact on Drupal's medium- and long-term future as a CMS with horizons that reach well beyond the humble web site.

© Preston So 2018

P. So, *Decoupled Drupal in Practice*, https://doi.org/10.1007/978-1-4842-4072-4_26

The Admin UI and JavaScript Modernization Initiative

In September 2017, at DrupalCon Vienna, a group of Drupal core contributors and JavaScript maintainers in the Drupal community agreed to adopt the React library for experimentation in administrative interfaces in Drupal core.[1] A lengthy process that began with this author's proposed adoption of a JavaScript framework in early 2016,[2] the adoption of React opened the door to fundamental changes in the way Drupal's administrative interface operates. Other alternatives considered included Angular, Ember, Vue.js, Elm, and other frameworks, and some in the community still support the consideration of Vue.js as an alternative owing to its adoption by the Laravel community and incremental adoptability (see Chapter 20).

The Admin UI and JavaScript Modernization Initiative is a joint effort between user experience specialists and designers in the Drupal community and JavaScript maintainers to reimagine Drupal's internal user experience to match the expectations of other editorial experiences that consist of single-page applications and seamless interactions. Since the release of Drupal 8, Drupal's administrative experience has mostly remained the same. A pertinent question is whether it has grown so obsolete as to threaten Drupal's primacy as a CMS.

The Admin UI and JavaScript Modernization Initiative is led by Angie Byron (webchick), Cristina Chumillas (ckrina), Matt Grill (drpal), and Sally Young (justafish), and has the following objectives, as found on the Drupal.org initiative page.[3]

1. Create a new "design system" for Drupal's editing and administrative interface, and implement this incrementally.

2. Create a decoupled, single-page React application that manages Drupal administration.

3. Modernize the underlying JavaScript code and enhance Drupal's APIs to better support all types of decoupled applications.

---

[1]Buytaert, Dries. "Drupal Looking to Adopt React." 2 October 2017. Accessed 8 September 2018. `http://dri.es/drupal-looking-to-adopt-react`

[2]"[META] Start Using Reactive Declarative JS Programming for Some New Core Admin UIs." 6 January 2016. Accessed 8 September 2018. `https://www.drupal.org/node/2645250`

[3]"Admin UI & JavaScript Modernisation." Drupal.org. Accessed 8 September 2018. `https://www.drupal.org/about/strategic-initiatives/admin-ui-js`

In recent years, Drupal has made significant strides in advancing its JavaScript development experience, including adoption of the Airbnb JavaScript style guide, the introduction of a JavaScript build process, and upgrades to the latest versions of jQuery and jQuery UI during the Drupal 8 release cycle. As of this writing, Drupal 8.6 also ships with support for Nightwatch.js, a common and popular tool for writing automated tests in JavaScript. This represents a significant improvement over the previous testing system, which lacked versatility on the client side, and replaces the now-deprecated PhantomJS.

In the Drupal 8.7 development cycle, several large-scale advancements are planned. Among them is the creation of a stand-alone single-page React application that replicates every extant Drupal administrative interface within a more dynamic user interface. This collaboration between the user experience and JavaScript teams in Drupal will yield not only an improved administrative experience, but also an opportunity to test the limits of Drupal's web services.[4]

Note   For more information about the Admin UI and JavaScript Modernization Initiative, consult the initiative page on Drupal.org at `https://www.drupal.org/about/strategic-initiatives/admin-ui-js` and the roadmap issue at `https://www.drupal.org/project/drupal/issues/2926656`.

The Future of the Drupal Front End

One of the primary reasons for Drupal's success thus far is that its value proposition satisfies a variety of personas. In other words, there is no single persona that benefits significantly more than the other. Drupal has long prided itself on its unique location at the nexus of three distinct personas.

1. The *developer*, who benefits from a flexible developer experience and high extensibility.

2. The *marketer*, who benefits from contextualized administration tools and editorial access.

3. The *user*, who benefits from whatever user experiences are built by both other personas.

---

[4]"[plan] Modernize Drupal's JavaScript." Drupal.org. 27 November 2017. Accessed 8 September 2018. `https://www.drupal.org/project/drupal/issues/2926656`

There are many ways in which the Drupal front end could figure in a future where decoupled Drupal becomes an increasingly preferred architecture for Drupal architectures. The most stable approach would be to retain the current state of the Drupal front end for those who prefer to make use of theme layer components like Twig and preprocess functions in Drupal. This would allow for the site-and-repository use case (see Chapter 4) to become the primary way in which Drupal is used.

Nonetheless, this comes with its own problems. Today, site builders and content editors have an expectation, however unrealistic, that the same tools that they use to create and lay out content in Drupal will be available for experiences that are not driven by the front end available in monolithic Drupal. Anecdotes abound of frustrated clients who selected fully decoupled Drupal as a solution, paired with a JavaScript application, only to discover that they are now unable to perform the same in-place editing and layout management that had been previously accessible.

For instance, some marketers might find it of paramount importance that the same layout tools used to position content on a web site be available for digital signage and augmented reality interfaces as well, despite the fact that both of these channels could depend on completely unrelated—and infrastructurally distinct—technologies.

This mismatch between the expectations of site builders and content editors and the dispersed reality of multiple channels relying on wildly variant technologies is what I term Drupal's new incongruity, which is illustrated in Figure 26-1. In particular, marketers who have come to accept that seamless experiences on multiple devices are a must-have have expectations that might be completely incongruous, and even irreconcilable, with the technologies underpinning them.

Figure 26-1. *As the number of channels that end users expect increases, a better outcome for end users relies on more custom work by developers to make user experiences work on more channels and leads to less flexibility for marketers*

Universal Editing

During the days of the Spark initiative in the early 2010s, when Drupal began to provide responsive administrative interfaces that worked seamlessly across mobile and desktop devices (as seen in Figure 26-2), it was still possible to imagine that content editors would be able to create and administer content on all devices. Colocating the editorial experience and the end-user experience on mobile devices in addition to the desktop was possible thanks to responsive design.

Figure 26-2. *The Spark initiative introduced mobile editing interfaces that reacted responsively to changes in the viewport*

However, this came with certain disadvantages. Because of limited screen real estate, the extent of functionality available to content editors and site builders was restrictive. Layout management, for instance, is difficult to imagine on mobile devices. The Spark initiative found that many users preferred to switch to desktop platforms to perform complex operations and that such mobile editing interfaces were of limited usefulness.

Today, with the advent of devices like the Apple Watch, it is clear that attempting to place editorial interfaces on every device is untenable. For marketing professionals with high expectations, though, it is similarly complicated to envision a desktop-based interface that can sufficiently administer and manipulate the range of end-user experiences now in existence.

In that sense, perhaps *universal editing* should refer to the concept of administering diverse experiences from a single desktop interface to attain the most versatility. Indeed, in early 2016, Drupal project lead Dries Buytaert argued in favor of an evolution of editorial interfaces in Drupal to be more *outside-in,* or decontextualized from the content of the page. Terrence Kevin O'Leary also referred to this as *Literal UI.*

In Drupal's traditional approaches to in-place editing and contextual links, these features are adjacent to the content they manipulate. This is an impossibility, though, when Drupal is employed to edit and preview content destined for other channels, such as JavaScript applications and digital signage driven by other technologies. By placing all of these formerly contextual tools in a separate area of the page where they do not interfere with the preview, we can open the door to administering other channels within the same space.

Nonetheless, the notion of providing high-fidelity previews of other channels within a Drupal-powered interface raises several important questions. What level of fidelity is attainable when the technologies underpinning digital signage or augmented reality interfaces are irreconcilable with web technologies? Is it possible to provide the necessary emulators, or are the infrastructural demands simply too prohibitive?[5]

Note   For more insight into this topic, see this author's DrupalCon Vienna talk, "Decoupled Site Building: Drupal's Next Challenge" at `https://events.drupal.org/vienna2017/sessions/decoupled-site-building-drupals-next-challenge`.

Progressive Decoupling and Decoupled Blocks

Whereas other channels require significant effort to support when it comes to matching the expectations that marketing professionals have in terms of editing and administering experiences besides web sites, JavaScript applications, like Drupal, are also based on web technologies and should theoretically be much easier to support within a Drupal context.

Progressive decoupling (see Chapter 4) has long been touted in the Drupal community as a balance between the needs of JavaScript developers yearning for a developer experience more attuned to their desires and the requirements of marketing professionals and content editors who demand a means to edit and lay out their pages

---

[5]So, Preston. "Decoupled Site Building: Drupal's Next Challenge." DrupalCon Vienna 2017. 28 September 2017. Accessed 10 September 2018. `https://events.drupal.org/vienna2017/sessions/decoupled-site-building-drupals-next-challenge`

as easily as they did traditionally in Drupal. It involves the interpolation of a single-page JavaScript application into the Drupal front end so that contextual tools such as block placement can still be leveraged, and ES6 and other modern development techniques can be employed to power more interactive experiences.

Nonetheless, as seen in Figure 26-3, progressive decoupling comes with its own issues, as not all of Drupal's vaunted contextual features are available to marketers and content editors. Moreover, progressive decoupling makes it more challenging for JavaScript developers to use server-side rendering in improving their applications' performance, as the Drupal front end is responsible for providing the JavaScript application's assets.

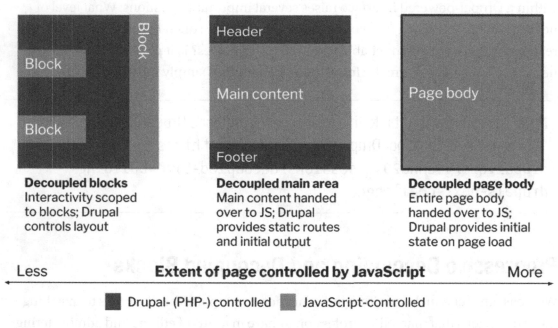

Figure 26-3. The spectrum of progressively decoupled Drupal approaches

Decoupled Blocks, a module developed by Matt Davis (mrjmd), is a framework-agnostic approach that forges an equilibrium between site builders and content editors who manipulate layouts and place content and front-end developers who need to be able to manipulate JavaScript behavior. In the Decoupled Blocks module, Drupal renders JavaScript components into blocks and allows for those JavaScript components to access certain block configurations that can provide state or other information.

Decoupled Blocks is a graceful solution to a difficult problem; it manages to compromise between the needs of site administrators who need to manage layout according to familiar drag-and-drop paradigms that have always existed in Drupal and the desires of JavaScript developers to exercise greater control over the behavior of interactive components on the page.

One significant problem is not unique to Decoupled Blocks and applies to all progressively decoupled Drupal implementations. Whereas certain features, such as block placement, remain intact, progressive decoupling leads to "black boxes" in which expected Drupal functionality such as in-place editing becomes unavailable. An illustration of this problem can be seen in Figure 26-4.

Site builder moves block from one area to another

This enables simple visual assembly for editors and site builders

But these JavaScript components are often "black boxes" and frustrating for editors

Figure 26-4. *The primary issue with progressive decoupling is the unavailability of certain Drupal functionality such as in-place editing within the portions of the page that are delegated to JavaScript*

Note Decoupled Blocks is available on Drupal.org at `https://www.drupal.org/project/pdb`. For more information about progressively decoupled Drupal approaches, also see this author's Acquia blog post, "Progressively Decoupled Drupal Approaches," at `https://dev.acquia.com/blog/progressively-decoupled-drupal-approaches/22/08/2016/16296`.

Shared Templating, Rendering, and Routing

Due to the substantial distance between JavaScript and Drupal development practices, community-driven efforts like the Admin UI and JavaScript Modernization Initiative emphasize an entirely separate approach to modernizing Drupal's administrative interfaces by producing a distinct React application that does not depend on any aspect of Drupal's front end; instead, it relies entirely on Drupal's available web services.

Nonetheless, some Drupal users have explored the possibility of sharing responsibilities across JavaScript and Drupal so that they can coexist on the Drupal front end. After all, one of the primary motivations for adopting universal JavaScript is to share code across the server- and client-side manifestations of JavaScript applications. What if there were a way to do the same across a server-side Drupal implementation and a client-side JavaScript application?

The ideal of *shared templating,* whereby Drupal and JavaScript both rely on the same templating system across server and client, is within the realm of possibility thanks to projects such as Twig.js, which is a JavaScript implementation of the Twig templating language used in Drupal 8. Nonetheless, Drupal 8's implementation of Twig includes many Drupal-specific nuances that significantly hinder any effort to provide a universal version of Twig across Drupal's rendering layer and a JavaScript-driven front end.

Shared rendering, in which Drupal and JavaScript both render the same way, has also been proposed as a solution to allow Drupal's front end to evolve into a more JavaScript-friendly environment. However, although this is possible in universal JavaScript due to the mutual intelligibility of the language across client and server, Drupal is written in PHP. Any endeavor to perform rendering across both the client and server in Drupal would require either a rewrite of the Drupal rendering layer into JavaScript (thus obligating the use of Node.js as a rendering proxy and the consideration of relevant infrastructural challenges) or the use of the library `php-v8-js`, which implements the V8 JavaScript engine in PHP but remains highly experimental.

Instead of pursuing these two untested directions, some Drupal users have instead opted to pursue *shared routing,* in which Drupal and a JavaScript framework share routes on a single domain but perform differentiated rendering. For instance, a JavaScript framework could render a particular route if it has that route available within the application, whereas Drupal could render routes that are not accounted for in the JavaScript application. This would allow for Drupal routes to serve as a fallback mechanism when JavaScript routes are unavailable. The notion of Drupal routes as a superset of JavaScript routes is illustrated in Figure 26-5.

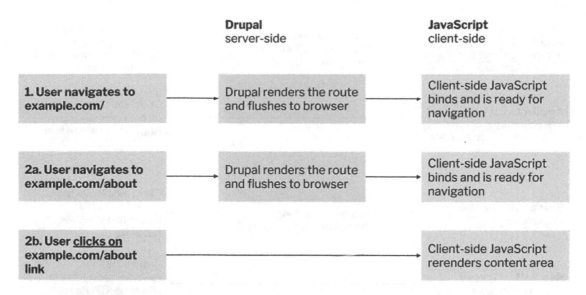

Figure 26-5. *Drupal routes as a superset of JavaScript routes*

Nonetheless, shared routing presents some additional difficulties, especially when client-side rendering becomes part of the picture. Template duplication will necessarily occur, because JavaScript frameworks perform dynamic rendering when users click links, whereas this sort of dynamic rendering only occurs in Drupal when a module such as RefreshLess (created by Wim Leers and inspired by the Turbolinks project in Ruby on Rails) is enabled.

Due to many users disabling JavaScript, there must be an alternative that provides server-side rendering in the event that JavaScript is unavailable. As a result, when JavaScript is disabled, a route would fall back to the Drupal version of the route, using the Twig template, but when JavaScript is enabled, the JavaScript template would be used instead. Although for some architects template duplication might not be a significant issue, it can lead to maintainability issues further down the road. This dilemma is illustrated in Figure 26-6.

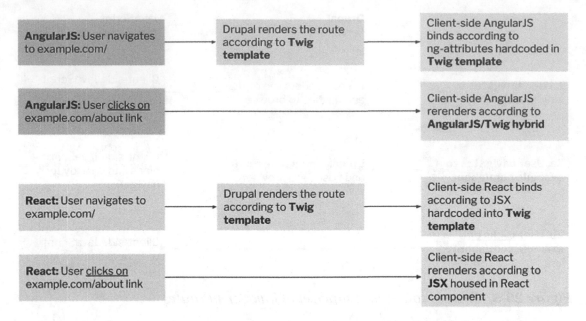

Figure 26-6. *Client-side rendering challenges the use of shared routing, because it creates template duplication when JavaScript can be enabled or disabled*

Note   The RefreshLess module is available on Drupal.org at `https://www.drupal.org/project/refreshless`. For more insight into this topic, see this author's DrupalCon Vienna talk, "Decoupled Site Building: Drupal's Next Challenge," at `https://events.drupal.org/vienna2017/sessions/decoupled-site-building-drupals-next-challenge`.

Decoupling Drupal by Design

As a result of the challenges that many architects face in attempting to have Drupal and JavaScript coexist in the same implementation, many users, this author included, have argued that Drupal should not attempt to integrate other technologies but instead should be *decoupled by design*, in which every single feature of Drupal possible today is available through web services or RPCs as well. In July 2018, Lauri Eskola (lauriii) and this author presented a session at Drupal Developer Days in Lisbon that articulated motivations and a vision for such a trajectory.

One of the most compelling rationales to decouple by design comes from the many challenges that developers face in Drupal's steep front-end learning curve and perceived obsoleteness. Developers by and large have flocked to decoupled Drupal architectures to pursue JavaScript implementations that adhere to development practices that are currently in vogue. Meanwhile, however, editors and site builders declaim the unavailability of contextual tools and other features in Drupal that require a monolithic orientation.

Decoupling Drupal by design would also provide that a Drupal installation process would offer to the user monolithic (Standard), enhanced monolithic (Standard plus API-first), and decoupled (API-first) profiles and thus result in three flavors of Drupal in wide usage. In the former, all Drupal functionality available on the front end would remain intact. In the latter, all Drupal functionality would instead be accessible through web services and RPCs, and contextual tools such as in-place editing would be disabled.

Note   In Drupal, *installation profiles* provide site features and functionality for a particular type of Drupal implementation that a developer intends to build. This is made available through a single download that includes Drupal core, any additional contributed modules, and prefabricated configuration.

However, the prospect of decoupling Drupal by design also presents several important unaddressed questions, such as the outlook for Drupal's user base. Does a Drupal that is decoupled by design translate into a permanent schism between JavaScript and other consumer developers on one side, creating universal JavaScript and native applications; and PHP developers leveraging Twig, enabling content creators, site builders, and themers on the other? Would contextual tools such as in-place editing and contextual links be unavailable in a decoupled context?

In a hypothetical decoupled installation profile in Drupal, every contributed module would need to provide API-first functionality through web services to match the functionality of core modules. The experience would be optimized particularly for the decoupled use case, thus obviating the need for all modules with front-end functionality such as Quick Edit (in-place editing) and Contextual Links. In the process, the Drupal community can ensure that there are fallbacks for cases in which a JavaScript-powered user interface is unavailable; we can instead leverage Twig and Drupal's Form API to produce the sort of flexibility required to support both models.

Whatever the result of the ongoing discussion regarding decoupling Drupal by design and the future of Drupal's administrative interface, one of the most important notions to take into account is that whereas developers yearn for Drupal architectures that are fully decoupled, editors and marketers still have strict requirements for a fully functional implementation out of the box, no matter what its architectural makeup. In that sense, perhaps Drupal needs to be *decoupled in architecture but monolithic in experience*, even if the latter is in perception only.[6]

Note   For more insight into this topic, see the Drupal Developer Days Lisbon 2018 presentation, "Drupal 9: Decoupled by Design?" by Lauri Eskola and this author at `https://lisbon2018.drupaldays.org/sessions/drupal-9-decoupled-design`.

Conclusion

In this chapter, we covered some of the issues that confront decoupled Drupal in the short, medium, and long term. First, concerning short-term endeavors, we described the present work of the Admin UI and JavaScript Modernization Initiative, whose efforts in the community have already yielded actionable results. Second, with regard to medium-term visions, we considered some of the ways in which the community has addressed richer integration with JavaScript.

Perhaps the most immediately relevant portion of this chapter to the Drupal community is that covering the potential of Drupal transforming itself into a truly API-first CMS. As Lauri Eskola and I argue, now that the benefits of web services are widely acknowledged in decoupled Drupal architectures, it is high time that we leverage this functionality within Drupal core and the contributed modules that comprise Drupal's ecosystem. By doing so, we can broaden Drupal's audience to include developers of novel experiences that we could not have imagined only a few years ago.

Here, our journey exploring decoupled Drupal comes to an end. We have roamed across a rapidly expanding and richly diverse universe, containing an astonishing range

---

[6]Eskola, Lauri, and Preston So. "Drupal 9: Decoupled by Design?" Drupal Developer Days Lisbon 2018. 6 July 2018. Accessed 10 September 2018. `https://lisbon2018.drupaldays.org/sessions/drupal-9-decoupled-design`

of possibilities that point to a promising frontier for Drupal. Nonetheless, Drupal's future is not yet guaranteed. Much work remains to cement Drupal's place among true API-first CMSs and to encourage developers in other ecosystems to adopt Drupal and its newly compelling features. Yet with the foundation built by countless contributors up to now, and with the eager early adoption of decoupled Drupal architectures across our industry, Drupal is at both a critical and a momentous inflection point in its history.

Countless contributors in the Drupal community have worked tirelessly to bring important functionality to decoupled Drupal practitioners around the world. Please consider helping the Drupal community map the future of those trajectories by joining contribution efforts, whether that means reporting bugs on issue queues, authoring documentation, reviewing patches and pull requests, or improving design and usability outcomes.

Thanks to decoupled Drupal, and thanks to the efforts of indefatigable contributors from every corner of the globe, the future of Drupal is bright and brimming with unbridled possibility.

Index

A

© Preston So 2018
P. So, *Decoupled Drupal in Practice*, https://doi.org/10.1007/978-1-4842-4072-4